Human Nature in Politics

Human Nature in Politics
the dynamics of political behavior

JAMES C. *Chowning* DAVIES

GREENWOOD PRESS, PUBLISHERS
WESTPORT, CONNECTICUT

Library of Congress Cataloging in Publication Data

Davies, James Chowning, 1918–
    Human nature in politics.

    Reprint of the ed. published by Wiley, New York.
    Bibliography: p.
    Includes indexes.
    1. Political psychology. 2. Social psychology.
3. Social history--Modern. I. Title.
[JA74.5.D38   1977]   320'.01'9   77-13870
ISBN 0-8371-9870-4

Reprinted with the permission of James C. Davies

Reprinted in 1978 by Greenwood Press, Inc.,
51 Riverside Avenue, Westport, CT. 06880

Printed in the United States of America

To my Mother and my Apa

Preface

The current state of knowledge of political behavior is on the one hand large and meticulous and elegant; on the other hand it is small, casual, and austere. The one hand is our knowledge of how people act within the framework of modern European and American democratic political institutions. The other hand is our knowledge of how people behave and misbehave when there are no such institutions to guide them.

The purpose of this book is to help close gaps between the areas we know well and those we know only slightly. To serve this purpose is to search for origins of political behavior. This makes it necessary to go deeper than is customary into basic mental processes and to range wider in time and space—back to the formative centuries of Western politics and out to parts of the world where the West has not meant the maturation of popularly responsible government so much as it has meant techniques of nonresponsible exploitation and control.

The search for origins thus takes us inescapably into the depths of the mind, in the search for common, universal causes of action. It is for the resulting emphasis that I have filched a title from Graham Wallas. My definition of human nature—the behavioral tendencies that are common to the species and rooted in the human organism— is logically incontestable. The tendencies that fit this definition are clearly disputable. In any event, I do not labor the phrase human nature, nor the shibboleth democracy.

Nevertheless I see no reason for tacitly accepting the assumption of John Locke and Karl Marx—the respective theorists of the middle class and of the working class—that the human mind is virtually a blank sheet on which culture writes whatever it chooses to write. The notion has underlain most social thought, ever since the study of society became as intense as it has in the last couple of generations. It needs re-examination, not reiteration.

As the mind relates to politics, this book is an attempt to consider what can and cannot be imprinted on the tabula non rasa. To me it seems necessary to do this to understand the origins of political action in the non-Western world. Indeed it seems necessary to do this to understand with more depth why people have developed the sorts of political institutions that prevail in Europe and America. But this book can be no definitive statement. Rather, it redirects attention to neglected lines of thought that were most explicitly related to politics by Thomas Hobbes three hundred, and by Graham Wallas almost threescore, years ago. Since these men wrote, psychology has advanced from a largely intuitive to a vigorously empirical science that can shed light on previously dark origins of political behavior.

Numerous people have in various ways helped me write this book. Five ladies: Mary Ellis Arnett, Lucille Lozoya, and Barbara Wilhite, who typed successive versions of it; and my wife Eleanor and my daughter Sarah, who jointly survived the writing from start to finish. Three onetime students: Peter J. Bickel, Robert M. Cadwell, and Alan P. Carlin, who spoke for the intelligent skepticism of scores of their contemporaries. One half-time research assistant, David M. Olson, whose intelligent persistence was not half-hearted. And the following critics and mentors.

In his reading of the completed manuscript, John H. Schaar was most sensitive and intelligent and stubborn, and generous of time and argument.

My major intellectual debt is to three psychologists, Sigmund Freud, Abraham Maslow, and David Krech. Each of them opened many doors and invited me in—in the first two cases without knowing me from Procrustes or Prometheus and in the third case without wanting me to become a follower. Any errors of fact and judgment contained herein are attributable not to Freud or Maslow or me but to Krech. When I asked him to read the manuscript, he said I should not now need to have him do it. If he had, this book would be free of fault.

Oddly, for one more interested in individuals than institutions, two institutions have at crucial times shown liberal material interest in me—the Social Science Research Council, when this book was taking early and then final shape; and the California Institute of Technology, when it was taking final form. They have thereby somewhat disproved Rousseau's notion that man is born free and is socially enchained. For reasons similarly liberal though not material, I am also deeply indebted to Peter H Odegard, Harold Winkler, Hallett Smith, and to John D. and Ewart K. Lewis.

No one who has not known Dwight Waldo well can appreciate how one person can lend his time, judgment, and kindly ear in helping another to stand intellectually on his own two feet. The writing could not have been done without his gentle, steady, and specific encouragement.

Most of all, I want to thank Julia Merrell Davies and Oscar Jászi, in whose memory the book is dedicated and sine quibus nihil.

JAMES C. DAVIES
Pasadena, California
11 May 1963

Contents

CHAPTER 1   *"You can't change human nature"*   *1*

2   *Social and individual nature*   *31*

3   *Political tension*   *64*

4   *Political perception*   *104*

5   *Proximal groups in politics*   *141*

6   *Distal groups in politics*   *183*

7   *Religion in politics*   *213*

8   *The politics of status*   *234*

9   *Political leaders and followers*   *274*

10   *The politics of instability*   *331*

List of sources   *367*

Authors' index   *383*

General index   *387*

xi

There is no liberty where there is hunger. . . .

LORD ACTON

City air makes a man free.

GERMAN PROVERB OF THE MIDDLE AGES

"You can't change human nature"

B = f(SO)

There is a legend that some second-generation Marxists in Moscow were debating whether to introduce private ownership of business enterprise into the Soviet Union. The arguments on the advantages of private versus public ownership grew so vigorous and persuasive that the issue was not at last settled until one man succinctly reviewed almost a half-century of Soviet socialist success and concluded, "You can't change human nature." In this legend Marxist environmental determinism comes full circle.

The circular, or more exactly the peripheral, reasoning employed in arguments between environmental and biological determinists in any case is apt to set up a rotary movement of thought. The difference between skilled broad-gauge writers and unskilled local sages on the issue is more apparent in rhetoric than in content. Some social philosophers write that only the broad cultural environment really determines how humans act. Others write that ultimately it is the great, innate fighting qualities of the Nordic or the Slavic or the Sinic race that will determine history. A modern, smoothfaced grandmother says that if it weren't for society and those terrible teachers her Johnny had as a child, he would be President now. An ancient, gnarled sheepherder, angry at the corruption of landlords and politicians, says it's just human nature and sends a fine young lamb to the village chieftain for a present.

The question is so inherently difficult that there is the temptation to ignore it, laugh at it, or conceptualize it out of existence. One social theorist, eschewing ignorance and laughter, almost conceptualizes human nature out of existence by calling it irrelevant. Abram Kardiner uses the phrase "basic personality structure" to include the traits characteristic of all people in a particular culture and finds this structure to be altogether the product of "all institutionalized practices" like relations between parents and children or men and women. Kardiner declines to probe more deeply, or more centrally.

He does not suggest that each member of a culture behaves in all respects like all other members of that culture. But he says that the only common traits are culture-wide and implies that there are no characteristics worth talking about that are common to broadly different people in widely separated regions. Yet without the universality of such phenomena as the relations between parents and children or men and women, it would be hard to explain the widespread fascination of comparative anthropology.[1] While recognizing the usefulness of abstraction on the level of common cultural characteristics, we need not assume that only such abstraction is possible or useful.

From Kurt Lewin and from Lasswell and Kaplan[2] we can derive a more abstract formula to conceptualize what causes people to act in the ways they do. The simple formula $B = f(SO)$ says that behavior is a function of the interaction of the situation and the organism. Anything less abstract than this loses conceptual precision. The formula has sometimes, as by Lewin, been written $B = f(PE)$, with P standing for person and E for environment. But this formulation unnecessarily mingles the two major categories of influence—heredity and environment. Common usage calls a "person" a highly structured, environmentally modified organism and does not much bother to dis-

[1] See, for example, Abram Kardiner, *The Individual and His Society: the Psychodynamics of Primitive Social Organization*, New York, Columbia University Press, 1939. See also Kardiner et al., *The Psychological Frontiers of Society*, New York, Columbia University Press, 1945. People are interested in different styles of childrearing and other social relations partly because such social relations are universal. Kardiner does not deny heredity but denies its importance. He says that "the capacity for repression is a phylogenetically determined characteristic" (i.e., it is inherited genetically), but implies that genetics would limit human adaptability to the animal level—as though human adaptability above the animal level were itself derived from the environment. See *The Individual and His Society*, 350–351.
[2] See Kurt Lewin, *Principles of Topological Psychology*, New York, McGraw-Hill Book Co., 1936, 12, 30–36, which uses the equation $B = f(PE)$, where P is person and E is environment. And see Harold D. Lasswell and Abraham Kaplan, *Power and Society*, New Haven, Yale University Press, 1950, 4–6, which uses E for environment and P for predisposition, "the nonenvironmental determinant of response."

tinguish organic structure from environmental modification. We do not usually call a baby a person but restrict the usage to an individual who has moved at least beyond infancy, talks, reads, writes, and has a name other than *Homo sapiens*.

Much, if not most, of the uniqueness of a person is a consequence of environmental influences. We have no units of analysis to quantify the two kinds of influence. But we can at least keep the formula qualitatively clean and our thought somewhat less muddled by using the concept *person* as the *sum* of his behaviors, not as one of the two basic *ingredients* of behavior. And we can say that most of the universality of a person, of his likeness to all other persons, is a consequence of organic influences. Let us then settle on the formula $B = f(SO)$. But even clean, abstract formulas—at least this side of mathematics—must have some use, some explanatory value—particularly in the study of politics, where formulas are treated with undue gullibility or suspicion.

It is indeed a long way from the human organism to the organization of government. And the question remains whether the first clause of the following sentence has any political meaning: "Every man is in certain respects like all other men, like some other men, like no other man." [3] More specifically, the question is whether there are any basic behavioral tendencies common to all human beings that become manifest in politics despite the obvious and enormous significance of environmental cultural influences that begin at birth. There is no useful purpose in considering the nature-nurture controversy, either to the gross point of trying to decide whether organic, innate characteristics ("heredity") are more important or less so than environmental ones [4] —or the fine and futile point of appraising whether innate characteristics account for 20% and acquired ones for 80%, or innate ones for 80% and acquired ones for 20%. But there is use in considering whether there are some behavioral tendencies whose origin is in the organism and which, through a long chain of causation, end up among the host of forces determining political behavior in individual human beings.

To sharpen the seldom-focused distinction between organic and environmental forces, we may well start with a brief aside on plant life.

---

[3] Clyde Kluckhohn and Henry A. Murray, *Personality in Nature, Society, and Culture,* New York, Alfred A. Knopf, 1948 ed., 35. The authors did not attempt to apply political meaning to their statement.

[4] Note the discussion of the concepts and of quantification in L. C. Dunn and Th. Dobzhansky, *Heredity, Race, and Society,* New York, Penguin Books, 1946, ch. 2.

No one doubts that live cells in the form of seeds must be planted in order for corn to grow. A barren field will not produce grain; neither can new grain be grown practically in a bag of seed. One cannot have the end product without both the organic characteristic of the chromosomes in the seed and the soil in which it sprouts and matures. What makes this self-evident analogy difficult to apply to human beings is that in our human species the impact of the environment is so great that the obvious aspects of human behavior are not at all like discrete chromosomes under a microscope but rather like such processed products as corn meal or bread whose heredity seems "obviously" irrelevant to explaining the food product.[5]

We surely cannot say that any manifest, observable act (political or otherwise) is instinctive, innate, organic, or "human nature." This is like saying a corn plant is its seed. But this by no means demonstrates that innate tendencies are not involved in behavior any more than the genetic make-up of a corn seed is unrelated to the mature plant. To help conceptualize the problem, let us consider a more direct and hypothetical human comparison. We observe a ceremony going on inside a Catholic Church in Honolulu, Hawaii. Tom Furumoto, an American born of Japanese ancestors, is kneeling beside Mary Fairgrieve, an American of Scotch-Irish Presbyterian descent and upbringing.

A variety of reasons might be proposed to explain this process. (1) They fell in love. (2) Tom was an ambitious young merchant and Mary saw the chance of becoming a wealthy woman. (3) Mary had been raised by parents who were hostile to all nonwhite people and she rebelled against them. (4) Tom wanted to assimilate to white society and had this opportunity to move respectably away from his racial background by way of a church that had evangelized his par-

---

[5] D. O. Hebb's Heredity and Environment in Mammalian Behavior, *British Journal of Animal Behavior,* **1**: 43–47 (1953) is a clear, brief treatment of the conceptual problem. See also Hebb, *The Organization of Behavior: a Neuropsychological Theory,* New York, John Wiley & Sons, 1949, 165–170. Herbert S. Langfeld, Heredity and Experience, *Année Psychologique,* **50**: 11–25 (1951) presents a history of the nature-nurture controversy among psychologists. Paul H. Schiller, Innate Constituents of Complex Processes, *Psychological Review,* **59**: 177–191 (1952) reports some meticulous observations of animal behavior to help distinguish innate and learned activity. See also Werner Muensterberger, On the Biopsychological Determinants of Social Life, in W. Muensterberger, ed., *Psychoanalysis and the Social Sciences,* New York, International Universities Press, 1955, vol. 4, 7–25.

ents in Japan with the belief that all men are brothers, regardless of race, color, or previous condition of servitude to false gods.

Behind each of these reasons we could trace back along the stream of causes to "ultimate" organic forces (and to "ultimate" situational ones), but we need not do so to make the point that in adolescence each of the parties to the marriage experienced the growth of an ineradicable and organic need for sex, which within the context of most if not all cultures may be met most acceptably by marriage. Whatever shaping the personalities of the two parties to the marriage had undergone, even to the point where sex may have been buried under a variety of less directly relevant factors, like social mobility, adolescent rebellion, and marriage customs in Western society, the basic need for sex remained a necessary force—probably the most crucial force unique to the maintenance of the social institution of marriage. It did not arise culturally even though the appropriate means for its satisfaction are among the most meticulously determined social rules in any culture—preliterate or literate, occidental or oriental. It took Freud a full generation to get people to recognize the importance of sex as a major organic determinant of human behavior and misbehavior, but, as he said, every nursemaid knew about it, just from watching the children.

Let us consider a more direct political example, again not for purposes of systematic analysis but to illustrate the concept of organic influences. The events are not hypothetical but historical. In mid-July 1863 in New York City a series of riots so seriously broke the fabric of metropolitan life that troops fresh (or tired) from the Battle of Gettysburg were brought in to re-establish order. The riots occurred immediately after the start of the selection of New Yorkers for the Civil War military draft, which had become law four months earlier. There was bitter hostility not only to the draft (partly because exemption from it could be bought for $300), but also to the growing Negro population. The hostility was most violent among semi-skilled and unskilled white (reportedly immigrant) workers for whom $20 per week was a high wage and for many of whom it was often a vicious fight with Negroes to get dockwork at $1.50 for a nine-hour day. Meanwhile wartime inflation was striking hard: roast beef doubling in price from 8 to 16 cents per pound and eggs rising from less than 12 cents a dozen to 25 cents in the period 1861–1863. From humble beginnings in the destruction of a conscription office, the riots fanned out to envelop police stations, to loot wealthy private homes, and in due course to kill and hang a few Negroes. It took police;

army infantry, cavalry, and artillery; and a Catholic archbishop to bring the riots to a sullen, exhausted end.

On the surface of things one could truly say that environmental factors caused the riots. When the draft act was passed with its provision for paying $300 to get exemption, when the call began in New York in July, and when Negroes up from slavery began competing for jobs with people almost as poor as themselves, the riot finally began. But underlying the manifest environmental causes are factors which bear the same relationship to the environment that seeds bear to soil, water, air, and sunshine in jointly producing a plant. The fear of loss of life in battle and of regression to semi-starvation in the contest for jobs were both involved. Reaction to these basic threats to life itself was built into the rioters and was among the causes of their manifest behavior, in the same sense as the need for sex is related to marriage. If they had possessed $300 to buy their way out of the draft or had secure jobs with a wage-scale tied to the cost of living, no doubt the workers would not have become rioters. When this deep military and economic threat to their survival developed, they took to the streets.[6]

Basic needs

With this brief presentation of instances where organic causes of manifest behavior seem relevant, we may consider more systematically the basic human wants as they relate, at the start of a long causal stream with many man-made dams and channels, to politics.

A want, need, or drive produces a tension which, to the individual, is generally more unpleasant than pleasant. He seeks to relieve the tension by achieving satisfaction of the need. It is not, however, accurate to say that people utterly dislike the sensation of wanting something and enjoy only the act of satisfying the want. They do derive satisfaction in the course of not only experiencing tension but of working *toward* its relief. Romeo and Juliet found parting such sweet sorrow that they wished to keep on parting till daybreak. Political

[6] See Irving Werstein, *July, 1863,* New York, Julian Messner, 1957, for a description of the riots. See also Jack F. Leach, *Conscription in the United States: Historical Background,* Rutland, Vermont and Tokyo, Japan, Charles E. Tuttle Publishing Co., 1952, 292–312. Aside from explanations that the riots were a conspiracy or were caused by "criminal elements," the economic competition between Irish stevedores and Negroes appears to be the most common explanation for the riots. There is an interesting point, namely the *time,* psychologically speaking, when the riots took place. The question of time is considered in Chapter 10 on the politics of instability.

candidates enjoy campaigns even though victory, the consummation they devoutly wish, may be denied them. Despite the pleasantness of tensions, people do strive to relieve them and then to create new tensions once the old ones are satisfied.

Freud initially believed there was but one basic need with different names: sex, libido, love, Eros. As his thinking developed, libido tended to become synonymous with a basic life urge. As he himself aged, he added the second and opposing urge to die. Eros and the death instinct became the grand duo. William James listed not two but thirty-two instincts. William McDougall, one of the first modern social psychologists, indicated seven major instincts plus some minor ones. Graham Wallas mentioned an instinct for property; desire for power and for "combat and adventure"; family affection; suspicion; curiosity; the desire to excel; and sex, food, anger, and fear.[7]

Henry Murray of the Harvard Psychological Clinic listed some twelve "viscerogenic" and some twenty-eight "psychogenic" needs. The viscerogenic needs in Murray's system are located in the organism but outside the brain and are the primary ones. The psychogenic needs have no ascertainable locus save in the central nervous system, and as secondary needs they are "presumably" derivable from the viscerogenic ones. The primary, viscerogenic needs are air, water, food, sex, lactation, urination, defecation, harmavoidance, heatavoidance, coldavoidance, noxavoidance, and sentience (the need for sensuous impressions). The secondary, psychogenic needs are acquisition, conservance, order, retention, construction, superiority, achievement, recognition, exhibition, inviolacy, infavoidance (need to avoid failure, ridicule, etc.), defendance, counteraction, dominance, deference, similance (need to identify with others), autonomy, contrarience (need to be unique), aggression, abasement, blamavoidance, affiliation, rejection, nurturance (need to nourish), succorance (need to seek aid), play, cognizance (need to explore, satisfy curiosity), and exposition (need to explain, interpret).[8] Murray does not suppose the psychogenic needs to be "fundamental, biological drives, though some may be innate."

Knowledge of human motivation is not yet adequate to establish the psychological equivalent of a periodic table of the elements. The garment of culture conceals the needs of the organism. There is no

[7] See his *Human Nature in Politics,* New York, Alfred A. Knopf, 3rd ed., 1921, 53–64.
[8] Henry A. Murray, *Explorations in Personality,* New York, Oxford University Press, 1938, 77–83.

argument on such organic needs as air, water, food, sex, and probably each of the other viscerogenic needs listed by Murray. But one can always justifiably and uneasily have the feeling that many supposedly basic needs are cultural derivatives. There is surely some doubt as to the existence of an organic basis for such psychogenic needs as abasement, blamavoidance, and exposition. We nevertheless should not be too surprised to see evidence among people anywhere on earth of some desire for order, for identification with others, and for the satisfaction of curiosity.

Freud and Murray as psychological theorists and empiricists represent polar positions on motivation, the one reductionist and the other perhaps elaborationist. The difficulty with Freud's theory is that it does not really help much to reduce political motivation to sex, even defining sex as the life force which he later came to call it. As one writer has said, it is almost impossible to overestimate the importance of sex in human behavior, but Freud achieved the impossible. A reading of Freud's *Totem and Taboo, Group Psychology and the Analysis of the Ego,* and *Civilization and Its Discontents* is indeed a stimulating, provocative experience, but it enlarges only one's speculative understanding of political behavior. Freud's unit of motivational analysis, Eros, is necessary though not sufficient to the understanding of direct, face-to-face interpersonal relations but does not furnish a long enough cantilever to bridge our chasm of ignorance of political dynamics in the individual human being.

One advantage of Murray's scheme over Freud's is that it implies a more complex human organism than does Freud's basic life-death etiology. The more we know about human behavior, the more complex it reveals itself to be—and the more Freud's sexualism becomes archaic reductionism like the basic elements of earth, air, fire, and water. To indicate, as Murray does, that affiliation, similance, and order are also rather basic psychogenic needs suggests that our units of analysis do not have to be reduced to a causal cause, or at least that they cannot be so reduced with what poor knowledge we now possess. But Murray's list as applied to the study of politics appears less viable than when used to assess in detail the personality of a particular human being in a particular culture. If Freud's theory is too simple for our purposes, Murray's is too intricate.

The work of Abraham Maslow provides a more useful basis than either Freud or Murray. In a 1943 publication [9] he set forth a system

[9] A. H. Maslow, A Theory of Human Motivation, *Psychological Review,* **50:** 370–396 (1943).

of basic needs, a system of great use in political analysis. He lists five main categories of needs:

1. Physical (water, food, sex, etc.);
2. Safety (order, predictability, dependability of the environment);
3. Love, affection, belongingness;
4. Self-esteem;
5. Self-actualization.

A second look at Murray's list of psychogenic needs shows that some of them readily relate to one of Maslow's basic categories (similance, affiliation, nurturance, and succorance to the third; infavoidance and superiority to the fourth; autonomy and contrarience to the fifth). It is also apparent that some of Murray's list fall into two or more classes (retention and construction into the second, fourth, and fifth; dominance into the third, fourth, and fifth). Maslow's list is not ostensibly political but makes it possible to describe political motivation in rather broad but nonetheless discrete terms. It is specific enough to avoid the Freudian reductionism.

In listing these five kinds of needs as the basic ones, Maslow asserts that the individual pursues them for their own sake in his lifelong process of behaving as a human being. Maslow is further saying that the failure to satisfy these needs, including the physical ones, diminishes and even atrophies an individual's mental life. These needs are not eradicable—not cultural artifacts—but organic, genetic forces which individuals can nurture but not create, control but never quite destroy, in either themselves or others.

One evident difficulty in the list is the inclusion of safety as a basic need. This is not to say that safety is not a need or that it lacks profound political importance, but rather that it appears to be an incongruous subset in an otherwise homogeneous set, like a menu that includes meat, potatoes, salad, milk, and "prepare everything so that it is appetizing." One does not want palatability but rather food that is palatable. The "physical" needs plus love, self-esteem, and self-actualization seem quite clearly to be pursued for their own sake, but it seems dubious that mentally healthy people pursue safety for its own sake. One does seek it as a precondition or as a means for gratification of the basic needs, but not because it is gratifying in the same sense in which one is gratified by a drink of water when thirsty, a hug by a loved one after a long absence, or freedom after imprisonment.

In other words what I am saying is that the pursuit and achievement of safety and security are instrumental to the basic needs: not ends themselves but means to an end. An individual will work and fight to be secure in his ability to satisfy his hunger and thirst, to be secure in his ability to gain love and impart it to others, etc., but not to be secure for the sake of being secure. It is a deeply disturbing experience to be deprived of a sense that the world is a relatively sure and predictable place where one's basic needs can be gratified. But this is so in the same sense in which one *prefers* palatable food, but basically *needs* food. It is more disturbing to be deprived of food than of the surety of its supply.

A reason for laboring this point a little is precisely that such aspects of the state of mind as the sense of security or insecurity are, for the most part, far more important politically than those aspects of the state of mind like hunger and the desire for love, self-esteem, and self-actualization. People generally do not turn to politics to satisfy hunger and to gain love, self-esteem and self-actualization; they go to the food market, pursue members of the opposite sex, show friends what they have done, and lose themselves in handicrafts, fishing, or contemplation—with rarely a thought about politics. If achievement of these goals is *threatened* by other individuals or groups too powerful to be dealt with privately, people then turn to politics to secure these ends. They want government to prevent murder, famine, or theft. They rarely expect the government to create life, food, and other goods, but do expect it to make safe their private pursuit. To *secure* their own ability to satisfy their individual wants, people will make demands on government. In day-to-day living they prefer to satisfy their wants by themselves and privately.[10] But this is anticipating some of the content of the rest of the book. We must return to the subject of basic needs before we get the wrongful notion that, because politics has generally an indirect and instrumental relationship to needs, we can now leave the subject of basic needs altogether, or, for example, assume an inescapable relationship between private enterprise as a means and basic needs as ends.

In his ordering of five kinds of needs, Maslow has introduced the notion of priority—some needs becoming manifest and demanding satisfaction before others emerge. This introduces the dimensions of time and maturation far more nicely than was the case with Freud— who elegantly analyzed the successive stages of sexual maturation but

[10] And they probably also seek security more often privately than through government. For example, they store food in the house, go by themselves to the doctor, gain security of affection in the family, etc. In this sense, this book about politics has to do with exceptional, nonroutine human behavior.

less fruitfully outlined the maturation of anything else. In Maslow's system physical needs have priority over the affectionate ones, and as the latter emerge they overlie but do not dissolve the former.

A common-sense observation will serve to indicate a priority even within the class of physical needs. A hungry person will be quite preoccupied with the pursuit of food: he will plan rationally how to get it, and when very hungry he will also have fantasies about tables loaded with delicious meat, vegetables, and fruit. But deprive him of water for a briefer time than he has been without food, and his thoughts and fantasies will turn to water. Take the further step of depriving him of air, and he will, within seconds, engage in action that is concentrated on the breath of life itself. Even a thirsty, hungry person under such circumstances will forget about everything except air.

Maslow's point on the hierarchy of needs is more subtle: until there is *substantial* and *relatively durable* satisfaction of the physical needs, the safety needs will not emerge; until the safety needs are *fairly* well met, the need for love and affection will not emerge; and so on. He qualifies his assertion by indicating that the artist starving in a garret is more apt than not to have had a *relatively* secure and physically satisfying childhood. We may add that the politician who stakes "everything" in the pursuit of public office is able to do so because his life history is more often than not one in which the world has been manageable, not beset by a constant search for food, safety, affection, and self-esteem. Setting aside, for the moment, the question whether a person wants to be sure about his food, love of and by others, etc. in the same sense that he wants food itself, love itself, and so on, let us consider the political relevance of the hierarchy concept. In the process of doing so, we will try to indicate the substantive political relevance of each of four successive basic sets of needs: the physical, the affectional, the self-esteem or dignity, and the self-actualization.[11]

The physical needs

In 1944–1945 at the University of Minnesota a number of conscientious objectors to military service subjected themselves to a series of

---

[11] Rostow touches on such priorities in discussing what happens "beyond consumption," and he notes that in Thomas Mann's *Buddenbrooks* the first generation of the family pursued wealth, the second social status, and the third music. [W. W. Rostow, *The Stages of Economic Growth*, Cambridge, The University Press, 1960, 11–12.]

starvation experiments. For the first twelve weeks (the control period) they were given an ample, well-balanced, but regulated diet averaging 3870 calories per day. For the next twenty-four weeks (the experimental period) they were given a semi-starvation diet averaging 1470 calories per day.[12] This period of nearly six months was followed by twelve weeks of rehabilitation, during which the average daily food intake was gradually increased to 1780 and then 2840 calories, after which the subjects' food intake was unrestricted and climbed to an over-normal average of 4740 calories per day. The experimenters made a variety of observations, mainly of medical significance, but the psychological ones are of basic political relevance.[13] Let us consider a "typical" case from this group of 32 whose experiences were observed throughout the year-long study.

"Don" was twenty-five years old, an architect, unmarried but with a girl friend to whom he wrote a letter almost every day. He was an active participant in the educational program these conscientious objectors had established to prepare themselves for post-war relief work outside the United States. During the control period his weight was 142 pounds (64.7 kg); during the experimental period it dropped finally to 115 pounds (52.1 kg); at the end of twelve weeks' rehabilitation it rose to 120 pounds (54.2 kg), and twenty-one weeks later to 163 pounds (74.1 kg), some 21 pounds (9.5 kg) more than he had weighed before the experiments began.

During the third experimental week his morale was high, and he maintained his interest and work in architecture. Although he had less desire to move about and tired easily when he did, his mental energy, along with his acumen, remained unimpaired. Unlike some of the other subjects, he was not preoccupied with thoughts of food,

---

[12] At Buchenwald, a Nazi concentration camp, an internee who became a member of the French Academy of Medicine after war's end reported the food allotment in 1944 to be usually some 1750 calories per day, decreasing "later" to about 1050. [C. Richet, Experiences of a Medical Prisoner at Buchenwald, in H. L. Tidy and J. M. B. Kutschbach, eds., *Inter-Allied Conferences on War Medicine*, London, Staples Press, Ltd., 1947, 454.]

[13] The comprehensive report is by Ancel Keys, J. Brozek, A. Henschel, O. Mickelson, H. L. Taylor, *The Biology of Human Starvation*, Minneapolis, University of Minnesota Press, 1950. The material here relevant is in vol. 2, notably chs. 37 and 38. See also J. Brozek, Semi-starvation and Nutritional Rehabilitation: A Qualitative Case Study, with Emphasis on Behavior, *Journal of Clinical Nutrition*, 1: 107–118 (1953) for a brief report on "Don," a "typical" individual who served as one of the experimental subjects and whose experiences are recounted in this chapter.

even during the fourth week. By the eighth week he reported having dreams about food. By the twelfth week not only his dreams but his conscious thoughts revolved around food as steadily as the earth around the sun. He got aches, pains, and cramps whether he exercised or not. He became more restless, irritable, and—in one of the ominous and universal symptoms of starvation—increasingly apathetic. He had difficulty concentrating on any activity for very long. He lost self-confidence to the point where he sought more control by the experimenters, saying, "I think it is a good idea to put strong checks on us." Writing in his diary during the twelfth week, he observed that he enjoyed being alone, that his thoughts and moods had turned inwards, that his interest in other individuals and in post-war relief work overseas had declined, and that what he now dreamed of was being an architect and leading "a personal home life" in a small-town or rural environment.[14]

By the sixteenth week he suffered severe hunger pangs and headaches. When his girl came several hundred miles to visit him two weeks later, he found the visit a strain and "felt that it had been impossible for him to achieve rapport with her." As Brozek further reported, "the egocentric effects of the semi-starvation, added to a new realization of the importance of personal security, led to a dropping of all relief study and training."[15] He began to spend most of his time "just sitting." By the end of the starvation period he had virtually stopped his studies and letter writing. In the final starvation interview he repeatedly expressed the hope that he would be placed in the one out of the four groups that was to get the most abundant rehabilitation diet.

At the start of the rehabilitation period he immediately felt better and wanted to do things. But during the third week he became obsessed with the belief he was not getting his allotted quota of food.[16] He spent his time going over his personal effects, read devotional religious literature, and had no wish to take part in group activities. Later he became interested in relief and rehabilitation work again, as his religious interest diminished, but he wanted to do this work in the

---

[14] See Brozek, *op. cit.*, 114.
[15] *Ibid.*
[16] People liberated from Nazi concentration camps initially experienced elation, and then "a let-down in spirits with increasing suspicion and anxiety for personal safety." [L. J. Thompson, German Concentration Camps: Psychological Aspects of the Camps, in H. L. Tidy and J. M. B. Kutschbach, eds., *Inter-Allied Conferences on War Medicine*, London, Staples Press, Ltd., 1947, 466–467.]

United States. Five months after the end of the starvation period, in Brozek's words, "the importance of attaining physical security had been sharply focussed by his semi-starvation experience," and "Don" had decided not to do relief work but go back to his architectural training and "get started on his own." [17] This was his mental condition despite his expressed greater awareness of the need to provide food for starving people everywhere.

As the major study reports, withdrawal and apathy symptoms among the subjects during the starvation period were accompanied by strong feelings of group identity, as starved ones against the well-fed world outside. But during rehabilitation, the discontents and suspicions that arose tended to have a nongroup flavor quite different from the strong group feeling before and during the experimental period.[18]

Reports of historical instances of widespread and chronic starvation lend color to the scientifically gray Minnesota findings.

On the Russian famine, 1918–1922: In the interest of obtaining better rations, children denounced their parents or other members of the family to the Cheka as anti-Communists.[19]

On starvation in the Nazi concentration camp at Belsen, 1944–1945: Loss of normal moral standards and sense of responsibility for the welfare of others was widespread; in severe cases interest in others did not extend beyond child or parent; eventually the instinct to survive alone remained, even to the extent of eating human flesh.[20]

---

[17] Brozek, *op. cit.*, 117.

[18] There was no evidence of impaired intelligence during the starvation period. Extensive intelligence tests indicated no substantial changes. But "spontaneous mental effort" did diminish. As one subject said: "I can talk intellectually, my mental ability has not decreased, but my will to use the ability has." [Keys et al., *op. cit.*, 853.] Other biological research on the effect of starvation reports a loss in brain weight of 3%, in the heart of 3%, in skeletal muscles of 31%, in testes of about 40%, and in fatty tissue of 97%; see also page 840. [Thomas Richard Parsons, *Fundamentals of Biochemistry in Relation to Human Physiology*, Cambridge, W. Heffer & Sons, Ltd., 6th ed., 1939, ch. 6, esp. 95–96.]

[19] P. A. Sorokin, *Man and Society in Calamity*, New York, E. P. Dutton & Co., 1942, 70. On the increase in theft, see page 73. Sorokin lived in the Soviet Union during this famine period.

[20] F. M. Lipscomb, German Concentration Camps: Diseases Encountered at Belsen, in H. L. Tidy and J. M. B. Kutschbach, eds., *Inter-Allied Conferences on War Medicine*, London, Staples Press, Ltd., 1947, 464. The daily caloric intake in concentration and prisoner-of-war camps evidently varied from about 800 to 1050 calories in the last months of the war. A "normal" diet in "normal" life circumstances is close to 3000 calories per day. See *ibid.*, 454, 476. See also, in this book, the table on page 27.

On French PWs, including some who were active in the anti-Nazi Resistance: These individuals . . . lost in the detention camps their interest in political questions and became concerned only with the immediate problems of the internment life and the possibility of escape. In the last stages the men were overcome with apathy and resignation.[21]

In large societies (including nations or parts of nations), when food becomes scarce there is thus a breakdown of social ties, of property rights, the devaluation of treasured objects and of virtue (including sexual) in the omnipotent physical desire for food. A momentary worsening of the food supply may produce local food riots, which may broaden and deepen into rebellion. But extreme hunger, as starvation approaches, produces apathy and manipulability. People become too weak and too busy staying alive to take either strong or concerted action against government.[22]

Physical needs and politics

There are two reasons for introducing a discussion of the political relevance of the physical needs by considering chronic hunger. The first is to describe a condition with which modern men in industrial society, notably including readers and writers of books, are rarely if ever familiar (except following either economic breakdown or deliberate action of government), and one with which contemporary men in many nonindustrial societies have occasionally or often been only too well acquainted. People who have always eaten regularly find it hard to comprehend the catastrophic consequences of hunger on thought and action, just as it is hard for virtually all people to experience vicariously and understand the consequences of a deprivation of air or water. But it is necessary to appreciate what starvation does to people in order to understand its political impact. This brings us to the second and significant reason: the depoliticization that follows deprivation.

We have noted several consequences of starvation: constant pre-

---

[21] Keys et al., *op. cit.*, 799–800. And see M. Lamy, M. Lamotte, and S. Lamotte-Barrillon, *La dénutrition, clinique-biologie-therapeutique,* Paris, G. Doin et Cie., 1948, 106, which Keys et al. here briefly summarize.

[22] See Sorokin, *op. cit.*, ch. 3. But there are exceptions to the breakdown of normal social ties, for example, in the Netherlands during the Second World War. [See Keys et al., *op. cit.*, 794.] For a clinical report on the period, see G. C. E. Burger, J. C. Drummond, and H. R. Sandstead, eds., *Malnutrition and Starvation in Western Netherlands, September 1944–July 1945, Part 1,* The Hague, General State Printing Office, 1948.

occupation with food, apathy, loss of self-confidence, a turning away from other individuals and society and a turning toward oneself, and a breakdown of social ties and moral standards. What in short we see is very much like what Thomas Hobbes, writing in cold bitterness in France about his reaction to the Puritan Revolution in England, described as the state of nature. There is the war of all against all and the solitary, brutish, short life of man. Only in a very primitive sense, except as in such instances as the Netherlands in 1944–1945, can there be anything like what we call society, let alone political society. To assume that ordinary or extraordinary persons in such a hungry condition can in any way concern themselves with matters of public policy is to assume a kind of madness that prefers order, justice, and individual responsibility therefor to survival itself—prefers means when ends cannot be met. The organism will not permit this. Politics cannot exist for people who are in such circumstances. The man with food to dispense can rule without protest. We have noted the desire of "Don," the Minnesota experimental subject, to have the experimenters "put strong checks on us."

Putting the problem of physical needs in broader context, we may state the proposition that the needs for food, clothing, shelter, health, and safety (i.e., freedom from bodily harm) do not ordinarily find *direct* political expression. With the exception of physical safety, the search for satisfaction of these needs is ordinarily carried on by social but nonpolitical means. Physical safety, in the form of protection against violence, is characteristically sought from government, but training for safety is often done privately in the family, when parents teach their children to be careful in crossing streets, walking alone in the dark, etc. Satisfaction of them is more a precondition of political participation than a cause of it, in the sense that good physical health is more a precondition than a cause of intellectual activity. When the means to satisfy physical needs are readily available through private channels, individuals do not look to government to provide the means. And when the means are so nearly unavailable that people are constantly preoccupied with eating, staying warm, dry, healthy, and alive, they have no time to consider public policy. Extreme physical need destroys politics for the needful. By this I mean that they can take no effective voluntary part in making any basic decisions of the sort that affect the whole community.

There is available some more lifelike and more systematic evidence on these phenomena. In their research on unemployment during the Great Depression that started in the late 1920s, Zawadzki and Lazarsfeld studied unemployed individuals in Warsaw and in the Austrian village of Marienthal.[23] They found a general desocialization and widespread resignation and apathy. In Marienthal more than four out of five persons were either resigned to unemployment or broken by it. No political activity was reported among any of the people. In summarizing their Warsaw findings they explained:

The masses cease to exist as such when the social bond—the consciousness of belonging together—does not bind any longer. There remain only scattered, loose, perplexed, and hopeless individuals. The unemployed are a mass only numerically, not socially.[24]

Without enough to eat there is not a society. Without a society, the adjective "political" has no noun to modify.

Another series of events also illustrates the phenomena of deprivation and depoliticization vs. gratification and politicization. After the Japanese bombing of Pearl Harbor, Hawaii on 7 December 1941, a military decision was made to evacuate all persons of Japanese birth or ancestry who were living on the West Coast of the United States. There was shock and bitter resentment among these evacuees, who were suddenly moved first to temporary assembly points on the West Coast and then to permanent centers in uncultivated and rather barren tracts of land away from the coast. Administrative conditions were chaotic, with enough of some items to last ten minutes and of others to last ten years. The initial problems for the evacuees centered mainly around shelter and clothing. The evacuees were provided with army-type barracks but typically with only a single unpartitioned large room for each family. Clothing was scarce, except for what the Japanese had brought with them. The usual services of a settled community, ranging from barber shops to shoe repair shops and schools, were slow in getting established. There was uncertainty as to what would happen to them, generally and specifically. Rumors were evidently the main commodity in abundant supply.

If there were ever a time when real grievances should have induced organized political action, it was either at the temporary assembly centers or at the camps when conditions were at their worst—that is, immediately after the evacuees arrived. But before political activity developed, there first took place some basic provision for physical

---

[23] B. Zawadzki and P. Lazarsfeld, The Psychological Consequences of Unemployment, *Journal of Social Psychology*, **6**: 224–251 (1935). P. F. Lazarsfeld, An Unemployed Village, *Character & Personality*, **1**: 147–151 (1932–1933).
[24] Zawadzki and Lazarsfeld, *op. cit.*, 245.

needs and then the establishment of an operative community, however informal. One of the camps, at Poston, Arizona, started receiving evacuees in early May 1942. Some 7500 had arrived by the end of the month; the peak population of about 18,000 was reached in August. In late June, at the instance of the Caucasian camp administration, some evacuees drew up a charter for municipal government. It won no real popular support. It was not until mid-November 1942 that a significant indication of indigenous political activity occurred, a general strike that lasted about six days. And this did not occur until a burgeoning of sundry private associations had provided the social coherence necessary for concerted political action.[25]

At another of the camps, Manzanar, near Lone Pine, California, under comparable conditions, a riot occurred even somewhat later, in early December 1942. At another center, Tule Lake, where internees started arriving three weeks later than at Poston, and where physical conditions and facilities were superior at least to those at Manzanar, a strike took place in August—again not when there was chaos but when the internees were threatened with the loss of whatever favorable conditions they had already gained in the camp. It was on the occasion of great insecurity, not of great physical deprivation, that these people struck against what amounted to their government.[26]

These phenomena are not limited to people in depressed villages and wartime detention camps. They occur in full-fledged political societies—that is, in nations. In the 1930s, 40s, and 50s, they occurred in periods of internal crisis, forced confessions, and forced protestations of loyalty in the U.S.S.R., the Hungarian People's Republic, and in areas controlled by the Chinese People's Republic. In the Soviet purges of the late 30s, candidates for confession were deprived of sleep and food for long and irregular periods. These fundamental needs became so pressing that the graceful gift of even an hour's sleep, after standing for an insufferable 48 or 72 or 96 hours in front of the interrogator, seemed to the candidates almost a present from God.

They became insecure because of the very irregularity with which

---

[25] See Alexander Leighton, *The Governing of Men*, Princeton, Princeton University Press, 1945, chs. 3 and 4 for the early chaotic conditions, chs. 5–9 on the beginnings of social organization, and chs. 10–13 for the strike and its aftermath.
[26] See Dorothy S. Thomas and Richard S. Nishimoto, *The Spoilage*, Berkeley and Los Angeles, University of California Press, 1946, ch. 2 on the disturbances at Manzanar, Tule Lake, and also Poston. See R. H. Wax, The Destruction of a Democratic Impulse, *Human Organization*, **12** (1): 11–21 (1953) on the separate stages of the rebellion at Tule Lake.

sleep, food, and rest from interrogation were granted. They were deprived of a sense of solidarity with fellow prisoners by being subjected to hearing the screams of other candidates being questioned and by the report that the others had confessed. They lost their sense of self-respect and dignity in the day-to-day prison routine of inescapable filth, rotten food, and dank, cold prison-cell walls. Their sole opportunity to become individuals again after the de-individualization process revolved around a brief career of private guilt, public shame during the subsequent trial, and a vague hope that they might in some humble way have been of use to the government, the Party, and to Society.

At no time did they in any usual sense actually become social or political. They confessed their sins against society not so much because of a sense of social responsibility as to get sleep and bread. They articulated their past political wrongs in public—their stupid interference in the governmental decision-making process, in which the government and the party made up its abstract mind about what should and should not be done for the good of mankind. They confessed not from a sense that they were stupid or meddlesome but because both the interrogation process and the sense of guilt which haunts all men (as John Calvin and Sigmund Freud have reminded us) were for them no longer endurable. In short, they had a stark, naked, physical need to survive, however hopeless, and to gain some sense of identity and worth, however contemptible.[27]

There is evidence showing a relationship between basic physical needs and political behavior in some data from the Soviet Union. Raymond Bauer and others of the Russian Research Center at Harvard University intensively and extensively questioned people who had become expatriates of the U.S.S.R. before or during the Second World War. The expatriates—only about 40% of whom had left the Soviet Union voluntarily—who were interviewed by the Harvard group included not only members of the intelligentsia but also nonelite skilled and unskilled workers and many peasants.[28] Unskilled workers and

---

[27] The Western world got its first vivid view of this process through the medium of fiction in Arthur Koestler's novel, *Darkness at Noon,* written (1938–1940) like Hobbes' treatise, *Leviathan* (1651), in Parisian exile, and again like the *Leviathan,* in light of immediate and vivid experience with the political system which the writer analyzed. The later factual though pseudonymous account of F. Beck and W. Godin, *Russian Purge and the Extraction of Confession,* London, Hurst & Blackett, Ltd., 1951, closely corroborates the Koestler analysis.

[28] The Beck and Godin study dealt with elitist defectors from the Communist party.

peasants expressed hostility to the government more often than skilled workers, and skilled workers more often than the intelligentsia. The commonest reasons for alienation from the Soviet system were not ideological or even primarily programmatic: the expatriates did not criticize Communism as such or the state-controlled health program or state ownership of heavy industry, transport, and communications—or the state guaranty of work for all.

The prime reasons expressed were the police terror and personal dissatisfaction with the jobs the expatriates had had. More specifically, the police terror meant arrest; job dissatisfaction meant inferior status and lack of opportunity to do the kind of work for which they felt competent. Almost all of the expatriate-respondents reported hostility to the police terror and to the collective farm system. Bauer further reports that 52% of those who had actually been arrested expressed hostility, 47% of those who had experienced the arrest of a member of their family did so, and only 27% of those who had experienced neither.[29]

It is also notable that only 28% of the expatriates who belonged to the intelligentsia expressed hostility to the Soviet regime, in contrast to 45% of the skilled workers and 58% of the combined category of unskilled workers and peasants. It should be no surprise that the Soviet intelligentsia (those with relatively high incomes and education) less frequently expressed hostility to a regime from which they were getting, in Lasswell's phrase, the most of what there is to get than did those who, as unskilled workers and peasants, were getting the least. It should also be no surprise that among the popular feelings shown toward confessed elitist traitors, who were placed on public trial during the 1930s, there were feelings of contempt, induced, perhaps, in part by jealousy.

At this stage of the argument of this chapter, the relevant point of Bauer's findings is that it was a primordial, primitive, and largely unconscious physical need that had such great portent for the stability of the Soviet political system in the 1930s and 40s. People withdrew their adherence to the system because they were deprived of physical safety—not because they found a discrepancy between the gospel as taught by Marx and as practiced by the Party. And it takes a highly abstracted reading of Khrushchev's speech to the Twentieth

[29] See R. A. Bauer, Some Trends in Sources of Alienation from the Soviet System, *Public Opinion Quarterly*, **19**: 279–291 (1955) and Raymond A. Bauer et al., *How the Soviet System Works*, Cambridge, Harvard University Press, 1956, chs. 12 and 13.

Party Congress in February 1956 [30] not to notice the sense of utter revulsion against the Stalinist purges.[31] Khrushchev was denying neither then nor later the validity of Marxist-Leninist ideology, which in the speech remained a major guidepost for his proposals. He was expressing his abhorrence of the physical suffering, degradation, and death of loyal comrades, which had nothing to do with official dogma. And he also appeared to be circumspectly exonerating himself for not having done much to stop Stalin's arbitrary rule.[32]

The reports that have been written on more recent brainwashing in Hungary and China indicate the same intensive educational techniques.[33] These studies describe a pattern of sleep and food deprivation, neglect of bodily disease (ranging from skin sores to gangrene)

[30] The speech is published in an annotated edition by *The New Leader* under the title The Crimes of the Stalin Era, New York, 1956.

[31] See the general comments of Herbert McClosky and John E. Turner in their study of *The Soviet Dictatorship*, New York, McGraw-Hill Book Co., 1960, 182–183.

[32] Khrushchev in the late 1930s did such a thorough job of liquidating nationalist tendencies in the Ukraine that in March 1939 Stalin rewarded him with full membership in the Politburo.

In Stalin's last years, he infrequently called even the Politburo into session. Khrushchev says [*op. cit., New Leader* ed., 61] that because of this "we will understand how difficult it was for any member of the Political Bureau to take a stand against one or another unjust or improper procedure. . . ." With reference to the spurious charges, a few months before Stalin's death, that several doctors had poisoned two leaders (Zhdanov and another) and tried to poison several others, Khrushchev reported that Stalin passed out copies of the doctors' confessions to members of the Politburo and, Khrushchev commented to the Twentieth Party Congress [*op. cit.,* 49–50]: "the case was so presented that no one could verify the facts on which the investigation was based. There was no possibility of trying to verify facts by contacting those who had made the confessions of guilt. We felt, however, that the case of the arrested doctors was questionable. We knew some of these people personally because they had once treated us. When we examined this 'case' after Stalin's death we found it to be fabricated from beginning to end." Unless one assumes that evidence of Stalin's actions did not exist until his death (instead of being in suppressed existence), it seems appropriate to suggest that Khrushchev and others were quite naturally afraid to discover the evidence.

[33] See Robert Jay Lifton, *Thought Reform and the Psychology of Totalism: a Study of 'Brainwashing' in China,* New York, W. W. Norton & Co., 1961, which is a most penetrating depth-analysis of the phenomenon. See also, for example, Edward Hunter, *Brainwashing: The Story of the Men Who Defied It,* New York, Farrar, Straus, & Cudahy, 1956, esp. ch. 8; and J. A. M. Meerloo, *The Rape of the Mind,* Cleveland and New York, The World Publishing Company, 1956, esp. chs. 9 and 4; Seymour M. Farber and Roger H. L. Wilson, eds., *Control of the Mind,* New York, McGraw-Hill Book Co., 1961.

and of physical discomfort, social isolation from fellow prisoners (physical and psychic separation from them), physical and social dependence on captors and inquisitors, and degradation that at best can be only vaguely sensed by the uninitiated reader. The informers and confessants who are the end result of the process readily and even with apparent eagerness report publicly that they have betrayed their buddies and their generous liberators (that is, captors), and above all that they themselves, the penitent from whose eyes the scales of innocence and guilt have been graciously removed to reveal true spontaneity and freedom, had been the blindest and guiltiest of all.[34]

We have now briefly considered inter alia the political behavior of two general categories of the physically deprived. In the first set, government made no appreciable effort to elicit or coerce either active or passive political participation. Government did not try—very hard at any rate—to induce political activity on the part of the conscientious objectors who were the subjects of the Minnesota experiments. It allowed them to dissent from the clearly majoritarian and clearly governmental decision to unite in the war effort against the enemies of all. Government did not attempt to make Japanese residents and citizens

---

[34] How they could be *both* blind *and* guilty remains a paradox as yet unresolved, perhaps not only by Marxism and Leninism but also by Calvinism or Freudianism. And the paradox has certainly not been resolved by Scientism or even science. Rousseau as a free-thinking Rationalist may have wanted men to be forced to freedom and Stalin as an economic Scientist to liberate men from decadent, bourgeois social influences, but science is no more capable of this than is reason. When self-styled rationalists and social scientists have tried to force things, the former for example in the French Revolution and the latter in the Russian and other Communist Revolutions, they have given indications of no more fundamental knowledge of human behavior than such premodern philosophers as Plato and Aristotle. Even their technical skill at coercion appears to amount only to misapplied behavioral science; else their success at coercion would last longer than is evidenced by the retractions of the confessors as soon as they are physically removed from the coercive environment. If it is not too completely denying the paradox of innocent sin, one may say that the error (or the sin) of self-styled rationalists or social scientists is the false notion that they have a complete understanding of reality and therefore (in a grand non sequitur) can rightly compel a man to behave in accordance with their "rational" or "scientific" understanding of reality. This is not to suggest that the category of those who coerce includes only "rationalists" and "social scientists." But in the eighteenth and twentieth centuries coercion has been justified on rationalist and scientific grounds, and the pursuit of freedom has been arrogated to themselves by elite groups on the same basically dogmatic grounds that have been used by elite groups that were frankly anti-rationalist or anti-scientific and had no interest in freedom for anything but the "state."

in America take a loyal part in the war effort. In fact the people and their government made it enormously difficult for them to do so. Government in Germany did not try very hard to make Jewish, Polish, and Russian concentration-camp internees develop a sense of affirmative participation in the war effort.

In the second set government tried very hard. Those high-ranking party activists who were believed to have become disloyal to the Stalinist regime in the 1930s were subjected to intensive indoctrination in prison—indoctrination that involved enormous expenditures of time and psychic energy on the part of the government through its agents, the secret police and the prison officials. Communications media of the period made vigorous efforts to establish popular loyalty to government by using the disloyal as examples of traitors who had rationally admitted their scientific errors (i.e., confessed their sin of dissent) and were now reshaped. Comparable efforts were made by government in China during the Korean War of 1950–1953, efforts directed at inducing active loyalty and participation among both the captured enemy and the Chinese public.

The result, I am here asserting, was in both kinds of situation to induce not active or passive political participation but to induce political apathy. And the chief reason I advance is that people in both circumstances were unavoidably so preoccupied with meeting their physical needs as to make political activity almost impossible, in any case quite improbable.

What political participation is

To clarify this argument, let me define two rather crucial terms—*political participation* and *political apathy*. The reader will then be able more readily to judge the sense or nonsense of the posited relationship between physical deprivation and political action. Political participation is taking part in making the basic decisions as to what are the common goals of one's society and as to the best ways to move towards these goals. Active political participation is the kind engaged in by the political elite—the people who are not quite accurately called the decision makers (and implementers)—the lawmakers (and the administrators). Passive political participation is the kind engaged in by the general public—the people who read newspapers; occasionally talk politics with neighbors; attend political rallies and cheer candidates, parties, or issues; and vote.

"Active" and "passive" are clearly both qualitative and quantitative distinctions. Abstractly they are analogous—and only analogous—to positive and negative charges (large or small) of electricity. Both are subsets of the same set. Both are necessary to the concept of political action, again only analogously, in the same sense that protons and electrons are necessary to the concept of the atom. The act of running for governmental office differs from that of voting for a candidate. The ordinary citizen is taking part in the process of making basic ends-and-means decisions for the members of the society, for all the people who are physically located within the boundaries of the state. So is the candidate. But the candidate differs from the voter in that he is responsible for articulating (i.e., giving coherent expression to) the publicly manifest needs of the members of the society and the public means appropriate for achieving their satisfaction. And the administrator of public policy (e.g., the head executive of a governmental bureau like the post office or the judge who administers justice under the constitutional and statutory laws of the society) also differs from the citizen in that he is the person who operates the agency which the ordinary member of the society from time to time uses for his own purposes—to send a message to a friend or to defend himself from the charge of doing a public wrong (committing a crime) or a private wrong (committing a tort). This role relationship between candidate and voter, administrator and citizen represents a qualitative distinction.

The degree of activity of both candidates and their supporters (or opponents) distinguishes people quantitatively. There are chiefs of state who are active, like Bismarck and Theodore Roosevelt; and rather inactive, like Hindenburg and Coolidge. There are administrators who are active, like Harold Ickes and David Lilienthal during the New Deal in the 1930s in America; and administrators who are inactive, like most local postmasters. There are citizens who are active, like Wendell Phillips, the magnificent agitator for equality between black and white and between employee and employer in nineteenth-century America, or Susan B. Anthony, the women's suffragist. And there are citizens who are inactive, like almost everyone else, almost all the time save when there is an election.

The distinction between activity and passivity is, in part, that arising from the role relationship, in which the elite are defined as those who present ends-and-means alternatives to the general public, who in turn choose among the various alternatives presented to them by the elite. But the distinction necessarily includes the degree of activity. A citizen like Wendell Phillips, never really a part of any government, was manifestly active and manifestly presented a program that had policy content. On the issue of abolishing slavery the public ultimately exercised a choice in its support of emancipation (among other things) when it re-elected Lincoln almost two years after the Emancipation Proclamation and some thirty years after Phillips began to talk against slavery.

The common characteristic of active and passive political participants is their *inter*action, their attraction *to one another*. Again the analogy in physics of mutual attraction between electrons and protons is appropriate, as is the mutual attraction between male and female in all species of plants and animals that are sexed. Indeed to speak of the attraction between male and female is in part tautological, because it is the attraction that partly establishes the distinction.

The distinction between active and passive participants may be further clarified by distinguishing both kinds from people who are politically apathetic. These are the ones who are not involved, who neither care about taking part nor actually take part in making or implementing social decisions on ends and means. In abstract and admittedly crude terms, this incloses the category of people who never vote in any election in which they *can* make a choice, evince no interest in politics (as, e.g., by reading only the sports page of the newspaper), and live immediately and only for themselves. Saint Simeon Stylites, perched atop the sixty-foot pillar of stone where he spent most of his adult life, would be a good example were it not for the fact that from his perch he preached; made converts, some of whom also came to perch on pillars; and took part in church politics. A more clear-cut example is a hermit who has renounced society or the isolated Japanese soldier who lives by himself on an island in the Pacific, ten or more years after the war with the United States has ended.

Since such relatively pure cases are rare and of micropolitical significance, we look for our everyday examples in ordinary societies. The everyday examples are those misery-laden people who form a manipulable "mass"—pliant or frangible in the hands of an elite and a general public. These apoliticals are the electronic vacuum tubes and transistors, the cogs and levers, or the sterile soil under a nuclear explosion: they are used, things are done to them, their form is changed. But politically they never use others, never act, never change themselves. In the pure case, indeed, it is doubtful that they have ever existed in more than minute numbers. In the real case, they are numbered in the millions.

The body and politics

After this statement of definitions, it should be clear why I posit a relationship between deprivation of physical needs and political apathy. The person who must concentrate all his energies merely on staying alive is in no position to concern himself actively or passively with policy decisions or their implementation. He is, in other words, for all practical purposes apolitical. "Don," the architect and conscientious objector in the Minnesota experiments, turned more and more inward as his chronic hunger persisted. He lost to a degree his ability to choose between the "right" of not violating the dietary rules and the "wrong" of cheating on them. He wanted to get more food than the others during the post-experimental rehabilitation period, and during this period he ate compulsively and gluttonously. He had lost interest in post-war social service abroad. He was to a disturbing degree amoral, asocial, and apolitical. He was not himself.

Neither indeed were those who were purged in Eastern Europe in the 1930s to 1950s, or those who lost themselves in the utterly involuntary, artificially brutalized society—or mass—in concentration camps. And a more sophisticated governmental and public opinion in America and elsewhere has adopted a more charitable and realistic view of prisoners in the Korean War. These captives, with an absence of free choice that is almost incomprehensible to most people in the prosperous, free Western world, expressed the views of their captors and became their pliant, shattered instruments, casually wired together for a useful moment and then discarded.

However, for a large portion of the world's inhabitants, existence is so marginal that the capacity for exercising discretionary judgment in politics, for making deliberate choices, is severely limited by the sheer necessity of staying alive. Far from having a standard of living, these people are alert only to the cruder index of survival, a task that quite preoccupies their daylight hours and, in the cold of winter, the dark hours when they should be asleep.

The chart that follows can give some crude indication why, for example, political activity in Peru has been confined to the elite and in Sweden is popularly widespread.

In his study of *Political Man,* Lipset makes a persuasive case for relating the stage of economic development in various countries to

Calorie and Protein Consumption in Selected Countries

	Calories per Person per Day	Required Calories per Person per Day	Actual as Percent of Required	Protein per Person per Year (1947–1948)	Index of Protein Consumption (Switzerland = 100)
I. Countries with inadequate diets					
Peru	2080	2540	−18.1	120.3	22
Tanganyika	1980	2420	−18.2	–	–
India	1850	2250	−17.8	162.8	30
Pakistan	2180	2300	−5.2	–	–
Egypt	2380	2390	−0.4	196.0	36
Union of South Africa	2650	2400	+10.4	287.2	52
II. Countries with adequate diets					
Sweden	2980	2840	+10.5	690.6	126
Netherlands	2910	2630	+10.6	402.4	73
U.S.S.R.	3020	2710	+11.4	–	–
Switzerland	3075	2720	+13.1	549.0	100
United States	3070	2640	+16.3	610.8	111
New Zealand	3310	2670	+23.8	663.8	121

Calorie data are from United Nations, *Report on the World Social Situation*, New York, United Nations, 1957, 61. Protein data are from W. S. Woytinsky and E. S. Woytinsky, *World Population & Production: Trends & Outlook*, New York, Twentieth Century Fund, 1953, 292–293. [The Woytinskys are not to be charged with the Index of Protein Consumption, which I independently computed from the Woytinsky table. The protein consumption per person per year represents the sum of a series of items in Woytinsky, including meat, milk and cheese, eggs, fish, pulses (beans, peas, lentils), and nuts.]

the degree of democratization.[35]   The indexes in the table are meant to suggest an earlier stage, that of pre- and protopoliticization of a society, that is, the stage before or during the first establishment of a political community.   There must be relatively adequate food in a country before it can develop a general public, a broad group that is

[35] Seymour Martin Lipset, *Political Man: the Social Bases of Politics*, Garden City, N. Y., Doubleday & Co., 1960, ch. 2, Economic Development and Democracy. Note also his article, Some Social Requisites of Democracy: Economic Development and Political Legitimacy, *American Political Science Review*, **53**: 69–105 (1959).   Economically developed but undemocratic nations like Germany and Japan before the Second World War limit the posited relationship, indicating non-economic factors are also relevant.

more than an unrelated agglomeration of people living within certain territorial boundaries. Before there can be government that in any real way interacts with the general public, there must be some significant kind of national consciousness, some sense of national community. A person who is compelled (or believes he is compelled) to focus his attention on the primitive production and consumption of food is not likely to know or—if he knows—to care about any community beyond his own little village. Long before there can be responsible or irresponsible popular government, long before the question of dictatorship or democracy can be taken up, the problem of survival must be solved so that a political community itself can develop, so that people can divert some of their attention to politics.

Just when this stage occurs cannot yet be determined, except post hoc.[36] From the table, it is reasonable to suggest that a political community does not yet exist in Peru and that any revolution there in, let us say, the 1960s is far more likely to be a contest between elites than one in which the elites are competing for and relying on broad popular support.

To put this discussion in perspective, we can now briefly mention matters of *style*, of political *means* as they are employed in a society that has rather limited government and a real constitution of sorts (India) and in a society that has a less limited government and not a very real sort of constitution (the Soviet Union). This brief discussion will serve only to indicate what this chapter is mainly *not* concerned with (style—the *kind* of participation) and what it *is* mainly concerned with (the existence or nonexistence of participation). To the extent that deprivation of physical needs makes for politics that is abnormal in the West European or American sense, this chapter is relevant to extreme political action in times of crisis in constitutional democracies and to political action and inaction in countries where people are chronically threatened with physical deprivation.

India raises a question about the relationship between physical needs of its people, which are very inadequately met, and a sense of national community and the form of government. By a monistic reading of the posited relationship, India should scarcely be a national community and surely nothing like the democracy which its free elections suggest it is. Surely the beginnings of a national community are

[36] This indeterminacy need not be considered appalling when we recall that public opinion polls in a highly developed democracy cannot yet predict the outcome of a close election and that economic statistics cannot yet precisely predict economic cycles.

in evidence and surely people exercise some political choice. But it seems most appropriate to say that there is substantial one-party rule, that there is not indeed a totalitarian state but something which may be called a constitutional oligarchy. The reasons for India's not being totalitarian like China are in part traceable to the different backgrounds of the two governing classes. India's elite has been trained in English political traditions, whereas China's has learned its political skills in the Soviet Union, the unacknowledged child of Russian autocracy. As far as popular preference is concerned—as far as the difference between the people being passive participants rather than apathetics—it appears very likely that the largely nonparticipant populations of both India and China would have accepted either totalitarian or constitutional leadership.

The Soviet Union presents an opposite question. Why should a country that is probably as well fed as the Netherlands and is increasingly able to satisfy the physical needs of the populace not be a democracy? Social scientists are able to provide profuse and persuasive arguments for the fact that it is not. The more precisely relevant question at this point is whether the dictatorship will continue to persist for an indefinite time period. The death of Stalin in 1953 was followed rather quickly by considerable relaxation of the most severe sanctions, in a society that for most of a century had been carefully watched and controlled by secret police responsible to an irresponsible oligarchy. First may come pressures from lower ranks of the elite to relax sanctions further. Then popular pressures for further relaxation of both the enforced austerity and the watchfulness of the police may develop, more openly than they have in Russia at any time since before the 1861 emancipation of serfs. The effect of economic betterment should therefore be to free people increasingly from economic preoccupations and to give them time and inclination to consider their political condition.

If this theoretical analysis makes sense, the consequences of failure and success to meet the pervasive and enduring physical needs remain relevant to a discussion of political behavior in both poor and prosperous countries. The problems of political behavior under such different circumstances get more detailed treatment in later chapters. We should now turn our attention to the relationship between other basic needs and political behavior.

Among these other needs we do not consider security until after the others. And then it is the subject of an entire chapter. This is because security, as I have already indicated, does not appear to be in the same category with the other needs which are pursued for their own sake and also because the political portent of personal security and insecurity is so enormous. This leaves us with three other basic needs which do appear to be pursued by normal human beings everywhere and for the inherent enjoyment which the pursuit and satisfaction of these needs involves. These three are the social needs, the need for self-esteem or self-respect, and the need for self-realization or -actualization. As we shall see, the pursuit and the satisfaction of each of these has political portent.

CHAPTER 2

Social and individual nature

The social needs

The social needs are those that arise from the deep desire people have to get together, be together, and stay together. Various manifestations of this urge have been analyzed and emphasized by philosophers, moral and religious leaders, sociologists, and psychologists since the time that man started to take a close look at himself. When he used the phrase "tenderness of her love" to describe the feeling of a wife for her husband, Plato was describing two kinds of affection: fondness and sexual desire. When he wrote about love [1] in his first letter to some followers in Corinth, the Apostle Paul said we are nothing if we lack charity, the ability to do unto others as we would have them do unto us, which was the central exhortation of Jesus. When Aristotle described man as zoön politikon, which may most appropriately be translated as "social animal with some political interests," he was emphasizing the broad social relationships between a person and members of the community at large, the polity. Each of these conceptuali-

[1] There are at least four Greek words which signify different connotations of the English word love: *philia,* meaning friendly love, affectionate regard, tenderness; *philotes,* meaning friendship, love, affection; *eros,* meaning basically sexual love or physical desire (but not simple lust, which is epithymia or lagneia); and *agape,* meaning altruism or charity, "Christian" love. Plato's phrase here quoted is "philia . . . ton erota" and Paul's, as paraphrased, "agapen de me ekho, ouden eimi." [Plato, *Symposium,* 179C (W. R. M. Lamb, transl.), London, William Heinemann Ltd., 1925, vol. 5, 104; and *The New Testament,* I Cor. 13:2–C. Tischendorf, ed., *Novum Testamentum Graece,* Lipsiae (Leipzig), J. D. Hinrichs, 1877, 772.]

31

zations is different from the other and each presupposes a common human desire.

The organic origins and loci of this desire have not yet been fixed. It is clear only that it exists and apparently is so fundamental to human beings (not to mention other species) that complete deprivation of it makes human behavior uncharacteristic, utterly abnormal. Freud described its essence as being the sexual urge, the desire of one sexual partner for another, but at one point [2] described the phenomenon so broadly as to make it include the tenderness, sex, and altruism connotations of the English word *love*. Until further research sheds more light on its origin, we must remain content and discontent with the notion that it is in a very complicated way located in the central nervous system, as this system is influenced by stimuli from both inside and outside the human organism.[3] This desire is one of the most basic and durable ones, not because it is so much discussed but because the evidence is so overwhelming that people cannot live alone, that they indeed are social animals. It is not simply that society could not exist but for this strong drive: man himself could not do so.[4]

I hope it is not belaboring a point already emphasized to suggest once more that these social needs appear to be neither prior to nor

---

[2] Sigmund Freud, *Group Psychology and the Analysis of the Ego*, London, The Hogarth Press, 1922, 37–40.

[3] See M. F. A. Montague, The Origin and Nature of Social Life and the Biological Basis of Cooperation, *Journal of Social Psychology*, **29**: 267–283 (1949); W. C. Allee, *Animal Aggregations*, Chicago, University of Chicago Press, 1931, ch. 19, Animal Aggregations and Social Life, and Allee, *Cooperation among Animals*, New York, Henry Schurman, 1951. In an intriguing report based on the study of ants, T. C. Schnierla, Problems in the Biopsychology of Social Organization, *Journal of Abnormal and Social Psychology*, **41**: 385–402 (1946), uses the term "trophallaxis" to designate "biological factors contributing to the facilitation of primary inter-individual stimulative relationships." In a more restricted sense, the term was used earlier. [Allee, *Animal Aggregations*, 338.] Allee did not claim discovery of the term or the basic proposition. But we still lack adequate knowledge of where the desire to get together, be together, and stay together rests in the organism.

[4] The reader is warned not to become so enamored of love as to shove other needs out of the organism and explain all behavior in terms of love's presence or absence. Like all monistic analyses, that one is easy on the mind and unfair to both Homo sapiens and his culture, however plausible it may be in societies where almost everyone's physical needs are satisfied. In the Second World War it was not only trophallaxis that beat the Axis. The desire to survive, and to survive with certain conditions protected, was also involved.

simultaneous with the physical needs, but rather that the social needs usually are subsequent to the physical. We have already noted the way "Don," the participant in the Minnesota starvation experiments, withdrew from others when his physical hunger came to dominate his life. We know that concentration camp inmates and prisoners subjected to severe physical deprivation in the brainwashing process became concerned with physical survival of themselves, usually quite regardless of the harm they did to others in order to survive. And we have some evidence that unemployment when persistent can change a coherent social group into a hungry, amorphous agglomerate.

Conversely, activation of the physical needs may intensify group feeling—activate the "subsequent" need to get, be, and stay together. Such events as wars, the threat of wars, economic crises, and disasters seem, more often than not, to enhance solidarity in groups ranging from the nuclear family to the national community (even allied nations in wartime). This enhanced solidarity, however, appears to be a reaction that occurs when the physical threat is not immediately severe to the individual [5] or, if severe, has passed its peak. There was a heightened sense of community in the United States and in Germany during the Great Depression of 1929–1939, after some sense had emerged that the problems of physical survival were manageable. There was a heightened sense of community in the U.S.S.R. after the German invasion of June 1941 and in the United States after the Japanese attack on Pearl Harbor in December 1941. The same phenomenon occurred following the Halifax disaster in December 1917.[6]

It is evident that the retrogression to behavior whose prime motivation is sheer individual survival is a less permanent change than one might suppose. Concentration camp inmates began their return to normal social relationships as soon as they were rescued. And so

[5] A series of laboratory experiments indicates that the threat of an electric shock or a hypodermic injection of glucose or the actual deprivation of food for about a day heightened the desire of the student-subjects to be together. [Stanley Schachter, *The Psychology of Affiliation,* Stanford, Stanford University Press, 1959.]

[6] See Samuel H. Prince, *Catastrophe and Social Change,* Columbia University Studies in History, Economics and Public Law, vol. 94, no. 1, 1920, 47–48. But note also that "the citizens of Halifax were almost entirely oblivious to the progress of the war and other matters of world interest, for many days after the disaster." [*Ibid.,* 77.] On the effect of sleep deprivation on group solidarity in the army in combat zones, see A. M. Rose, Social Psychological Effects of Physical Deprivation, *Journal of Health and Human Behavior,* 1: 285–289 (1960).

did those Westerners brainwashed in China.[7]   To explain both the mental regression and recovery on habit or on social conditioning—quite apart from any organic tendencies—scarcely seems adequate.   If the physical needs were not operating when a person entered a concentration camp, death rather than survival should have been the universal consequence of such a profoundly shocking change in the environment.   If the social needs did not re-emerge upon release from the camps, the traumatic conditioning to activity concerned with survival should have kept the liberated ones in the Hobbesian condition far longer than it did.

Nevertheless, political action would be as impossible without the need of people to get, be, and stay together as it would without prior, continuous, and more than minimal satisfaction of the physical needs. Satisfaction of the physical needs is a condition precedent for politics; existence of the social needs is both a condition precedent and a condition concurrent.   People become involved in public affairs both because some of their social needs have been otherwise met and because they find *some* inherent social satisfaction in political involvement.

Some satisfaction of the social needs in other than political ways is thus probably necessary to make it possible for people to take part in the process of deciding what are the common goals of their society and how best to achieve them.   People who are so lonely, so bereft of human contact, that they are preoccupied with meeting this particular need will probably have to meet it first by the simple process of associating with others in nonpolitical groups.   And before they can do even this, people must have acquired a minimal sense of belonging in the family itself.   At the other end, logically speaking, people break apart—disaffiliate—when they engage in political contests.   They do this for a variety of reasons, not all of them social.   But as long as they are *engaged,* the social need is involved, its sign having changed from positive to negative.

[7] "Recovery of normal behavior ran parallel with improvement of bodily health and was often surprisingly rapid, leaving only a feeling akin to that of having had a bad dream."   [F. M. Lipscomb, German Concentration Camps: Diseases Encountered at Belsen, in H. L. Tidy and J. M. B. Kutschbach, eds., *Inter-Allied Conferences on War Medicine,* London, Staples Press, Ltd., 1947, 462–465 at 464.] On the more enduring though impermanent changes among Westerners brainwashed in Communist China, see Robert Jay Lifton, *Thought Reform and the Psychology of Totalism,* New York, W. W. Norton & Co., 1961.   Lifton concludes that only one of the twenty-five Westerners he interviewed was "a truly successful convert."   [*Ibid.,* 237.]

The family, the progenitor of all other social units,[8] is in many ways more significant politically than such readily recognizable political groupings as business, labor, and farm pressure groups—and political parties themselves. If an individual does not develop, *within the family*, the sense of belonging, dignity, and indeed individuality, which are necessary for him to become a relatively autonomous and unique person, he is more likely to end up a complete social isolate than a participant in anything.

We will reserve for full discussion in a separate chapter the *ways* in which the family and other face-to-face groups form the political attitudes and behavior of the individual. The relevant point here is that the family, whether nuclear or extended, is necessary for the individual to become social and therefore political: that is, the family is a major determinant not only for the style in which a person becomes politically involved, but also for the involvement as such. A person who has not achieved the basic sense of both belonging and of being an individual will be even less able to take part in making political decisions than an isolated farmer in the vastness of the Great Plains of western United States, because such a creature will not be either social or individual. Only in the biological and not psychological sense will he be even a human being.[9]

It follows logically, from the definition given earlier of political participation, and psychologically, as indicated in the paragraph immediately above, that we can, by and large, exclude from the category of participants those people whose family life is relatively nonexistent as a result of parental death and orphaned upbringing and those whom totalitarian governments seek to raise in state orphanages altogether away from their natural or adopted parents. The dreams of such governments to raise a new generation of true servants of the state are probably impossible to realize except on a very small scale. The products of such a regimen are deliberately made into political

[8] By this I do not mean to imply any *necessary* relationship between the role structure (the pattern of interpersonal relationships) within a family in a particular culture and the role structure in other groups, even though the pattern of parent-child relationships probably does have some influence on the structure of other groups. (Note that Aristotle depreciates the frequent failure to recognize a qualitative distinction between the family and other communities—and then, like Hobbes after him, proceeds to make the state an organism of which individuals are members, like feet or hands.) [Aristotle, *Politics*, Bk. I (H. Rackham, transl.), London, William Heinemann Ltd., 1932, 3–13.]

[9] Evidence for this broad assertion is discussed in Chapter 5.

apathetics, nonparticipants, the useful vacuum tubes we have already mentioned. However active they may be in serving public policy—and the governments demand an active compliance from their subjects—they have nothing to do with making it.

The growth of agrarian political activity in late nineteenth-century America illustrates the relationship between nonfamilial but still rather archetypical social activity and political involvement. Isolated farm families were confronted with the personally devastating economic consequences of crop surpluses, declining commodity prices, a steadily deflating currency, and debt. Before they finally were able to take effective political action, they took joint social action through the Granges (which specifically disavowed politics) in the form of economic boycotts, purchasing and marketing cooperatives, and the exchange of technical information on how best to raise crops and manage the business aspects of farming.

Before they did this, farmers simply got together, in the company that misery loves. If we can credit careful historians of agrarianism, the first get-togethers were scarcely political at all. They held picnics and rallies to which whole families came, often with box lunches for all-day socializing.[10] Only when they had thus developed a community sense—become a social group rather than a mere scattered rural population—did they turn their minds to the political possibilities of solving problems that hitherto had been common to all individuals but not communal, subjectively private but not consciously public. Lest the importance of this socializing process be minimized, be it remembered that it took the better part of a full generation—from the 1860s to the 1890s—for farmers to develop the degree of political organization that was cohesive, articulate, and powerful enough to make their demands a matter of major worry to the national political parties. This of course does not mean that the formation of a group was the only factor producing the farm bloc: socializing was a necessary but not sufficient cause for political action.

One manifestation of the social needs is of such enormous political portent as to require special comment at this point. It is the phenomenon of identification. Freud, who was probably the first to consider it systematically, traced its origins to the relationship of the child to his mother. A child from infancy leaned towards his mother in the process of childhood dependence. His leaning grew to love—as Freud

[10] John D. Hicks, *The Populist Revolt*, Minneapolis, University of Minnesota Press, 1931, ch. 5, Alliance Activities, esp. 128–141.

called it, genital love—and then the growing child developed a sense of rivalry towards his father, whose relationships with his mother the child unconsciously wanted to assume. So his love toward his mother and his love and envy of his father combined to establish fundamental emotional patterns within the family that became rather permanent prototypes for broader relationships with the other people, that is, with society.[11]

We do not have to accept altogether the sexual etiology to recognize the great significance of identification and of the particular, very intricate, and complicated ways in which enduring patterns of identification are established in childhood. People *do* identify with others in a very intimate way, however conscious or unconscious they are of doing so, and the process has tremendous political consequences. Identification occurs both positively and negatively: individuals become emotionally bound up with other individuals as objects of either love or hatred or—more likely than either—as individual objects of both love and hatred. We are both attracted to and repelled by the same person, even though we seldom are willing to face this aspect of reality, partly because it is likely to mean we are to ourselves both attractive and repellent.

The phenomenon of identification is the tendency of an individual (A) to put himself in another's (B's) place or, more exactly, mentally to *be* that other person and to defend or attack B as though B *were* A. One archetype of this phenomenon is the tendency common to mothers, and even sometimes fathers, to smile and laugh with sheer joy when their child does likewise for the first time (and thereafter). Another example—more archetypical—is the tendency of the child to smile and laugh as a mere uneducated infant when those big people, whom he comes to know and puzzle over as his parents, in a similarly uneducated manner smile and laugh. The here-relevant characteristic of this interaction is precisely that it is spontaneous, uneducated, and natural.

And so is the reaction, more truly the interaction, in which individual members of an audience watching a motion picture so completely identify with the characters on the screen that they as individuals rejoice at the success of others with whom they affirmatively identify and show sorrow, anger, and contempt at the success of others with whom they negatively identify. People who read books are

---

[11] For a lucid and indeed authentic statement of the Freudian position, see Sigmund Freud, *Group Psychology and the Analysis of the Ego,* London. The Hogarth Press, 1922, ch. 7, Identification.

amused at the antics of the legendary cowboy in the movie theater who yells "Give him hell" to the hero and shoots his gun in the direction of the villain on the screen. But the reaction (or interaction) of the more sophisticated who so subtly understand the profound and tragic conflict that faced Hamlet or Macbeth or Faust or Rubashov differs in being subtle, not in the tendency to identify. It is the adjective, not the noun, that here distinguishes the cowboy from the intellectual.

In the theater [12] a further identification process goes on. A, the observer-participant sitting in the audience, is identifying not only with B_1 and B_2, the hero and the villain of the drama, but also with A_2, A_3, through A_n—the other members of the audience. He tends to be pleased and displeased when $A_{2...n}$ are so too, and not to be displeased and pleased when they are not displeased and pleased. His reaction to the drama gets its emotional tone from those who are watching it with him. If the others like the show, he will applaud with them; if they like it and he does not, he is apt to remain silent or be very quiet in showing his disapproval, in part because he wants —needs—to be and go with $A_{2...n}$ and finds it very lonesome to be and go against them. And if he does go against them, he consciously or unconsciously will tend to seek support for his views from members of a different audience, one whose taste and discrimination are superior to that of the audience present, that is, another group of people who are like him. This identification phenomenon does not of course apply only to the sophisticated. The cowboy who may be laughed at for shooting the screen villain will take refuge, get emotional support, by reminding himself that other good cowboys (ones like himself) would have done the same thing.

This conflict in identifications—and conflict between identification and what the individual in his own mind regards as good or evil—is one of the most profound and enduring that man is confronted with, starting when he first realizes that he wants to be with others (to merge the self with the other) and to be himself (to distinguish the self from the other). Indeed, the conflict starts earlier than does the realization of its existence: it begins with the child who sometimes depends on the love of his parents and others, and who at other times wants to be free from smothering parental affection, frustrating pa-

---

[12] Both "legitimate" and "motion picture." I do not mean to imply anything uniquely spurious or illegitimate about movies. Neither "Hollywood" nor "Broadway" has a monopoly on the authentic or the phony, but the usage of "legitimate" is old, indeed effete, enough to be venerated without affect.

rental moral admonition, and the active concern for his welfare on the part of other people—including society—who often demand conformity and affection as the price for this concern. He need not know that he must be both together and alone: he feels it.

Projection is one kind of identification that occurs between one individual and others.[13] Although in its most common Freudian usage, projection has been employed to explain neurosis, mild mental abnormality or illness, it is also useful to explain behavior that is quite common (normal), however unhealthy it might be for the individual who projects. A little girl who in play wants to wear the adult-styled and -sized dresses and high-heeled shoes that she extracts from her mother's wardrobe is identifying with her mother. She is also identifying with her mother when she punishes (with words or hands) a little doll that has in fantasy wet her doll crib. When, close to dinner time, the little girl reports that her doll is hungry, she is projecting into the doll her own desire to eat. When a somewhat older boy watching a wild west movie says "bang-bang" as the hero is threatened by the villain, he is identifying. When the boy indicates anger at that bad cowboy who was mean to that poor Indian, he may be not only identifying with the Indian but also projecting, as a consequence of being punished for making nasty comments about that dark-skinned man who came to the door yesterday. The child (A) imputes to the cowboy (B) his own (A's) prejudice and punishes B because A got punished. The girl who reports that her doll is hungry is making an affirmative projection—the girl wants to eat. The boy who gets angry with the bad cowboy is making a negative projection—the boy does not want to be punished and is displacing onto the cowboy the racial prejudice he does not want to face in himself.[14]

[13] Like identification, projection is a term and phenomenon that Freud gave currency to, but projection was given more emphasis by his daughter Anna in the searching analysis she did of *The Ego and the Mechanisms of Defence*, New York, International Universities Press, 1946. (The volume first appeared in German in 1936 when her father was eighty years old, three years before he died.) I claim neither Freudian orthodoxy nor unorthodoxy in my analysis of projection or any other mental process.

[14] For an extended consideration of projection, see A. Freud, *op. cit.*, especially ch. 9, Identification with the Aggressor, and ch. 10, A Form of Altruism. The illustrative cases of the hungry girl and the prejudiced boy are far too complicated to be adequately explained in terms of identification and projection. For example, the girl may have had a compulsive desire to eat because of a history of chronic infantile hunger; the boy may have been severely beaten by a swarthy playmate at school. My present purpose is not to analyze holistically the children but to isolate conceptually the two psychic processes under consideration.

Now let us briefly revert to our farmers in America in the late nineteenth century, a group whose political movement has with gross oversimplification been called populism. We got them together with the help of the social needs. Or more exactly, *they* got together, in part because of their natural social need. Now let us for a moment consider how they identified and projected.

When they got together, farmers felt that they were with their own kind of people and that these were—as Jefferson had said—God's chosen people, who since the burgeoning of industries and cities no longer enjoyed universal public acceptance as the elect of Jefferson and of God. They felt a kind of kinship not merely in being together with other members of the human race but also in being with other people who were like themselves and different from those others, the bad ones. Farmers were looked upon as oafs, bumpkins (or was it pumpkins?), maladroit and uncoordinated musclemen who were not quite so clumsy at hopping from one clod to another as they were at expressing their grievances in speech and writing. Before being able to attack this image of themselves, which seems to have been clearly the dominant one in the cities, among ordinary citizens and elitists alike,[15] farmers had to build an image which in their own minds indicated they were significant and intelligent people. They were able to do this by a process of enlarging their world in the same way that anyone does who sees a movie or a play or reads a newspaper or a book. At their get-togethers they were told that they were their own best friends, perhaps their only true friends, and that they had common enemies. They heard these things from spokesmen whose backgrounds were no more typically rural than their education but who had passionately adopted the farmers' interests as their own.[16]

---

[15] It is only since the 1930s that written and spoken jokes about stupid and clumsy farmers appear to have lost their currency and respectability in America.

[16] James B. Weaver, the Populist candidate for the Presidency in 1892, graduated from law school at the age of 21 and practiced law in Iowa before and after the Civil War, in which he attained the brevetted rank of brigadier general. [Hicks, *op. cit.*, 164.] Ignatius Donnelly moved from Pennsylvania as a young man to Minnesota, where he practiced law, ran for public office (serving three terms in Congress), and became successful as an orator and writer rather than as a farmer. [*Ibid.*, 162–163.] Thomas E. Watson of Georgia, a poor farm boy, by his own great early efforts left the soil to become a school teacher, lawyer, and legislator. [*Ibid.*, 176–177.] "Pitchfork" Ben Tillman of South Carolina was the son of a slaveholding but socially marginal planter; he was given a 400-acre farm by his enterprising mother shortly after the Civil War. [*Ibid.*, 143–144.] Senator William A. Peffer of Kansas started as a school teacher and farmer but by the

When farmers identified with each other, they were doing so on the realistic basis of common interest. They were poor and the victims of a political system still pretty largely beyond their control. Their spokesmen were aiding in the establishment of this nonrational sense of identification. It was quite rational to establish this, because without such a sense of common interest their political action would have been fragmentary, individual, and a failure. When farmers identified with their leaders as men of vigor, determination, and courage, they were also socializing in a way that was relevant to their common purpose. When, however, they made their leaders into heroes—and therefore themselves into heroes—their identification with the leaders lost contact with reality in the sense that neither farmers nor their leaders were probably any more or less heroic than anyone else would be under comparable circumstances of victimization by "bad guys." When this step was reached, life became like the movies. The farmers in their own minds embodied all the essential virtues and their political opponents all the significant vices. In their minds, life in the open country became, as Jefferson had seen it, the good life, and life in the cramped, fetid city became evil—save perhaps for the downtrodden in the cities who were also exploited by the bad guys. And these downtrodden were more likely than not farm-raised young people whom circumstances (the "interests") had forced into cities and sin.

We can get some clue as to the projections which people, including farmers, were making in late nineteenth-century America from a novel written by Ignatius Donnelly, one of the most articulate and revered of the populists. *Caesar's Column,* of which over 260,000 copies had been printed when the total population of the United States was about 85.4 million,[17] presents a picture of Victorian innocence and innocents

age of about thirty-five was occupied mainly with practicing law and then editing a local paper before he entered politics. [*Ibid.,* 179–180.] And William Jennings Bryan apparently never laid hands on a plow or pitchfork, save as a political campaigner. After attending college and law school he went straight into law and politics. [M. R. Werner, *Bryan,* New York, Harcourt, Brace & Co., 1929, is a full and fair-minded biography.] This is no criticism of these agrarian leaders. Had they really worked in the land, they could hardly have become such articulate and effective farm spokesmen, any more than a person who is racked by a chronic illness can practice medicine. Nor is it a criticism of farmers, whose attachment to their leaders was as natural as that of a patient to his doctor.

[17] First published in 1890, 260,000 copies of this book were printed by 1906. The 1906 total population of the United States was 85.4 million. Comparable 1960 publication would amount to 550,000 copies, given a total population of 180 million.

betrayed and used by a small group of dark and cunning men who led a life of fulfillment in New York, with an abominable, titillating, intriguing indulgence in sex, money, and power. The degraded populace rises in a proletarian revolt, destroys this oligarchy, and then falls prey to the leader, a new Caesar as vicious as the destroyed oligarchs. The most powerful of the oligarchs, a Jew, when mortally wounded, pays a rough fellow $100,000 to finish him off. The good, ordinary people, defeated and "Semitized" by men of great talent,[18] now fall prey to the canaille and are faced with anarchy, chaos, and despair. The heroes are valiant: they battle without stint to exhaustion and defeat; the vicious villains, whether of the elite or the mob, are of course not valiant but implacable. The new hope is a small émigré society in Africa, with a wall thirty feet high to keep the outside world out.

The content of this novel and its very wide readership suggest—and only suggest—that popular beliefs of the time included a sense of self-righteousness and of the righteousness of innocence. The writing reflects a simple polarity not just between abstract good and abstract evil, but between real people of perfect virtue and perfect iniquity. The novel and its popularity also suggest, but do not conclusively demonstrate, that adherents of populism had a secret yearning for the enjoyment of illicit sex, money, and power. If this indeed was so, adherents of populism were projecting impulses which they consciously recognized as being wrongful but which they nonetheless unconsciously held. They were transporting the content of their own mental barnyards to the cities and throwing it at the dark and dangerous men who were lurking there. And yet this occasionally lascivious book has an engaging, fresh air of affection and of faith that social harmony can be readily realized.

In the twentieth century, projection appears to operate rather often in international politics. Hitler and the Nazis became quite innocent about announcing the aggressive tendencies of (actually irresolute) France in the Rhineland before moving in German troops, and about the threat that the "so-called" free city of Danzig constituted for Germany before Danzig was absorbed. It was not hard to predict the take-over of Czechoslovakia after Nazis called to public attention the depredations against Sudeten Germans by Czechoslovakia. Other, more ambivalent cases: the Soviet charge in 1961 that the United

---

[18] On the anti-Semitism of populism, see Richard Hofstadter, *The Age of Reform: From Bryan to F. D. R.*, New York, Alfred A. Knopf, 1955, 77–81.

States was planning nuclear tests, whereupon the Soviet Union went ahead with a series of tests; the Chinese charge that India was aggressing against China in 1959, whereupon China crossed into territory on the border between Tibet and India that had long been at least passively recognized by China as Indian; the reciprocal charges of aggressive intent by India and Pakistan with respect to the Kashmir in the 1950s and 60s; the charge of imperialism by India against Portugal, followed by the taking in December 1961 of Goa, Damão, and Diu; the reciprocal charges of aggressive intent by Israel and Egypt, notably before the 1956 conflict; the American imputation of unbridled tyranny on the part of Spain against Cuba in 1898 shortly before launching war against Spain, and the reciprocal charges of aggressive intent by the United States and Cuba starting in 1960.

The phenomena of identification and projection did not, of course, start to occur only in the nineteenth century, though an approach to their understanding has come, after Freud, only in the twentieth. When Cortes and his 400-odd fellow Spaniards took up in 1517 the incredible task of conquering Mexico, two of their expressed reasons were Christianizing the Indian population and subjecting it to the rule of their Holy Roman Emperor, Charles V. These Spaniards were devout Christians who became increasingly repelled by the brutalities of Aztec civilization. As the expedition progressed from one principality to another, Cortes not only accepted food, women, and elaborate gold objects of obvious immediate attractiveness; he also asked that the Indians stop their human sacrifices, stop their depredations on neighboring communities, stop worshiping their "cursed Idols," and adopt Christianity.[19] The Spaniards were clearly identifying with the Christian Church, the Holy Trinity, and the Emperor, "Don Carlos." How much, if any, they were projecting any guilt they may have felt as conquerors who killed is not clear. The mental association between their own killing in battle and ritual killing by the Aztecs may have operated reciprocally: the Spaniards may have projected their own guilt by expressing horror at human sacrifice; they may have fought so bravely and cruelly not because of a sense of guilt but because of their horror. There is not much evidence of a sense of guilt. Indeed, the Spaniards after each battle treated the wounds of their men and

[19] Bernal Diaz, *The Discovery and Conquest of Mexico: 1517–1521*, G. Garcia, ed. (A. P. Maudslay, transl.), London, George Routledge & Sons, Ltd., 1928, ch. 22, 111 (in the territory of Tabasco), ch. 35, 159–164 (in Cingapacinga), ch. 52, 224–225 (in Tlaxcala), and ch. 70, 326 (in the city of Mexico, which, under Montezuma, then feudally dominated most of what is now Mexico).

horses with fat cut from the body of a dead Indian. Diaz' account is quite devoid of any sensitivity in noting the practice.[20]

There may be some evidence of projection when Cortes' men advise him to use treachery to capture Montezuma in his own palace, immediately after describing the planned treachery of Montezuma and his court.[21] Diaz concludes this part of his account with the observation: "All that night we were praying to God that our plan might tend to his Holy Service." [22]

Identification with the symbols, images, and living leaders of communities they professed to serve (the Church and the Holy Roman Empire) doubtless was a major factor giving Cortes and his men the incredible courage to face fantastic odds as they moved across Mexico. This identification process was fundamentally like that which encouraged farmers in late nineteenth-century America to pursue politics. In their race, religion, and national origin, the Cortes forces felt the strength of community. In their revulsion at human sacrifice they may in addition have been projecting a sense of guilt about the conquest of a less advanced culture in battles where their technical advantage outweighed the numerical superiority of the Indians. But it is easier to infer the presence of *these* unconscious mental processes among nineteenth-century Americans than among the Spanish conquistadors. It is reasonable only to suggest that the unconscious *sense* of guilt, which long preceded the *study* of it, may have induced sixteenth-century conquerors as well as nineteenth-century farmers to pour their sins into the hearts of the others, the evil members of the outgroup.

I do not make this suggestion in the interests of a moral relativism, whereby the love of material things among farmers is equally reprehensible with the greed of market manipulators, middle-men, manufacturers, and financiers—or whereby the killing of Aztec Indians by Spaniards in battle is as bad as the ritual killing of Indians by Indians. Farmers in America had been wronged by a political system which until the 1890s substantially ignored their interests and excluded their participation. Spanish conquest of Mexico, even with the Inquisition,

[20] *Ibid.*, 106, 187. A legend still circulates in Indian communities in the Peruvian Andes about white men who abduct little children, kill them, and take grease from their bodies—not for treating wounds but for lubricating machinery. See Richard W. Patch, Life in a Peruvian Indian Community, *American Universities Field Staff Reports,* West Coast South America Series, vol. 9, no. 1, 1962, 29n.
[21] Diaz, *op. cit.*, 312–314.
[22] *Ibid.*, 314.

did succeed gradually in stopping a barbaric custom that had cost the lives of hundreds of thousands. The point here is that it appears necessary for people, when they seek to change practices no longer acceptable, as civilization advances by political processes, to identify themselves with completely virtuous groups and to shield themselves from guilt by attributing insufferable motives within themselves to the evil ones. If men were to wait until they were altogether pure in heart before acting, they might never do so. If they lacked the capacity to carry the firmly held conviction that they are quite pure, they might be the prey in politics, as elsewhere, of those who deny the existence of right and wrong.[23] In centuries to come, people in politics may have an unexaggerated sense of this virtue without becoming amoral or immoral, but there seems thus far to be an ineluctable tendency to overdraw one's own virtue. And Marx, Lenin, and Stalin could exhibit cold fury at those who denied the manifest validity of scientific socialism. Even the amoral in such instances were self-righteous. This human dilemma persists, grotesquely sporting the olive branch on one horn and arrows on the other.

The need for equality

Interlocked with the strong urge to have a sense of belonging, of solidarity with others, is the desire to have a sense of equality, related to what Maslow calls self-esteem. This is the need for self-respect, in which the individual says: I am as good as anybody else; I may not be as clever or hard-working as you are, but I am as good as you are. The social needs are so closely associated in behavior with the need for equality that the two kinds are often not distinguished. Students of society and ordinary members of society alike tend to fuse and confuse the desire for identity and the desire for separation—the desire to be a part and the desire to be apart.

The confusion arises because, paradoxically, people are unable to have a sense of wholeness, of completion, if they are altogether soli-

---

[23] Note the comments on populist values in R. Hofstadter, *op. cit.*, Introduction, 3–22, esp. 16–19. For a consideration of the morality of Aztec human sacrifice and of the Spanish Inquisition, see William H. Prescott, *History of the Conquest of Mexico and History of the Conquest of Peru,* New York, Random House (Modern Library), n.d., 46–52. Neither Hofstadter nor Prescott adopts moral relativism, yet each points out the equivocal consequences of behavior in which the actors were unequivocally convinced of their righteousness. Both are generally sympathetic to the reforms which the righteous introduced.

tary. Solitude destroys, among other things, the sense of being someone in the eyes of others. Complete submission to others destroys the sense of being someone in one's own eyes. People find it unnatural —a cause for discomfort, unease, anxiety—to be quite alone. They also experience anxiety if they become completely absorbed, identified with others. The paradox is recognized in David Riesman's poignantly epitomized "lonely crowd" in which people try to lose themselves but succeed only at the painful cost of deep anxiety—because the individual's desire to be himself is suffocated by his desire to be with others, and because his guidance by the values and morals (or immorals) of others is in conflict with his desire to be guided by his own values.

It should be clear that I am implying that not all morals and values are social in origin, that many of them—in fact the profoundest of them—arise from within the individual himself. In other words, I am saying that not all values are only the result of social consensus as to what is desirable and undesirable, right and wrong, good and bad; but are rather an ultimate result of the inherent characteristics of man himself as an organism.[24]

The desire for equality is not only confused with the desire for identity, it is also confused in its subjective and objective manifestations. That is, social theorists sometimes say that people wish to be regarded by others and by themselves as possessing equality in competence and responsibility, and that people want to have tangible evidence of such equal capacity. In his intensive and empirical study of attitudes toward these objective kinds of equality, Lane [25] casts serious doubt on the implicit or explicit belief of utopian writers and actors that people even want to be equal in competence, responsibility, and worldly goods. When Robert Owen in New Lanark, Scotland and New Harmony, Indiana and Karl Marx in the British Museum envisioned a happy world in which all share everything equally, they

---

[24] The assertion is no inference from a hypothetical public opinion survey of all mankind, even though (hypothetically) a universal public opinion poll might indicate common responses to the same questions on certain values. The statement no more depends on the expressed attitudes of people than the assertion that water is composed of hydrogen and oxygen depends on a survey of the opinion of hydrogen and oxygen atoms, even though expressed attitudes probably are symptomatic of reality. I make the assertion not to imply that it is proved but to specify the logical—and I think empirically sound—premise for much of the argument of this chapter.

[25] Robert E. Lane, The Fear of Equality, *American Political Science Review*, **53**: 35–51 (1959) or Lane, *Political Ideology*, New York, The Free Press of Glencoe, 1962, ch. 4.

were presupposing the desire of people to have this kind and degree of equality. Writing as they did during an era of gross inequality of both material opportunity and possessions, they logically and perhaps inescapably supposed that the wish to achieve greater objective equality meant the desire to achieve absolute objective equality. The routine failure of utopian communities, from Brook Farm to New Harmony to Fourier's phalanxes, provides even more unsettling evidence for the lack of such desire than do the manifestations of the (to be sure, open) class system in the classless society of the Soviet Union. Lane's observations, among people who are objectively more equal to those of great wealth than their nineteenth-century counterparts, do not support the notion that people really want to be objectively quite equal.

But subjective equality is a different matter. People do have a strong desire to be regarded as equal in worth, value, and dignity—each of these words in this context meaning the same thing. Their wish for equal opportunity to achieve wealth, status, and power in accordance with their inherent capacity stems from this and is one of the links between subjective and objective equality. Their desire, that is, to have such opportunity stems not from a belief that each individual should have his wealth, status, and power equated to that of all others, but equated to the inherent capacities of each individual—that the balance should not be socially but individually determined.

It may be argued that an individual's subjective appraisal of his own potential can be so out of harmony with an objective, social appraisal of his potential as to render useless the individual's subjective self-appraisal. Again Lane's observations under microcosmic empirical conditions cast doubt on this argument. Doubt is more generally cast by the fact that societies in which social (including political) limits are established to individuals' opportunities for equal access to wealth, etc., have historically been less stable than those societies in which such opportunities have been comparatively equal, even though the equality has not been in possessions but in opportunity. The Soviet Union of the 1930s and 40s was more stable than was Russia before 1917; the Second World War did not precipitate revolution in Russia, whereas the First World War did. The United States since 1783 has been more stable than were the thirteen colonies before 1775. The Northern states of the United States compose a more stable society in the 1950s and 60s than do the Southern states, with the persistently unequal objective social status of Negroes in the South. And the severe sanctions in the Soviet Union of the 1940s and

50s against any efforts among the ordinary people to gain equal political power with the elite suggests that there are tensions within the
Soviet Union arising from unfulfilled demands for subjective equality.
The Soviet Union, more stable than the Russian Empire, is less stable
than the United States. But this is getting ahead of the argument
as it is pursued in later chapters.

This notion of subjective equality has a long history in the Western
world. When it has been stated, the expression has sometimes been
as a moral imperative and sometimes as a scientific hypothesis about
the characteristics of the human organism—as a claimable right or as
a hypothetical natural phenomenon. At the 1947 meeting of the
Council of Foreign Ministers in Moscow, George C. Marshall, then
Secretary of State of the United States, said, "we believe that human
beings have certain inalienable rights—that is, rights which may not be
given or taken away. They include the right of every individual to
develop his mind and his soul in the ways of his own choice. . . ." [26]
In this context, the crucial phrase is "the right of *every* individual." In
1863, Abraham Lincoln spoke of the American dedication in 1776 "to
the proposition that all men are created equal." In 1776, Thomas
Jefferson wrote of the "self-evident" truth "that all men are created
equal." In the same Age of Enlightenment that produced Jefferson,
Immanuel Kant had stated—as a moral imperative, not a scientific
hypothesis—that one should so act as to regard oneself and others "as
an end withal and never as a means only." The ancestry of these
expressions in the Western world goes at least back to Christ when
He said, "Thou shalt love thy neighbor as thyself" (Mark 12:31). A
century before Christ, Cicero had foretold the growing recognition of
equality in saying, "Nay, if bad habits and false beliefs did not twist
the weaker minds and turn them in whatever direction they are inclined, no one would be so like his own self as all men would be like
all others." [27]

In his *Nicomachean Ethics,* Aristotle refers to a saying that "friendship [or love or affection] is equality." [28] Some seven centuries before

[26] Quoted in H. M. Bishop and S. Hendel, eds., *Basic Issues of American Democracy,* New York, Appleton-Century-Crofts, 2nd ed., 1951, 23–24.
[27] Quoted in George H. Sabine, *A History of Political Theory,* New York, Henry
Holt & Co., 1937, 165.
[28] In the original the saying has an aphoristic rhyme and rhythm: "philotes isotes."
[Aristotle, *The Nicomachean Ethics* (H. Rackham, transl.), London, William
Heinemann Ltd., rev. ed., 1934, 470.] At another point Aristotle says that in
"friendships of equality . . . both parties render the same benefit and wish the

Christ, in one of the great Jewish law books, the precept was written: "Thou shalt love thy neighbor as thyself" (Leviticus 19:18).[29]

More significant by far than the recurrent expressions of human equality, dignity, and worth is the profound attraction the idea has had. It does not seem to matter whether the expression is a moral imperative, as in the instances of Christ and Kant, or an ostensibly empirical hypothesis about the characteristics of man, as in the cases of Jefferson and Lincoln. The appeal has been enormous, particularly among those who suffered from social inequality.

The earliest popular appeal of Christ was to the poor and downtrodden. This well-known fact was expressed in modern sociological and psychological language by Erich Fromm in a 1930 essay.[30] Describing the main adherents of primitive Christianity, he said

It was the mass of ill-bred poor people, the working men of Jerusalem and the rural peasants who—because of increasing political and economic oppression, because of social distance and contempt in this growing mass—were filled with the drive and longing for a change in the existing relationships. . . .[31]

The earliest Christians in the Roman empire outside Palestine likewise were the poor, attracted among other things by the sense of inherent individual dignity and worth that is so central to Christianity.

It is altogether too simple to explain the Protestant Reformation in terms of the desire for equality, but two central aspects of the Reformation found widespread popular resonance: the new emphasis on the priesthood of all believers and the very radical act of translating the Bible into popular tongues. These changes reflected a belief that all men were not only equal in the sight of God but were also able to establish contact with Him without the intervention and intercession of an elitist group, the members of the clergy. To understand the Reformation one must include an explanation for the pervasive and enduring equalitarianism which it represented and elicited. Social and intellectual historians are wont to neglect the radical consequences for

---

same good to each other" [*op. cit.*, 475] and says "it is those who wish the good of their friends for their friends' sake who are friends in the fullest sense. . . ." [*op. cit.*, 461.]

[29] See Roy B. Chamberlin and Herman Feldman, eds., *The Dartmouth Bible*, Boston, Houghton Mifflin Co., 1950, 967, on the history of the Golden Rule.

[30] E. Fromm, Die Entwicklung des Christusdogmas, *Imago*, **16**: 305–373 (1930).

[31] *Ibid.*, 329. The translation is mine. Early Christians were so poor they could not afford parchment on which to write down what became the New Testament, which was first written on perishable and cheap papyrus. For the attitude toward the rich, see, for example, James 5: 1–5.

the changed image that individuals had of themselves when they came to believe they were fundamentally equal to the clergy in the sight of God. Yet this changed self-image had more political portent than the American and French Revolutions.

Again with a warning against oversimplification, we may without overemphasis suggest that the phrase "all men are created equal" has had more than ephemeral appeal, particularly since Jefferson recast the idea that is over two thousand years old. Let us just mention a few of the major political advances in America that have derived much of their impetus from the need for equality.

One of the first manifestations was the demand for the right to vote. Even before the War of Independence was won, the suffrage implication of the equality of men had been spelled out in law in five states. The Constitutional Convention of 1787, struggle as it did with a host of conflicting demands, avoided the question altogether by leaving qualifications for voting up to the individual states. As new states in the frontier West came into the Union, they provided for universal suffrage, but the older states resisted. On one ground or another (property ownership or payment of taxes), various states continued to restrict the right to vote. Massachusetts, for example, did not gain— or permit—substantially universal suffrage until 1820. The Rhode Island government did not concede it until after an abortive little revolution in 1842 that was stillborn only because, after decades-long agitation for suffrage, it was hastily granted, when agitation was succeeded by action.

Suffrage was not universal, of course, but those who had won it were now satisfied with their new dignity and now were resistant to importunities from the unenfranchised, just as had been those men of substance from whom they had exacted the right to vote. These men now had attained suffrage and, like their predecessors, in some manner thought they constituted the entire category of those who had the intelligence, interest, prudence, and sagacity to rule. In succession, women and then Negroes insisted on the logical extension to themselves of the principle of equality. By the 1920s in America women were suffered to vote; by the 1940s Negroes were gradually being suffered to vote.

Some of the other public manifestations of the pressure for equality are in the realm of equalizing opportunity—for example, in the provision of universal free education at public expense; the facilitation of organizing business enterprises under general statutes of incorporation which limit financial liability to the assets of the enterprise itself; and income and inheritance tax laws which make it difficult to accumulate and keep vast fortunes.

Still others are exemplified by divorce and community property laws, which enforce a greater reciprocity between man and wife; laws providing public defenders for those who cannot afford to hire an attorney to defend themselves against a criminal charge; and the removal of statutory and constitutional discrimination against ethnic groups in the right to own land. The list is so extensive as to suggest that all law has to do with spelling out additional implications of the principles that all men are equal in dignity and worth. This is not true (witness, for example, class legislation, which discriminates in favor of old people, women, children, those who work in hazardous occupations, farmers, businessmen, laborers, etc.), but the persistent demands of all groups to get from politics what they consider their equal share of public welfare seems often to have behind it the notion that hitherto each group has been discriminated *against* (and pendulously now must be discriminated *for*).

The suffrage remains one of the most basic recognitions of the need for equality. Indeed, the existence of universal suffrage is sometimes considered synonymous with equalitarianism. To the ingenuous sophisticate or nonsophisticate—to those crypto-Platonic realists for whom ideas are more real than reality—the actual grant of universal suffrage may appear to be the ultimate political achievement, with which all other goals may be reached because the crucial instrumentality is now available to the entire population and to all segments of it, whether farmers, workers, businessmen, old people, lawyers, doctors, or sports enthusiasts.

The difficulty is that having the right to vote is no guaranty, even when the right is exercised, of the right to take part in the process of making policy decisions in a society. Having a vote ("Stimme" in German, meaning "voice") in an election ("Wahl" in German, meaning "choice") is no assurance that one has more than the voice of a spectator at an athletic event in which there may be only one team in the field. It is not quite true that politics ceased to exist in Germany during the Nazi period. Decisions between alternative public policies were made, but they were made in private and only occasionally were announced publicly. The right of the German public to vote had nothing to do with the political process, or at least no more to do with it than the enthusiasm of the spectators at an athletic event has to do with the performance of the players.

The grant of universal manhood suffrage in the 1936 Soviet Constitution has had nothing to do with the making of political decisions in the Soviet Union.   This grant perhaps allayed popular unrest during the early Draconic part of the Stalinist era, but only among the crypto-Platonists.   The regime does seek popular support, because profound apathy could make impossible the implementation of privately made public policy.   But widespread popular participation in the 1960s has remained a chimera.

There appears hope of gradual equalitarianism in Soviet politics, more as a result of the growing restlessness of the new, nonparty elite in factories, collective farms, universities, and the governmental bureaucracy than in consequence of popular pressure.   If this elite should fail to become the vanguard of Soviet political equalitarianism, it will be acting differently from the way the bourgeoisie did in France in the late eighteenth and early nineteenth centuries, the way the middle classes of England and the United States have acted, indeed from the way skilled tradesmen acted in America during the political struggle for the recognition of labor.   The battlecry will be equality and justice; the new Soviet elite that does not now share political power will get it and become content; and then a new set of unequal nonparticipants will seek their share.   And so will go on the process of spelling out the logical implications of the now almost universally recognized principle of equality.

To those better acquainted than I with the intellectual history of the Western world, these observations about the 2000-year development of equality no doubt sound like nothing but ill-disguised natural law, following a path that starts with the Stoics and—by way of Thomas Aquinas, Jean Bodin, and Hobbes—arrives at the eighteenth-century rationalism of Kant, Locke, Rousseau, and Jefferson.   In a sense this is obviously true and the tradition is one from which I should not want to be disassociated.   The difference is that now the appropriate area for establishing and testing hypotheses relevant to political equality is less in the study of literature than in the study of human behavior. The energy behind the continuous (dormant or active) demand for equality is not to be found solely among those who read.   It appears to be deeply imbedded in all human beings and to emerge among all who have advanced beyond the level of mere physical and social survival.   If so, an investigation of the dynamics of the human mind is in order.   A contemporary writer has said that the source of the idea of equality is not in natural law but "in the private man's sense of his own infinite worth." [32]

One may say, to put the horse before the cart, that the statement (and the appeal) of a major segment of natural law lies in the subjective sense of equality and that natural-law doctrine is deficient not in its reasonableness, or even validity, but rather in its relative nonempiricism. It has not been subjected to empirical test and therefore remains more a faith than a tested theory. The task ahead is not to examine the ideas but the minds, the psyches, of men. And, if the above discussion makes sense, the need for equality is not just one of men's ideas but one of their profoundest characteristics. However, let both the reader and the writer of this be reminded that the statement of a relationship—in this case a hypothesized organic ingredient in the desire for equality—does not demonstrate the relationship. The statement can do a service if it helps formulate a notion to be tested; it does a disservice if it is grasped as being either logically or empirically obvious.

The need for self-actualization

We have thus far discussed three of the five needs that Maslow regards as basic. Early in the discussion I outlined why I think the need for security is basic but not of the same order as the physical, social, and equality needs. It does not appear that people pursue security for its own sake, in contrast to the way they seek to satisfy the other basic demands of their organisms. They seek for security *in* the predictable, controllable satisfaction of the other needs. They want to feel secure in getting enough to eat, in the affection of others, and in the self-respect that derives from being regarded as equal. But they do not normally seem to want to be secure for the sake of being secure. Indeed, most people become politically concerned only when their security in meeting basic needs is threatened. For most people politics is thus almost purely instrumental. [33]

This assertion as to the largely apolitical—though not asocial—character of the general public is based on several factors. For one thing, most people do in fact seem to turn their attention to politics when

[32] H. A. Myers, *Are Men Equal?*, Ithaca, Cornell University Press, 1955.

[33] In substantially identical form, this section on self-actualization appeared under the title A Note on Political Motivation in the *Western Political Quarterly*, **12**: 410–416 (1959) and is here used with the permission of the *Quarterly*.

they are a little unsure about being able to pay for the next meal, the next pair of pants, or the winter fuel supply—or when they fear domestic insurrection or war which threatens them or their kin. For another, relatively few people seem to get concerned with politics even when tyranny threatens them with arbitrary government, perhaps because tyranny seldom, if ever, seeks to gain or maintain control on any platform other than full employment, full stomachs, and protection from all enemies foreign and domestic. Again, it seems evident that most of the relatively few who do get concerned with tyranny that threatens individual autonomy become so in consequence of some event which threatens their own individual security or which tends to ostracize them from their normal group relations in the broadest sense. (Aside from politicians, generally it is the scientist, engineer, or other employee ousted from his job as a security risk—or the individual who becomes a social pariah when stigmatized as a foreigner or Communist —who develops an unusual degree of political involvement.)   And lastly, most of those who are political leaders are much above average in income and social integration: for them, the needs for physical security and a sense of social belonging are well satisfied.

If it sounds alarming to suggest what appears to be a selfish, inhuman, stomach-and-herd motivation pattern for the politics of most people, we need only consider the dismal alternative of the entire general public taking part in politics in order to determine by democratic majorities who should go into which occupations, what religion should be the legal one, and the maximum or minimum number of hours that must be spent daily in watching television. How then would we dispose of the wretched apolitical deviant who worked, worshiped, and relaxed contrary to law?

Although most people are apolitical most of the time, the large majority of people do at election time consider politics to be relevant to being *secure* in the satisfaction of their basic needs. But the overwhelming majority do not relate to politics their interest in those activities which are not directed toward securing the satisfaction of physical, social, or esteem needs but are pursued for inherent satisfaction—activities engaged in for their own sake, in the pursuit of happiness. The patterns of individual self-actualization are so varied that the group seeing political and governmental action as related thereto may become so small as to be politically impotent or inactive.

The person interested in recreational fishing will vote against a ballot proposition designed to open more fishing areas to commercial operation. As a fisherman, he may not be expected to have any political attitude on whether or not freedom of intellectual inquiry and expression should be restricted by sanctions against unorthodoxy. The businessman politically concerned with maximizing his freedom of action in economic matters may not be expected as a businessman to get aroused against investigations of teachers who are accused of devious indoctrination. There need be no surprise at the working-man who is secure on his job and who shows no spontaneous agitation at the fact that his union boss may have to sign a loyalty oath in order to hold his job. Only if the fisherman, businessman, or working-man is required to attest his own loyalty in order to engage in his chosen activity may he be expected to form a political opinion and engage in political action for or against oaths. If taking such action threatens his own security he very likely will not oppose oaths.

If these speculations are reasonable, they indicate limits to the amount of political action that individuals will take to *prevent* action by their governments. They may be expected to get aroused when state action threatens realization of their particular individual or group values. To expect more is to assume a measure of involvement, perspicacity, farsightedness, and perhaps meddlesomeness that is not the endowment of ordinary mortals. The implication of this is that the achievement and preservation of restrained political institutions which maximize the opportunities for individual self-actualization are a responsibility of relatively small groups influencing the action of public officials, each of which groups may be expected to engage in action designed to gain or maintain freedom from governmental interference for the group alone. In this sense, "free" as distinguished from "popularly responsible" government is the product of conflict between pairs of small groups—teachers vs. school boards; editors, writers, clergymen, and (paradoxically) government workers as individuals or as group members vs. congressional committees; and Jehovah's Witnesses vs. local police departments—as much if not more than free government is the consequence of political participation by the general public.

There is one sense in which perhaps the large majority of people do relate their political participation to self-actualization. On any comparative basis it is clear that the standard of living in the industrialized Western world is high and that people, by and large, are relatively secure in what they have. Yet they want more and sometimes seek more through their government. The relatively poor Frenchman who seeks a higher housing subsidy, the similar American who votes for the candidate who advocates a higher minimum wage or shorter hours, and any citizen who votes for a candidate who promises a reduction in personal income taxes are all well-off when compared with the unindustrialized, poor, and politically inactive Persian or Arab.

In these situations, the motivation appears to be related indirectly to the need for self-actualization, in the sense that they want a better living standard and more security generally: not for the inherent satisfaction of better quality food or steadier retirement income but in order to be able to buy a (newer) car, take a trip (or a longer one than they did last year), get a new fishing rod, or replace the table radio with a high-fidelity instrument on which they can enjoy fine music. Their political activity ostensibly has the same purpose as that of the insecure. They seek many of the same things that are sought by the insecure (minimum-wage and maximum-hours legislation, lower taxes, etc.). Yet in wanting more, one ultimate motivation appears to be a demand that government provide conditions under which they may pursue a line of activity which is related not to security but to self-actualization—to fishing rather than to fish or other food.

The relation between politics and self-actualization is here deemed largely negative for the large majority of people not just in America, with its ideological adherence to the principle of laissez faire, but in other industrial countries as well. People do agitate politically for legislation that will provide them not only security but also the time and money to pursue inherently satisfying activity. But they pursue this goal in nonpolitical ways. They look to government to provide the ground rules and sometimes the machinery, but they get their increase usually by negotiating directly for higher wages, shorter hours, etc., with employers. Or they get their increase by becoming skilled scientists, engineers, lawyers, doctors, or by a business venture.

They may turn to government to settle labor-management disputes by mediation, adjudication, or violent force. They may turn to government for a state-supported law school or a veterans' education subsidy. But the actual getting process is most of the time for most people a matter of interaction between individuals and private groups, or between different private groups, rather than between these two categories and the government. Yet it is ordinarily only when people feel insecure in the provision of food, clothing, shelter, health, and safety—when they fear arbitrary dismissal from a job, when private economic enterprise is unstable or breaks down, or when war threatens—that they turn to government.

There remains for consideration the very small minority of the general public—precinct workers, elected officeholders, and so on—for whom political participation is not readily explicable primarily in terms of the needs for security. Although this category of people is proportionally very small—as a guess, perhaps 5 or 10 million out of an adult population of 100 million in the United States in 1960—their significance is great because they are the exceptionally active individuals and almost by definition the leaders in politics.

It would be possible to explain their extraordinary political involvement as being only quantitatively different from that of the great majority if it were evident that the exceptional individuals differ from the average only in the greater intensity with which they feel the necessity of being secure in food, clothing, shelter, health, and safety, and of being accepted and loved by the groups to which they belong. In the University of Michigan Survey Research Center's study of the 1952 election there is evidence that tends to validate the paradox that those who are most active in politics are not those who by an objective judgment are most in need of more security. People with the highest incomes, the most intricately skilled occupations, and the most education almost without exception are the ones who vote most regularly and frequently and who express the belief that voting is worth the trouble and that they have an obligation as citizens to do so. Similarly, the opposites of these people—the ones with least income, skill, and education—generally vote the least and care about it the least.[34] It is, also, now rather clearly evident that elected public officials, ranging from President to governors to congressmen to state legislators, much more often than not are among the wealthiest, most highly skilled, and highly educated people in the society.[35] Why do proportionally more of them become very active politically?

Lasswell's early study of agitators and administrators as political personality types [36] was a pioneering effort in analysis of the motivation for political elites. One limitation of the analysis, however, is that describing motivation for politics as the displacement of private

---

[34] Angus Campbell, Gerald Gurin and Warren E. Miller, *The Voter Decides,* Evanston, Row, Peterson & Co., 1954, 70–73, Table 5.1, "Relation of Demographic Characteristics to Presidential Preference in 1948 and 1952 Elections," and 187–199, Appendices A and B, "Sense of Political Efficacy" and "Sense of Citizen Duty."

[35] See Donald R. Matthews, *The Social Background of Political Decision-Makers,* Garden City, Doubleday & Co., 1954, 23 (Table 1), 29 (Table 6), and 30 (Table 7), on the socioeconomic status of politicians in America, and 42–55 on the same for politicians in Great Britain, Germany, and the Soviet Union.

[36] Harold D. Lasswell, *Psychopathology and Politics,* Chicago, University of Chicago Press, 1930.

aggressions on public objects or as the extraordinary need for deference or as the urge for power does little to distinguish politicians from others—or to compare them with one another. Can it not with equal validity be claimed that Karl Marx displaced his private aggressions on public objects, that movie actresses have an extraordinary need for deference, and that Nicholas Biddle enjoyed power? And cannot wide differences be seen between the relatively serene personal background of Jefferson and the turbulent one of Jackson? Did they both equally have private aggressions, the former suppressing them or giving vent to them quietly, while the latter differed only in the volume of noise he made? Did John Quincy Adams and Theodore Roosevelt equally share the desire for public deference? Did Woodrow Wilson and Warren Harding equally share the desire for power?

Individual politicians like Peter the Great, Stalin, Jackson, Lincoln, Gladstone, Churchill, Bismarck, Hitler, Petain, and de Gaulle are a very heterogeneous lot. They tempt one to the occasionally voiced statement that there is no common set of factors characterizing people of extraordinary political activity. This is an easy and plausible generalization which contains a disturbing amount of truth. Both the politician, because of his subjective image of himself, and the biographer, because of his intimate involvement with the politician, are likely to encourage this impression of uniqueness.

There are large environmental influences on those people that make it incredible to imagine the often cruel techniques of Peter the Great being employed in early nineteenth-century America, or Jefferson successful in establishing parliamentary government in early eighteenth-century Imperial Russia. And the striking individuality of some political leaders makes it hard to imagine Germany being unified quite in the way it was without the particular personality of Bismarck, or to envision the temporary defeat of divisive forces within the American union in the 1830s without the unique figure of Andrew Jackson, who, in a style different from Peter the Great, offered to hang as high as Haman the leaders of a group that descended on Washington to demand restoration of government funds to the Bank of the United States. In a sense it seems to be true that the political events of a particular period are a unique and never-repeated consequence of the interaction of a vast array of forces, which include among other things individual political leaders, who in turn are personally shaped by almost as vast an array.

Many motivations for intense political participation do appear to be individual yet causally plausible. One person may be a precinct worker because he feels a particular loyalty to the candidate for whom he is working. Another such worker may distribute campaign literature because he wants to learn the game of precinct politics so that he can more effectively run for office himself. Still another may do so because he is compensating for guilt feelings induced by the shadow of his father, who was a corrupt political boss. Still another may feel that the particular political issues involved demand his active participation, even though he is cool toward the candidate, has no ambition to hold office, and his father is a universally respected member of the city council. Some or all of these individuals may also be partly motivated by a strong desire to be of public service, to do good.

Along this path of motivational investigation lies madness. Categories of motivation could be abstracted and classified in a manner that would be either meaninglessly simple and general or so complex as to addle the latest electronic computer. This is not to say that such idiosyncratic motivations are not a real part of the complex of causes for intense political activity in a particular individual. But they are so numerous, different, and likely to be so individually intertwined as to defy any kind of quantitative analysis.

The only factor which appears to be a reasonable postulate for common motivation of intense political participation is the need for self-actualization. Its manifestations, political or nonpolitical, are as varied as the number of human beings on earth and are only rarely political. Its characteristic is that it is activity in which the individual happily loses himself—getting so absorbed that, at certain times and in some situations, he is able to forget himself in the performance of activity which he enjoys primarily for its own sake and not primarily because he thereby feeds or protects himself, his family, his community—or because he can give socially acceptable vent to his aggressions, gain great deference, or bend people to his will. The choice of this activity may be conscious or unconscious, intentional or accidental, made by the individual himself or, perhaps, even for the individual by others. It is inseparable from competence, because a person cannot develop his potentialities in activity in which he is regularly a failure, and from energy level—both of which are conceptually though not behaviorally separable from motivation. Consequently some people who have competence for physical sport and a low energy level may get great inherent satisfaction out of watching a ball game on television. Others may love music, be tone deaf, and have a high energy level—all of which lead them to sponsor and subsidize a local symphony. Others get their greatest inherent satisfaction from politics, ending up as precinct workers, state legislators, constitutional heads of state, or dictators.

There might be a temptation to regard the need for self-actualization as a residual category, used to explain political activity when there is inadequate evidence that an individual is participating because of the needs for security or a place in the group. This makes the need for self-actualization either a card catalog of phenomenal, overtly expressed needs like the compensation for a corrupt father or the desire to do a favor for an old friend; or else a very empty void. Evidence for political manifestations of the need for self-actualization should be found by determining what it is that an individual likes to do best after his elemental needs for food, shelter, etc., are reasonably well secured. It is not just a matter of hobbies, because many individuals are basically happy with their work, whether it be as a machinist, business administrator, or full-time professional politician. For a substantial majority of people, politics does probably have some inherent interest, for example, during a political campaign or crisis. But for those few who do participate intensely in politics, the most reasonable, common, fundamental, and basically organic factor appears to be the inherent and profound pleasure which, for them, the game of statecraft contains.

We need not be misled by the statements of politicians that they really want to go back to the farm or edit a newspaper. If this is what they wanted more than politics, they would indeed have become farmers or editors. Charles V of the Holy Roman Empire became the equivalent after some thirty-seven years of power; Edward VIII of England after only eleven months. Most politicians prefer to die in harness or at least to serve out their full constitutional terms. There are few if any occupations, at least in our era, that give an individual a more abundant chance to realize his fullest potentialities for good or evil than politics. And it is to politics that highly ambitious people turn in the twentieth century, as such people turned to the Catholic Church in the Middle Ages and to the business world in late nineteenth-century America.

A hierarchy of needs?

The question remains whether basic needs do, as Maslow has said, fall into a priority so that people will generally seek satisfaction of their physical needs before their social, social before their equality or self-esteem needs, and equality before self-actualization. From his intensive studies of individuals, Maslow believes a hierarchy exists. Does the hierarchy exist among individuals in such large social and political aggregates as nations?

In general the burden of my argument as to physical needs has been that when they are not satisfied, people turn away from politics (or do not turn to it) in a political apathy that is the consequence of the intensive preoccupation with survival. As to social needs, the argument has been that they do not emerge until there is substantial satisfaction of the physical needs and that political participation cannot furthermore become common, that is, nation-wide, until people do develop a sense of community—of a common identity that makes possible joint political action. As to the need for equality, the inference from hierarchization is that people will not become concerned with equality until they have found a community and that equality will gain prominence as a political value only thereafter. In other words, once a sense of communal identity as such has been established, people will then and only then begin to demand that they be regarded as items of intrinsic worth, meriting a dignity that recognizes they are not only means to the ends of government but withal individual ends in themselves.

It is at this point that they become concerned with the kind of political oppression that is involved in discriminating against individuals on individual grounds. At this point the property-less deny the argument that only those with property can take part in making basic policy decisions; women deny that politics is for men only, and Negroes that only whites can rule. As to the need for self-actualization, the argument is that most people will pursue their own entelechy in nonpolitical channels, resisting political interference with their desire to pursue their own development only when government specifically threatens them. It is further argued at this point that the common motivation for political actives is the sheer enjoyment they get from it.

Let the following charts, schematizing Maslow's hierarchy as modified by the elimination of security, serve to illustrate the conceptualization. The vertical axis presents the *relative* saliency of the individual's needs. The horizontal axis presents mental development through time. The curved lines represent very roughly the relative mental preoccupation as the individual moves through his life. The first chart

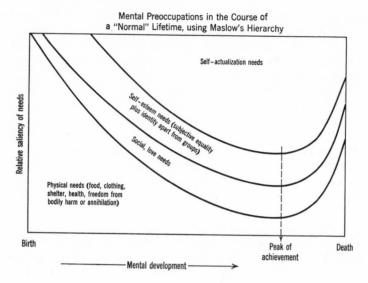

Mental Preoccupations in the Course of
a "Normal" Lifetime, using Maslow's Hierarchy

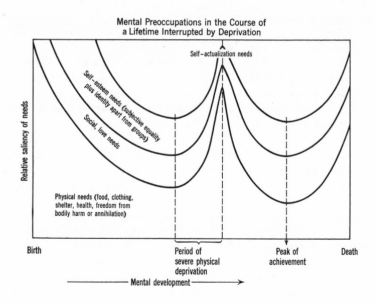

Mental Preoccupations in the Course of
a Lifetime Interrupted by Deprivation

shows a "normal" process of development.[37]   The second suggests what happens when there is some kind of physical deprivation.   In such a severe condition, the individual would least of all be thinking of politics.

It would be anticipating one of the main theses of this book to argue the hierarchy more intensively at this point. In the interests of accurately analyzing political reality, it is appropriate here only to suggest that political phenomena be viewed, among other ways, in light of this major hypothesis—and to suggest that the reader neither now nor at the end of the book consider the evidence to be conclusive in favor of the hypothesis or conclusive in opposition to it. Let the reader and the author at this point remain content with accepting the possibility that a consideration of the basic needs and of their priority may help explain many phenomena that hitherto have not made much sense in relation to each other—that the hierarchization of needs may help explain different stages of political development and help determine approximately the order in which different kinds of politics are likely to emerge.

[37] For an alternative and earlier schema, see David Krech, Richard S. Crutchfield, and Egerton L. Ballachey, *Individual in Society*, New York, McGraw-Hill Book Co., 1962, 77 and Krech and Crutchfield, *Elements of Psychology*, New York, Alfred A. Knopf, 1958, 627.

CHAPTER 3

Political tension

A conceptual caveat

This chapter deals with a difficult but useful concept. As I will use the term tension it includes insecurity, anxiety, and frustration, but it includes both the disagreeable *and* the agreeable sensations of wanting. I use the term to describe a general, somewhat diffuse mental state that is not identical with the need or needs that produced it. This usage differs from Maslow's, in that he places security as a need in his hierarchy, with the need for security emerging after the physical needs are fairly well satisfied and before the social or love needs emerge.

My reasons for distinguishing *tension* from *need* are basically these. For one thing, it appears that one is usually tense, about a variety of needs, but usually not about tension itself. One can be tense though well-fed; tense though beloved; tense though in pursuit of an active career, even though well-fed and beloved, etc. A tension is characteristically derived from a specific need and released in some kind of activity relevant to a particular need, even though the activity may not be functional to the "real" relief of the tension. A hungry person may eat food or, less appropriately, he may sleep or eat dirt. A lonely person may find friends or escape into romantic fiction. A person who wants to be prime minister may become one or an adviser to prime ministers. But he will not ordinarily act without some object for the release of his tension, an object relevant to some specific need category. As we will see in describing some experiments by Pavlov and Maier, there may be behavior that relates only to the relief of a kind of unattached tension. It is too early in the chapter to say, and too early in the development of knowledge of the human central nervous system to say for sure.

The second reason for using the term tension is precisely that it is not always discharged in ways that appear relevant to the particular need that has been excited. A person in need of affection may become a compulsive eater. A person with a frustrated talent for art may go into politics and revel in the hate of enemies he has created for himself.[1] It may be possible to eliminate use of tension and related words and thus to deal directly with the consequences of excitation of a need for food, affection, etc. But the diffuseness of the mental state that follows excitation of a need makes the general term *tension* useful. The mental condition spills over in the mind: it is not always precise about what caused the tension and how to relieve it with respect to the specific cause. This makes it possible to consider security a need itself, but in so conceiving it, one tends to avoid the search for causes of insecurity and for solutions which are appropriate and functional or inappropriate and dysfunctional. Freud attributed civilization to the deflected and sublimated libidinal urge. As long as there are these deflected, seemingly inappropriate gratifications, the term remains

A difficult and useful concept.

Tension—a state in which one force opposes another force—occurs everywhere in nature. The moon stays in orbit around the earth as a result of the opposing forces of the earth's gravity and the moon's inertia in its orbit. The particles within an atom stay together not because they are without dynamic force but because the forces that attract them to each other are more potent than the forces which would cause them to break out of their orbits within the atom. Tension also is a characteristic of human life and of human behavior, and it is a characteristic of that aspect of human behavior which is called politics.

Just what is mental or psychic tension? It is not a need in the sense in which the organism has a need for food, clothing, and shelter; or a need for affection; or a need for a sense of dignity. But it is a consequence of the generation of these needs. When the organism needs something, the condition of mental tension arises. An infant that needs food cries. This creates tension in the mother, who then comes

[1] For the diffuseness of behavior in a person who is insecure, see A. H. Maslow, The Dynamics of Psychological Security-Insecurity, *Character and Personality*, **10:** 331–344 (1942).

to feed the infant. An adult who is in need of affection will seek out friends and a spouse in order to relieve this tension. An adult who has become a citizen—a member of the political community—will seek political relief for internal tensions resulting from such needs as physical hunger, social hunger, hunger for self-esteem, and so on, when he sees political means as appropriate or necessary devices to relieve his tensions.

The living human organism is not content with a state of complete absence of tension. That is, once a need has been satisfied—often even before—another one is generated. Once a person has a full belly and the assurance that he can continue to fill it periodically, he develops new needs and therefore new tensions. Some positive, pleasant aspects of tension (like pursuing a career), along with some unusual and strongly negative ones (like food-hunger), were the major concern of the previous discussion on human needs in politics. This present discussion has more to do with more usual tensions in more normal circumstances, which are nonetheless unpleasant.

The problem of unpleasant tension has been a major concern of students of the human mind at least since Freud. Freud himself was unhappy with his inability to conceptualize in a definitive form the problem of tension and so have been his successors. Various names have been applied to unpleasant kinds of tension, names like anxiety, frustration, insecurity, and fear. For our purposes the two most useful terms relating to unpleasant mental tension are anxiety and fear. Fear is intense, short in duration, specific, and is usually related to physical survival. For example, if a mountaineer saw a bear running down the trail in his direction he might fear that the bear would kill him. Anxiety, on the other hand, is chronic, relatively low level (that is, not intense), and vague. For example, a fellow might be anxious about whether his girl really was going to marry him or not. It would make little sense to describe his state of mind as one of fear rather than anxiety.

Without violating common usage we can say that a person is insecure when he is anxious and vice versa: the two terms are roughly synonymous. But the term frustration in its common usage is not precisely synonymous with anxiety or insecurity. Frustration usually connotes the interruption of an action by external forces, after its beginning in a need and before its consummation in the satisfaction of that need. ("My girl frustrates me." "That pile of work frustrates me.") Anxiety connotes a mental condition of uncertainty about the satisfaction of the need. Anxiety, in common usage, emphasizes internal causes of the state of mind, and frustration emphasizes external causes.

For our purposes it is probably just as well to consider anxiety and frustration as being almost synonymous terms, in light of the basic supposition that all behavior is a function of the interaction of the organism and the environment. The differing connotations of the term are useful but not vital. If the organism had no need it would not be frustrated: the existence of a need is as essential to frustration as is the interference with the satisfaction of that need by some external force. Attractive but unattentive young women do not usually frustrate octogenarian men. Work does not disturb a happy hobo. Furthermore, it seems clear that a need can be frustrated not simply as a result of external forces—environmental forces—but also as a result of a conflict between different organic needs, like the need for food and the need for affection.

Vague anxiety and specific fear

The distinction between anxiety and fear is far more important. Fear is apt to produce a prompt reaction either to remove the object of fear from oneself or oneself from the object of fear. For example, the mountaineer approached by a bear would either try to hide, run away, or shoot. Anxiety on the other hand is chronic and vague. It endures over a long period of time and is harder to locate than even a black bear in a dark forest. It produces a different kind of reaction. One does not know quite what is the cause for his anxiety and, partly for that reason, he does not know quite what to do.

Unlike the hero in the wild-west movie who has no trouble in distinguishing the villain by his dark beard and sinister look, the person who is anxious cannot readily picture what his problem is, what the source of his anxiety is. For example, he may not know whether to marry the girl or not. He does not know her well enough and she doesn't know him and he doesn't know himself well enough. Should a mother spank a child or not? Should she send him to bed for punishment or not? The immediate result of spanking or of sending to bed may be apparent but the consequences of it are not. And only by the slow process of trial-and-error learning, plus a somewhat anxious reading of the latest literature on child raising, is a mother relieved to a very limited degree of the anxiety she has about how to raise a child—how to reward him and how to punish him.

In politics one is seldom faced directly with issues that arouse fear and is often faced with problems that arouse anxiety of a mild or severe sort. For example, should one vote for candidate X or candidate Y in a crucial election? In a crucial time in the history of one's country, should he align himself with the past or with the future, in opposition to or support of a revolution? If so, which past? What truly uncertain or falsely certain future? The very nature of policy decisions in a society makes for a state of anxiety. The very issues that are up for public consideration and decision are those which are most difficult to make because the source of the difficulty is uncertain and the solution for it is even more so. Following the French Revolution, the control of policy decisions passed to a broad middle class from a semi-feudal class linked with the clergy and the court. There was no precedent for doing this. Both bourgeoisie (the new, broad popular base for the new ruling class) and the new rulers themselves were unaccustomed to the exercise of political power. Once this exciting but anxiety-inducing problem was solved and suffrage later became universal, new worries arose, like the problem of tyranny supported by a broad populace. When suffrage became universal one could not deny the problem by saying that now everybody is taking part in the governmental process and that everybody cannot be a tyrant—in France or anywhere else.

The following diagram indicates how these concepts are related to each other in the ensuing discussion. At the same time this diagram indicates what degree of anxiety or fear is related to effectiveness of response to the threat involved. A starting notion—little more than a tautology—is this: the more specific the threat, the more fear-inducing it is; the more vague the threat, the more anxiety-inducing it is. A further notion is that when the threat is very vague *or* very specific, that is, induces a high degree of anxiety *or* fear, a person is less likely to take effective action in response to the threat than when the threat is less vague or less specific. A person can, so to speak, die from terror of ghosts or from fear of an onrushing bear. Correlatively, the modal point of the curve running from extreme anxiety to extreme fear suggests that a moderate degree of anxiety or fear is necessary for the person to take effective action in response to the threat. In other words, if he lacks the kind of tension in a real but moderate degree that is called mild anxiety or mild fear, he will do nothing effective. Tension of one sort or the other is necessary for the individual to take effective action in response to the threat.

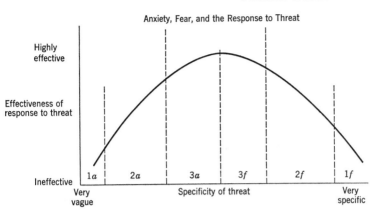

Examples:

1*a*—A person believes he is utterly incapable of coping with life's problems; re-
lapses into apathy or despair.

—A person believes he can do nothing about broad public problems and neither
can government; withdraws his attention from politics.

1*f*—A person is suddenly confronted by a maniac with a knife; just stands there,
or faints.

—A person is convinced atomic holocaust will take place next Thursday; abandons all activity. A person is picked up by state police for political reasons
and then released; avoids all political involvement.

2*a*—A person feels too regularly defeated by problems he once could solve but
now cannot; talks with friends, the priest or minister, or a psychiatrist.

—A person feels impotent to prevent unemployment but thinks government
can; joins authoritarian political movement.

2*f*—A person driving a car at 70 mph (113 kph) sees two cars collide on the
highway; slows down to 60 mph (97 kph).

—A person fears invasion of his country by armed forces of a truculent neighboring country; ceases opposing the draft or even volunteers for military service.

3*a*—A person is anxious about a heart attack; takes out an insurance policy and
gets regular medical check-ups.

—A person has a job and unemployment insurance but is anxious about unemployment; votes for a candidate who says he will boost the economy.

3*f*—A person is confronted by a robber; either hits him or runs away.

—A person fears a hostile country is gaining a clear lead in military prepared-
ness; agrees to greater government expenditures for new weapons and to
higher taxes.

More or less, but not all or none

If this conceptualization of these kinds of tensions makes sense it then follows, logically and psychologically speaking, that the organism cannot truly be said to be in search of complete security or the cessation of anxiety or fear but rather in search of a modal course in which there is tension, but not hypertension: fear, but not panic; anxiety, but not collapse. This notion runs counter to the belief that the main thing people want in life is security, that is, complete freedom from anxiety or fear. At the same time it runs counter to the notion that people want no security, that is, want to maintain a continuous state of either severe anxiety or deep fear. This notion further contradicts the belief that people pursue security for its own sake, that is, are concerned primarily with the relief of tension just for the sake of relief of tension. People pursue the relief of tension in order to satisfy the basic needs (the physical, social, self-esteem, and self-actualization needs. When they have satisfied one need or have become secure in the ability to satisfy that need, they are ready to pursue another one, reverting to concern with that prior need only when it is itself threatened. The goal of the organism is not the relief of tension as such but the achievement of a state of optimum tension which avoids the extremes of utter deprivation on the one hand and of paralyzing fear or anxiety on the other. Utter lack of need *and* of need satisfaction is one way to define death itself.

A continuing state of fear of a severe sort on the one hand or profound anxiety on the other is apt to throw the organism into a state of mental collapse. It might even be more appropriate to say that a severe state of fear is likely to produce a mental explosion into the panic of violent action, and that a severe, profound state of anxiety is apt to produce a mental implosion into apathy and despair. The important point is that severe fear or severe anxiety, more likely than moderate fear or anxiety, produces action or inaction which is dysfunctional to the health and continued existence of the organism in its lifelong process of satisfying needs, ranging from the physical all the way to the self-actualization.

The etiology of anxiety and fear

What has been said thus far serves to conceptualize political tension. It does not, except by unavoided implication, explain either its causes or its consequences. In this section I will indicate what seem to be the most common causes of anxiety and fear and in the next section consider some of their manifestations, first on an experimental and abstract level, mainly from psychological writings, and then on a social and political level.

Earlier in this chapter I indicated that the deprivation or frustration of a basic need (that is, an internal organic need, whether physical or mental) is a cause of anxiety. Freud conceived of anxiety as a manifestation of internal danger, resulting for example, from a frustration of the demands of the libido and the superego. Freud further said that anxiety is a reaction to internal danger and that fear is a reaction to external danger.

Following the formula $B = f(SO)$, we may more appropriately say that the deprivation or frustration of a basic need can originate either within or without the organism and necessarily involves the interaction between the organism and the environment. For example, we know that the organism has a need for air: it must breathe. The profound fear state—approaching panic—that the organism manifests when it is deprived of air is a consequence of the organism's need for air. On the other hand, if the supply of air from the environment is uninterrupted the organism's need is satisfied. We thus can say equally well that the cause for the extreme anxiety or fear state following deprivation of air is environmental in origin. The more modern followers of Freud like Erich Fromm, Karen Horney, and Harry Stack Sullivan have, unlike Freud, tended to be preoccupied with the environment as the source of anxiety, saying in effect that anxiety is not a danger signal from within, but a danger signal from without.

The sense of the matter seems to lie in neither direction—in concentrating exclusively on the environment *or* the organism. It seems, in other words, better to say that mental tension is a result of an activated need within the organism, interacting with a depriving environment in such a way as to produce an anxiety or fear state. As long as we are aware of this basic interrelation between the organism and the environment we can appropriately, for shorthand purposes, say that the cause for an anxiety is social in origin. We can say this, however, only when there is *not* the generation of a new need within the organism but only the deprivation of an existing need—and we can say this only for shorthand purposes when we wish to focus our attention on frustrating environment.

Anxiety and fear may arise from the conflict between two or more needs. For example, a person may need both food and affection and be torn between gratifying one or the other when he cannot gratify both: a person who is hungry may not know whether to snatch a bite of food or to give the bite of food to a child or to a parent. Similarly a person may be torn between a need for affection and a need for esteem in the eyes of others. That is, he may be in conflict over the deprivation of affection of others that is involved in his standing out from others—for example, excelling in a particular task which produces envy on the part of others and therefore deprives him of their affection. There might be a conflict in the mind of a person between his needs for food and for self-actualization. The classic case is the artist or writer starving in a garret in order to paint or write. The decision-making process for the person who wants to exceed and gain social esteem without losing the affection of others is bound to produce an anxiety state, at least until the decision is made to pursue one need or the other. So also will the person be anxious who likes to eat and likes to paint and, when he has to choose between the two occupations, cannot make up his mind.

Anxiety may also arise from a conflict between a basic need and internalized social rules. No child is taught that it is wrong to eat. At the same time children in most societies are taught that it is wrong to steal food. If a person is hungry and sees stealing as the only way by which he can get food, he will be in an anxiety state until he makes up his mind either to remain hungry or to steal the food. If he steals, he probably will be in an anxiety state afterwards, as a result minimally of the mild fear of being caught and maximally of the guilt he feels as a result of doing something which, by the rules he has learned and absorbed and made his own, he believes he must not do.

Anxiety may also arise from a conflict between different social values. For example, in a particular society there may be the conflicting values of success and excellence on the one hand and conformity and togetherness on the other. If a society values both these things and values them very highly and if they are in conflict—which inherently they seem to be—a person who succeeds has the problem of indicating to others that he is really no different from those who have not succeeded. The person who has not succeeded but has conformed has a problem of indicating to the society that he has succeeded at the same time that he has conformed, and he may try to put on a good show of success to convince others and himself that he is meeting not just one but both of the social values in his particular society.

Another kind of conflict among different social values is that between respect for authority and for freedom. In any orderly society authority has a high value. In any good orderly society, freedom also has a high value. What does a person do when authority says he should do one thing and his desire to be free says he should do another? This internal desire is reinforced by the value placed on it by society. Does he disobey the law? Does he even, as a revolutionary, disobey the written or unwritten constitution in order to be free, or does he disobey the social value placed on freedom and resign himself to a simple obedience to authority? Again, until such a conflict is resolved by a person either obeying authority or pursuing freedom, the individual is bound to be anxious.

Another source of anxiety is the conflict between habit and custom on the one hand and emergent needs on the other. This is distinguished from the previous category, in which there is a conflict between different social values, in that habits and customs are rather satisfying, and a person who wants to govern his life by habit and custom can do so with a high degree of security. However, if he persists in the satisfaction of things within the framework of habit and custom he may be thwarting a set of needs within him which demand that he break away from habit and custom. When he is faced with this dilemma he will develop anxiety.

One example of this is the African raised in a tribal background who has come in contact with a missionary or some other European who has introduced into the African's tribal society a new set of individualistic values, including equal human dignity and self-actualization. Another instance of such a conflict between habit and custom and emerging needs is involved in the social class system. If the class structure has become increasingly—more precisely, uncomfortably—rigid, is it to be allowed to persist or are efforts to be made to introduce either a new class system or an open, classless society? In such a case the person gets a sense of security within a social class just as did the African within his tribe, but again he is in conflict with his desires—with potentialities he has—which cannot be realized within his status in the existing social class system. What is he going to do—will he stay within his class, remain content with it for his life and the life of the children to come, or will he become an advocate or at least an adherent of a social movement which calls for establishing an open class system or a classless society?

In very broad terms the same thing was involved in the changeover during the Protestant Reformation from the religious monopoly, at a time when evidently a great amount of frustration had been stored up in individuals throughout Western Europe. They opposed this religious monopoly because in the sixteenth century it seemed so stifling to the development of things which the individuals in these societies now wanted to develop. The church had probably not changed so much as had individuals' expectations. This problem, again as in the previous examples, is one in which individuals by the millions or at least thousands had to decide what they were to do. Were they to remain within the religious institution which they had inherited and which had existed for over a thousand years, or were they to give it up and venture onto the dangerous shores of religious pluralism and—even more anxiety-inducing—individualism of a rank sort?

Tension may also arise when there is a considerable discrepancy between one's aspirations and his capacity to achieve them. When this is blamed by the individual on the existing social structure and political power structure, the tensions generated may induce the person to accept social and political change, so that he may realize his aspirations.

One example of this is the person who during a depression has had to forego his plans for getting an education in order to get a job and support his family. Another case is the obvious one of a person in a rebellious state of mind in a society where he feels hemmed in, pushed down, and pushed back by the social system as it is maintained by the established upper classes of the society. Still another illustration, a rather special one, is that of the individual of extraordinary energy and extraordinary aspirations who feels that the social system and power structure of the society have denied him his appropriate place as a leader within a constitutional society. A closely related example is the demagogue or revolutionary leader who uses the aspirations of others, similarly repressed but less gifted than he is, to further his own ambitions.

General tension and dysfunctional action

The most significant thing about tension is that it is a general state of mind derived from the unsatisfied condition of basic needs but not necessarily from any particular one of the several basic needs. To use an example from the physical world, a rock may become warm or hot either as a result of being in a fire or as a result of long exposure to the sun on a hot summer day. The heat of the rock is measurable in degrees quite regardless of the source. Similarly a person may become anxious or frustrated as a result of the deprivation of a physical need, conflict between two or more needs, conflict between different social values, and so on. But his state of mind is the same: like the rock that is warm or hot, he is internally agitated about something outside himself. The heat within him is politically relevant when the forces that he blames for inhibiting his desires are social and political. He wants to reduce this intolerable state of tension by whatever means he can, often with little regard for how appropriate or inappropriate the means of relieving the tensions are.

This is not to say that his action will be necessarily dysfunctional, or irrational. At least momentarily, it will relieve his tension. To take a nonpolitical example, a child punished by her mother for refusing to eat and throwing food on the floor may, being unable to react against her mother, spank or kick or verbally punish her doll. Such action is probably inappropriate with respect to the cause of tension, the punishment received from the mother, but may nevertheless relieve the tension. And the child may then proceed to eat her food. Similarly, when a young man is angry with his father for denying him an education, he may blame the government; conversely, if he does not get an education and is angry with the government for not providing it, he may renounce his father. What this does mean is that, as the anxiety state becomes more profound and endures for a longer period of time, an individual is more likely to engage in action which is dysfunctional. He is more likely, so to speak, to blame his father when the government is at fault or to blame the government when his father is at fault.

An appropriate political example is the case of an African tribesman who forsakes his village in order to become free in a town. He is abandoning something which is of clear positive value to him—the predictability of an orderly society run in a constitutional manner—in order to gain freedom and independence. If his reaction were precisely functional to a variety of things he wanted he would not abandon his adherence to constitutionalism as such in the interest of gaining freedom, but would insist that he have both constitutionalism and freedom in the city where he goes. He does not in fact get both: he loses constitutionalism in order to gain a kind of freedom, because his interest in constitutionalism, that is, in a predictable political process, is outweighed by the frustrations which accompanied the constitutional system in the tribal village.

In a sense dysfunctionality or irrational behavior is the dangerous consequence of social hypertension. If the tensions which are normal in a society become too aggravated they are likely to produce behavior which indeed may relieve the frustration rather well but replace it with other frustrations that were nonexistent in the previous social conditions. Later we will consider this more fully. Now let us consider some experimental and abstract observations about anxiety and then look at some social and political manifestations of these findings.

Experiments with anxiety

Starting in Russia about 1900 Ivan Petrovich Pavlov began a series of experiments in conditioned reflexes, using dogs as the subjects. The general results of his experiments are well known, namely, that establishing an association in the dog's mind between an artificial stimulus and the reward of food caused the dog to salivate when only the artificial stimulus was introduced. The dog, which normally salivated only when it saw or smelled food, now salivated when a bell was rung or a light went on or when he received some other associated stimulus.

In one of the experiments a dog developed a conditioned reflex of salivating when his skin was stimulated at the rate of 24 impulses per minute. The dog was also trained to stop drooling when touched at the rate of 12 times per minute. Under both sets of circumstances the dog behaved in a predictable fashion: it regularly salivated when touched at the rate of 24 times per minute and regularly stopped when touched at the rate of 12 times per minute.

In one variation of the experimental procedure, the dog was touched at the rate of 12 times per minute and immediately thereafter touched at the rate of 24 times per minute. Under the previous behavior of the dog it should not have salivated during the first part of this procedure and then should have started to salivate when the rate was doubled. But in this case the dog stopped salivating altogether despite the normal stimulus for salivation and also stopped responding positively to other kinds of stimulus which had previously produced salivation—a whistle, a lamp, and a metronome.

Why did this occur? The rate of stimulation for both salivating and not salivating had previously been clearly distinguishable by the dog, and it had responded in a predictable fashion. Now suddenly the dog acts in a strange manner. The explanation advanced by Pavlov is that this unusual response was "due to a conflict between the processes

of excitation and inhibition which the cortex finds difficult to resolve." [2]
To put it in terms used in this chapter the dog was suffering from a
state of intolerable tension such that its response was not to act in a
rational or functional manner but rather to withdraw from the problem altogether.

An American psychologist, N. R. F. Maier, has conducted a set of
experiments that more explicitly examine this phenomenon which
Pavlov noted, namely, the behavior of animals under highly stressful,
frustrating circumstances. Maier's experimental situation included a
small platform fastened underneath to a vertical rod. A rat placed
on the platform could not get off it, save by jumping. Approximately 6
to 12 inches from this pedestal were two doors covered by cardboard
cards. If the rat jumped to one door it was rewarded with food. If
it jumped to the other door it got a bump on the nose and fell to a
canvas suspended on springs about two feet below the platform. After
training the rats so that they were used to going to one door where
they would get food, the experimenter then began to randomize the
process so that half the time when the rat jumped to the door beyond
which he was accustomed to find food he got the food; the other half
of the time he got a bump on the nose and fell to the canvas below.

As a result of this the rats tended to freeze on the platform and to
refuse to jump, when they only had a 50–50 chance of getting food.
To encourage them to jump, the experimenter attached a hose to the
platform which sent an uncomfortable blast of air against the rear of
the rat. A curious thing then developed. The rats would continue to
jump to the door to which they were accustomed, whether or not
they got bumped. They would not try to redirect their behavior in a
manner which would produce the reward of food and avoid the punishment of getting bumped on the nose. They did make one change:
they jumped towards the accustomed place and hit it with the side
of their bodies rather than with their nose, thereupon falling to the
canvas.

Maier describes this phenomenon as behavior that is a consequence
not of motivation but of frustration. The rat no longer has the apparent desire to get food but rather has the desire merely to relieve
its frustrations and does so by jumping, in slightly changed manner,
toward the door which he knows may or may not be blocked. That is,

---

[2] I. P. Pavlov, *Conditioned Reflexes: An Investigation of the Physiological Activity of the Cerebral Cortex* (G. V. Anrep, transl.), London, Oxford University
Press, 1927, 302.

he knows the food situation is unpredictable, but by jumping off the platform he knows he can escape the blast of air on his rear. Maier does not adequately consider that escaping the blast was itself a goal, but this goal does not altogether account for the rat's action.[3]

An adequate explanation of Pavlov's and Maier's experiments would have to consider forces that existed before the tension that was deliberately produced in the capricious experimental circumstances. But whatever the etiology of these two kinds of behavior, it seems clear that at least the immediately prior determinant of this behavior was the frustrating situation itself, that is, the inability of the organism to resolve external forces which were operating in opposite directions.

An experimental study of anxiety was undertaken by Janis and Feshbach to find out the effect of anxiety on toothbrushing habits. Using high school students as subjects, the experimenters gave identical instructions to all critical groups in the experiment on how they should take care of their teeth. They then told one group of subjects that if they failed to take good care of their teeth they would get cavities and gum infections. They told another group that they would risk damage to their eyes, heart, joints, and kidneys and might even go totally blind. The result was that both the (former) minimally threatened group and the (latter) maximally threatened group re-

---

[3] Norman R. F. Maier, *Frustration: The Study of Behavior without a Goal*, New York, McGraw-Hill Book Co., 1949. In an experiment conducted with seven monkeys, Masserman and Pechtel put a rubber snake in the monkeys' food box at feeding time. Monkeys are very much afraid of snakes regardless, apparently, of whether they have ever seen a snake before or not. In this experiment the monkeys, experiencing conflict between hunger and fear, developed persistent tension and anxiety. In the authors' words they all developed "various inhibitions, regressions, phobias, compulsions, organic dysfunctions, neuromuscular disabilities, sexual deviations and alterations in social relationships, and these symptoms were sufficiently persistent and progressive to constitute an experimental neurosis which seriously interfered with the health and well-being of the animal." Animals that had been at the top of the social hierarchy lost their dominant position to the others and food could be taken from them as readily as from those lower in the hierarchy. The hierarchy became flattened so that the group became rather tightly a group seeking escape and protection as a joint enterprise. The animals would cling to each other in fright. There was apparently no control group, though the conditioned response had been established successfully over a minimum of eight months. The investigators do not indicate how many times they had to introduce the rubber snake into the feed box before the neurosis developed. My summary gives only a brief hint of the various specific reactions to conflict as these are described in the report. [J. H. Masserman and C. Pechtel, Conflict-engendered Neurotic and Psychotic Behavior in Monkeys, *Journal of Nervous and Mental Disease*, **118**: 408–411 (1953).]

tained the same amount of *information* on proper care of the teeth. But people in the minimally threatened group changed their toothbrushing habits more significantly, in accordance with the instructions given for tooth care, than did people in the maximally threatened group.[4]

In an experiment by Smock the subjects were first shown a card with a vague configuration and then successive cards with increasing definition of the figure (e.g., the figures of a cat, the numeral 5, a vase, and a girl getting out of a bathtub). The critical group of subjects was put in a state of experimental stress. The subjects were then asked to tell what the figure was. The critical (stress) group came to an earlier conclusion than did the control (secure) group, and had to see more cards before they correctly identified the figures.[5]

All of these experiments involved tension induced by the experimenter. In each, severe tension impaired performance. The question still remains whether tension not so induced—anxiety that reflects an enduring state of the personality—will produce the same results as anxiety that is briefly and experimentally induced. Does, in other words, the chronically and generally anxious state of mind produce irrational or dysfunctional results?

Else Frenkel-Brunswik posited the notion that, under some circumstances at least, it does. The experimental group that she studied were socially marginal public school students aged 11 to 16 who came from racially prejudiced families. She found that the subjects whose parents were marginal in their social status and prejudiced could not express subtle or ambivalent opinions of their parents. They had a tendency to express freely to the interviewer rather stereotyped opinions about how their parents looked. On projective tests, which exposed impulses that they could not acknowledge in public, they exhibited considerable aggressive reactions to their parents.

Frenkel-Brunswik also used a figure-recognition test on these subjects. A distinct picture of a dog was gradually changed to an amor-

[4] I. L. Janis and S. Feshbach, Effects of Fear-arousing Communications, *Journal of Abnormal and Social Psychology*, **48**: 78–92 (1953).

[5] C. D. Smock, The Influence of Psychological Stress on the Intolerance of Ambiguity, *Journal of Abnormal and Social Psychology*, **50**: 177–182 (1955). See also E. L. Cowen, The Influence of Varying Degrees of Psychological Stress on Problem-solving Rigidity, *Journal of Abnormal and Social Psychology*, **47**: 512–519 (1952). This study tried three groups on the Luchins water-jar test of mental set: a control group, a mild stress group, and a severe stress group. The control group was less rigid in solving this problem than the mild stress group, and the mild stress group less rigid than the severe stress group.

phous picture which then gradually emerged into the clear figure of a cat. She found that, as the dog became less clearly dog-like, the marginal-prejudiced children persisted in calling it a dog longer than did the subjects used as a control group.[6]   Other experiments have tended to corroborate the findings of Frenkel-Brunswik.[7]   Another experiment indicates that subjects with a pre-existing high-anxiety state performed better on a learning task than did those with a low level of anxiety, but that when stress was applied to these two categories during the experiment, the performance of those with pre-existing anxiety suffered more than did that of the low-anxiety category.[8]

Tension quantified

These data ranging from Pavlov to Frenkel-Brunswik and those who have worked within her frame of reference are in a real sense non-quantitative.   With the exception of the toothbrush and water-jar tests, these experimenters evidently assume that a person is either very anxious or not very anxious at all and tend therefore to assume, without really stating it, that they are talking about anxiety versus nonanxiety, about security versus insecurity.   A more reasonable hypothesis as to the effect of anxiety is this: high anxiety produces greater distortions of perception than does low anxiety, and the optimal level is not the minimal but rather a moderate level of anxiety.

Part of the problem is related to the reluctance or inability of psychologists to tolerate an ambiguous conceptualization of anxiety, seeing it as either existing or not existing in a particular person rather than existing at some level between minimum and maximum.   A brief experiment involving a rather small number of cases reports that those who have a high anxiety level tend to read news of personal tragedy

[6] E. Frenkel-Brunswik, Intolerance of Ambiguity as an Emotional and Perceptual Personality Variable, *Journal of Personality,* **18**: 108–143, at 128 (1949).

[7] See for example J. A. Taylor and K. W. Spence, The Relationship of Anxiety Level to Performance in Serial Learning, *Journal of Experimental Psychology,* **44**: 61–64 (1952), which indicates that subjects who rated high in a test of manifest anxiety were slower to learn an experimental task than the "nonanxious" group; and V. Cervin, Experimental Investigation of Behaviour in Social Situations: I.   Behaviour under Opposition, *Canadian Journal of Psychology,* **9**: 107–116 (1955), which indicates that "emotionally unstable" subjects were less likely than stable ones to shift their opinions during a discussion.

[8] J. A. Taylor, The Effects of Anxiety Level and Psychological Stress on Verbal Learning, *Journal of Abnormal and Social Psychology,* **57**: 55–60 (1958).

relevant to themselves and not to be interested in news about problems outside themselves. In reading news relevant to themselves these people are identifying themselves with people who have had comparable problems outside. Most people who are at a middle level of anxiety, so the experiment indicates, select news to read in a manner reflecting their desire to solve problems which are not directly personal. The low-level anxiety people split their news reading between personal and nonpersonal stories but read less of the nonpersonal news than do the middle-level anxiety people.[9]

Far more persuasive than this brief but highly relevant finding is an intensive study of surgical patients.[10] Using psychiatric procedures, Janis studied patients who were hospitalized for surgery of a moderately severe sort but not the kind that had a low recovery rate. The study was conducted over a five-month period and included 22 cases divided into high-, moderate-, and low-fear categories. He found consistently that the moderate-fear groups were better able than the high- and low-fear groups to stand the anticipation of the operation and its consequences during the recovery period.

The desirability of a moderate degree of tension is argued at great length by Rollo May in his theoretical and clinical analysis of the anxiety problem.[11] The argument which he advances is based on the speculative writings of Soren Kierkegaard, Erich Fromm, and several other modern psychoanalysts. He also presents facts which are comparable to the Janis data and indicate on a clinical basis that a moderate degree of anxiety is better than either no anxiety or a very intense degree of it.

Anxiety and identity

One fundamental characteristic of anxiety is loss of a sense of identity, of the distinction between the self and the outside world—that is, between the ego and the personal or natural environment, the environment of people or things. In its extreme form this symptom produces what Freud called the "oceanic feeling."[12] There is a "feeling of oneness with the universe." This means that the threat from without or

---

[9] H. Kay, Toward an Understanding of News-reading Behavior, *Journalism Quarterly*, **31**: 15–32 (1954).

[10] Irving L. Janis, *Psychological Stress*, New York, John Wiley and Sons, 1958.

[11] Rollo May, *The Meaning of Anxiety*, New York, The Ronald Press Co., 1950.

[12] Sigmund Freud, *Civilization and Its Discontents*, London, The Hogarth Press, Ltd., 1930, 12–14, 21.

from within is no longer distinguished but is denied by being merged with the outside world. Freud describes this feeling as a return to the infantile state in which the child does not clearly distinguish between its self and the objects around it. Arthur Koestler in his reminiscence on experiences during the Spanish Civil War indicates that he had arrived at such a state, after a period during which he never knew whether he would survive or be shot by a firing squad. He described his mental condition at times as one of "inner peace which I have known neither before nor since." [13] This extreme loss of identity as a symptom of extreme anxiety seems to be a symptom of even moderate anxiety and fear. When an individual senses over a considerable time period that he cannot resolve a conflict between his needs and the environment, etc., he has an intolerable sense of failure and tends to merge himself with the environment either by withdrawing from society or by pushing himself into the outside world. In either case he is distorting himself and the outside world by breaking down the distinction between himself and it.[14]

Rational and irrational responses to anxiety

The irrational ways in which people cope with this phenomenon of anxiety, the ways they relieve the symptoms but not the illness itself, run the gamut probably of all neurotic behavior. They range from such phenomena as compulsion, projection of guilt outward, aggression, displacement of aggression, ridicule of the cause of tension, identification with the aggressor, identification with the defender (in which one delegates power not to the aggressive enemy but to the defender of one's amorphous self), and to a withdrawal from the real world into a world of fantasy where the problems either do not exist or are automatically solved by magic helpers.[15] Aggression is another often

---

[13] Richard Crossman, ed., *The God That Failed*, New York, Bantam Books, 1952, 68. For a fuller account of this profound experience, see Arthur Koestler, *The Invisible Writing*, Beacon Paperback ed., 1955, ch. 33, The Hours by the Window, 345–353.

[14] For an exquisite consideration of identification anxiety as it beset a rather prominent future reformer, during his formative years, see Erik H. Erikson, *Young Man Luther*, New York, W. W. Norton & Co., 1958.

[15] See Anna Freud, *The Ego and the Mechanisms of Defence*, New York, International Universities Press, 1946. This analysis by Freud's daughter marks a real advance over his speculations and observations on neurosis.

irrational reaction to the kind of tension that is called frustration.[16] Defense is another way in which the organism meets a threat from without and, as one writer points out,[17] may often be confused with aggression. What to an outsider may appear to be aggressive action on the part of an actor, may in the mind of the actor be nothing other than defense. Hitler was disturbed at the Czechoslovakian threat before the Second World War; Stalin feared aggression from Yugoslavia in 1948. In the armed clash in October 1962 between Indian and Chinese forces on the border between Tibet and India, both sides said they were acting in self-defense.

All of these various ways of irrationally dealing with the problem of anxiety may also operate to relieve not simply the symptoms but also—temporarily—the anxiety itself. For example, a person who is compulsive about honesty may get at least some relief from his anxiety state by recognition and praise on the part of others of his honesty. A person who feels inadequate to solving a particular problem may, by identifying either with an aggressor or a defender, at least for a time gain enough self-confidence to be able momentarily to stand on his own feet. But these solutions that relieve symptoms of tension are like aspirin or antihistamines, which relieve the symptoms of a head cold. The real, that is the effective, rational, or functional relief from tension necessarily involves meeting the causes and not the symptoms of the causes. For example, a person who has anxiety about whether or not his girl really will marry him can relieve the tension by having her accept or—alternatively—reject him. The uncertainty of the situation cannot long be resolved by withdrawing into a symptom-relieving, fantasy world of romantic novels or romantic movies.

The different kinds of rational response to tension are doubtless as numerous as the problems which induce it. In private life this means pursuing or fleeing from the girl until she rejects, accepts, or pursues him. In public life, that is in politics, one means of dealing with the source of aggression is by changing the aggressor to a friend. Another is to avoid him. Still another is to destroy him.

In any event the solution would not develop if the person has so completely distorted reality by withdrawing from it as to give up completely his own power to solve the problem. The citizen who feels that public problems are too complex for his understanding, and too large

[16] John Dollard et al., *Frustration and Aggression,* New Haven, Yale University Press, 1939.
[17] G. Ichheiser, Frustration and Aggression or Frustration and Defense: A Counter-hypothesis, *Journal of General Psychology,* **43:** 125–129 (1950).

for him to be involved in making policy or selecting policymakers, does not really solve the problem by leaving these problems and their solutions to a political leader whom he trusts uncritically and completely. The person who identifies with the aggressor, like the concentration camp inmate who adopts the clothes and mannerisms of the guard, may get temporary relief from tension. But in the long run no solution is possible, short of ending the concentration camp situation by liberation or death. A person who speaks angrily in his home of the stupidity or malice of a politician or of an enemy country does nothing really to solve the problem, unless such talk is precursor to action, such as voting against the politician he dislikes or supporting action by his government which may control the foreign aggressor.

The fundamental point here is that where there is no tension, even in the unpleasant form of anxiety or fear, there cannot be any recognition of the problem that calls for solution. Whether some kinds of tension are more productive than others of problem-solving cannot be even guessed. All that I suggest here is that moderate tension is more productive than either very high or very low tension. People without tension are like those who have gone to sleep in the middle of a road. If they fail to wake up before the first car comes along they are not likely to survive. Even if they exaggerate the danger by seeing an approaching car as either a freight train or as Armageddon headed directly for them, they are more likely to take effective action than if they are asleep. Now let us consider the social and political manifestations of the unpleasant tension we call anxiety and fear.

Social and political manifestations

Up to this point we have looked mainly at mental tension in individuals reacting in controlled, closely observed circumstances. We have found a common pattern of behavior among a variety of experimental subjects in a variety of situations. We have found that Pavlov's dogs, Maier's rats, and also the human subjects under experimentally induced tension have exhibited more or less irrational, dysfunctional reactions. In each of these cases the behavior that was a consequence of tension was not appropriate to a reduction of the tension, at least not of its real cause. We have looked at some experimental and hypothetical cases of irrational and rational relief of anxiety among people.

Now we shall consider whether the same phenomena occur on a larger, real-life scale in broad social and cultural contexts. Do the phenomena of tension occur in the same ways when the circumstances in which the individual acts are the looser, more tenuous ones relating to one's role as a member of society and as a citizen, that is, a member of the polity? If the phenomena do not operate in the same way in the broad social and political context that they do in the laboratory, then there is no real relationship between the two worlds.

An inarticulate premise of the work of physicists is that what they see in the laboratory is like the world outside. If light rays from some source bend as they pass through a prism, he then expects them to act so whether the light source is a candle, an electric lamp, or the sun millions of miles away. If a particular pattern on a spectrogram of a small flame indicates the presence of hydrogen in laboratory circumstances, he then assumes that the same spectrogram taken from light coming through a telescope indicates the presence of hydrogen in a star being observed from a distance of millions of light-years. Unless the broad social world is not comparable to the small private world of the individual, and in that sense is unlike the natural world in its phenomena, we should expect to find comparable patterns of behavior under conditions of tension in both experimental and in natural, non-experimental social circumstances.

Let us first look at some individual political leaders whose childhood involved rather severe tension and then look at some behavior of ordinary citizens to see whether tension affects them the same as it does the political leaders.

Five tense men who went into politics

Abraham Lincoln was born on the American frontier, where existence itself was sometimes marginal. When his father was a child of about six he had witnessed the killing of his own father by Indians and had himself barely escaped death. Lincoln's father, never very successful in farming, moved from one place to another in search for something better, for a somewhat better condition of survival and not much more. The ancestry of Lincoln's father was rather uncertain although he traced it back to a particular place in Pennsylvania. His mother's ancestry was also uncertain but, Lincoln was sure, she was the illegitimate daughter of a Virginia gentleman. His ancestry on both sides was not likely to induce a sense of dignity and social belonging. Lincoln's mother died of an uncertain illness when he was not yet ten years old and he had to help bury her. He was thus shocked and motherless at a very impressionable age.

These various kinds of insecurity—insecurity as to survival itself, insecurity as to ancestry, insecurity as to personal affection (a sense of belonging to somebody)—were very severe in Lincoln's case and induced a state of tension which persisted through his life. Had it not been for the deep devotion and understanding of his stepmother, his "angel-mother," it is hard to imagine Lincoln's psychic survival. As life turned out for Lincoln, we may say that the quantum of tension he experienced and endured was probably a necessary ingredient of his great achievement. As life turned out for his father, we may say the quantum of tension was a necessary ingredient of his failure.[18] More specifically, the loss of a mother is not the usual fate of children, but the loss of father at the hands of mysterious, "wild" Indians is a probable cause of more intense anxiety. Lincoln experienced the lesser, his father the greater, of these two traumata.

In the ten or fifteen years before he became President, Lincoln had an opportunity to think out thoroughly and come to his own conclusions on the major issues facing the country at the time, one of them being slavery and the other the perpetuation of the union. There was no particular need for a person raised in his background to face so directly and intelligently the problems of his time. The relevant point here is that the tensions which became part of his personality appear to have contributed to causing him to develop a solution for these problems and to have the necessary energy available to work out their solution during the terrible war years. The tension produced the energy that induced him to face things; it did not necessarily cause him to face *these* particular problems and certainly had nothing to do with the content of his solutions for them.

To paraphrase Lasswell, Lincoln displaced his private tensions on public objects. Instead of resting satisfied with a successful career as an attorney, he had to find or seek relief for his tensions in a broader arena. In the process, he made it from the periphery to the center of his society and culture. Bereft as Lincoln markedly was of private affection uninterrupted by death and illness—both as a child and as an adult in a not serenely happy marriage—and bereft as a frontiersman of a mental condition of social identity in the greater American society, may it not be that these tensions and the ability to endure them were

---

[18] This assertion must naturally exclude the contributions he willy-nilly made to the survival and growth of the only son of his who survived infancy. For Lincoln's sense of duty and apathy or antipathy toward his father, see the letter Lincoln wrote to his stepbrother, three days before his very ill father died. [Roy P. Basler, *Abraham Lincoln: His Speeches and Writings*, Cleveland & New York, The World Publishing Co., 1946, 259.] Lincoln did not attend his father's funeral.

necessary factors in composing the man who became the beloved President of a very powerful country during its worst crisis?

A hundred years later, the story of Senator Joe McCarthy's life had much in common with that of Lincoln. McCarthy too was born in a poor farming family, in a section of the country that was still rural and at a time when industry had pretty well swept even his native state of Wisconsin. His family had just moved from a log cabin to a frame house—moved from the bottom of the housing scale to a point somewhat higher on the scale—before Joe, the fifth of nine children, was born. His American-born father was half-Irish, half-German. His mother was born in Ireland. Like Lincoln, McCarthy was an awkward, shy, highly sensitive, physically unattractive child. Taunted by his fellow pupils, he was socially backward in and out of school. He withdrew into himself. Again like Lincoln, he knew constant hard work on a farm where the problem was not one of differing degrees of prosperity but one of survival. His first success came as an adolescent when he started raising chickens. He did so for four years, with enormous success. Then as a result of illness, he had to turn the chicken farm over to the care of inexperienced friends who allowed the chickens to take sick and die. Success was topped by failure.

The various frustrations of his life up to this point helped build up such an enormous degree of tension within him that for the balance of his career his high energy was productive of great fame and success. In his case it was not until four years after he became a senator that he hit upon the problem of domestic Communism, which had already so agitated his countrymen. For the next four years he occupied increasingly and so completely the attention of the public that almost all other problems were subordinated to the one which he gave voice to. It seems reasonable to suppose that, like Lincoln, he was displacing his private tensions on public objects and in the process making it from the periphery to the center of his society and culture.

Thomas Masaryk, the founder of the Czechoslovak republic, came from a background that was so lowly as scarcely to be marginal to anything below it. His father was a serf who worked on a crown estate belonging to the Austrian Imperial government. He was born seven months after his parents' marriage. His father was a Slovene and his mother a Germanized Czech who could read German but not Czech. As a child he had day-to-day reminders of the great social gap separating him from those whom his father and he had to serve. His record in school was excellent and he was headed for a teaching career, but the project had to be abandoned after two years in a technical school (Realschule) because of the family's poverty. He then became, in succession, the apprentice of a locksmith and of a blacksmith. These jobs had such limited prospects as to portend returning to the static status of his father after losing the chance to rise socially as a teacher.

This young man, a countryboy in background like Lincoln and McCarthy, finally made it to the center of the society of his time, to Vienna, by dint of his scholarly excellence. His marginality was ancestral and social, as the son of a Slavic serf and as a member of an ethnic minority that was looked upon with contempt by the dignified Germanic culture of Vienna. In a sense the public life of Masaryk was a continuing record of his reaction against the tensions induced by his social and ethnic marginality as a boy and young man. He developed a strong pride in his cultural and social background as a Czechoslovak. At the same time he realized the marginal position of his own culture, which was squeezed between the Culture of Eastern Europe under the leadership of Russia and Western Europe under the leadership of Austria, Germany, France, and England. He gained political prominence at last during the First World War, when the Austro-Hungarian empire started to crumble, and he succeeded in getting the support of Woodrow Wilson and others in establishing the new Czechoslovak republic.

It seems more reasonable to suppose that he developed the political personality that he did partly because of the marginality of his background than to suppose no connection between the two. The tension that he had as a child and young man found relief in the form of intense political activity.

Adolf Hitler came from similarly marginal circumstances—marginal not only socially but also emotionally. His father, Alois, was the illegitimate son of an itinerant miller and a 42-year-old peasant woman who died when Alois was 10 years old—5 years after the marriage had been celebrated. Adolf's grandfather did not legally acknowledge that he was the father of Alois until Adolf's father, Alois, was 39 years old. Alois was raised by his father's brother, a peasant married to a peasant woman 15 years older than himself. Following the pattern of his foster parents, Adolf's father first married a woman 14 years older than himself. His second marriage was to a young hotel cook whom he had started living with before his wife's death and whom he married thereafter. His third marriage was to a second cousin 28 years younger than he. Adolf was the third and oldest surviving child of this marriage. When Adolf was born his father was already 53 years old and distant, not only temporally but also emotionally, from his son. Constantly criticized and depreciated by his father, Adolf was as constantly indulged by his doting mother. She perhaps found in her son a source of affection which was unavailable in her husband, who was indeed more than twice as old as she when Adolf was born. Having risen from social squalor, Adolf's father was determined that his son acquire the status and prestige which he had as a minor official of the government, rather than sink back into ancestral wretchedness or become a worthless artist. When Adolf was 13 years old his father died, leaving him freer to pursue his own artistic talents. His mother's weak insistence that Adolf follow in the footsteps of his father passed for naught.

As a young yokel of indefinite talent and definite emotional insta-bility, Adolf went to Vienna to study art a few years before the First World War broke out. He had little success in studying art (and architecture), but he had enormous success in developing a twisted understanding of the social life, racial heterogeneity, and politics of polycultural Vienna. His mother died a year after Adolf got to Vienna, leaving him now bereft of the one source of personal affection which he had known throughout his life. On the eve of the war he was virtually an orphan not just in the physical but also in the emotional sense. A failure at art and a failure in social relations, he was in essence a profound personal failure.

When the war came he at last had an opportunity to find himself —in combat, not as a soldier of his native Austria but in the army of the Germany he admired so greatly. His physical injuries suffered in the dedicated service of his adopted fatherland gave him a manifest excuse for developing the political outlook which he did—an outlook which is almost the epitome of frustration. Born across the river from Germany, raised by an unapproachable father and a weak and doting mother, rejected in Vienna as a submarginal artist, rejected even in the German army by his fellow soldiers as a fanatical superpatriot, and after the war a wounded veteran who neurotically seemed to have no real desire to satisfy the usual needs of a thirty-year-old bachelor but merely to perpetuate his frustrations, Hitler became the embodiment of a frustrated nation.

It is conceivable that a person born on the German side of the river with a father who was not so much older than he, with a mother who was stronger, and with a little more talent in art could have become a successful politician. It is much more likely that such a person would have become a moderately successful artist or architect. As in the case of Lincoln, McCarthy, and Masaryk the frustrations which Hitler endured as a child and as a young man seem inescapably to constitute one cause for his becoming the kind of political leader that he did.

Ultimately the frustrations found release in a classic case of the Freudian death instinct, with Hitler pursuing his own destruction because of the inability to find affirmative satisfaction for his strong emotional and artistic needs. He seemed bent not only on self-destruction but also on the destruction of the German nation. Determined to make the process of self-destruction a social one, he gained—or at least felt that he had gained—in the mid-1930s a measure of emotional acceptance, of love, from the German people that relieved the frustration of his childhood and youth in Vienna. But in his rage he found it impossible to give a constructive turn to this emotional attachment he had developed, and so had to destroy it and himself in the process of waging a fatal war. Unable to love others (with the exception of his mother and later his niece, Geli Raubal, the daughter of his half sister), he turned to hatred. Unable to create artistically and to build architecturally, he sought first the destruction of the outside world, then of Germany, and finally himself. Even when compared with McCarthy it is hard to imagine a clearer case of displacing private aggressions on public objects than that presented by Hitler: frustration produced not only aggression but also death.

Our fifth political leader, Vladimir Ulyanov (Lenin), was indeed, like the four others, born in the provinces—but of a family that was highly respected in the local community, on grounds not of hereditary distinction but of actual accomplishment. Lenin's father came from a petty-bourgeois background that evidently carried greater prestige than that of the fathers of the four previous leaders. He finished his university education with the help of an older brother and became a school inspector, the head educational figure in a province southeast of Moscow during the time of educational expansion after the emancipation of serfs in 1861. Lenin's mother was the daughter of a Volga-German physician. The stable, prestigious social background of Lenin is in striking contrast to the poor, even squalid background of each of the other four leaders.

Lenin's childhood was not generally frustrated. He respected his father and loved his mother, and these relationships were apparently reciprocal between parents and child. He had a very close and favorable emotional relationship with his siblings, particularly with his brilliant, hypersensitive brother Alexander and his most gifted sister Olga.

The frustrations for Lenin came significantly later, not in childhood but in adolescence. His father died when he was sixteen years old, five years after the political reaction that followed the assassination of Alexander II in 1881. Lenin witnessed the effects on his father of the partial destruction by governmental reaction of the work of a lifetime in building a provincial educational system. A year after his father's death Lenin experienced the execution of his beloved brother Alexander for implication in a plot to assassinate Alexander III. This profound shock occurred while Lenin was finishing gymnasium in preparation for entrance into a university. Three months after he was finally admitted in 1887 to the University of Kazan he was expelled from the university and the city, partly because of his brother's terrorist activities and execution. In 1888 he finally was able to continue his education in Kazan, but not at the university, as a result of his mother's negotiations with friends of her deceased husband. Within three years Lenin was just starting to take the final examinations in law at the University of St. Petersburg when his sister Olga, also studying at the university, died of typhoid.

The striking difference between Lenin and the four others is that his anxiety and frustration more clearly and objectively came not only from private but also from broad social circumstances maintained by the ruling class. Whereas psychic traumata had occurred to the four others at a very early age, Lenin had a background of relative security and self-confidence as a child. As an adolescent he was faced with the world crashing down about his ears. For him there was a striking contrast between deep emotional security as a child and profound insecurity as an adolescent following the death of his father, brother, and sister.

Lenin developed a unique set of attitudes and behavior patterns induced by his anxieties and frustrations. The conflict between him and society, unlike that of the previous leaders, was not so emotionally personal. It was not hard or inappropriate for him *not* to blame himself for failure. His conflict could become impersonal and objective as a result of his ability—realistically explainable—to blame his own frustrations on the ruling structure of the society in which as a young man he was preparing for a career. Like Hitler, whose action pattern was rather largely destructive, even nihilistic, and only to a limited degree constructive, Lenin reacted to personal frustration by seeking destruction of the established ruling class; but unlike Hitler he reacted by helping to create a new society which would supposedly avoid the injustices of the old, and freely provide to everyone the opportunities which had been denied to him.

Had he experienced not childhood fulfillment but the emotional deprivation which Hitler experienced, and to a lesser degree McCarthy, it is conceivable that Lenin would have devoted his career merely to the destruction of the existing social and political order rather than going on as he did to the construction of a new order. The pattern of his political action nevertheless calls for an explanation in terms of irrational consequences of his frustration, just as in the case of the others.

If the irrational sources of his action were not in a profoundly frustrated childhood, in contrast to our other leaders, nonetheless his violent reactions to the frustrations of his adolescence were irrational—unless one assumes that the only choices available to him as a political leader during the decades before October 1917 were the ones which he made. He showed little if any restraint as he presided over the destruction of the old order and showed no more restraint in the destruction of the moderate, Menshevik revolutionary leadership. After the Bolshevik group came to power and he became the recognized leader, he did show restraint in avoiding the destruction of fellow revolutionaries who came in conflict with each other and with him. Had his pattern of frustration been one that went back to birth rather than just to adolescence—if he had been frustrated as profoundly as Hitler—it is conceivable that he would not have been as tolerant of dissension, of resistance to his own will, among his fellow revolutionaries as he in fact was.

Sources of their tensions

In each of these five instances there is good evidence of a relationship between private anxiety—anxiety which was personal—and public consequences of this anxiety. But the effect of these tensions on these five leaders need not lead us to the conclusion that these early experiences were sufficient causes for their styles of rule or that social-status marginality is the only source for tension that finds an outlet in a political career. It is unlikely that Lincoln, whose political successes began fairly early and did not meet with any serious early frustrations, would have followed the same style of rule as did Lenin if Lincoln had been the leader of the Russian revolution. He would have no more been able to stem the tides of destruction of the old order than he could have stopped a springtime flood on the Ohio River.

It is hard to conceive of Hitler's having the enormous success that he did over a long period of time if the country which he ruled was not Germany but the United States. For one thing, McCarthy—his closest American counterpart—came to prominence not in a period of postwar defeat and depression but in a period of postwar victory and prosperity. A person with Hitler's background might have well gained political prominence in America, but it is doubtful that he would have succeeded as well as Hitler did in Germany or better than McCarthy in America and gained complete control of the government.

Among factors shaping their individual style of rule it is also reasonable to assume that the particular genetic make-up of these five leaders was also of tremendous significance. A person in other respects like Hitler but lacking his intense, sometimes psychopathic, reaction to childhood and adolescent experiences more likely would have lived out his life in quiet frustration as peasant or innkeeper or customs inspector, like his father before him. A person who had Lincoln's childhood experiences of despair but lacked the intense reaction to them might have become a moderately successful and contented farmer or small-town attorney in Illinois. Thomas Masaryk with his extraordinary intelligence would more likely have become a dignified and respected professor in the absence of his high energy level and therefore not have gone on from academic to political life after becoming highly successful in the former. Lacking the profound intelligence and intellectual curiosity of Marx, Lenin in the absence of a high energy level may have become a mediocrity in Russian society, a man broken by the adolescent experience of losing in close succession his father, his beloved brother, and his sister.

Thus, without their particular genetic make-up, our leaders would have been quite different: the organism would not have resisted the external pressures which inhibited its development, but rather would have given in to them. The analogy in the natural world would be a hammer dropping into a pan of dough rather than striking an anvil, or a star continuing on its path through space rather than colliding with another star. The intimate, lifelong interaction of the intense ambitions of these five men with frustrating environments helps explain their careers. If one force had not opposed but had yielded to another force there would have been no tension.

Among these five tense men, the consequence of their prominence was in two cases mainly beneficial and constructive, in two others mainly harmful and destructive. In the fifth case it is hard to decide whether the constructiveness outweighed the destructiveness. In our intolerance of ambiguity about saints and sinners we are apt to feel mild anxiety about comparing such people as Lincoln and Masaryk with McCarthy and Hitler. This mild tension need not inhibit—indeed may facilitate—our understanding of the relationships between child-hood and adolescent frustration and political behavior of such leaders as these. Neither is it necessary that the establishment of a catalogue of saints and sinners keep us from looking for the origins of their moral and immoral actions. For the nonce—for a generation or more—the human species will have to tolerate tension in nurturing and assessing leaders. We cannot be sure that childhood misery will produce Lincoln or Masaryk rather than McCarthy or Hitler, and we do not solve the social problems which produced Lenin's dictatorial rule by damning his autocratic, often arbitrary style of rule. Until we know more about the psyche, we will surely have to welcome or put up with possible Lincolns, Masaryks, McCarthys, Hitlers, and Lenins. The alternative is to expose, in the manner of ancient Greece, and in their infancy, all potentially useless or harmful children.

With our poor present knowledge of the human psyche and soma, we can, however, do some possibly fruitful hypothesizing on the dynamic forces that produced the personalities of such men as these. But we know well that the factors mentioned are inadequate explana-tions of these men, and even more surely we know that such forces cannot predict who will be the politicians of the future. Being unable to identify every causal factor—and its intensity—we can say only that the causes of personality development are not interchangeable from one person to another.

The study of political leadership, where one is examining in intimate detail the highly individual case, remains far more complicated than the study of ordinary citizens, where one is concerned with only one or a few facets of the personalities of people who in other, politically quite irrelevant ways, are as complicated as political leaders. With this retrospective caveat, let us have a look at popular tension, or more discretely, at tension among the general public. We will consider chiefs-of-state more fully later, but, for the nonce, will let them rest in a state of un-tension.

Tension in the populace

To establish the political portent of tension we have to examine individuals who form large populations of unprominent people. When these large populations are restlessly, inarticulately pervaded by ten-sions and when this tension is activated by articulate political leaders such as Lincoln or Lenin, tremendous energy is aroused which produces intense political action. We must examine how these people become tense—how with lesser energy than their leaders they give political forms to their anxieties, frustrations, and insecurities and then proceed to act. We will seek the same sources among average people that we have sought among our highly energized leaders: the denial of need satisfactions and the consequent build-up of tension.

One characteristic which we have emphasized in our leaders is marginality. They were men who were caught, in time and status, on various boundaries and moved across them. These men were moving from one social status to another and from one historic period to another and their tension throughout life both caused their individual move and resulted from it. The failure of need satisfaction in childhood and adolescence induced movement and left permanent, active (benign or malignant) lesions that kept these men in tension forever after.

A comparable process appears to occur among a citizenry. The citizenry is unstable and tense because of frustrated and unfulfilled needs. In seeking satisfaction by political means, their interests and those of the leaders become resonant, like harmonic chords on a piano when one vibrating string causes other strings to vibrate. The subject of resonance is a particular aspect of the relations between leaders and led and is considered in Chapter 9 on leaders and followers. Endemic tension within a broad political society is the subject of the present discussion.

Primitive cultures and political culture

In what is now Malagasy (formerly Madagascar), there dwelt before the coming of the white man two different tribes, both supposedly of Indonesian origin. The basic social unit in the original culture patterns of both tribes consisted of extended families grouped in villages. The primal social organization was patrilineal, with provision of food by common familial cultivation of rice in plots that were cut out of the jungle, tilled for a couple of years, and then allowed to revert to jungle for some ten to fifteen years.

At an undetermined time one tribe changed from this peripatetic pattern of rice culture to a system of continuous planting, in fields used every year. One result was to induce transition-anxiety, as the now fixed property gradually came under the control of the king, whose personal power replaced the paternal familial land-control system.

During the transition period this anxiety became so intolerable that one clan in the tribe abandoned the new rice culture altogether, blaming the abandonment on an enemy attack which scattered the menfolk and so caused a labor shortage. This anxiety sounds vaguely like that which followed the establishment of state farms and collective farms in the Soviet Union in the 1920s and 30s. The other kind of anxiety that developed as the second tribe settled on a fixed pattern of rice cultivation resulted from the dependency relationship with the king, who was all-powerful and could give or withhold food from his subjects. The former communal checks on the power of the father who headed the family were now absent. One's fortunes now depended on subservience to the king and on his grace. The individual was supported less by family and custom and was more dependent on his own resources, activity, luck, and success in cultivating both the soil and the king. These anxieties persisted from generation to generation and truly became endemic. They are comparable to the anxieties which existed in the relationships between subjects and tsar in Russia before the 1917 revolution and between citizens and Communist party after the revolution.[19]

To those who habitually associate mental stress with highly complex industrialized society, it may seem incongruous that anxiety should become manifest in the supposedly serene life of a simple subsistence economy in a preliterate society. The tribe that adopted the more dependable cultivation of the same land year after year lost some of the anxiety resulting from food scarcity but gained anxiety when subsistence became more dependent on the whim of a powerful king. In other preliterate cultures there have been other patterns of anxiety. Scarcity of food and an abnormally high ratio of men to women in the Marquesas Islands produced anxieties of subsistence, affection, and sex.[20] Food scarcity and treachery produced anxiety among the Dobuans in the East Indies.[21] In Alor, also in the East Indies, anxieties were derived not from food scarcity but from a lack of steady affection of the mother toward the children and from the cultural value of chicanery in the transfer of personal property (mainly in the form of pigs) and from constant haggling over debts (because debts

---

[19] On the social consequences of the change in method of rice culture, see Abram Kardiner, *The Individual and His Society,* New York, Columbia University Press, 1939, chs. 7 and 8.

[20] *Ibid.,* chs. 5 and 6.

[21] Ruth Benedict, *Patterns of Culture,* New York, New American Library of World Literature (Mentor Books Edition), 1949, ch. 5.

give a creditor power over a debtor).[22] Among the Kwakiutl Indians in British Columbia anxiety arose from the relationship between prestige and property which was acquired by gift or marriage. The main function of the society seemed to be to exalt prestige by the manipulation and periodic destruction of wealth, which made one group superior to its rivals.[23]

Social stability and individual tension

The anxieties in these static, primitive cultures indicate that societies that have been stable for generations can and do generate tensions. These tensions relate to the frustrations of basic needs, in ways that have little if anything to do with the complex social problems of highly fluid modern societies undergoing industrialization and the new patterns of social integration which the process entails. Some other sources of tensions than those mentioned—tensions which may vary from vague anxiety to sharply focused fear—are these: the possibility of sudden death or slow starvation following storm, flood, drought, and disease; uncertainty or inadequacy of affection in consequence of parental neglect or capricious attention; fear of death or social estrangement as a result of a belief system that calls for propitiation of gods and dead ancestors by human sacrifice, and by removal from society of persons possessed of evil spirits. Related as are these sources of tensions to survival itself or to membership in society, it is hard to assume that the serene atmosphere of preliterate society really is so serene. In comparison with modern sources of tensions these, which are of such a fundamental sort, seem to be far more severe. Food anxiety is rare in industrial societies.

But another general sort of tension in primitive societies results from the frustration of unfulfilled expectations, from the stultifying of development by a culture that is largely controlled by the whims of nature, the mortifying hand of the past, and by the often severe authority of a father or tribal head.[24] Unlike the tensions related to subsistence and affection, these are not likely to be activated in a static society until it comes in contact with radically different socio-economic and technical cultural patterns having values which give or promise

[22] Abram Kardiner, *The Psychological Frontiers of Society,* New York, Columbia University Press, 1945, chs. 5 and 6.

[23] R. Benedict, *op. cit.,* ch. 6.

[24] Fereidoun Esfandiary, Is It the Mysterious—or Neurotic—East?, *New York Times Magazine,* 24 March 1957, 13 ff.

dignity to the individual and a chance for him to realize his potential. When this occurs, when the arid seeds are watered, there is then a prospect of real civil disturbance—of riots that reflect the release of tensions fundamentally caused by a static society, but with aggressive action directed helter-skelter at the established government, whether that government was imposed by colonial power or by an indigenous ruling group. It is not government as such which is the cause for the aggression but rather the entire frustrating social structure and value system, which the government both rests on and supports. The government and in a sense the existing social structure become the object for aggression which has its origin in the frustration of the chance to establish individual dignity and self-actualization.

Tension is also the product of cultural transition, as we have seen in the case of the Madagascar tribes that Kardiner described. The abandonment of tradition, the rejection of the past with its built-in anxieties and frustrations, itself produces tension. The social system in primitive culture produces a measure of security by showing what can be done to survive under the ordinarily capricious rule of nature and by maintaining close personal ties between people. To the primitive individual, the world is hostile, his distant neighbors may be hostile, but he does not face these threats alone.

Social transition and individual tension

A static social system provides protection for the individual in the primitive world of the past, but it has little adaptive value when he moves into the new world. This movement occurs when a young man goes to the city and gets a job. Although physically free of restraints imposed by the static culture of his forefathers, the village headsmen, and his own parents, he can never in his lifetime quite erase the effect of these restraints on his personality. The struggle against restraint continues after the ex-tribesman has emerged from the dark past in the city: he fights the past when its presence is more mental than real, more in his memory and habit than in his current experience. This is the tension resulting from an individual's pangs of rebirth, of renaissance.

But intolerably confining as the womb of the past has become, the former tribesman is alone now in the bright new world with its excitement and freedom of movement. This solitude creates a new set of tensions even before the old tensions have begun to subside. His welfare is now his own responsibility, not the responsibility of his parents, his village, or his tribe. He can enjoy the excitement of new friends in the city but he lacks the dependability of old friends and parental warmth. He can get new girl friends but will have trouble getting an urban wife who does not rebel rather than submit to the male authority which he brings with him as a habit of the past. To gain love, he must show love—a phenomenon that neither he nor his girl more than vaguely experienced in the smothering village customs of arranged marriages and dominant, inequalitarian, superior husbands.

And to gain a steady income with its prospects of a fuller life the man from the tribal village must develop new habits of regular appearance on the job. He can no longer sleep when he feels like it, go fishing or hunting when the mood strikes him. He must work steadily and in close cooperation with others, in a factory system dominated by a boss who generates hostility by re-establishing a fatherlike authority, which the tribesman came to the city to escape. The boss may be a white man or trained in the ways of a white man, generating further hostility as he becomes associated in the newcomer's mind with a system of heartless exploitation.

Fear of hostile and capricious gods, who are remote and intangible, is replaced by frustration at no less hostile, capricious, and far closer bosses, and a government run by (or at least for) the exploiters. When the man in transition breaks down under the heavy stress of change, he reverts to the habit of his childhood and blames evil forces outside himself. The failure is not his but the system's, just as a crop failure in his home territory was an act of the gods and not of his fellow tribesmen or himself.[25]

At this point the lonely individual in transition becomes prey to the demagogue who promises simple solutions to complex problems and a vicarious, often spurious affection, and who imparts a sense of social solidarity to replace the comforts of family life in the village of the lonely one's childhood. He cannot really go back home and indeed usually does not, as the rapid growth of cities in Africa and Asia indicates. What is more, he does not really want to go back because the

---

[25] For a careful clinical analysis of the cultural background of mental illness among those in transition from tribal to urban life in Kenya, see J. C. Carothers, A Study of Mental Derangement in Africans, and an Attempt to Explain Its Peculiarities, More Especially in Relation to the African Attitude to Life, *Psychiatry*, 11: 47–86 (1948). The author blames the greater individual and private responsibility of urban life for the higher mental breakdown rate among Africans in cities than among those in tribal villages. *Ibid.*, 81–84.

anxieties and frustrations of modern urban life are less intolerable than those left behind in the village. But the new tensions demand relief and the new leader offers relief. The foreigner will be expelled, the exploiter expropriated, and new opportunities will be created. And it will all be done by the new leader, his followers, and the new party— the new omnipotent forces that will replace the village magic and destroy the evil foreigner. The new urban ex-tribesman need not develop responsibilities and conscience. He need only overthrow the old. Freer and happier than before, he is free and happy only on a scale which starts with the utterly stifling restraint and misery of life in the tribal village.

As societies, like those in Western Europe and North America, advance toward closer integration and coordination on industrial bases, and their members become increasingly free as individuals, the sources of tension change from the gross mental conflicts involved in transition from tightly knit village life to those generated in a looser, freer, more individual existence in the modern industrialized city. As this stage is reached, the individual is now less concerned with throwing off the old and more concerned with preserving the new and preserving himself in the new social context. Freer now to live as he chooses, he cannot escape a greater measure of personal responsibility for his own welfare. Unlikely to starve, he nevertheless may fear regression to a state of relative poverty if he loses his job. Relatively free to advance socially on the basis of his own performance, he acquires new tensions if his aspirations for status and prestige do not accord with his actual attainments. And to keep his wife, protected now by laws equalizing her status and her rights, from divorcing him, he must show her an unaccustomed degree of deference and respect. If he treats her poorly, she can leave him, no longer having to reconcile herself to a miserable subordination.

The new sources of anxiety, which do not altogether supplant the old, are thus the more refined, even exquisite, ones of a person who has made great strides and fears retrogression. He may lose his job, his status, his wife. Anxiety about such losses does not throw him back to a primitive condition, but it does cause tension of enormous political portent. These are the social conditions of anxiety that can produce the counter-revolution of such advanced people as the Southern plantationers in the United States in the rebellion of 1861 and the Germans during the Nazi period of the 1930s. The major difference is not that they are rejecting the miserable past, like people in transition from rural village to urban society, but that they are rejecting the worrisome present in favor of a glorified, unreal past. They want to regain something they have lost rather than gain something they have never had.

In private life the tensions take the form of worry over loss of status, loss of marital happiness, and loss of clear and present opportunities to progress further. They are associated with what Durkheim called the anomy (sense of rootlessness and normlessness) that comes with the loss of dependency on a stable, regulating order of life. The individual finds it impossible to shoulder the burden of responsibility that comes with the internalization of rules of conduct that in the past have been imposed by external authority.

In public life these tensions take the form of a desire to escape from individual responsibility for the proper functioning of a highly complex, tightly integrated socio-economic system. Unable to face this public responsibility, which is easier to evade than the private responsibility for the welfare of himself and family, he finds it easier to blame the system for the incompetence of past political leaders and to hand to a new and forceful leader the intolerable burden of individual responsibility for public policy.

The frame of mind that induces the tendency to follow a leader in a society in transition from the primitive to the modern is thus the same as the mental outlook produced by tensions which cause a mature society to turn to a leader—anxiety about basic needs which never have been satisfied or which, in the later case, it is feared may be denied in the future.

The more basic the threat the more frantic becomes the tension. If a gray-flannel junior executive fails to become a corporation president or a blue-jeaned machine operator does not become a shop foreman, he may tolerate the failure. If he loses his job or fears such a grave loss, he will less likely tolerate the tension. If he is profoundly beset with fear not just of loss of status and a high standard of living but of life itself as the result of war, his mental state may become one of panic. This is particularly so when he sees others around him in the same circumstance. Unique private misfortune is more tolerable than misfortune that becomes general in a society. Shared misfortune spreads like a plague.

In any case the measure of tension is not the objective degree of advancement or decline but the subjective degree of a *sense* of threat. A middle-class businessman threatened with loss of prestige and status may react politically with no more rationality than a detribalized African fired from his clerical job in an export company owned by citizens of the colonial power. The degree of political fever is thus not a function of the objective social circumstances but of the subjective individual appraisal of what he has lost or may lose. And a person in a primitive, highly stifling culture with no outside social contact may fear loss less and have less potential for the irrational action that is a consequence of hypertension than ex-tribesmen in the city or the member of a highly advanced, individualistic society.

Industrial society and individual tension

When an industrial society functions properly without economic or social dislocation in a peaceful world, its insecurities are far fewer and less intense than those of a primitive or transitional society. But when the industrial system or the social system which contains it has a breakdown, the tension can be even greater than a breakdown of an intimate primitive society. What is more, once it does break down the same profound anxieties relating to survival and a sense of social belonging are reactivated and cause the society—despite its external appearances—to revert to the same set of anxieties which prevail among primitive men.

The tension induced by the threat of invasion and war has at times had tragic and atavistic political consequences. The Soviet purges of the 1930s reflected and exploited the tension in the Soviet Union following the rise of Nazism and produced a frantic conformity that was demanded by both the party rulers and the general public itself. McCarthyism in America in the 1950s in part was a consequence of the nagging uncertainty of the ongoing war in Korea, the fear that it might entail severe losses and spread into world conflict. The Korean War in 1950 also brought to the attention of perhaps most of the American public the deprivations of war so recently ended in 1945. This safely non-European war also made it possible to satisfy the desire of Germans, Irish, Italians, and Catholics in America to find release for the imputed disloyalty of the former three during the Second World War and for the social marginality of the latter in a Protestant country. Germans, Irish, Italians, and Catholics (the religious and ethnic categories overlapped but were not coextensive), after two wars in which their old- and new-world loyalties conflicted, could now candidly be patriotic.[26]

---

[26] See Samuel Lubell, *Revolt of the Moderates,* New York, Harper & Bros., 1956, ch. 3 and 80–83.

The reaction on both sides of the long subversive argument after the Second World War was dysfunctional and irrational. When the national government categorically denied the existence of any subversives within the executive departments, it accepted the unstated premise of the McCarthyite opposition that it would be possible in such a vast organization not to have some doubtful characters. The denial that there were any motes and the subsequent discovery of large motes proved, to millions, the existence of monstrous beams in the governmental eye. This reaction produced a state of mind that diminished preoccupation with strengthening the nation and that imagined a purge of the few domestic subversives and alleged subversives would solve a problem not internal but external in origin. In the time of the Soviet purges of the 1930s, Germany—not domestic deviationism—was the major enemy. In the American case, the Soviet Union—not domestic deviationism—was the major enemy. In the late 1930s in the Soviet Union and the early 1950s in the United States the major enemy probably benefited by the preoccupation with the minor enemy. The only sure dominant force was not patriotism or intelligence or prudence or cunning or integrity: it was hypertension.

Most of what has been written hitherto in this chapter might lead one to the conclusion that political anxiety and frustration are per se bad; that the good society and polity are the utterly secure, relaxed ones altogether free of tension. But without social tension there would be no social and political evolution; without a gap between what people want and what they have there would be no growth. Even tensions that go by the unhealthy names of anxiety, insecurity, and frustration are spurs to productive action in which individuals and their society progress toward a greater realization of their potential. Tension therefore is necessary. It is only when it becomes hypertension in the form of panic or collapse that it is not a salubrious but rather a dangerous social and political condition.[27] The more specific consequences of tension in primitive societies in transition and of tensions within an industrial culture itself are reserved for later discussion. Before turning to these consequences, we should first have a long look at how people perceive in general and specifically how they look at politics. It will become apparent that in looking at perception we have not abandoned needs and tensions, because it is through these mental processes that all reality has to filter, like sunshine through a dense forest.

[27] See Rollo May, *The Meaning of Anxiety,* New York, The Ronald Press Co., 1950, 226–234, 350–356.

CHAPTER 4

Political perception

Some obvious observations

Everyone is born with a potential set of standard sensory devices, which as an adult he now knows how to use just as he knows how to use his motor devices in walking, tying shoes, and handling tools (knife and fork, pen and paper, bicycle, ox and wagon, etc.). He scarcely sees the need to consider the self-evident process he has been using continuously since birth. The things he sees are obviously real and unequivocal and true, and he sees them clearly. We are so accustomed to believing what we see that we find it hard to credit—save in a very general way—that we also see what we believe.

To indicate why it is politically most important to perceive how we perceive, I will start this chapter at the roots of perception, with the hunger for (sensory) stimulation. Self-evident and politically unimportant as this may seem to people in the rather serene and constitutional Western world, knowledge of this hunger has been turned to political purpose over and over again in modern dictatorships (oriental and occidental). In going to these roots, I am reporting tendencies which are probably common to the human species and which have extraordinary political implications—even in countries that have achieved effective limitations on the power of their rulers, but even more so in the great majority of nations where the limitations are either few or, by constitutional standards, virtually nonexistent.

In succession I will take up the desire to be stimulated—akin to what Murray calls the need for cognition (see pp. 7–8); the relation of perception to other needs; how percepts are organized in the central nervous system; the relation between values and perception; the personal and nonpersonal carriers of percepts; and the content of percepts

104

themselves. In abstracting and considering serially these aspects of perception, it may be a little easier to see ourselves individually as others see us and see others as we see ourselves. Without this self-consciousness, political perceptions (like other perceptions) remain too much akin—qualitatively too close—to the quite unconscious process by which an amoeba senses food, wraps itself around the food, digests it, and then activates its perceptual processes in search for more. The amoeba can do this, we may suppose, with nary a thought passing through its nucleus. It is done without mirrors.

The hungry eye

From birth we are constantly surrounded by a varied and stimulating environment which we can escape only by sleeping. We take this environment as much for granted as we do the air. Very few of us really have ever experienced what it would be like not to be constantly stimulated. Sick people experience it somewhat, after the locus of their illness diminishes its stimulation of the brain and before they return to normal living. Prisoners in solitary confinement, including military prisoners being brainwashed, experience a psychically cataclysmic collapse of the environment.

In the 1950s for the first time a series of systematic experiments was conducted to find out what happens to an individual in a rather stimulus-free environment. The experiments of course did not achieve complete freedom from external stimuli but came close enough to give all of us a good fright.

The first of these experiments was conducted at McGill University under the direction of D. O. Hebb and his associates. The experimental subjects were placed alone in a small room on a bed where they stayed, except when eating or going to the bathroom, for a period of 96 hours. The room was lighted, but the subjects' vision was limited by a translucent visor over the face. Hearing was limited by a U-shaped pillow which covered the ears, so that only the hum of the sound of the air conditioner could be heard. The subjects wore cardboard sleeves and cotton gloves to limit their sense of touch.

At first the subjects were relieved at not having a sometimes burdening stimulus world about them. They could permit their minds to drift and spontaneous images to appear: rows of dots and then more complicated repetitive patterns like wallpaper and then animated cartoons. One of the subjects reported "seeing" squirrels with sacks over their shoulders marching across his field of vision. But soon the subjects no longer could grant or deny permission to their minds to wander. Their minds took charge. The scenes that appeared would move in bizarre ways, sometimes pivoting on an axis, like patterns in a rotated kaleidoscope. The real eyes would get tired trying to focus on the imaginary figures that appeared. The subjects experienced difficulty in concentrating on either the scene or anything else that they tried to bring to mind.[1]

They developed an intolerable restlessness and nausea. They began to experience a kind of separation from self, a sense of "otherness" or "bodily strangeness." One subject reported that "something seemed to be sucking my mind out through my eyes." Although they were told not to talk to the experimenters except in emergency, the subjects would try to draw the experimenters into conversation either through the microphone or when they left the experimental bed for brief periods.

After the experiments ended, the subjects for a time could not see things normally. A conventional plus sign would become distorted so that one of the legs of the cross appeared longer than the other. Near objects appeared large; distant objects appeared small. The room would undulate, walls and people would bulge and shrink, and when the eyes alone were moved it seemed as though objects in front of them were moving. Straight lines appeared curved, colors appeared saturated and even luminescent, and people with normal skin coloration appeared to be wearing rouge. The subjects experienced nausea more intense than they had when they were in the isolation phase of the experiment.[2]

[1] Note the same inability to concentrate by a person in a state of semi-starvation (p. 13).

[2] Woodburn Heron, The Pathology of Boredom, *Scientific American,* **196** (1): 52–56 (January 1957). W. Heron, B. K. Doane, and T. H. Scott, Visual Disturbances after Prolonged Perceptual Isolation, *Canadian Journal of Psychology,* **10:** 13–18 (1956). W. Heron, W. H. Bexton, and D. O. Hebb, Cognitive Effects of a Decreased Variation in the Sensory Environment, *American Psychologist,* **8:** 366 (1953). For the effect of limiting auditory stimuli, see D. O. Hebb, E. S. Heath, and E. A. Stuart, Experimental Deafness, *Canadian Journal of Psychology,* **8:** 152–156 (1954), the most common consequence being a tendency to withdraw and to be irritable.

Hebb and his associates found that their subjects in isolation did not perform so well on simple arithmetic learning tests as did a control group. They were slower at copying and generally found it an effort to think about anything at all. There may, however, at least be some time during such confinement in isolation when subjects find their learning ability improved rather than diminished. See J. Vernon and J. Hoffman, Effect of Sensory Deprivation on Learning; Rate in

Another experiment under the direction of John C. Lilly took place under an even more completely stimulus-free environment. The subjects were placed alone in a tank of tepid water that felt quite neutral —neither hot nor cold. In other words, it "felt" as minimally as possible. They wore only a black mask through which they could breathe and in emergency communicate with the experimenter. Sound stimuli were limited to the mechanical noises of the equipment used to keep the tank of water at the proper temperature. Gravity pressures were minimized because the subjects were supported not by a mattress but by the surrounding water.

At first the subjects had thoughts about recent events and then a sense of relaxation and enjoyment at having nothing to do. Soon they developed a tension which Lilly calls "stimulus-action hunger." This tension became so strong that if prolonged made it impossible for the subjects to stay in the tank. At first experiencing recollections and fantasies of highly emotional content, the subjects then experienced the same kind of oceanic disassociation from self that Hebb's subjects did. As Lilly explains it, bodily energy rises rapidly when there is no opportunity for its discharge. "At this stage, given any opportunities for action or stimulation by external reality, the healthy ego seizes them." [3]

These experimenters argue very persuasively that there is an inescapable desire of the organism to be excited by external stimuli and that when the environment is so free of stimulus as to provide inadequate relief for the resulting tension within the organism, there is pent-up energy which seeks release and tries to grasp stimuli at any opportunity. In other words, we want to perceive, even when we have no other wants. We have an apparently innate desire to ob-

Human Beings, *Science*, **123**: 1074–1075 (1956), in which the circumstances of sensory deprivation were quite different from Hebb's layout and the period of confinement was 48 hours.

[3] J. C. Lilly, Mental Effects of Reduction of Ordinary Levels of Physical Stimuli on Intact, Healthy Persons, *Psychiatric Research Reports*, **5**: 1–9 and discussion, 10–28 (June 1956). One of the discussants of Lilly's research had been in solitary confinement for over 14 days in a windowless, lightless room. He established contact by tapping with some person or creature in an adjoining part of the prison, but was never able to establish a common code language. This simple, nonverbal communication of mere existence became of major importance to him. [*Ibid.*, 22–23.] This reminds us of Rubashov's companionship with the never-seen prisoner in the adjoining cell, in *Darkness at Noon*. The human voice, to a person so isolated, "sounds marvelous," said Lilly in a lecture at the University of California, Berkeley, 14 May 1962. He also reported that the subjects became extremely dependent on the observer.

serve and make sense out of the wide variety of stimuli to which we are subjected from birth.[4]

Perception and physical needs

Even though we have this basic, residual desire simply to be stimulated, to sense and make sense out of the environment, in ordinary life we usually perceive in the pursuit of other wants. Perception is ordinarily instrumental to other needs. In earlier chapters we have considered at some length the basic needs—the physical, social, equality, and self-actualization needs. At the present point in the argument of the book it is sufficient to indicate only briefly how these various needs influence our perceptual processes.

We have already considered the effects of starvation on perception as these became clear in the Minnesota experiments—hallucinations and dreams about food and increasing inability to think sensibly about anything else. In this sense the preoccupation with thoughts about food when the organism is hungry is analogous to the preoccupation with thought for its own sake that occurred in the experiments conducted by Hebb and Lilly. We need add only at this point that when the organism is confronted with symbols which can be related to the hunger need, the perceiver tends to distort reality in the direction of his need for food. In an experiment using picture and word association, the vague pictures that might or might not suggest food more often suggested food-words to hungry subjects than to those who had just eaten. And when the subjects were shown words that might or might not elicit a word association of food, those who were hungry tended to respond with a food-related word.[5]

[4] For a broad consideration of the theoretical and experimental problems involved, see H. F. Harlow, Mice, Monkeys, Men, and Motives, *Psychological Review*, **60**: 23–32 (1953). The discussion is confused a bit by the definitional notion that the only primary drives are the physical ones, but this straw man in the discourse does not cast too long a shadow on an otherwise abundant crop of ideas, which contains few sour apples. If we note that Harlow recognizes that human learning is "motivation aroused by external stimuli" (p. 29), we can interact nicely with a stimulus-laden essay. See also A. R. Cohen, E. Stotland, and D. M. Wolfe, An Experimental Investigation of Need for Cognition, *Journal of Abnormal and Social Psychology*, **51**: 291–294 (1955), which ingeniously tests the desire to structure ambiguous stimuli quite apart from the relevance of such structuring to any other need.

[5] R. N. Sanford, The Effects of Abstinence from Food upon Imaginal Processes, *Journal of Psychology*, **2**: 129–136 (1936). In a similar experiment hungry and nonhungry subjects were presented for very brief periods with pictures of food

This tendency of hungry people to see objects related to their hunger has clear political content during periods of economic depression. In these times political organizations are established whose purpose is to provide money and therefore food for hungry people. One such organization in California, which proposed during the Great Depression providing money to needy citizens every week, was appropriately named the Ham-and-Eggers. To people who are in severe economic straits such organizations have particular interest. (To others they may seem laughable, even incomprehensible.) Similarly those who are unemployed or threatened with unemployment and those faced with a serious health problem will focus their attention in politics on programs which are designed to relieve unemployment and provide medical care at a nominal cost. Only those who are quite secure themselves in their jobs and in their health will not pay attention to political programs of this sort and will regard them as nonsensical.

The threat of physical destruction itself raises interesting questions. If hungry people are quick to see signs of food, if people who are unemployed or threatened with serious illness pay particular attention to unemployment and health insurance problems, then surely people who are threatened with physical destruction as a result of nuclear warfare should be preoccupied with this problem. Quite the contrary, most people seem relatively unconcerned about this problem, to the bafflement not only of a simple explanation for their unconcern but also to publicists, civil defense officials, and others who are very much worried with the problem. One suggested explanation for this lack of concern is that people experience a kind of "hysterical paralysis" in the face of this overwhelming danger—that is, the problem is so incredibly dangerous that people escape from it by denying its existence.[6]

The "hysterical paralysis" explanation is psychologically plausible, but there is another explanation which may be as near reality as this: namely, the threat is so great as to make it effectively impossible for any small group of governmental leaders—military or civilian—of any nation to start the process which would inevitably lead to widespread

objects by means of a tachistoscope, a projector which allows the flashing of images on a screen for controlled periods of small fractions of seconds, somewhat like a camera in reverse. Subjects that were hungry saw the food objects more quickly —that is with fewer exposures on the tachistoscope—than did the nonhungry subjects. See R. S. Lazarus et al., Hunger and Perception, *Journal of Personality*, **21**: 312–328 (1953).

[6] Philip Wylie, Panic, Psychology, and the Bomb, *Bulletin of the Atomic Scientists*, **10**: 37–40 (1954).

destruction. To initiate atomic warfare, in other words, is to commit suicide, which few normal people prefer to do. The explanation on grounds of hysterical paralysis is paradoxical, that is, the danger is so great that people cannot face it. The alternative explanation is also paradoxical because it says the danger is so great it will not ever arise. Quite aside from the problem of nuclear destruction itself, the psychological problem of explaining why there is such widespread apathy to the danger of destruction remains unsolved.

Perception and other needs

The very basic desires to perceive and to satisfy physical needs are indeed capable of directly influencing perceptual processes—that is, without the intervention of any other agencies. But most of our perception occurs in social context and is related to our social needs— our needs to get together, be together, and stay together. We learn most of what we know or believe through human agents. The first of these are parents, then playmates, then adolescent and mature associates ranging from teachers in schools, ministers, rabbis, and priests in churches, and political candidates operating usually within political parties.

Our association with people has much to do with the style and content of all our perceptions and actions, since political processes always take place within the context of nonpolitical association. We will consider this broad social problem separately and at length in the next chapter. Suffice it to say here that the ties between individuals have enormous effect on how we perceive situations.

For the moment let us mention only one case that strikingly illustrates the effect of an intimate kind of social need—the love between mother and son—on perceptual processes and on behavior. In April 1960 a 123-pound (56 kg) woman in the United States saw the 3600-pound (1640 kg) family station wagon slip off the jack that was holding up one side of it, trapping her son underneath the car. The mother picked up the one corner of the station wagon and held it long enough so that her son could escape from under the car. The visual stimuli that touched her retina were not at all like the sensation of pain when one touches a hot object or of discomfort when one is hungry. But the perception of her own son trapped under the car, combined with her strong affection for him, was enough to cause incredible exertion, which freed her son and cracked some of her vertebrae. To cite a political example, with a warning that the example is a complicated one, about three-fourths of all adults in the United States are members of the same political party as their parents (see ch. 6, p. 208).

The need for equality particularly affects the perceptual world of those who feel that they are discriminated against. A Negro walking on a city street and encountering a white man may feel slighted if the white person turns his eyes away from him, regardless of whether the white person was turning his eyes away from the Negro or merely admiring a shapely female. An Egyptian, listening to Nasser pour contempt on the American Secretary of State, after negotiations are broken off between the United States and Egypt for construction of the Aswan dam in 1956, will cheer enthusiastically. He hears Nasser in effect proclaiming the equality and dignity of Egyptians with Americans. An American reading the report in the newspaper will see the incident only as the mad aberration of a demagogue.

The need for self-actualization is more tenuously involved in political perceptions. It is, however, a reasonable hypothesis that only a person whose physical, social, and equality needs are relatively well met will become concerned with public affairs that have to do with individual liberty. Thus unemployed persons scanning the newspaper will read the help-wanted columns plus news relating to government action designed to gain jobs for people. From the same news source, the college-educated person who has a job, etc. will more likely pay less attention to these things than to such incidents as court decisions which allow for censorship of movies and allow or prohibit the right of free speech to a particular organization. These latter news items are not likely to strike the attention of a hungry person. They can preoccupy the attention of the person who is not hungry precisely because he is not hungry. Absence of chronically active physical needs is not a sufficient but a necessary condition of such preoccupation.[7]

The consideration of basic needs as they affect both political perceptions and political behavior can most appropriately be considered in the chapters (1, 2, 5, 6, and 8) relating to these needs. In the balance

---

[7] Note the consistently greater concern for civil liberty (in the form of allowing religious, economic, and political dissenters to speak) among community leaders in large American cities than among the general public. [Samuel H. Stouffer, *Communism, Conformity, and Civil Liberties*, Garden City, Doubleday & Co., 1955, ch. 2.] Among these community leaders who were more tolerant than the general public were Regents of the Daughters of the American Revolution, Republican County Central Committee Chairmen, presidents of city bar associations, and newspaper publishers. The posited relationship between satisfaction of physical needs and concern for individual freedom of course presupposes that these leaders have less than average concern with their physical needs.

of this chapter we can most appropriately consider some more strictly perceptual processes.

How perceptions are organized

One of the commonest tendencies in organizing our pictures of the world is to make these pictures complete, so that—symmetrical or not—they provide a total explanation for reality in a manageable, not over-complicated form. Even in very simple ways we tend to distort reality to make it consistent with sensible pictures with which we may or may not have been familiar before. For example, as the adjoining figure 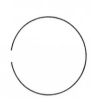 indicates, a circle missing a fraction of its total circumference is not seen as a long arc but as an almost complete circle. When one reads the following words—Repulican, reactiouary, radicel, Demcrat —he is unlikely at first glance to see that these four words in their context have been misspelled. He sees them not as they are printed but as incorrectly written symbols describing already familiar objects. The horse put his foot in the eye of the fleabells loudly listening to the oceanclouds by the light of the silvery sandstormtrooper. This sentence is so puzzling that a person does not try to reduce it to sense, but quickly moves beyond this nonsense, perhaps with the judgment that the writer is a modern impressionist in need of psychiatric help. In no ordinary sense does the sentence make sense to anyone.

From childhood onward, we have a strong desire to get a complete picture of things. If a mother reads a story to a small child, he gets indignant if she breaks off reading the story midway before finishing it. If we go to even a mediocre movie we are far more likely to stay to the end to see what happened to the villain and the hero than to leave before we find out. People find it difficult to tolerate unresolved situations not only in stories but also in political news. They tire of unresolved issues; they are unwilling to tolerate the tension which this irresolution entails. As Allport and Faden said, the higher the tension "the stronger will be the demand for closure." [8]

In politics this tendency toward completeness and simplicity means that we seek and accept simple categorical solutions to inherently

[8] G. W. Allport and J. M. Faden, The Psychology of Newspapers: Five Tentative Laws, *Public Opinion Quarterly*, **4**: 687–703 (1940).

complicated public problems. This tendency shows itself particularly when people are in a condition of political or economical stress. In such circumstances they are far more willing to listen to a person who advocates the simple solution, like the single tax on land, a solution which is supposed to cure not only the tax problem for government but also the distribution of wealth amongst all people of this society. When tense, they are far more willing to consider the free coinage of silver as a solution to a similar set of political problems. When tense, they are far more likely to blame Negroes, Jews, capitalists, communists or any other handy set of symbols for their political ills. When tense, they are far more likely to see the American Way, National Independence, Marxism, or Democracy as symbols which—depending on their particular social context—represent the only means of solving problems that are very complicated in any social context.

Another common tendency in perceptual organization is to categorize and classify things into coherent, consistent entities. For example, in appraising people, one uses the total set of impressions about them to form a unified whole, in which each part of the total set is interrelated to the others. Any incongruous aspects tend to be ignored or depreciated. This has been shown in a study by Asch, who presented two different experimental groups with lists that were identical in their descriptions of hypothetical people, except for one word. The first list included these adjectives in this order: intelligent, skillful, industrious, warm, determined, practical, cautious. The second list contained these words: intelligent, skillful, industrious, cold, determined, practical, cautious. The two experimental groups came out with radically different descriptions of the person described by the two sets of adjectives, which were identical except for the change from "warm" to "cold." These two words changed even the quality of the other six words as they added up to descriptions of persons having these formal word descriptions.[9]

[9] S. E. Asch, Forming Impressions of Personality, *Journal of Abnormal and Social Psychology,* **41**: 258–290 (1946). A comparable result was obtained when a hypothetical person was described by the following words or phrases: "works in a factory, reads a newspaper, goes to movies, average height, cracks jokes, intelligent, strong, active." The adjective "intelligent" was the puzzler for the subjects of this second experiment. They tended either to ignore the word or to say that this factory worker was a good "joe," etc., but lacked drive and education; or, for example, they promoted him to a foreman. Only three of the forty-three subjects frankly acknowledged that they considered it incongruous that a factory worker be intelligent. [M. Haire and W. F. Grunes, Perceptual Defenses: Proc-

Quite aside from the logic of prior attitudes, one of the most common bases for categorizing (for perceptual organization) is the liking or disliking, acceptance or rejection (in Freudian terms, positive or negative cathexis) of the object categorized. We like and accept things which are familiar to us: our comfortable surroundings, our friends, our familiar ideas and loyalties. We dislike and reject the opposites of these. Negroes are most at ease with Negroes, Republicans are most comfortable with Republicans. Catholics are likely to harbor suspicion or dislike or other negative cathexis for Protestants and other disbelievers. Frenchmen are apt to be suspicious of Germans. Portuguese have mixed feelings for Spaniards. Americans in the middle of the twentieth century are prone to suspicion of un-American, particularly communist, notions and people. Mid-century Russians are apt to be suspicious of anything associated with the American government or capitalists.

A third tendency of perceptual organization, related to the previous two, is to persist in established views. One word that describes this is habit. A nice phrase which describes the same thing is the "need to minimize surprise." [10] Some psychological experiments, quite free of emotional overtone, indicate how basic is this tendency to persist in established views.[11]

One experiment, lacking political content, nevertheless has political portent. The experimenters presented to a group of pre-law students evidence from a celebrated American bigamy trial that had taken place over a hundred years earlier. The evidence for and against the charge of bigamy was presented to different groups of the experimental subjects in different sequence: (1) in the order presented at the

esses Protecting an Organized Perception of Another Personality, *Human Relations,* **3:** 403–412 (1950).]

[10] M. Brewster Smith, Jerome S. Bruner, Robert W. White, *Opinions and Personality,* New York, John Wiley & Sons, 1956, 261.

[11] In the first case subjects were shown, by a tachistoscope, playing cards which were incongruous. For example, out of five cards one would contain a red spade and another a black heart. The normal cards, like a red heart or a black spade, were recognized roughly four times as quickly as were the incongruous cards. [J. S. Bruner and L. Postman, On The Perception of Incongruity: a Paradigm, *Journal of Personality,* **18:** 206–223 (1949).] In another experiment, the experimenter cut two different figures from the same piece of green material. One of the figures was a donkey and the other a leaf. These two figures were shown to the subject in identical red light. Most of the subjects of the experiment saw the leaf as being greener than the donkey. [K. Duncker, The Influence of Past Experience upon Perceptual Properties, *American Journal of Psychology,* **52:** 255–265 (1939).]

actual trial (prosecution, defense, prosecution, defense); (2) some of the prosecution evidence, then all of the defense evidence, and then a conclusion of the prosecution evidence; (3) all of the evidence for the prosecution, then all of the evidence for the defense; (4) all of the evidence for the defense except for one crucial item, then all for the prosecution, and then the crucial defense item. The subjects were given a nine-point scale in which they could indicate their certainty as to the guilt of the defendant, varying from complete certainty of guilt all the way to complete certainty of innocence.

From the beginning the subjects exhibited a slight tendency to believe that the defendant was guilty, merely because he was formally charged with the crime. But the order in which the testimony was presented made a remarkable difference. In the first variation of the experiment the subjects as a total group were quite well convinced that the defendant was guilty after they heard the first portion of the prosecution's testimony. Their belief in his guilt dropped by almost half after hearing the first testimony for the defendant, went back almost to the previous point of belief in guilt after hearing the second argument for the prosecution and then dropped down almost to complete belief in innocence when the second defense testimony had been presented.

In each succeeding version of the experiment (that is, when the order of presenting the evidence was changed) belief in the innocence or guilt of the defendant varied as a function of the last evidence presented to the pre-law students. A transitory mental set, arising solely from the experiment, was clearly established. The task of establishing guilt or innocence is highly complicated. But the very simple facts of establishing a mental set and reacting to the most recent set of stimuli were significant factors in determining whether or not the accused was guilty.[12]

The mental sets established in ordinary life are probably far more resistant to change than those established in the minds of experimental subjects. In some cases the animus behind the resistance to new percepts indicates strong emotional involvement in the desire to maintain established views.[13] In the cathedral in Toledo, Spain, the form of

---

[12] H. P. Weld and M. Roff, A Study in the Formation of Opinion Based upon Legal Evidence, *American Journal of Psychology,* **51**: 609–628 (1938).

[13] A classic instance of this occurred when Freud was a young man starting his medical career in Vienna. He reported to a society of doctors some cases of hysteria, a mental disorder which was then believed to be suffered only by women.

the mass and liturgy is different from the orthodox Catholic mass and has had a curious continuous history of uniqueness for centuries, in the face of the strong pressures for uniformity in a predominantly Catholic and orthodox Catholic country. The mass and liturgy employed in the Toledo cathedral are believed to be the same mass and liturgy spoken by a group of Christians who were allowed to remain such when Spain was captured by the Moors, in the eighth century. When Toledo was recaptured from Mohammedanism, in the eleventh century, these Mozarabic Christians were asked to abandon their old liturgy in favor of the orthodox Roman one. The story is that they agreed to do so if two champions of the Roman liturgy were defeated in ordeals by combat and fire with protagonists of this Mozarabic liturgy. When the Roman protagonists failed, the rites continued and are still practiced daily in the Toledo cathedral—at least 1200 years after they first were practiced.[14]

A similar conflict occurred in Russia between the old and the new, starting in the seventeenth century when the Patriarch Nikon introduced a series of reforms in the Russian Orthodox Church, basing these changes on a return to older but newly discovered and more authentic scriptural texts, from which church doctrine had unwittingly deviated for centuries. One of the most significant reforms that he introduced involved changing from two to three fingers in making the sign of the cross, the three fingers symbolizing the trinity in contrast to the two-finger symbolism of the duality of Christ. Another major change involved deletion of the first two words of the phrase "true and vivifying." These changes were resisted bitterly during the four-year period (1653–1656) that the prayer book and liturgy were being changed. The resistance was met with severe repression of those who came to be known as the Old Ritualists. Their leader Avvakum was burned at the stake for his opposition to the new and official doctrine. Unimportant as the changes seem to outsiders, they were so important to the Old Ritualists that even as late as 1850 some nine million of them still were practicing their accustomed rites.[15]

Freud said some of his hysterical patients were men. The response of one of the people listening was to say this was impossible: there could not be male hysterics because the word hysteria comes from the Greek word hystera which means uterus, so that by definition no man could have the illness. Sigmund Freud, *An Autobiographical Study*, London, The Hogarth Press, 1935, 25.

[14] H. V. Morton, *A Stranger in Spain*, New York, Dodd, Mead & Co., 1955, 108–110.

[15] George Vernadsky, *A History of Russia*, fourth edition, New Haven, Yale University Press, 1954, 131–133, 180–182.

In both the Spanish and Russian instances, religious habit—the accustomed ways of worshipping God—had enormous political consequences. It is easy for people in the twentieth century to smile at
such persistence in the face of such moderate change as occurred in
the ritual of the Roman Catholic Church in Spain and of the Greek
Orthodox Church in Russia. Besides, some might say, judging biga-
mists innocent and persisting in antique church ritual in pre-modern
Russia or an embalmed Spanish town have nothing to do with political perception.

But in the Western world, in politics, there is the same tendency to
resist with great passion the introduction of even such verbal changes.
So, for example, if the label socialistic is applied to something, it is
presumed to be evil in the United States. When a great dam was
authorized by Congress and approved by Calvin Coolidge, one of the
most conservative Presidents in American history, its construction at
public expense, its operation by the government, and its naming in
honor of Herbert Hoover, another conservative President, presumably
had nothing to do with socialism. At least there was no serious opposition to it on that score.

When, however, a few years later in the Tennessee Valley a series
of dams was constructed and operated by the same government but
under the nonconservative Franklin Roosevelt, this was deemed socialistic by its opponents. By its friends—particularly in the Tennessee
Valley—the project was not at all socialistic. Similarly, a governmental
subsidy to the shipping industry is not considered socialistic, but unemployment insurance and health insurance have in the past been
considered socialistic, until they became official doctrine of the conservative party.

By the same token when the piecework system was introduced into
socialist industry in the Soviet Union it was not called what American
labor calls it: the speed-up and the dog-eat-dog system of production;
in the Union of Soviet Socialist Republics it became socialist competition. The speed-up has been one of the most bitterly opposed features of private enterprise in American society, a feature which continues to be slowly eliminated. It became officially accepted dogma
in the classless, socialist society ruled by the vanguard of the working
class. The emotionalism generated over the mere symbols themselves,
quite apart from any content, appears to be almost as much a part of
public consideration of issues now as it was three centuries ago in
Russia. There have not been any burnings of dissenters among con-

stitutional democracies in recent years, though there have been instances of restrained, nonlethal brutality against dissenters.

All people have a tendency to persist in established views and in established ways of doing things and all people resist change. But it seems quite clear that people differ in the degree to which they persist in established views and resist change. If many millions of people in Russia persisted in their adherence to the Old Ritual, many more millions were willing to abandon the so-called Old Ritual. If millions of people in America during the 1930s resisted efforts to introduce new ideas and practices in government, millions of others were willing to do so.

Do people differ deeply and enduringly in their readiness or reluctance to accept change? An extensive study by McClosky of conservatives and liberals has reported some striking differences in various facets of their personalities. He found that conservatives, in contrast to liberals, had a relatively high sense of social alienation, pessimism, anomy, and guilt. He found them to be less socially responsible and less self-confident. He further found them to be less well-informed, less educated, and perhaps lower in intelligence.[16] Relative reluctance to accept change was one of the defined characteristics of conservatives in the study.

One early study of more limited scope found virtually no correlation between political liberalism and level of information, although on some specific policy issues, liberals turned out to have more factual knowledge than conservatives.[17] Another study found that conservative students had about the same amount of factual information as radical students but had somewhat more misinformation than the radicals and less willingness to withhold judgment even on matters of fact. Furthermore, conservatives had lower academic grades.[18] Still an-

[16] H. McClosky, Conservatism and Personality, *American Political Science Review,* **52:** 27–45 (1958).

[17] C. R. Pace, The Relationship between Liberalism and Knowledge of Current Affairs, *Journal of Social Psychology,* **10:** 247–258 (1939). Liberals were better informed on labor unions, war, Trotsky, and the WPA work-relief program; conservatives on the plan of Roosevelt to reorganize the Supreme Court and the Spanish Civil War.

[18] G. W. Allport, The Composition of Political Attitudes, *American Journal of Sociology,* **35:** 220–238 (1929). Another investigator found some slight relationship between intelligence and what he calls "alterationism," a tendency to want and accept social change. [M. Sanai, The Relation between Social Attitudes and Characteristics of Personality, *Journal of Social Psychology,* **36:** 3–13 (1952).]

other study found a slight relationship between intelligence and liberalism.[19]

An intensive study of ten individuals who were all above average in intelligence—nine of the ten were in the top 10% of the total population—found remarkable differences between these ten individuals in what could be called political liberalism and conservatism. This study of course has no significance as a cross section of the entire population or of people who are well above average in intelligence. It indicates only that among very intelligence people there can be a wide range of generally conservative or liberal attitudes.[20]

It is clear that people do differ in their resistance to change. It is clear also that this variation in the resistance to change is related to personality characteristics. Just what these personality characteristics are, what the reasons are for these differences in personality characteristics and therefore differences in resistances to change, remains in doubt.

A more adequate explanation for resistance to change may in time be found in its relationship to anxiety, frustration, and other forms of tension. The most common reaction to a new threat is to use procedures that worked well on a prior threat. A person suffering from physical illness or injury usually regresses in some degree to childlike behavior. The physical threat to his organism is so severe that he cannot cope with it by himself and he falls back on a dependency relationship to doctors and nurses—a relationship that takes him back to the days when he was cared for as a child. A person unable to face changed social and economic circumstances may similarly fall back on stereotyped catch phrases and old techniques for solution to the new political problems. Nations prepare for new wars by perfecting techniques that were successful in former wars.

What little psychological research has been carried out on the relationship between anxiety and mental rigidity tends to support the notion.[21] "Intolerance of ambiguity" is the concept used to describe

[19] G. Rubin-Rabson, Intelligence and Conservative-Liberal Attitudes, *Journal of Psychology*, **37**: 151–154 (1954). The slight positive relationship between intelligence and liberalism almost disappeared when attitude toward Negroes was excluded from the correlation. Note Table 1, p. 152.

[20] M. B. Smith et al., *Opinions and Personality*, New York, John Wiley & Sons, 1956. Note Table 3, p. 254, and ch. 10, passim.

[21] See J. C. Beam, Serial Learning and Conditioning under Real-life Stress, *Journal of Abnormal and Social Psychology*, **51**: 543–551 (1955), which found that subjects when under stress (such as pending doctoral examinations in graduate school) made half again as many errors and took about half again as long to learn

a major aspect of mental rigidity by Frenkel-Brunswik. She relates this intolerance mainly to racial prejudice, but also to anxiety.[22]

One of the major problems in research on mental rigidity is the failure to distinguish different areas and levels of personality and therefore not to consider whether a person can be inflexible in some areas and flexible in others, inflexible at some levels and flexible at others. We have noted some inconclusive evidence of a relation between mental rigidity, racial prejudice, and dogmatism, and a finding of correlation between social conservatism on the one hand and alienation, pessimism, anomy, and guilt on the other.[23] We have seen evidence far less conclusive of the relationship between intelligence and mental flexibility. The fault is one of mental inflexibility about the problem of mental inflexibility, the tendency to extrapolate from flexibility or rigidity, liberalism or conservatism, in one area to one or more other tendencies in another. Even though people do tend to differ generally in their flexibility it is still unsafe to make broad generalizations as to the exact areas in which individuals are inflexible and in what other areas they are not. A clerk selling tickets in a railway station may exhibit a high degree of rationality and flexibility as a ticket clerk but be quite rigid outside his own particular competence. On the other hand, natural scientists may have a high degree of flexibility in their own field and yet may exhibit a high degree of dogmatism, which is one aspect of mental rigidity, when it comes to social problems. And

the correct order in which twelve successive nonsense syllables were presented as when they were not under the stress condition. Another study found a positive but low correlation between dogmatism and anxiety. [M. Rokeach and B. Fruchter, A Factorial Study of Dogmatism and Related Concepts, *Journal of Abnormal and Social Psychology*, **53**: 356–360 (1956).]

[22] E. Frenkel-Brunswik, Intolerance of Ambiguity as an Emotional and Perceptual Personality Variable, *Journal of Personality*, **18**: 108–143 (1949). A curious comment by Frenkel-Brunswik indicates that intolerance of ambiguity can also be a characteristic of the people who study it. At one point she says "today as never before we witness a contrasting crystallization of the two patterns, although they may frequently be interwoven. Power orientation, anti-intellectualism, externalization, hostile exclusion, rigid stereotyping, and dogmatism are on the one side; understanding, thoughtfulness, empathy, compassion, insight, flexibility, justice, reason, and scholarship are on the other." [Interaction of Psychological and Sociological Factors in Political Behavior, *American Political Science Review*, **46**: 44–65 (1952).]

[23] Note the contrast in findings between the following: M. Rokeach, Generalized Mental Rigidity as a Factor in Ethnocentrism, *Journal of Abnormal and Social Psychology*, **43**: 259–278 (1948), and L. D. Goodstein, Intellectual Rigidity and Social Attitudes, *Journal of Abnormal and Social Psychology*, **48**: 345–353 (1953).

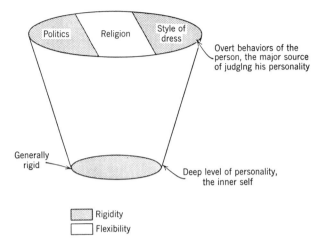

Overt behaviors of the person, the major source of judging his personality

Generally rigid

Deep level of personality, the inner self

Rigidity

Flexibility

even a highly sophisticated psychologist can be aware of mental rigidity and find it in others without recognizing its existence in himself. The diagram above will serve to illustrate the conceptual problem of mental rigidity as an aspect of personality.

Values and perception

We have indicated the relation between the basic needs and perception and how the activation of a particular basic, organic need will cause people to select and even distort aspects of the environment which are related to that basic need. There is also a relation between culturally determined values and perception. The phenomenon is manifest in a wide range of values from quite apolitical to political. Investigations have demonstrated that people distort their perception of money and other symbols of high or low value, such as obscene words. And people who are exceptionally high or low in racial prejudice are more apt than others to recognize words and other signs relating to minority groups.[24]

People's values obtrude not only in apolitical ways, like those just described, but also in their reading of politics. Subjects in one experiment were presented with a speech which contained a carefully equalized amount of pro- and anti-New Deal material. The subjects who

[24] See the summary of Some Experiments on Perceptions Distorted by Values at the end of this chapter, pp. 137, 140.

were by previous test pro-New Deal remembered more of the pro-New Deal material in the speech. Those who were anti-New Deal remembered more of the anti-New Deal material.[25] It has also been found that people react more vigorously to labels than they do to content. For example, "a non-college population of 336 subjects" tested before the Second World War rejected fascist and communist labels on ideas but were far less critical of specific but unlabeled fascist and communist doctrine.[26]

Painting on a larger canvas, we can imagine an account of the American Revolution as it might have been written by a patriotic English chronicler in 1786, during the reign of George III.

Agitated at being asked by their mother country to help support the cost of their own government and of protection from Indians, some of the settlers in the central North American colonies drifted farther and farther away from respect for law and order. They mobbed English officials, refused to quarter English troops sent to guard the frontier, deliberately destroyed shipments of English tea, and formed a network of subversive political clubs under the leadership of cunning, unprincipled agitators like the notorious Samuel Adams.

Pretending to believe in broad principles of natural law and justice which were plagiarized from English philosophers like John Locke, they arrogantly proclaimed their right to independence in a demagogic Declaration which, if it is ever remembered, will go down in history for its infamous defamations of English justice. The traitorous English subjects who led this rebellion—including the land speculator George Washington, the homespun printer and tinkerer Benjamin Franklin, and the slaveowner who professed belief in human liberty and equality, Thomas Jefferson—cynically exploited popular discontent by employing the rabble-rousing, faithless English schoolmaster Thomas Paine.

The well-disciplined, courageous British troops sent to put down the little rebellion were finally defeated only as a result of the intervention of the French army and navy, which provided a majority of the forces marshaled at Georgetown. Only by an opportunistic and frantic appeal to a decadent, backward, and absolutist monarchy were the dissident elements able to overthrow constitutional English rule. The rebellious colonies have already shown signs of internal collapse because of the same shortsighted, self-serving provincialism that started the rebellion in the first instance. The masses

[25] A. L. Edwards, Political Frames of Reference as a Factor Influencing Recognition, *Journal of Abnormal and Social Psychology*, **36**: 34–50 (1941). Similar results were achieved when the material was pro- and anti-Soviet Union. [J. M. Levine and G. Murphy, The Learning and Forgetting of Controversial Material, *Journal of Abnormal and Social Psychology*, **38**: 507–517 (1943).]

[26] D. Katz and H. Cantril, An Analysis of Attitudes toward Fascism and Communism, *Journal of Abnormal and Social Psychology*, **35**: 356–366 at 362–365 (1940).

of American yeomen, who thought they were gaining freedom, have only changed their just English rulers for a crude lot of adventurers grown rich from the English trade and oppressive from the unaccustomed exercise of power without constitutional restraint.

In politics, efforts are almost invariably made to euphemize the unpleasant. Japan described its war in China in the 1930s as the China Incident. The mild nonviolent move in Poland toward independent action vis-à-vis the Soviet Union in 1956 has been described in Poland as "the October event" rather than "the revolution" or "the Polish October." It seemed more appropriate to avoid the trouble that would be involved in associating Poland's efforts at gaining independence with the holy Russian revolution of October 1917. The violent revolution in Hungary in 1956 is referred to as "the event" by those who are anti-Soviet in Hungary and as the "counter-revolution" by those who are sympathetic to the Soviet Union. In the Soviet Union itself, after the death of Stalin, the term "Stalinist" became for a while a synonym for "bad." Subsequently the synonym for "bad" changed to "reactionary" and then "dogmatist." In the international communist language, the inflexible and orthodox are referred to as rightists, as Stalinists were in the period after Stalin's death. Those favoring change are called leftists, if they stay away from extremes; if they are extreme leftists they are called revisionists or liberals or, even worse, bourgeois.[27]

Quite aside from the tendency to distort opinions about the New Deal or about the Soviet Union or about capitalism or socialism, there is a tendency for our values to intrude on the simple recollection of straight political facts. A study based on interviews conducted in 1947 found that Americans who had a favorable attitude towards the Soviet Union tended to think the Soviet Union had declared war on Japan just before the first atomic bomb was dropped on Japan, and those unfavorable to the Soviet Union tended to reverse this sequence of events.[28]

National values are deep-seated and deeply cherished: they are usually unquestioned and unquestionable. When they are violated

---

[27] Flora Lewis, Clues to the Communist Lingo, *New York Times Magazine,* 1 September 1957, 11. For other consequences on language and logic of imposing totalitarian ideology, see the lectures by a Swiss philologist, Hannes Mäder, reprinted under the title The Tongues of Tyrants in *Atlas,* 4: 92–99 (August 1962).

[28] M. B. Smith, The Personal Setting of Public Opinions: A Study of Attitudes toward Russia, *Public Opinion Quarterly,* 11: 507–523 (1947).

by our fellow citizens, the effect is profoundly disturbing. When violated by our families, the fact is so shocking as sometimes to be quite unacceptable: the reality itself is denied. When two young employees of the National Security Agency of the United States defected to the Soviet Union in the summer of 1960, the father of one of them was apparently able to accept the fact but unable to understand why. The father of the other refused to believe in the defection, saying that his son must have been kidnaped or drugged.

The depth and intensity of these national values may be indicated by a dramatic instance in which a person abandoned them. The Japanese pilot who led the attack of 353 planes on Pearl Harbor, 7 December 1941, was then 39 years old, well past the stage of pliant, impressionable youth. He said "my heart was filled with hate and revenge when I led the attack."

When placed on trial as a war criminal, he stoutly justified Japan's actions throughout the entire war. He was acquitted. In 1949 he met an old friend who had been captured during the war and imprisoned in Arizona but denied that he had been maltreated by the Americans. This friend told him that the daughter of an American missionary who had been killed by Japanese in the Philippines during the war had worked as a prisoner's aid in the Arizona prison camp. The leader of the attack on Pearl Harbor then read about other American prisoners who had suffered maltreatment in Japanese prison camps but had come to the point of no longer hating their captors. From this point in his thinking, he went to a study of the Bible and became a dedicated, active Christian lay-missionary. The national values which had been so deeply imprinted in his personality up to 1949 were replaced by an altogether different set of values. His abandonment of national values was quite literally an aspect of religious conversion.[29]

The carriers of things perceived

Like all other mental phenomena, perceptual processes are a function of the interaction of the organism and the environment. Hitherto we have concentrated on the processes occurring within the perceiver himself—his basic, organic needs, his perceptual processes as such, his relative mental flexibility or rigidity in facing new ideas and new ways of solving problems, and the effect of predispositions, including values,

[29] Oakland *Tribune,* 27 December 1959; Los Angeles *Times,* 25 March 1962, Section H, page 3.

on his percepts. Regardless of the immediate context in which we see things and regardless of the characteristics of the object perceived, these characteristics of the perceiver have great but not total influence on how we see things.

Now let us consider a major aspect of the environment that forms part of the interaction process between the organism and the environment. This aspect is the context—the carrier, the vehicle—in which percepts reach us. All percepts are received in some context—even abstract things like mathematical symbols and formulas. One broad category of context is the social one—individuals and groups which carry percepts to us and the groups within which we receive them. This category is so broad as to merit extensive consideration on its own in the following chapters on social influences on political behavior. The present discussion deals only with the more immediate personal contexts in which we receive percepts.

The competence, the authority, of the carrier—whether it be a person or an object like a book or periodical—is a significant factor that helps determine how hospitably we receive the percept. This fact is often employed by advertisers who inform us that experts (physicians, dentists) have tested a particular antiseptic or toothpaste and find it twice as effective as all others, or twice as effective as ever before. We are far more inclined to accept an idea or a product if it is favored or recommended by an authorized source. If a noted scientist argues that nuclear powered submarines are practicable, we are far more willing to accept the argument than if it is advanced by a newspaper with a broad reputation for spreading dubious opinions. If a committee of economists forecasts a long-range shortage of electrical power, we accept it as true more readily than if a newspaper writer says the same thing.[30]

The trustworthiness of a carrier—again whether a person or an object—also influences our acceptance of a percept. If we sense he or it is honest, fair, and disinterested, quite apart from his expertness, we are more inclined to believe what he says than if we doubt his integ-

[30] C. I. Hovland and W. Weiss, The Influence of Source Credibility on Communication Effectiveness, *Public Opinion Quarterly*, **15**: 635–650 (1951). In this experiment identical arguments on various issues were presented to pairs of subjects, one group being told that the arguments were made by named experts (scientists, a committee of economists, etc.) and the other being told that the arguments were made by named inexperts. The arguments when attributed to the experts were believed more readily than when the identical arguments were attributed to inexperts.

rity. This phenomenon is close to but distinct from the reaction to experts. We may, for example, be influenced by the expertise of two different scientists or economists. But if the speaker or writer has a reputation for arguing from the standpoint of a particular interest group or of his own self-interest, we are less inclined to accept his arguments.[31]

With our habitual tendency to credit what a person says rather than discredit it—to be gullible rather than skeptical—we are influenced by the bias which a speaker reports, particularly when he announces a bias which is congenial to us. That is, if one can announce that he wants an audience to have a favorable impression of a particular person and then proceeds to a strong but polite criticism of the person, he will change more opinions in the intended but unannounced direction than when he says he is critical of the person he is criticizing. However false it is, we are more apt to believe a bias that is announced than one that remains unstated by the carrier.[32]

This phenomenon, in a nonlaboratory, political situation, occurred during the siege of Paris in the Franco-Prussian War. A French general had been seized by a large crowd which believed he had been caught trying to take fortification plans to the Prussians. The crowd took him to the government office in Paris and demanded his immediate execution. Instead of pleading for abstract justice or calmness, instead of telling the crowd that in fact the general had helped build

[31] See *ibid.*, which fails to distinguish experimentally between expertness and trustworthiness, but indicates that both variables are involved. More direct evidence is contained in an experiment involving the presentation of identical arguments favoring lenient handling of juvenile delinquency, first by a hypothetical judge in a juvenile court, then by a neutral (an inexpert) person, and then by a hypothetical former juvenile delinquent who gave indications, before he started reading the identical argument presented by the judge, of disrespect for the law and his parents and of interest in lenient treatment because of his own record. This experiment by Kelman and Hovland is reported in C. I. Hovland, I. L. Janis, and H. H. Kelly, *Communication and Persuasion*, New Haven, Yale University Press, 1953, 31–32. See also N. Pastore and M. W. Horowitz, The Influence of Attributed Motive on the Acceptance of Statement, *Journal of Abnormal and Social Psychology*, **51**: 331–332 (1955), which finds that subjects more readily accepted a statement when the motive for it as stated by the experimenter was a "positive" one than when the motive was "negative."

[32] When subjects in one experimental group were presented with criticism of Henry Ford by the experimenter who said he wanted to present a favorable picture of Ford, they were more moved to be critical of Ford than when the experimenter, using the same criticism, said he wanted to present an unfavorable image. [Ewing, reported in Hovland, Janis, and Kelly, *op. cit.*, 25–27.]

the fortifications and that the plans could be bought at any bookstore, the spokesman for the government in substance said "justice shall be done," and added, as he moved toward the prisoner, "pitiless justice. Let the Government of the National Defense conclude your inquiry. In the meantime we will keep the prisoner in custody." The crowd dispersed and soon the general was able to depart in safety.[33]

Apart from his authority and his trustworthiness, apparently the simple attractiveness of the speaker to the listener will dispose people favorably toward what he (or she) has to say. This phenomenon is obvious in the effective use of beautiful and smiling young ladies to advertise everything from automobiles to double beds, beer, cigarettes, and headache powders. The phenomenon also occurred in dramatic form when, during the Second World War, a widely popular singer, Kate Smith, underwent a marathon, 18-hour radio broadcast selling war bonds. In an elaborate study of audience reaction, Merton found that listeners were deeply impressed with her selfless patriotism and sincerity and empathized strongly with her for the "stress and strain" of the grueling broadcast.[34]

The same phenomenon is likely to occur when an audience can identify with a political candidate or officeholder who has subjected himself to an exhausting campaign or long speech, for example, to a television marathon in which the candidate answers questions telephoned in from near and far. The phenomenon presumably has some impact when a speaker like Nikita Khrushchev makes a marathon, two-day speech before the Supreme Soviet. The audience is not simply listening in a rational fashion to the candidate's discussion of the questions but is also empathizing with his suffering through such a severe test of his physical endurance.

Once the percept has become established in the mind of the perceiver, he tends to remember it rather than its source and, in a curious delayed reaction, tends to be *increasingly* influenced by it as time passes—and therefore indirectly by the source, even though the source

[33] G. LeBon, *The Crowd* (1896), London, Ernest Benn, Ltd., 1952 printing, 113.
[34] Robert K. Merton, *Mass Persuasion: The Social Psychology of a War Bond Drive*, New York, Harper and Bros., 1946, ch. 4. As one of Merton's respondents said, recollecting Smith's marathon, "I felt, I can't stand this any longer. [The announcer's] statement about her being so exhausted affected me so much that I just couldn't bear it." Another said, "My heart ached for her." These quotations are on pages 90–91. The broadcast was of course on radio, not television. Some $39 million in war bonds were sold during the one-day broadcast. The audience was estimated at some 20 million people. [*Ibid.*, 2–3.]

was initially discredited. This phenomenon, called the "sleeper effect" by those who discovered it, involves a dissociation of source and content. When subjects were tested for retention of views presented, it was found that if the source of the opinions was deemed trustworthy, subjects actually came to agree *less* with the opinions after four weeks than they did right after hearing them, and, if the source was not deemed trustworthy, to agree *more* than they had initially. Further, the subjects who had disagreed with the views expressed by a source they did not trust had a harder time recalling the name of the untrustworthy source toward whose opinions they had moved during the four-week period. When reminded of the source, they quickly moved their opinions back in the direction of their initial reaction, disbelieving the opinions of the untrustworthy source and believing those of the trustworthy source.[35]

The content of the percept itself

Once percepts have been established in our minds they tend to become part of us, part of the personality which resists the incongruous and resists change itself. In becoming so established these percepts come to be regarded as interchangeable with reality. Often the percepts have a validity superior to reality. Anything which conflicts with established percepts is regarded as unreality and—unless it is of overwhelming validity—has to be rejected. The self-image of men impels them to believe they absorb fact and only fact in a reasoned matter that is quite unaffected by any such distorting influences as hunger, mental inflexibility, or any predisposition they may have toward the carrier of the percept itself.

Once people become aware of these nonrational influences, they often over-react, rejecting altogether the notion that people can ever see things as they are. Having lost the belief in pure, cameralike perception, they reject its possibility altogether. This in effect means that they reject the possibility of the self-awareness that is part of the process of seeing reality as it is. Intolerant of ambiguity, they reject the possibility of rationally testing reality just as they previously re-

---

[35] Hovland and Weiss, *op. cit.* in footnote 30 above. See also W. Weiss, A "Sleeper" Effect in Opinion Change, *Journal of Abnormal and Social Psychology,* **48**: 173–180 (1953), in which there was *less* loss over a six-week period, and therefore a "sleeper" effect, among subjects advised at the beginning of the six-week period to take the communications they had just received with a grain of salt, than among subjects not so advised.

jected the influence of nonrational forces.   Like David Hume, who saw the tendency to establish a cause-and-effect relationship between various phenomena as a consequence of the habit of associating things, they fall into the habit of explaining the way people see things in *altogether* nonrational terms.[36]

We need not return to innocence to recognize the possibility of accepting and absorbing ideas and phenomena that conflict with what we want to see.   If hungry people tend to see an amorphous picture as loaves of bread, or if jarring and threatening experiences are hard to absorb, we need not assume that we do not at least partially absorb them.   It is fact that people suffering from extreme hunger have been known to eat dirt; thirsty people to drink salt water; people in despair do escape from reality in such fantasies as Armageddon, flying saucers, or acceptance of the inevitable Wave of the Future—be it fascism, communism, or some other concept serving as a magic carpet on which to fly away from reality.

However, in less catastrophic, more usual economic, social, and mental circumstances, common sense and systematic evidence show that we do not so completely flee from reality.   The pictures we form in our heads are not always idle or busy fancies or inert stereotypes.   When we see two or more things that occur together in either time or space, it is not just habit that causes us to establish a relationship between them.   When we hold a match to the wick of a candle or lamp and the oil bursts into flame, it is not just habit that causes us to say there is a causal relationship between the burning match and the lighted candle.   When we flick a light switch and the light turns on, it is not simply habit which causes us to establish a cause-and-effect relationship between flicking the switch and the light turning on.

Pavlov's dogs were trained to drool in anticipation of food when they heard a sound, saw a light, or felt some stimulus (like heat, electric shock, or an object) through the skin.   This training was a habit, a classical, supposedly quite irrational tendency to associate a cue that inherently had nothing to do with the food itself.[37]   But the dogs lost the conditioned reflexes after they were no longer rewarded with food.

[36] Without being aware of it, Hume fell into his own trap.   He had become so accustomed to his own habit of thinking about how people establish cause-and-effect associations that he failed to realize he was proposing a cause-and-effect relationship between habit and the belief in cause and effect.

[37] Note especially I. P. Pavlov, *Conditioned Reflexes,* Oxford University Press, 1927, Lecture IV, 48–67.

Two points are relevant: establishing the conditioned reflexes of salivation required that the dog be rewarded with food when he received
a particular stimulus; and discontinuing the reward made the conditioned reflex die out. Instead of behaving "irrationally" the dog was
behaving "rationally" in both establishing and extinguishing a reflex—
even though the relationship between the stimulus and the food was
purely symbolic.

Humans are creditable with at least as much ability as dogs to relate
symbols to reality. If we see two series *aab, aab,* we expect the third
series to be *aab.* If it turns out instead to be *bba,* we psychologically
may expect the series of three to be not *aab, aab, aab,* but rather *aab,
aab, bba* and may expect this series to be repeated at regular intervals
unless some more complicated series is presented. If during a war we
find that the sounding of a siren is followed by airplanes and bombs,
we become conditioned to the stimulus and head automatically for a
bomb shelter. If, after a war, we hear a siren, we may for a time act
or think as though an air raid were about to occur, but the response
in due course will become extinguished. It would be irrational in
wartime not to associate the sound of the siren with an air raid; after
the war it is irrational to do so. Our behavior gradually adjusts accordingly, even though we know in both cases there is only a symbolic
—not cause-and-effect—relationship between the sound of the siren
and either air raid or no air raid.

Similar phenomena occurred in politics during the First World War.
It was a relatively immobile conflict along clearly demarcated battle
lines, in which the ability to resist became associated with the strength
of trench fortifications. This association, which had not only symbolic
but also real value during the First World War, lost altogether its real
value but retained a strong symbolic value for Frenchmen as the
Second World War approached. A long, powerful, impregnable
Maginot Line was built, in the confident expectation that it would
be able to turn any enemy who might approach from the East. The
fortification failed, of course, because in the Second World War the
strategy of warfare changed to one of high mobility which included
circumvention of the Maginot Line on the ground and in the air. But
having failed in this attempt to establish a real cause for an historic
effect, Frenchmen rather quickly adapted to the realities of the 1940s.
They adapted so successfully that they were able to carry out very
effectively an unprecedented underground warfare while their country was occupied by Germany.

The flexible, adaptable response of broad general publics to gross events has been tested in such a way as to indicate that broad publics are able to make reasonable conclusions from observed phenomena. In the United States in February 1948, a severe slump in commodity market prices occurred. The drop was so precipitous that in less than a year the price of wheat had dropped by a third and that of corn by more than a half. Such an event was bound to have significance for a broad population which has to pay for products derived from wheat and corn.

As it happened, the Survey Research Center of the University of Michigan was conducting an economic survey using a cross section of the adult United States population during the period when the slump first started. It was therefore possible to compare the responses of people interviewed before and after the slump. Without anticipating the slump, the survey questionnaire contained the question: "What do you think will happen to the prices of the things you buy during 1948—do you think they will go up, or down, or stay about where they are now?" About three-fourths of the people interviewed before the slump said they expected prices to go up; after the slump only about a fourth of the people interviewed indicated they expected prices to go up. All segments of the population changed their price expectations —rich and poor, farmers and city dwellers, and those with and without education. But those with no education seemed to be less sensitive to the slump than were those with a college education. Before the slump 80% of the respondents with no education thought prices would go up. After the slump 42% of those with no education still thought prices would go up. In contrast 74% of those with college education thought prices would go up before the slump, but only 20% thought so after the slump. As things turned out, the majority of both educated and uneducated were wrong after the slump. In the year after the slump, food prices did drop about 1%, but this drop was offset by price increases in all other consumer items, including clothing, rent, fuel and electricity, and house furnishings.

It is curious to note that those with no education turned out to be more accurate in their forecast than those with college education. The reasons for this may have been altogether accidental: those with no education may simply not have heard about the commodity slump or may have failed to recognize the possible consequence of a commodity market slump. On the other hand, those with no education may indeed have been in better touch with reality, unaffected by what turned out to be inaccurate manipulation of symbols and other prognostic devices by those with college education. Regardless of whether elite groups can continue to comfort themselves with the belief that they are better forecasters of the future than are nonelite groups, the relevant point here is that all segments of the population appear to have become aware in greater or lesser degree of the commodity market slump and to have reacted to it in a sensible—however wrong— manner.[38]

Seeing such a cause-and-effect relationship between one phenomenon and another is relatively easy in the case of something like a commodity market slump. It was a simple event and its consequences were rather easily predictable, or at least imaginable. The difficulty is that in politics relationships of a cause-and-effect sort are ordinarily far more complicated than a relationship between commodity prices and consumer prices. It is easy to state the problem—simply look at the facts and find out what causes what effect. It is easy, having verbalized the problem, to assume that one has solved it. It is enormously difficult to ascertain what reality is and what does cause what effect.

However discouraging the fact may be to literate or illiterate misanthropes, human beings can and do learn highly complicated relationships in politics, even to the point, for example, of tolerating taxation for such remote benefits as space exploration and economic aid. And it is not altogether clear that human beings with a high degree of education are a lot better at examining these relationships than are ordinary people. At least for every group of ordinary persons that has an odd view of political reality, there is a highly educated person who has the same odd view. We cannot say the problem is one of an educated elite which understands politics and an uneducated mass that does not.

Consider the difference in the ways of thinking of John C. Calhoun and Abraham Lincoln before the American Civil War. Neither of these statesmen has ever been accused of having an ordinary mind. Both were among the most intelligent people of their era. But as the conflict between the North and South developed, over a variety of issues including the moral problem of slavery and the exclusion of slavery from territories in the West, John Calhoun with his Yale education almost refused to recognize the most glaring fact of all—that slavery was the central issue. He saw the growing breakdown of relations between the North and South as a consequence of the government

[38] J. C. Davies, Some Relations between Events and Attitudes, *American Political Science Review*, **46:** 777–789 (1952).

in Washington seeking to destroy the independent power of the states. He saw it as a conspiracy of the North and the West against the South—a deliberate, concerted plan to destroy the South.

As a solution he proposed something that no logician in his right mind would think of expressing, namely, the principle of concurrent majority. Calhoun was a brilliant logician, but when it came to defending the interests of the South, logic failed him and he resorted to illogical rhetoric. He failed to see or to recognize that only a majority and a minority can concur and that within a finite political system there cannot be two majorities on the same issue. Majority rule for him meant nothing less than unanimous consent, which is precisely the negation of majority rule. Few people in the South had more education than John C. Calhoun, but few people in the South had less ability to reason about the South, with attention either to logic or to objective reality, than did Calhoun.[39]

Lincoln, with his one year of schooling, on the other hand, appeared to have far greater contact with reality and a better ability to reason about it. He understood that the task of reconciling forces in the North and the South was not simple but enormously complex— quite apart from a differing value system which in his case caused him to place union and freedom above separatism and a continuation of the institution of slavery. Both Lincoln and Calhoun were representative of broad publics. This fact in a sense was more significant than the quality of their minds. Not logicians but representatives become leaders, a category which includes dictators as well as elected rulers.

A more recent and equally notable example occurred at the end of the First World War when the United States debated whether or not it should enter the League of Nations. The two leading antagonists were men of extraordinary mental powers and high education. Woodrow Wilson, the author and advocate of the League of Nations, argued with great force, logic, and intransigence for American entry into the League. Henry Cabot Lodge with great force, logic, and intransigence argued against American entry into the League.

In both cases the intransigence of the two men was a consequence not of a rational appraisal of reality but of personal forces which

[39] Note the force with which Calhoun beguiled a twentieth-century editor in John Fischer, Government by Concurrent Majority, a 1948 article in *Harper's Magazine,* reprinted in H. M. Bishop and S. Hendel, *Basic Issues of American Democracy,* New York, Appleton-Century-Crofts, 4th ed., 1961, 266–278.

pitted the two men in a political contest on quite apolitical and almost completely irrational grounds. Wilson said that the Senate had to be forced into acceptance of the League, had to "take its medicine." Lodge adopted a posture of truculent negation. The position of both men found strong adherents among wide segments of the population. It is clear in other words both from the divided state of elite and of public opinion before the Civil War, and at the end of the First World War, that it is not only the "mass" which can be in error but also the "elite" itself. Politics is so complicated and so subject to opinion and unamenable to inadequate fact that not only irrational but also usually reasonable men differ continually on what is good public policy. Until there is not only complete consensus but complete knowledge, the dialogue that politics amounts to will have to continue. The gap between the knowing and the ignorant on public policy remains small.

The uncertitude, ambiguity, and ambivalence of political phenomena are so endemic as to lead some people to the view that a manipulator of public opinion has virtually infinite freedom to change the pictures in the heads of ordinary people. Broad as the limits are, they are considerably this side of infinity. A propagandist cannot so distort reality that common sense and everyday observation belie what the propagandist says. We need not fall back on such fables as that about the "king's new clothes" to recognize this. German propaganda for domestic consumption during the Second World War for a long time continued to distort reality by emphasizing Germany's victories, and either de-emphasizing or denying Germany's defeats. But Goebbels was unable at last to deny to the German public that its armies had suffered a severe defeat in Africa and later that it was suffering severe damage in air raids. In the first case soldiers were writing home about the battles they had been in and were coming home from Africa to report to their families. In the second case the air raids were experienced not through the newspapers or over the radio but in person. Goebbels himself finally came to the conclusion that the best propaganda was not a polemical editorial but slanted news.

Propaganda cannot paint a picture which conflicts with reality as it is seen by individuals in the light of their basic needs. A person during a depression who continues to be hungry from day to day is unimpressed by exhortation that prosperity is just around the corner. He is unlikely also to be moved favorably by exhortation to abide by the constitution and by due process of law when he is hungry. Such a person will say "you can't eat free enterprise" or "you can't eat the constitution." In similar circumstances, in other lands—for example, after a famine year—an ordinary person is as likely to say "you can't eat dialectical materialism." Nasser was successful in giving release for the tensions of Egyptians when he poured contempt on America and its Secretary of State on the occasion of the American refusal to grant a loan for the Aswan dam and Nasser's seizure of the Suez Canal. But he recognized that—however palatable a denunciation of America and Dulles was—such a verbal diet was a poor substitute for real food to a hungry population.

Nkrumah of Ghana expressed this problem in a very realistic way:

> Independence of itself does not change this world. It simply creates the right political atmosphere for a real effort of national regeneration. But it does not supply all the economic and social tools. The leaders are now expected, simply as a result of having acquired independence, to work miracles. The people look for the new schools, new towns, new factories. They expect political equality to bring economic equality. They do not realize what it may cost. In this situation, however poor the country, the new government cannot sit and do nothing. . . .
> . . . We cannot tell our peoples that material benefits in growth and modern progress are not for them. If we do, they will throw us out and seek other leaders who promise more. . . . We have to modernize. Either we shall do so with the interest and support of the West or we shall be compelled to turn elsewhere. This is not a warning or a threat, but a straight statement of political reality.[40]

Even though limits exist to what the political propagandist can say in his picturing of reality for his public, his limits on some matters are very broad. If in a dictatorship a propagandist tries to control public access to reality by having control of the press, radio, and so on, he can establish rather durable mental sets which shield people from disturbing outside influences. He cannot shield them from the price of food and other domestic events communicable by direct or interpersonal contact. But if the dictatorship uses violent means of coercion he can make the need to avoid death and pain and solitude the central reality. He can degrade them and deprive them of all opportunity, as O'Brien deprived Smith of all reason for existence in Orwell's *1984* and as the Chinese brainwashers have done.

In the short run, a propagandist in an open society who lacks complete control of communication and means of violence cannot surely succeed. That is, a propagandist operating in a constitutional situation has a relatively short time in which to produce real results. Facts

---

[40] K. Nkrumah, African Prospect, *Foreign Affairs,* **37**: 45–53 (1958). Quoted by permission. Copyright by the Council on Foreign Relations.

that contradict his picture of reality will destroy it. In the long run, the same thing is true of those who do have such control in a dictatorship. Short of killing, they cannot completely alter or destroy the basic human needs and the ability to observe reality which are built into the organism. It is not just children but also adults, not just ordinary people but also members of the elite, who, in the last analysis, truly learn what clothes if any the king is wearing. But just how long the long run is, in the penultimate analysis, is rather hard to say. People possessed of what they believe to be the ultimate truth are seldom reluctant to broadcast the proximate falsehood. And anxious people are too often ready to believe in both.

A plea

In this chapter we have seen or tried to see how it is that people see things and how they at least try to see things as they are. We also saw the general limitations that make it so very difficult for people to see things as they are. The discussion has been based on the findings of psychological research rather than the ageless arguments for and against a belief that mankind is rational and capable of seeing reality as it is. I have tried to avoid other enormously difficult questions, like defining objectivity and subjectivity. Rationality, objectivity, and subjectivity are real problems, but can in this study best be considered in light of psychological evidence rather than philosophical argument.

Anyone who wishes to jump to one conclusion or the other—that men are or are not capable of seeing reality as it is—is free to do so. But first he should himself define reality, so that we can know what it is men are or are not capable of seeing as it is. And I urge you to recall that any such conclusions are based not on what this chapter has said, but on preconceptions which you brought to the chapter.[41] At least one of us, myself, is not at all sure from presently available evidence whether mankind is completely capable of rationality or not. I am sure only that mankind has not yet achieved perfect rationality, not even the segment of mankind (including me—and thee too) who read and write books or in any other ways study reality. Which brings us to another aspect thereof, social groups, which we shall now try to comprehend—or apprehend.

[41] I do not claim freedom from preconceptions in writing it.

APPENDIX 1

Some Experiments on Perceptions Distorted by Values

When poor and rich children are asked to judge the size of coins, poor children, consistently more often than rich children, have shown a tendency to misjudge the size of the coin as being larger than it is. [J. S. Bruner and C. C. Goodman, Value and Need as Organizing Factors in Perception, *Journal of Abnormal and Social Psychology*, **42**: 33–44 (1947).] Curiously enough, the same tendency to overestimate the size of money applies when play money in a contrived gambling game is being judged, and the overestimation of size occurs when the play money has both negative value and positive value. [W. F. Dukes and W. Bevan, Jr., Size Estimation and Monetary Value: a Correlation, *Journal of Psychology*, **34**: 43–53 (1952).] When the object is not money but another kind of simple symbol, there is the same tendency to distort. Subjects were shown three different symbols, a dollar sign, a swastika, and a square containing a diagonal cross. The subjects saw each of the three symbols as larger than it actually was and saw the dollar sign and the swastika as being markedly larger than the neutral square with a cross in it. The dollar sign was seen as being larger than the swastika. Stated in more abstract terms, the experiment indicated that both positively and negatively valued symbols will be exaggerated more than a neutral symbol and that the positively valued symbol will be exaggerated more than a negatively valued symbol. [J. S. Bruner and L. Postman, Symbolic Value as an Organizing Factor in Perception, *Journal of Social Psychology*, **27**: 203–208 (1948).]

There is also a tendency to deny that we have seen things which we value negatively. One experiment indicates that people are slower to recognize relatively common, obscene, taboo words experimentally presented without warning than they are even relatively uncommon nontaboo words. [W. Lacy et al., Foreknowledge as a Factor Affecting Perceptual Defense and Alertness, *Journal of Experimental Psychology*, **45**: 169–174 (1953).] When the subjects were warned in advance that they would see taboo words, they were quicker to recognize them. The experimenters did not speculate whether the subjects, male graduate students, may have had delusions about the reluctance of psychologists to recognize the existence of dirty words. [E. McGinnies, Emotionality and Perceptual Defense, *Psychological Review*, **56**: 244–251 (1949).] Evidently a mild kind of shock and avoidance reaction occurs when these words are seen because in another experiment, subjects were slower to see ordinary words after having seen the taboo words than they were in seeing the same ordinary words, after seeing nontaboo words. [E. McGinnies and H. Sherman, Generalization of Perceptual Defense, *Journal of Abnormal and Social Psychology*, **47**: 81–85 (1952).]

Even when relatively neutral words are seen in an emotionally laden context people tend to be slower to recognize such neutral, harmless words than words which have positive or negative value. [J. C. Gilchrist et al., Values as Determinants of Word-Recognition Thresholds, *Journal of Ab-*

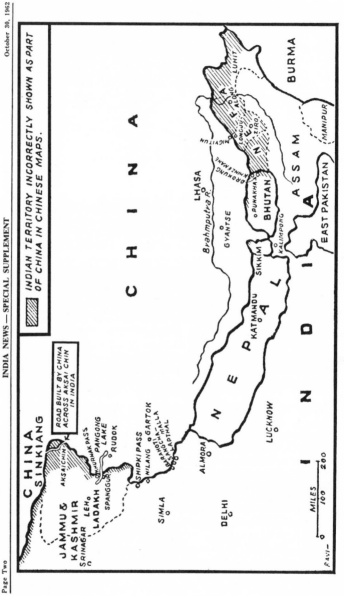

An Indian Cognitive Map

SKETCH MAP: SITES REFERRED TO IN THE CHINESE FOREIGN MINISTRY'S NOTE OF AUGUST 12, 1961 AND
IN THE NOTE OF THE INDIAN MINISTRY OF EXTERNAL AFFAIRS OF OCTOBER 31, 1961

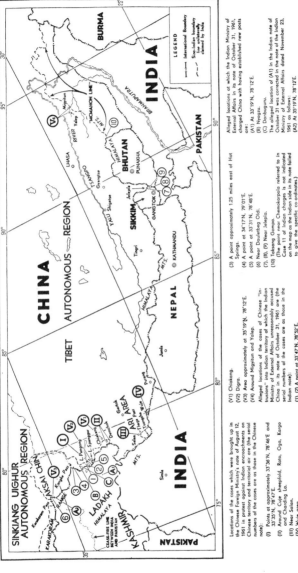

Locations of the cases which were brought up in the Chinese Foreign Ministry's note of August 12, 1961 in protest against Indian encroachments on Chinese territory and territorial air are (the serial numbers of the cases are as those in the Chinese note):

(I) Points at approximately 33°36'N, 78°46'E and 33°35'N, 78°47'E.
(II) Around Cuje sheepfold, Roto, Ogo, Kargo and Charding La.
(III) Near Solan.
(IV) Wuje area.

(V1) Chiakang.
(V2) Digra.
(V3) Area approximately at 35°19'N, 78°12'E.
(V4) Around Migyitun and Yalep.

Alleged locations of the cases of Chinese "intrusions" into Indian territory of which the Indian Ministry of External Affairs unreasonably accused China in its note of October 31, 1961 are (the serial numbers of the cases are as those in the Indian note):

(I), (2) A point at 33°47'N, 78°52'E.

(3) A point approximately 125 miles east of Hot Springs.
(4) A point at 34°17'N, 79°01'E.
(5) A point at 33°31'N, 78°48'E.
(6) Near Doulatbeg Oldi.
(7), (8), (9) Near Jelepla.
(10) Tsakang Gompa.
(The point near Chemakarpola referred to in Case 11 of Indian charges is not indicated on the map as the Indian side in its note failed to give the specific co-ordinates.)

Peking Review

Alleged locations at which the Indian Ministry of External Affairs in its note of October 31, 1961, charged China with having established new posts are:
(A1) At 33°19'N, 78°12'E.
(B) Nyagzu.
(C) Domburu.
The alleged location of (A1) in the Indian note of October 31 was corrected in the note of the Indian Ministry of External Affairs dated November 23, 1961 as follows:
(A2) At 35°19'N, 78°12'E.

December 15, 1961

A Chinese Cognitive Map

normal and Social Psychology, **49:** 423–426 (1954).] The experimenters used as subjects people who were either very high or very low in the degree of their anti-Semitism. The subjects were shown cards with neutral words sandwiched between the word "Jew" printed twice on some of the cards and neutral words between the word "ink" printed twice on other cards. Both the high and low prejudiced subjects were slower to recognize the neutral words in the context "Jew" than they were in the context "ink." No control group of subjects, between those who were high or low in prejudice towards Jews, was used in this experiment. Evidence of perceptual emphasis related to emotion has been found where it is not abstract symbols, verbal or otherwise, but people who are being judged. [P. F. Secord et al., The Negro Stereotype and Perceptual Accentuation, *Journal of Abnormal and Social Psychology,* **53:** 78–83 (1956).] In this experiment pro- and anti-Negro groups were shown pictures of ten Negroes who differed in the degree of their negroid features. Both the pro- and anti-Negro groups tended to emphasize negroid features in the pictures more than did the neutral group.

When values become more personal and less abstract or general the relationship still holds. People again tend to be slow in identifying words in categories representing things to which they attach little value. A person who depreciated religion, when shown on a tachistoscope the word "sacred" reported seeing the words "sucked," "sacked," and "shocked" before he finally gave the correct word. A person who depreciated economic values, when shown the word "income" wandered even farther afield, reporting that he saw the word "learning," "tomorrow," "knowledge," "literature," and "loving" before he finally saw the word correctly. [L. Postman, J. Bruner, and E. McGinnies, Personal Values as Selective Factors in Perception, *Journal of Abnormal and Social Psychology,* **43:** 142–154 (1948).]

APPENDIX 2

A Couple of Cognitive Maps

The two maps (pp. 138–139) cover almost exactly the same segment of the earth. The main natural feature is the Brahmaputra river. On one map it is called the Brahm[a]putra in Tibet and on the other the Yalu Tsangpo river. On one map, on the *right-hand side,* is a shaded area, labeled Nefa, on the Indian side of the boundary between India and China. On the other map the same territory, containing arrows pointing to the "McMahon Line," is on the Chinese side of the boundary between China and India. These are the cognitive maps which Indians and Chinese had in their heads as they exchanged not words or maps but rifle fire along the border in the Autumn of 1962. To each combatant, the true boundary is as its map indicates. Since the real boundary cannot be determined by the words or the maps in the minds of the combatants, how is the reality determined? At least we know that we see what we are determined to see. How do we determine reality? The first map appeared in an official publication of the Indian government; the second appeared in an English-language journal published in China.

CHAPTER 5

Proximal groups in politics

Some definitions

One of the most fundamental characteristics of perceptual processes is that they take place within society. Perception is social. But almost everything that mankind does is social or at least takes place within society, and it is inconceivable that man would be man outside society. In this chapter our attention shifts from a noun to an adjective, from perception to social, which modifies not only perception but almost everything else we do. The individuals, and therefore the groups, with which we are passively and actively associated help determine not only our individual and social identity but also our political affiliation. As Lazarsfeld has said, "social characteristics determine political preference." [1] This true statement should not be taken for more than it merely says. It is not true that social characteristics are the solitary determinant of political preference, even though there is a tendency among students of society to make the object of their attention the king of all determinants of behavior. For example, in his discussion of the division of labor, Emile Durkheim says,

> Common life is attractive as well as coercive. . . . as [man] learns the charm of this new life, he contracts the need for it. . . . That is why when individuals who are found to have common interests associate, it is not only to defend these interests, it is to associate. . . . [2]

[1] The specific context—class status—in which Lazarsfeld made this statement becomes the subject matter of Chapter 8, The Politics of Status.

[2] E. Durkheim, *The Division of Labor in Society*, Glencoe, Ill., The Free Press, 1933, 15.

141

Durkheim avoids saying that society determines everything, but he does say that society determines our conscience, our sense of right and wrong, and does so without the intervention of any other forces. In other places Durkheim qualifies his statement a little bit more but still makes society the king of determinants of behavior.[3]

As long as we are self-conscious about the tendency of people who study anything to regard that thing as of predominant importance, because it *is* of most interest to the person who studies it, we can safely acknowledge that relations with other people do constitute a major determinant of all behavior. All our action takes place in social context and—it cannot be overemphasized—people become free not by being group members but as a direct result of being group members. Groups do not simply establish conformity to the values, norms, beliefs of the group. They also make individuality and nonconformity possible.

It is best to start off with some definitions, in order at least not to add to the confusion that is apt to prevail when people talk about society without being very precise in what they mean by it. A group is a set of organisms in a state of interaction with each other. Only when they are interacting do they constitute a group; when they are not interacting, they are not a group but a set, a category, a class. The actual members of a group, however, do not need to be together, in one another's presence, in order to interact. A person can be far removed from those other individuals which form the groups with which he identifies and still be profoundly influenced by them.[4]

Some examples may make clear the distinction between group and category. In the natural state, a cluster of bacteria, a forest of trees, a school of fish, a flock of birds, a herd of antelope, a family of primates or of men—each is a group. In the cultivated state, that is in the condition cultivated by man, a culture of bacteria, an orchard, fish in a hatchery, chickens in a barnyard, cattle raised for milk, beef or companionship, and children in school are groups. In biological taxonomy, a genus, for example, oak trees (*Quercus*) composed of species, for example, red oak (*Quercus rubra*) and white oak (*Quercus alba, Quercus sessiliflora*) is not a group but a category. Members of

---

[3] *Ibid.*, 14–15, 350.

[4] In order to indicate that interaction is a general phenomenon, let it be mentioned that two magnets within each other's field can be properly called a pair of magnets, whereas two magnets outside one another's field—even though they have the potential for interaction—are not a pair but simply two separate magnets.

the same species may form a kind of group when they are together physically in a grove of trees.

At least in the higher animal kingdom but probably also in the lower animal kingdom, two members of the same species widely separated may amount to nothing more than a category, but may form a group immediately when placed together—despite the absence of any prior contact whatsoever. For example, two animals may be placed together in the zoo, one of which came from a place hundreds of miles from where the other one came, and immediately interact. What this suggests is that the tendency to form groups is innate, requires no prior social conditioning, and that members of the same species have a ready, a spontaneous, tendency to interact when placed together.

Among human beings, people who, for example, commit a particular crime are nothing more than a category per se, but when such people are tried and convicted for a particular (civil or political) crime (like murder or opposing the government), they may actually form a prison group in death row and engage in common group activity, such as jointly going on a hunger strike or trying to get the warden to fire the cook. Small businessmen whose enterprises fail are a category but conceivably may unite into a group whose major purposes include mutual commiseration and joint action against big business, big trade unions, and big government. People who eat irregularly through no choice of their own may be a category, but when they begin to share their consciousness of unforeseeable hunger they can become a group that has enormous power to get what it wants, by social—including political—means.

People are not really people unless they are together. They are like haploid (germ) cells in that they are isolated and incomplete, in contrast to diploid (somatic) cells composed of or descended from two compatible germ cells that have joined together. But we need not think, since society is necessary to make people, that when people get together a good society is formed. When people interact, even intensely, they need not be doing so to their mutual benefit and to produce the completion, fulfillment, or happiness of both or all. To take an extreme case, two people who are fighting constitute a group just as much as two people who are in love.

A group can change from mutual affection and trust to mutual hate, suspicion, etc., and back again while still remaining a group. The prime small-group instance of this is a married couple who change from a state of strong affection and happy attachment to a condition in which the interaction pattern is one of vigorous hostility, even of hatred for brief periods. A larger case is exemplified by the broad social group composed of Western, Central, and Eastern Europe. When Germany engaged in two successive world wars with the allies, the nations fighting each other were no less a group than when, after these wars, Germany was in a more or less peaceful relationship with the former enemy nations. This raises the question of the character of the relationship between members of the group.

A master and a slave (M_1 and S_1), a landlord and a peasant (L_1 and P_1), a boss and a worker (B_1 and W_1)—each pair constitutes a group no less than one master talking with another (M_1 and M_2) about his trouble with slaves ($S_{1...n}$), S_1 and S_2 talking over their grievances against M_1, B_1 telling B_2 about his troubles with W_1 and W_2. One basic difference between groups composed of M and S, L and P on the one hand and those composed of $W_{1\&2}$, $B_{1\&2}$, etc., on the other is that the area of opposite and conflicting interest is greater in the former category of superiors and subordinates and the area of identical and complementary interest is greater in the latter category of equals. It should be borne in mind that these two different kinds of groups are only abstracted polar types, and it cannot be truly said that a group composed of superiors and subordinates is necessarily a very unstable group. But it does suggest the hypothesis that there is less likelihood of the latter equalitarian kind becoming a hostile group which destroys itself or one or more of its members, and more likelihood that this group will survive and grow. This is hypothesized as a consequence of the greater area of *common* interest in groups of equals, even though like *individual* interests may produce not just cooperation but conflict.[5]

At this stage it is well to recall one of the major premises of this book: that togetherness, group formation, is not the only or the immediate or ultimate goal of organisms, even though it is one of the profoundest of their urges. It is well to recall also that the origin of forces which cause people to interact is the same—rooted in the same place—as are the origins of other basic but antisocial human urges, that is, in the organism. One implication of this is that in any actual group there are likely to be forces that seek to break it up, not just forces that seek to hold it together. This statement in turn is another way

---

[5] From this paragraph the reader—and the writer—may note how difficult it is to separate definition from hypothesis and will, I trust, be on guard—though I hope not en garde—against the tendency to regard definitions, hypotheses, and evidence as congruent.

of saying that the interests of the individual members of groups are in no instance coextensive forever or for very long. Some people talk about the conflict of interest between the individual and the group. It is more appropriate to talk about the mental conflict between the interest of an individual as an individual and the interest of that same individual as a group member, that is, in his social relationship. No individual can maintain his identity if he identifies his interests completely with those of the group, and no individual can establish his identity without being a group member. And, if Maslow is right, no one can become himself without satisfying his physical needs—in a social context.[6] In the first two cases he would be respectively an undifferentiated portion of a homogeneous mass (a condition that has never existed despite the reifying efforts of writers about the masses) or socially dead and thus not a person but a stunted animal. In the last case he would be physically dead and therefore not a person but an ex-person, a corpse.

Why the terms proximal and distal?

A major distinction must be made at this point between the two major categories of groups: proximal groups and distal groups. In the ways that these two terms are used in the ensuing discussion, they approximately equal the more usual designation of primary and secondary groups. The reason for choosing the terms proximal and distal is most easily stated by anatomic analogy. The proximal bone of one's thumb is the bone closest to the hand; the distal bone, attached to the proximal bone, is the one more distant and requires the mediation of the proximal bone in order to carry out its various sensory and motor functions. The social denotation of this anatomic connotation is this: proximal groups are those which are mentally next to the individual. In consequence, these are the ones with which he is *subjectively* in most strong, affective relationship, either positively or negatively. Usually such groups are the ones which he sees face-to-face. However, a proximal group—that is, one which mediates external influences

---

[6] The relative priority and the interaction of physical and social needs showed up clearly in a Nazi concentration camp. According to one report, in a camp where the food and housing conditions were not as bad as in others, comradeship developed. The report also shows that the individuals who were members of a small, closely knit group of prisoners that shared things equally survived better than individuals who were isolated. [C. Bondy, Problems of Internment Camps, *Journal of Abnormal and Social Psychology*, **38**: 453–475 (1943).]

from distal groups and in addition has some enormously significant group functions, other than mediation—need not always be face-to-face at a particular point in time and space when it helps determine how the proximal-group member acts. A distal group, on the other hand, always has its influence mediated by a proximal group: no distal group identifications are ever established without the mediation at some point of a proximal group.[7]

The fourfold table which follows will serve to illustrate what I mean by the difference between proximal and distal groups, including those which are present and those not present at the time they influence behavior. If the reader still prefers the modifiers face-to-face and non-face-to-face, there is no loss in using them as long as he remains aware of the essential mediating role of proximal (face-to-face) groups with respect to distal (non-face-to-face) groups.

These distinctions between proximal and distal groups are arbitrary but not therefore absurd. It may be hard indeed to distinguish qualitatively between the influence which the parish priest or the local party boss has on a person and the influence of the church itself. It is probably as yet impossible to distinguish these influences quantitatively. But we can certainly recognize that the influence of all distal groups has to be mediated in some way or another through proximal groups, through individuals with whom the influenced individual himself has direct, immediate contact.

Why groups form and endure

With these distinctions in mind between groups on the one hand and categories on the other, and between proximal and distal groups, we can briefly consider why groups form, grow, endure, and die. Fundamentally they do all but the last of these things because they serve one or more innate human needs, including the needs for food, clothing, shelter, health, physical safety; social needs, including sex (which is part physical as well); self-esteem or dignity; and self-actualization. We can readily see how necessary groups are for the satisfaction of the physical needs. And without stretching the imagination we can see how these vast, largely distal groups called nations become coordinated to satisfy physical needs which in primitive tribal

[7] Here again, as before, definition and hypothesis are intermingled. Be on guard. The forces of direct and mediated contact and of close and distant contact remain a paradox—distinct yet intertwined, and not quite conceptually resolvable.

Social Groups

Some Examples of Proximal Groups
(Those with Which One Has Direct Contact)

Present at Time of Influencing Behavior	Not Present at Time of Influencing Behavior

Family, in broad sense
Neighbors
Friends
Work associates
Priest, rabbi, minister
Individuals one has met only once or briefly, like the rude and dirty "foreigner," the generous seat-partner on a train, etc.
The speaker at a public meeting
Pseudo-proximal (actually distal)
   The speaker on radio or television (actually mediated electronically)
   The sympathetic or hostile character in a novel or folk legend (actually mediated by an author or the person who tells the legend)
	One's mental association with parents, grandparents, et al., days or years after these associations have physically taken place
	One's past associations with neighbors and friends
	One's past associations with churchmen (pastor, priest, et al.) and with other manifestations of the church organization
	Pseudo-proximal (actually distal)
	   One's fanciful or imagined associations with ideal figures
	      Identification with great men, rulers, gods, Christ, or God
	   The remembered speaker on radio or television (actually mediated electronically)
	   The remembered sympathetic or hostile character in a novel or folk legend (actually mediated by an author or the person who tells the legend)

Some Examples of Distal Groups
(Those with Which Contact is Mediated by Proximal Groups)

Present at Time of Influencing Behavior	Not Present at Time of Influencing Behavior
Political parties Pressure groups News media (papers, radio, TV) Tribe Clan Race Church Region Nation	The history of one's country, region, clan, etc. The history of one's church The history of one's party, social club, trade union The history of one's culture—the generic term within which can be included all of the preceding distal examples

or medieval manorial society are largely satisfied in a nuclear (father, mother, children) or extended (father, sons and their wives and children) family. In national groups, we buy food raised by an unknown farmer and are protected by anonymous policemen and judges and armies. Can we then say that social needs are altogether derivative and secondary, that people form groups solely for the sake of other needs? Experimental evidence indicates that this is unlikely to be so —particularly intraspecies—not only among humans but also among primates and some higher vertebrates.

In one sensitive experiment, new hens were individually placed in an already established flock of chickens. The initial interaction consisted of fighting and chasing, between the old members of the flock and the new member. After this subsided, for some days the new hen could still be identified by the distance she kept and the unique pattern of similance and avoidance with respect to the other hens. After six to ten days the strangeness of the new hen was no longer apparent; it had become an established member of the flock.[8]

In a similar experiment, strange dogs were introduced into an established group of dogs, indicating the basis on which a new dog is accepted or rejected. The amount of aggressiveness and hostility shown toward a new dog varied according to several factors. The old dogs reacted to the new dog most aggressively if he was "of the same breed and sex." They reacted somewhat less aggressively if the stranger was of the "same sex but different breed," even less aggressively if it was of the "same breed but different sex" and least aggressively if the new dog was of a "different breed and sex." The tighter the social hierarchy previously established, the more frequent was the rejection of the new dog. And the dog whose integration was being forced tried to avoid the established group and get close to the human observer.[9]

In both the hen and the dog experiments, we observed sociability as such to be a major factor in what happened within the group. The mere fact of not being a group member made a difference in how the group behaved when the new individual animal was introduced to

[8] David M. Levy, The Strange Hen, *American Journal of Orthopsychiatry,* **20**: 355–362 (1950). Levy noted that the need to belong "appears to take precedence over the dominance drive, the drive we perceive in humans as the need for self-assertion." [*Ibid.,* 358.] And he noted that it took longer for older hens to get assimilated than very young chickens.

[9] J. A. King, Closed Social Groups among Domestic Dogs, *Proceedings of the American Philosophical Society,* **98**: 327–336 (1954).

the group. There is more direct evidence for the effects on an individual of not being a group member, and therefore by implication a demonstration of the social need.

Social nature without nurture

One of the main purposes of a series of experiments under the direction of Harlow at the University of Wisconsin was to carefully observe the relation between mother rhesus monkeys and their offspring, to find out how necessary it was—if necessary at all—for monkeys to have actual mothers. In the experimental setup, monkeys from birth were separated from their actual mothers and bottle-fed from either a bare wire figure that was shaped like a mother or a sponge-rubber and terrycloth covered mother. The baby monkeys did indeed seek out food from the wire mother, but aside from their need for food they had a preference for the cloth-covered mother.[10]

Monkeys so raised did not develop normally and had strange social reactions. Some would "rage" at passers-by or "rage" internally by biting themselves; others exhibited apathy. None of them exhibited normal social reactions. At the age of 6 months they were unable to play normally with other monkeys; they could not play with one another and could not manipulate toys. In contrast, at the age of 4 months, monkeys raised by real mothers did play together and with toys. When they became adults and were placed together with other monkeys that were breeding, the monkeys that had "matured" with mother surrogates did not breed.[11]

[10] If the experiment seems cruel, bear in mind that humans are more important than monkeys—or should be—and that Harlow and his associates, in studying these Madison monkeys, probably have contributed to our understanding of ourselves. Of course this itself may constitute cruelty, but of a lesser sort than persistent ignorance of ourselves. At least we assume that the truth will make us free. And it is not psychologists but rightist and leftist dictatorships that have made monkeys out of human beings.

[11] A full and felicitous account of the research as of 1958 is contained in Harry F. Harlow, The Nature of Love, *The American Psychologist,* **13**: 673–685 (December 1958). See also H. F. Harlow and R. R. Zimmerman, The Development of Affectional Responses in Infant Monkeys, *Proceedings of the American Philosophical Society,* **102**: 501–509 (1958). There is a sensitive report of the research by L. Engel, The Troubled Monkeys of Madison, in the *New York Times Magazine,* 29 January 1961. For a comparison of the social behavior of monkeys born in natural surroundings and of those born in a primate laboratory and restricted in social contact, see W. A. Mason, The Effects of Social Restriction on the Behavior of Rhesus Monkeys, I. Free Social Behavior, *Journal of Compara-*

Harlow explains this process as one of social conditioning. He attributes the abnormal behavior purely to the environmental forces of the babyhood of the monkeys. If the abnormality of the monkeys raised without normal mothers was a process of social conditioning, why then was the social conditioning incurred after these monkeys were placed with normally raised monkeys not successful in changing, in normalizing, the behavior of the experimental monkeys? Why must the imprinting process occur at certain (early) stages of mental growth?

What seems to be missing from the explanation can best be illustrated by noting the effect of foot-binding among Chinese gentlewomen during their childhood so that as adults they would have tiny feet. It is indeed true that the tiny feet were a direct result of environmental factors and had nothing to do with heredity. It is also true that the feet were not able to grow to normal size once the period of normal growth for feet had been passed, despite the unbinding of the feet. By the same token, the behavior of Harlow's monkeys cannot be quite explained by the fact that they did not get social conditioning from a normal mother. We must also add the fact that social conditioning to be effective has to come at a certain time during the organism's development, because the organism is so constituted as to be unable to interact with the environment in the same way at all stages of development. Organic factors, in other words, continue to interact with environmental factors and are crucial to the development of the individual.

Clinical evidence as to a small child in India that apparently had a socially abnormal infancy and early childhood tends also to refute the monistic nature of environmental influences on the maturation process. This child, who was fifteen years old at the time the report was written about him, had been found at the age of nine in a very disheveled state—unable to speak, unable to walk normally, unable to behave normally in almost any sense. The popular supposition in India was that he was another one of the fabulous wolf children.

---

tive and Physiological Psychology, **53**: 582–589 (1960) and W. A. Mason, *ibid.,* II. Tests of Gregariousness, *op. cit.,* **54**: 287–290 (1961).

O. Weininger, Mortality of Albino Rats under Stress as a Function of Early Handling, *Canadian Journal of Psychology,* **7**: 111–114 (1953) reports that albino rats which were not handled when they were young died when subject to prolonged deprivation (mainly of food and water), whereas rats that had been handled when they were young survived the same deprivation.

Whatever or whoever had been involved in his early childhood, it is clear that he had been raised in surroundings not at all similar to a normal human environment. He was quite incapable of any kind of communication, any kind of verbal communication with human beings. Tests indicated that his brain development at birth was normal, that whatever had caused him to become what he was had occurred since birth as a result of abnormal social interaction, whether with wolves or with human beings. Again, as in the case of Harlow's monkeys, apparently the "wolf" child was incapable of becoming a normal human being, once the period of normal social development had passed without normal human relationships and despite continuous efforts over a six-year period to train him in normal behavior patterns.[12]

More clear-cut data are available in the case of a psychotic nine-year-old child, whose prior history became known to the investigator. In his early childhood, this child had received no affection, and when he had cried was allowed to cry endlessly without being comforted. He was well-fed, well-clothed, and otherwise not neglected, except in terms of affection and other normal interactions between parents and children. When he first got psychiatric attention, this child had come to think of himself as a machine. He could eat, defecate, etc., only if he properly plugged himself into imaginary devices on the wall, table, or what not. After three years of therapy, when he was twelve, some progress had been made toward returning him to normal social interaction, but he still was to a very large degree abnormal, even though he had now rejected the notion that he was a machine and was very anxious to establish affectional patterns with other people.[13]

A study of infant children raised in a nursery by their own mothers and of infant children raised in a foundling home without mothers revealed rather striking differences in the behavior of these two categories of children. The children raised in a nursery with their own mothers became normal, healthy individuals; none of them died. The children raised without their mothers in the foundling home were emotionally starved and "never learned to speak, to walk, to feed themselves." All but one or two of the 91 in the foundling home became "human wrecks who behaved either in the manner of agitated or of apathetic idiots." In contrast to 100% survival of the nursery-

[12] Paul Grimes, India's "Wolf Boy," *New York Times Magazine*, 30 October 1960.
[13] Bruno Bettelheim, Joey: A "Mechanical Boy," *Scientific American*, **200** (3): 116–128 (March 1959).

raised children, the mortality rate among these foundling-home children was 37% at the end of the second year, and those who survived remained either apathetic or hyperexcitable.[14]

These clinical findings do not conclusively demonstrate that there is a social need, that there is an innate desire on the part of individuals from birth to associate with other human individuals, but at least they corroborate what is taken for granted by virtually all parents —that children need affection and that if the environment denies it, the consequences are catastrophic. To reiterate a segment of Chapter 2, groups do not form just for the purpose of satisfying other needs, such as the physical needs for food, clothing, etc., but also form for the sake of getting individuals together. Being together is not simply inherently satisfying, fun for its own sake, but also necessary to the normal development of what we know human beings to be as adults.

Groups help meet the physical and meet the social needs. For this reason groups form, grow, and endure. Correlatively they cease to exist when they no longer help meet these various needs. This assertion is not so self-evident as on its logical face it may seem to be. It denies both that there is a functional autonomy of—or acquired need for—groups as such and also that they are autonomous, spontaneous entities apart from the various members who compose them.

The functional autonomy principle argues that the individual has only to be exposed to group membership in order to generate a need for association. This position seems to be as incomplete as saying that there need only be sensitization for a photograph to be taken. There can be no sensitization if there is no light outside and no photosensitive film inside the camera. A camera never becomes functionally autonomous; it always needs light outside and film inside to work as a camera. In this sense society remains a concept, not an actual force, and only the characteristics of human beings make society what it is. This does not mean that there is no point in studying society

[14] R. A. Spitz, The Role of Ecological Factors in Emotional Development in Infancy, *Child Development,* **20:** 145–155 (1949). The author asserts that emotional discrimination precedes other perceptual development. The infant at 3 months responds with a smile to its "human partner" but does not recognize food till 2 months later. At 8 months a child distinguishes familiar from strange people and is anxious in the presence of strangers but does not distinguish toys and other objects from each other until 10 months. [*Ibid.,* 147.] See also John Bowlby, *Maternal Care and Mental Health,* Geneva, World Health Organization, 1952, which summarizes much research on the consequences of abnormal or absent mother-infant relationships.

as it is—as an abstraction, like such other abstractions as perception or motivation—but just that we remember that society is an abstraction and not all of reality and is not even a self-contained abstract system. Without the innate social need, neither society nor the individual is conceivable.

The brothers Furumoto [15]

When we were considering basic human needs we brought up the hypothetical case of Tom Furumoto and Mary Fairgrieve who had just been married in a Catholic church in Hawaii. Having created this couple just a few chapters ago, we now have no difficulty making long leaps through some thirty years' time to find out what has happened to them. We find out for one thing that they have had two sons, both of whom are now quite grown. One of them has just entered law practice in a firm with a large-corporation clientele in Hawaii, after graduating from law school in the University of California at Berkeley. A second son has just been kicked out of Swarthmore College for causing the pregnancy of a co-ed, the daughter of a prominent playwright in New York. How these events came about and what happened since the wedding of Tom Furumoto and Mary Fairgrieve is now our concern, as a matter having to do with proximal group influence.

Tom and Mary Furumoto left the church for an extended honeymoon. Both were quite passionately and almost desperately in love. They forgot about the doubts of his parents who, with age, grew increasingly attached to the old ways of the Japanese village of their childhood and increasingly doubtful of the rootless new generation. And they ignored the hot indignation of Mary's father and the cold disdain of her mother. The couple's enormous zest and happiness continued for months after Mary discovered she was going to have a child. Then there was some discussion as to where the child should be baptized. Tom reminded Mary that the priest had made them

[15] The following fictional account of the Furumoto family is presented to lend coherence and comprehensibility to a variety of psychological findings discussed in the chapter. The reader who boggles at fictionalizing can skip the Furumotos without loss of content but may suffer from a notion that human behavior is as compartmentalized as psychologists must look at it in sensibly carrying out research. An excellent critical synthesis of research is contained in Sidney Verba, *Small Groups and Political Behavior,* Princeton, Princeton University Press, 1961, chs. 2–4.

promise to baptize the child in the Catholic church. Mary was vigorously reluctant and agreed to do so only if the child were a boy, which it was. Before the child's birth, Mary argued with apparent success that those of their children who were boys would be raised Catholic and the girls outside the church.

The first child was baptized Thomas Fairgrieve Furumoto after his father and mother. The second was named Kentaro Kawashima Furumoto after the father of Tom's mother. Two years later when Mary was pregnant with their third child she contracted the mumps and lost the child and almost died herself. Within six months after her recovery, Mary wrote her father that she had joined the Catholic church. Her father wired Mary that John Knox at least was spared the shame of siring a Mary Stuart. Mary now broke with her parents completely.

Some thirty years after the marriage we find that young Tom has married a Portuguese-Hawaiian restaurant owner's daughter, whom he met years before at the University of Hawaii, and that Ken, living and writing in New York, remains unmarried. Tom's career is headed towards politics in the Republican party. His catalogue of saints includes Abraham Lincoln, his two grandfathers, his father, and whoever is the current or most recent Republican U. S. Senator from Hawaii. His catalogue of sinners includes Adolf Hitler, the South African white supremacists, the unprincipled Japanese political boss in the Democratic party in Honolulu, and Japanese citizens of the United States who live in Hawaii and who have a taste for Zen Buddhism and a distate for Hawaiian music as played in the best tourist hotels.

Ken moved to the Harlem district of New York after leaving his classmates in Swarthmore. He studied English literature for a while at Columbia, left, and became a writer of delicate, hybridized love poems, which reflect a sensitivity to both Japanese verse and English love poems of the Cavalier period. He has had a steady succession of affairs but never married because of his constant search for the ideal woman, who is a composite of his mother, the playwright's daughter, Ruth the Moabitess, Marx's devoted wife Jenny, and of his own veneration of the unequivocally sexual, physically mature Greek goddess Aphrodite. His ego ideals are Leo Tolstoi, Peter Kropotkin, and Franz Kafka. His bêtes noires are the Nazi ideologue Alfred Rosenberg; the Japanese wartime premier Hideki Tojo; white people whose best friends are deserving Negroes, Puerto Ricans, Chinese, Japanese, and Indonesians; and any compromisers with justice (which

includes all politicians, statesmen, agitators, and violent revolutionaries) and with truth (which includes almost all magazine editors).

It would be easy and a little comforting to explain these results by
stating some correlations—that for example children accept (or occasionally reject) the politics of their parents. Or we could say that the
adoption of political views is only one facet of the general enculturation process that parents carry out as mediators between the big
society and their children. These and like statements are true and
not very explanatory: they say how but not why.

But how, in terms of the central, familial part of proximal social
influences can we explain such phenomena as the lives and outlooks
of young Thomas and Kentaro Furumoto? Both were raised with
formally identical genes, in the same nuclear and extended family,
and in the same culture. Why do they differ? Why is one intensely
political and why does the other regard himself as intensely apolitical,
even antipolitical? Using these contrasting hypothetical brothers to
provide a basis for systematic analysis of group influences, let us start
with the familial among the proximal group influences and then consider the nonfamilial proximal influences.

Togetherness and aparthood

One of the least disputed facts in social science is that the familial
influences usually constitute the strongest of the social influences in
the shaping of the personality of an individual, in the making of an
adult human being out of the squalling new organism that parents
find so fascinating and pleasurable but which is in psychological terms
only potentially human. We can best get at the shaping of an adult
human by putting ourselves not in the position of parents but in the
position of the newborn child, because it is into his central nervous
system that the influences pass and are selectively absorbed and cast
off in the maturation process.

The earliest social experience, which is surely on the unconscious,
inarticulated level, is of oneness with the very limited environment,
whose most prominent feature is the almost ever-present mother. An
infant does not distinguish himself from his environment. In time,
an infant becomes gradually aware of the distinction, partly because
of the occasional failure of the environment to satisfy his needs when
they send signals of discomfort to his brain. The central nerves get
signals from his empty or distended stomach, his wet and smelly bot-

tom, or from those peripheral and central neural regions that tell his brain he needs to be held, fondled, and played with—or that he has been held, fondled, and played with too much. The gap between need and satisfaction forms gradually the gap between self and other.

A dialogue develops in the background of his other activities—a dialogue that becomes noticeable to others—parents, especially—during the first few weeks or months and perhaps not too much later to the child itself. As he eats, sings to himself, and plays, a conflict grows that roughly parallels, but in a sense is identical with, the gradual separation from his parents over the long period of childhood. After he becomes aware of his own separate identity, the conflict is between deliberately identifying with his parents and others and becoming his own detached, autonomous, self-sustaining self. He is never really able to be his mother or (later) his father, either physically or mentally,[16] but in his mind he inevitably thinks as though he indeed were his mother or his father. He is never able in his mind to be altogether separated from his proximal groups, beginning with his parents. As he emerges and continues to emerge into self-consciousness, he does so ineluctably from the context of a particular mother or father who in his perception were once part of him and he of them. The subjective and objective, united at birth, are never wholly separated or separable. Whether he is at work in school or in play at home, the growing child, consciously or unconsciously, is never altogether without his parents.

The identification process also includes the adoption of the parents' attitude toward people, society, God, the universe, right and wrong, and everything else that parents deliberately or inadvertently, in thought and action, impress upon their children. These conceptual, ideational matters are part of the environment, directly mediated by those people from whom the child does not quite distinguish himself. Some observers who have noted these phenomena have concluded that this absorption of culture is a passive, indiscriminate one in which the growing child is like a piece of clay in the hands of the sculpturing enculturators. This extreme environmentalist view has been shared by Lockeans, Lamarckian evolutionists, psychological behaviorists, and Marxists alike (not to mention advertising agencies). Quite without relationship to their political ideology, the view has polemical

---

[16] He never truly was, for the sex cells which produced his body were never part of the anatomy of either parent but only contained therein and only nurtured during gestation by his mother.

point in emphasizing the tremendous, almost unique, impressibility of the human organism.[17]

But this process of absorbing and assimilating the environment is by no means a passive one, in which old wine is poured into new wineskins, any more than the digestive tract indiscriminately absorbs everything that the child swallows. The mind mediates between a continuing barrage of stimuli, not all of which are from outside the organism. The mind—the ego in Freud's terms—has to mediate, by acceptance, rejection, and compromise, in order to maintain some kind of coherence in the personality of the individual.[18] Among people of normal desire for a greater satisfaction of needs, including the need for better relationships with parents and for more comfortable autonomy, there is never complete satisfaction with the way one's parents have done things, with the way parents think and act. And as no two organisms are identical, even with formally the same genetic composition, so are no two sets of environmental influences identical, even for children raised by the same parents, teachers, fellow students, and others. Parents change from year to year, and the rest of the environment usually changes much more than do parents.

The father and mother of the brothers

Now let us apply the proximal group influences to a supposititious explanation of the political outlook of the brothers Furumoto. This makes it necessary for us to peer into the minds of Tom and Mary Furumoto, the parents, and at least to glance into the minds of both sets of grandparents.

We have noted an adoption of the conventional values of the Westernized, Americanized, Christianized Hawaiian society by Thomas Fairgrieve Furumoto and a rejection of many of the same values by his younger brother Kentaro. Why this difference in reaction pattern?

Tom (the father) Furumoto as a child had had occasional close school contacts with Caucasians whom he enjoyed playing with, except sometimes when they got angry or mean and called him a "dirty little Jap." He was so lost in play on such occasions that he was startled at being called a dirty little Jap. He not only did not regard himself as particularly dirty, small, or Japanese but also resented be-

---

[17] For Freud's formulation of the process see particularly his *New Introductory Lectures on Psychoanalysis,* London, The Hogarth Press, 1933, Lecture 31, 78–106, especially 78–90.
[18] See *ibid.*, 105.

ing accused of these three iniquities. After these experiences Tom would sometimes tell his parents. They would get upset and see to it that he bathed more regularly than boys bathe even in Japan, ate as much as he could of good food to help him grow tall, and studied assiduously his English speaking and writing. The parents were upset because to them Tom was not very Japanese at all, spoke only broken Japanese, and seemed to speak English with no accent whatever. They also told him he should be proud that he was Japanese. Tom was an energetic, perceptive child and young man. He saw that it was difficult to adopt and be adopted into Western culture, but he also saw that it was impossible to return in any sense to Japan. With vigor and minimal equivocation, he chose to assimilate.

He left the Buddhist temple of his parents when he left home for Honolulu and the University. From a Caucasian friend, who usually regarded him not as Japanese but as a good fellow, he gained solace in companionate atheism, but when his good friend after Pearl Harbor burst out in hatred of "those sneaky Japs," Tom gradually moved into the Catholic church and became very devout. Displacing in the most acceptable fashion his hostility to the white community, he came to hate the land of his ancestors for the contempt and suspicion directed toward him by his fellow students during the first year of the war. He enlisted in the army, served in military intelligence in the Pacific until September 1945, and in the occupation forces in Japan until he was discharged a year after the war. He did well at his job, though at a high price in what he had come to regard as his own false, unChristian pride. The Japanese with whom he talked in Tokyo in 1946 greeted his American-accented Japanese pronunciation with smiles illconcealed under their hands, and seemed to think him a traitor of sorts. And once he overheard the wife of an American officer say to her husband, after seeing Tom reading a Japanese book in a railroad station, "Are you sure that that Jap in American uniform is not a spy?" His anger and frustration he swallowed successfully, with the help of the priest, who reminded him that the meek would inherit the earth.

Tom's parents had secretly rejoiced at Japanese battle victories in the early years of the war, in the same deep and shallow way that Cambridge University graduates all over the world rejoice when a Cambridge man becomes prime minister of the United Kingdom. When Tom came back from Japan and was discharged from the army, his parents were privately and publicly proud of their son who had made good in American society, and they counted the high cost even less than had Tom.

He worked as a clerk for a while in a trading company and then went into partnership with a Caucasian in the wholesale fish market in Honolulu. Once on a double date with his partner, he met the partner's girl friend, an acquaintance who was spending the Christmas vacation of her last college-year in Hawaii with her Nisei roommate at Vassar. Tom's partner was bored and nervous with the two Vassar girls' tendency to discuss Prokofiev, Franklin Roosevelt, Hitler, and race prejudice. But Mary was struck by the energetic, confident Tom and he by her and so the son of Japanese immigrants to Hawaii and the daughter of a highly successful and intelligent men's clothier in Pittsburgh were married after her June graduation. Her father, Adam Fairgrieve, was a thoroughly humane sort who had heartily rejected the subordination of women that had killed his own mother with drudgery and child-bearing. He recognized the implications of women's suffrage. Nonetheless he was apoplectic at the marriage of his daughter to a poor Hawaiian Japanese, and in a Catholic church at that. What did they teach those girls at Vassar, anyhow?

Mary Williams Fairgrieve had never as a child in the late 1920s known the poverty and discrimination that her future husband was experiencing thousands of miles from the Pittsburgh suburb where she was raised. Her father was not an immigrant but the son of an immigrant from Scotland. He had worked his way through Princeton, and met and courted the daughter of a distinguished dean, who traced his ancestry proudly back to Roger Williams of Rhode Island. The dean was dubious of this ambitious young upstart whose father had been a mill hand and an Owenite in Scotland, and who despite poor grades and a certain self-righteous smugness proposed to marry his bored, beautiful daughter and frankly aspired to go into business and become wealthy. Young Fairgrieve was quite free of the radical foolishness of his father, whom he deferentially dismissed as impractical, and the distinguished dean was relieved to find that young Fairgrieve had none of those old world ideas about the subordination of women. So Dean Williams gave his gratuitous consent, early in the unbuttoned 1920s. Fairgrieve prospered, and took his wife and two daughters around the world in 1938, just before the younger and unbeautiful daughter Mary was about to enter high school. They spent two weeks in Japan, and Mary fell in love with a land and a people.

With no real grounds for hostility against society at large, Mary's problems were not related to assimilation but were a projection of the mixed feelings she had toward her parents. She respected her mother, who came to return the respect. The mother was a just-minded, cold woman. She taught her daughters manners and polite interest for ideas and learning, and never really loved them or her husband—a merchant who could never measure up to her handsome and academically distinguished father. Mary loved her father dearly, but the love was unrequited. Her father kept forever trying to convince his wife he was worthy of her, with constant unsuccess. So he transferred his affections to his eldest daughter, who resembled her mother. He displaced many of his aggressions against his wife on Mary, his own living image. The mother and the elder daughter he indulged.

Mary was relentlessly educated by both parents. From her mother she learned to disdain the cheap and the false; from her father she learned to respect hard work, authority, the best people, and the great, now safely dead and buried Celtic radical, Roger Williams. And she never felt either loved or indulged. In high school she consistently made the honor roll and had no dates. Her sister disdained the honor roll and dated a little more often than her parents knew. The older sister went to a small college near Baltimore, flunked out, and eventually married a young Harvard graduate who was an ensign in the wartime Navy. Mary went to a very serious girls' college and again was an honor student.

But it was the depression and her thwarted affection and her resulting unconscious hostility to both parents that combined to produce a socio-political reaction in Mary. On what to her were manifestly quite rational grounds, she began to suffer for brutalized mankind. She spent a summer doing social work among steel workers in Pittsburgh. In college she chose as an older roommate the daughter of a clothing manufacturer who was Jewish. When this girl graduated, Mary volunteered to take as a roommate the daughter of a prominent Los Angeles merchant who as a Japanese had been interned in a relocation center for the duration of the war.

Mary's mother seemed much less disturbed by the changes in her Vassar daughter than was Mr. Fairgrieve. Perhaps because he was so upset by this radicalism, Mrs. Fairgrieve made light of it all and said Mary would eventually settle down and marry a doctor or a lawyer, after seeing the futility of graduate school. Mr. Fairgrieve from time to time dropped comments: "But what will the men at the club say if they find out about Mary?" and "You can pass off this nonsense about a Jewish roommate, even though it is embarrassing, but the daughter of a possible saboteur, and Japanese at that!" or "I understand the Jap girl's from a Buddhist family turned Catholic. I bet Mary isn't even a Christian any more. Has she said anything about going to church lately?" and "Now she says she's going to vote for Roosevelt, first chance she gets. Haven't I given her everything she wants?"

And so on her last college fling, a trip to Hawaii, Mary met her roommate's date and at last married a Catholic Japanese up-and-coming businessman. Tom was not Presbyterian, not Scotch and not yet rich, but otherwise he was just like Mary's father, except that Tom was ardent and really seemed to love her, which her own father never had. In this young Catholic was the same puritanical dedication to betterment that tensed the minds of members of the American middle-class in the late nineteenth and early twentieth centuries and their counterparts in the U.S.S.R. starting in the 1930s and in China in the 1960s. In this young Vassar graduate was the same self-assurance of high social status that was the precious commodity purchased at great sacrifice by puritans of whatever race or religion for future delivery to their descendants. By marrying her, Tom got distal contact through his proximal wife of this assurance, but only his strikingly handsome children would proximally experience even a modicum of it.

The apolitical and the political

Their first son, young Tom, was the idol of his father to such an extent that his mother vaguely sensed the same neglect that so upset her in her own father. Young Tom grew up in the new Hawaii, where Japanese now were finally and condescendingly admitted to the best clubs and where his father had ever-growing influence in the business community. His father, awed himself by his own success as a one-time poor boy, infused in his eldest son a sense of awe for men of power. "If you want to get ahead," old Tom had often said to young Tom, "you have got to have the right connections. And don't emphasize your differences. Deal with people not as a part-Japanese but as a businessman." Tom the younger had never examined the major premise of getting ahead or of the other advice. He accepted it and shifted only his occupation, from business to law. This pleased his father, who at times said wistfully that nowadays it wasn't the businessman who had the prestige but the politician.

The elder Tom's life was a monotonic theme proving to his parents, his wife's parents, himself and his wife that he could succeed. The refrain of lavish devotion to their older son Thomas Fairgrieve made Mary turn her affection toward their hypersensitive second son Kenny.

There were no longer the racist fist-fights that her husband had experienced in his childhood, but there was still more than a trace of prejudice. Young Tom had the fortunate and thick hide of a future politician. He turned prejudice back on itself and sometimes nicely shamed his classmates into electing him to office to show they were not prejudiced. And Ken was hurt deeply by slights that his older brother barely noticed. When he was in high school, Ken fell in love with the beautiful daughter of a Caucasian neighbor who was a defeated candidate for Congress. She seemed to love Kenny, too, but as the excuses mounted for refusing to go to dances with him, he sensed her parents' objections, and as usual at last broke down to tell his troubles to his mother.

Tom ended up in law, with political aspirations in the conservative Republican party after his steady success at the University of Hawaii and at the law school in Berkeley. Ken was packed off to Swarthmore, which packed him and the playwright's daughter off campus. He went to New York and fell without protest into the tender care of a succession of women whose natural desire to love and to nurture found in him a strong catalyst and warm object.

In 1980, young Tom became his party's candidate for United States Senator from Hawaii. He was not at all embarrassed by his mixed ancestry, which was again a political asset, but he was embarrassed by the opposition effort to cast reflection on his decency and patriotism by describing the antics of his younger brother in New York. Kentaro had occasionally made the headlines for solitarily picketing the United Nations General Assembly. He demanded that the vote for universal fingerprinting of all human beings be reversed, as an invasion of privacy. The delegations of the United States of America, the Union of Soviet Socialist Republics, and the People's Republic of China issued a joint statement defending the plan to accumulate careful records on all people everywhere, for the protection of universal and equal man.

The United Nations press secretary issued copies of this joint statement of the great powers, on which India, Portugal, and the Transvaal Republic maintained a preoccupied neutrality. He called attention to Furumoto's previous immature exhibitionism when he had protested the unanimous passage of an agreement that all humans aged eighteen or older must wear a stainless steel identification tag, whose usefulness had been dramatically demonstrated in a recent intercontinental passenger rocket disaster, in which the only thing left to identify some of those who had died was their identification tags. Angered by Furumoto's dramatic protest, a Bantustan delegate proposed to order scientists to investigate the bloodlines of natural scientists and radicals. His argument was that scientists, the true servants of mankind, were most frequently found among ethnically pure individuals (regardless of what the pure race was) and that only hybrids like Kentaro Furumoto caused radical trouble for governments. When another delegate pointed out that such an investigation should not be made, because data on parentage were still unavailable for 73% of mankind, this proposal was temporarily shelved.

Thus we see that the elder Furumoto brother had become quite political and the younger altogether antipolitical. Or so it seemed at first glance. At second glance the opposite appeared. Young Tom was campaigning for a Senate seat on a standard set of issues on which he and his opponent disagreed only in the vigor with which each would carry out the program. They were concerned not with policy but with administration. Ken on the other hand, with neither aspiration nor competence for even a candidacy for elected office, was highly political in his solitary opposition to worldwide public policy, on which consensus on the need for universal records had become well-nigh universal. Only a dissident group of students at the University of California in Berkeley and at the University of Moscow were opposed to such registration proposals. News commentators labeled these students psychoceramics, and they were distinguishable because they shaved their entire faces, contrary to the now universal, manly, and equalitarian practice of letting the beard grow.

A retrospective explanation of causes

It is impossible to trace in detail all the proximal influences that shape the pattern of political behavior in any one or two individuals. It is further impossible to predict from knowledge about two individual cases how any large number of individuals—a substantial population—will behave politically. But some data are available with which we can understand not only the ideography of particular cases but also the nomothetic characteristics of both individual, unique patterns and general, common patterns.

Multiplicity of influences naturally makes for a greater diversity of results. If the organism from birth has greater opportunity for selection, more varied development occurs in each individual case. More specifically, where a mother and father differ in their social outlook and come from diverse backgrounds, there is more likely to be diversity in their children.[19] A corollary of this is that children raised in working-class families are more likely to have uniform working-class political attitudes than children raised in middle-class families are likely to have standard middle-class attitudes.[20] A postwar study of Germans who had been anti-Nazi during the war indicates that the parents of an abnormal number of these anti-Nazis had married outside their own ethnic, national, or religious groups; or the anti-Nazis themselves had done so. In fact the investigator found that, in the earlier lives of all the anti-Nazis studied, there had been deviation from routine pedagogy and experience. And in all but three of the cases, there were at least three deviations from the standard, in one of these five experiences: the pattern of relationships between the subject and his mother or father; the subject's being a favored child; crossing ethnic, national, or religious lines in marriage; subject exposed to anti-Nazi influence by parents or friends; or traveling or reading widely.[21]

Diversity of parental background (and therefore less mutual reinforcement of values by both parents) or unusual relationships between parents and children are apt to produce greater diversity, greater nonconformity. More consistently domineering parents are apt to produce great conformity among their children, who are more alike in their outlook and have a higher respect for authority.[22] Such parent-child relationships take place in the background of the largely nuclear families in America. What the effects are of the more diffuse adult authority pattern which prevails in the kibbutzim in Israel probably cannot be foretold. Before any valid generalization can be made, we will have to wait for the maturation of a generation of individuals who have been altogether raised in kibbutzim. Only about 20

[19] T. Lidz et al., The Intrafamilial Environment of the Schizophrenic Patient: IV. Parental Personalities and Family Interaction, *American Journal of Orthopsychiatry*, **28**: 764–776 (1958).

[20] See Angus Campbell et al., *The American Voter*, New York, John Wiley and Sons, 1960, 348 note, which suggests there is more solidary political-party loyalty among working-class than among middle-class groups.

[21] See David M. Levy, Anti-Nazis: Criteria of Differentiation, in Alfred H. Stanton and Stewart E. Perry, eds., *Personality and Political Crisis*, Glencoe, Ill., The Free Press, 1951, 151–227, esp. 155–159.

[22] T. W. Adorno et al., *The Authoritarian Personality*, New York, Harper and Brothers, 1950, ch. 10. M. L. Hoffman, Some Psychodynamic Factors in Compulsive Conformity, *Journal of Abnormal and Social Psychology*, **48**: 383–393 (1953). R. Stagner, Attitude toward Authority: an Exploratory Study, *Journal of Social Psychology*, **40**: 197–210 (1954).

to 30 of the adults in the kibbutz studied by Spiro had been raised in it.[23]

How do we apply these data in explaining the Furumoto family? Both parents in their similar values reflected their own dissimilar upbringing. The elder Tom, raised affectionately in an authoritarian home, still sought integration into the larger society. Mary Fairgrieve, raised with scant affection in a nonauthoritarian home, sought identification with mankind and with an affectionate oriental member of mankind (her husband), thereby telling her occidental parents that she resented their cold neglect. At the same time she had the profound social security that made such a successful interracial marriage possible; she did not have to gain admittance to society in order to gain self-confidence: she already did belong and therefore already had a basic self-confidence of sorts. Each son adopted a basic outlook that varied from the other's outlook as a function of which parental influence was stronger. The older Tom Furumoto paid more attention to young Tom, who showed at least conventional tendencies and an acceptance of the established authority pattern. Mary paid more attention to Ken, who showed strong anti-authoritarian tendencies. Both sons exhibited mild anxieties but showed a strong tendency to identify with one parent or the other.[24]

The shaping of the two Furumoto brothers took place within American culture at a time when permissive views of pedagogy were influencing both parents, but especially the mother. The father recognized

[23] See Melford E. Spiro, *Kibbutz,* Cambridge, Harvard University Press, 1956, 60–63; and also see A. I. Rabin, Some Psychosexual Differences between Kibbutz and Non-Kibbutz Israeli Boys, *Journal of Projective Techniques,* **22**: 328–332 (1958). Comparing 27 boys aged about ten years and raised in a kibbutz with 27 similar boys raised in normal patriarchal families in Israel, Rabin found less rivalry between children and fathers, less identification of children with fathers, and less rivalry between siblings, among the kibbutz-reared boys. The kibbutz pattern of diffuse proximal-group contacts is reminiscent of the extended family pedagogy among Navajo Indians and various Oceanic peoples. See Spiro, *op. cit.,* vii, 90, 98–99 (on the lack of privacy). But note that the association of parents and children in the kibbutz is very intense. *Ibid.,* 123–125.

[24] In a study of 76 people, aged 17–35 and mostly without secondary education, who attended the International People's College in Denmark, 1946–1948, an investigator tentatively established the far greater importance of parents, relatives, friends, etc. in forming political attitudes over other contacts, for example, with politicians or with organizations. Unfortunately the number of cases is inadequate to make profound conclusions. [H. Iisager, Factors Influencing the Formation and Change of Political and Religious Attitudes, *Journal of Social Psychology,* **29**: 253–265 (1949).]

intellectually the desirability of more equalitarian and permissive relations between parents and children, but, with his strong ties to his own parents, he retained strong tendencies to dominate the household. With his wife, his struggle to dominate was a stand-off. With his first son, the elder Tom gained authority and both gave and received affection. With his younger son he gained hostility to authority and no affection. To young Tom, his mother was a useful and respected person, but a woman nonetheless and so a little inferior; to Ken she became the embodiment of most motherly and feminine virtues, in a classic Freudian case of the Oedipus complex. And she never discussed politics, deferring to her husband on this one issue as she had to her father, in her childhood but not in her adolescence.

So seen, the rejection by Kentaro of his father's assimilationist and conservative politics may have been a facet of his rejection of his father, just as young Tom's acceptance of his father's politics was a facet of his rather total acceptance of his father. To this extent, the social-political views of neither son were rational, even though we may try to explain their views rationally.

It is commonplace that an overwhelming proportion of children adopt the politics of their parents, and in our hypothetical case the Ken Furumoto reaction is statistically infrequent. Roughly three-fourths of all Americans in the 1950s shared the political views of their parents, when both their parents identified themselves with the same party.[25] But it may be that this parental political influence, though as consistent perhaps as parental religious influence, prevails only in stable, pluralistic societies. Quantitative data are lacking on the relative influence and stability of influence of German parents on their children during the Nazi era, but the influence of the government was without question very strong. Whether it was actually stronger than parental influence for the entire population remains undetermined. In many cases the parental and Nazi influences operated in the same direction. In many cases the influence of the Nazi government outweighed opposition of the parents.

On a statistical basis, McClosky and Dahlgren come closer to explaining the Ken Furumoto reaction in noting that people who have "become alienated or separated from their families tend either to renounce its initial political affiliations entirely or to retain them more

---

[25] Angus Campbell, Gerald Gurin, and Warren E. Miller, *The Voter Decides,* Evanston, Ill., Row, Peterson and Co., 1954, 99. A. Campbell et al., *The American Voter,* 147.

tenuously." [26]   The finding helps explain not only Ken's reaction to his parents but also the reactions of Mary Fairgrieve's father who had renounced the radicalism and customs of his Scotch father when he set out on the path of assimilation.   Difficult as it was for Fairgrieve, even in a culture that minimized differences between Scotch and American, it was far more difficult for his future son-in-law, who had to renounce a far different culture in favor of one that moved from mild contempt, then to hostility and suspicion, then to an initially abashed and patronizing commitment—at first more in principle than in practice—to racial equality, during the elder Tom Furumoto's formative years.   The social pressures to conform were great.   Paying the price in loss of dignity, the elder Tom sought to establish a conformity in his sons that accepted the American values of equality and material enrichment, and made no complaints.

The family, crisis, and dictatorship

In modern totalitarian dictatorships, which invariably interfere with the family, pressure to conform is not internalized to the degree that it is among those assimilating to an alien culture.   The totalitarian pressure more clearly and frankly comes from without and attacks family solidarity with an intensity seldom felt in the voluntarily assimilating family.   The parents in an assimilating family are more likely, though with mixed feelings, to share the desire of their children to lose their old customs and adopt a new conformity than are the parents in a totalitarian society.   The influence of a dictatorship at times rather completely destroys the intrafamilial authority pattern. The political rebellion of children, having now the highest political sanctions, becomes total and spills over into broad social, antiparental rebellion.   In most cases the power of the government is or seems to be so strong as to result in surrender by the parents of their authority, so that they become nurturant, however unwilling, servants of youth— feeding, clothing, and sheltering the new generation out of fear for their own lives, while the beneficiary of this servitude is the government.

There is a tendency for families to be depoliticized by crisis, but this is by no means always true nor always accompanied by either an increase or a decrease in family solidarity.   Not enough is yet

[26] H. McClosky and H. E. Dahlgren, Primary Group Influence on Party Loyalty, *American Political Science Review*, **53**: 757–776 (1959), at 766.

known to tell the intra- and extrafamilial circumstances in which the one phenomenon or the other occurs. There is a set of relationships, but they have not yet been spelled out. There is evidence that economic crisis has a severe impact on family solidarity. The pattern of intrafamilial influence changes, displacing the father, as breadwinner and head of the family, with the mother, as the one who keeps the family together—while disintegration is blamed on the father.[27] One study further indicates that a breakdown in family solidarity occurred in materially deprived families in the U.S.S.R. But when there was an arrest or other repressive act against a family member by the government, families so attacked became more closely knit.[28] Such occasions are comparable to those in which a member of an immigrant or minority family experiences physical or mental attack by some outsider.

Disruption of the family (by economic or political intervention) often makes for depoliticization.[29] The effect of external forces in depoliticizing the family is an apparent consequence of the tendency to huddle together and maintain these primordial family ties in the face of external threats. It is illustrated in most extreme form in the impact of natural disasters on a community. Studies of communities immediately after they were hit by explosion or tornado indicate that the catastrophe makes people seek to protect and be protected by their immediate family and to quite forget the broader community welfare. Those who are active in meeting the multiple problems imposed by disaster are the ones without family ties or the ones who know their families could not be in danger. As Killian put it "much of the initial confusion, disorder, and seemingly complete disorganization reported in the disaster communities was the result of the rush of individuals to find and rejoin their families." [30]

---

[27] E. Wight Bakke, *Citizens without Work*, New Haven, Yale University Press, 1940, ch. 6, The Family Confronts Unemployment. See also P. Eisenberg and P. F. Lazarsfeld, The Psychological Effects of Unemployment, *Psychological Bulletin*, **35**: 358–390 (1938) and Ross Stagner, *The Psychology of Personality*, New York, McGraw-Hill Book Co., 1937, 399.

[28] K. Geiger, Deprivation and Solidarity in the Soviet Urban Family, *American Sociological Review*, **20**: 57–68 (1955).

[29] In the sense of reducing participation in the making of decisions on broad public policy.

[30] L. M. Killian, The Significance of Multiple-Group Memberships in Disaster, *American Journal of Sociology*, **57**: 309–314 (1952), reprinted in Dorwin Cartwright and Alvin Zander, *Group Dynamics: Research and Theory*, Evanston, Ill., Row, Peterson & Co., 1953, 249–256, at 251–252.

A man-made crisis that disrupts the established social and political order seems to have the same effects on the family as a disaster. In an effort to strengthen the closest, most proximal group ties—those of the family—people turn away from the broader society, which thereby becomes disunited, and crisis makes possible the control of the society by a determined new political group.

Thus when there is international or "internal" war, people huddle together in their families, just as they do in a case of an explosion or tornado. Those who are free from such family ties, or who know their families are unaffected, are the category from which leadership emerges, as in the case of natural crisis.[31] A mild crisis like an economic depression can have the same consequence of making the family preoccupied with its own survival and weakening ties to the larger community, thereby easing the path to power for the autocrat. These directly political crises are discussed in a later chapter. The presently important point is that the psychic consequence of an external threat to the family may be to draw it together internally and to insulate it from the rest of society, desocializing and depoliticizing it.[32]

And even milder crisis affecting the family, like the chronic crisis of assimilation facing a family that has moved into a new society, seems to have the same desocializing, depoliticizing effect, although less intensely and over a more protracted period. This is the crisis which we have typified in the generations-long process by which the Furumoto family became assimilated. Old Tom's parents were too busy providing for the family to worry about the larger society, which was at once a constant threat and a constant challenge to them. Old Tom, reaching maturity during the Second World War and thereafter, was able to move out into the larger society, marry into it and show wistful signs of political interest. His two sons became, in their antithetical ways, highly political. At any rate, one of them thought he was entering politics and the other thought he was staying out.

Proximity and misperception in the laboratory

The pattern of direct interaction between people probably is much the same outside the family as it is within, the major variation being

---

[31] For the effect of such a crisis on the emergence of leadership from a category of people relatively free of responsibility, see G. Wada and J. C. Davies, Riots and Rioters, *Western Political Quarterly*, **10**: 864–874 (1957).

[32] See Sidney Verba, *Small Groups and Political Behavior*, Princeton, Princeton University Press, 1961, 53–54.

the much lesser intensity of interaction between people who are not members of the same family. But we need not raise or settle the question of whether the nuclear family is the prototype of all other groups, and whether parent-child relationships are the prototype of social authority patterns. We need only recognize that some research in nonfamily proximal groups is more extensive than that in family groups. When the kind of research that has been done in small groups of people who before the experiment are strangers to each other is applied to research in family groups, we will then better be able to argue the generality of laws of group influences.

The influence of nonfamilial proximal groups on perception and on the expression of opinions has been dramatically demonstrated in a succession of experiments. Sherif showed that the tendency of the eye to see motion in a fixed point of light, when there is no reference point to indicate relationships of the point of light to other objects (the "autokinetic effect"), is socially influenced. He placed two and three subjects in darkened rooms. In four successive trials he then asked each subject in turn to indicate aloud how far he thought the point of light had moved. The subjects showed a clear tendency to follow the lead of the first person who had orally said how far the light appeared to move. Furthermore, once a "social norm" had been established, individuals tended to stick to it when they later made judgments alone.[33]

The absence of a background against which to judge movement is a necessary part of the autokinetic effect and makes plausible the argument that, in this contrived experiment, there was no objective limitation of the strength of proximal group influence. This, we could argue, proves not the strength of group influence but merely that it could control perception completely because there was no counterforce. A blob of wet sand cannot react like a concrete block when confronted with a hammer blow. If there had been even the vaguest reference point in the dark room, the subjects would not have reported the fixed point of light as moving, even in order to feel more at ease with other subjects of the experiment. When stiffened and supported not by a social but a visual frame of reference—so one could argue—they would resist the strong, sometimes abrupt, pressure of proximal groups.

[33] M. Sherif, *The Psychology of Social Norms,* New York, Harper and Brothers, 1936. M. Sherif, Group Influences upon the Formation of Norms and Attitudes, in T. M. Newcomb and E. L. Hartley, *Readings in Social Psychology,* New York, Henry Holt and Co., 1947, 77–90.

A series of experiments by Asch indicates further the strength of group influence. The stimulus situation was not a single point of light with no visual reference but a set of three black lines on a white card, three feet from which was a reference card with a standard line exactly the same length as one of the three lines on the first card. The experimenter found that the college students when alone in the experimental room could tell, with virtually no error, which of the three lines on the second card was as long as the standard line. In one of the experimental situations, a row of subjects was asked to judge which line was like the standard one, the only difference being they were all asked to judge in the presence of others. All but one of the subjects were collaborators of the experimenter and were told to make a wrong judgment; the one innocent subject was not asked for his judgment until the others had stated theirs. Numerous trials with numerous naive subjects indicated that virtually complete accuracy in private now was replaced with remarkably increased errors in public: 32% of the naive judgments (not of the naive judges) were wrong. One-third of the naive judge-subjects made errors in at least half of the runs, and only one-fourth of them showed complete immunity to group influence.

Optimistic jumpers to political conclusions from psychological research can assimilate this experiment comfortably into their system of beliefs and values by noting that two-thirds of the judgments were correct. They can get further solace by noting that when the experimenter added just one innocent subject—so that each of the innocent subjects could get support from one other person in their rational appraisal of reality—errors dropped to 6%.

Pessimistic jumpers to political conclusions can just as comfortably ingest and digest these data by emphasizing that one-third of the judgments—of supposedly mature people with good eyesight, seeing so obvious and value-free a stimulus—were badly distorted just because the group was against them. They can get further solace for their pessimism by noting that when a solitary collaborator first gave correct answers and then betrayed his naive friend by deliberately giving wrong judgments, the errors of the innocent went back up almost to the original proportion of 32%.[34]

[34] Solomon E. Asch, *Social Psychology*, New York, Prentice-Hall, 1952, ch. 16, Group Forces in the Modification and Distortion of Judgments. For further research on perceptual conformity, see, for example, the report of Crutchfield's work at the University of California, in David Krech, Richard S. Crutchfield, and

Both categories of jumpers themselves become solidary opposing groups, each citing as authority the beliefs and values of the other members of their respective group of philosophers and sociologists and psychologists to prove conclusively or at least effusively that men are rational or are not.

Proximity and misperception in real life

Hopefully not altogether contaminated by past and present associations, both proximal and distal, the little distal group composed of the reader and the writer of this book can try to withhold judgment without depreciating either the importance of the age-old question or the research that remotely bears on it. In considering a further experiment, we get considerably closer to real-life circumstances and to politics, but probably no closer to a valid direct answer to the rationality question.

In this experiment [35] the subjects were twenty-four actual members of a cooperative rooming and boarding house at a university. The co-op group members were casual, mostly not close, friends but saw each other regularly. The experimenter, who was also a member of the cooperative, asked the twenty-four subjects to fill out privately a questionnaire in which they indicated their opinions about the Soviet Union. Later he asked them to state orally, in the presence of other cooperative members, their opinions on the same question. Immediately after responding orally to each question they were asked to indicate on a check-sheet what they thought was the average opinion of cooperative members on the question just answered.[36]

In 21 of the 24 cases the orally, publicly expressed opinions—whether pro- or anti-Soviet Union—were different from those expressed privately. Thirteen moderated their opinion when they stated it before other members of the group; eight expressed their opinion more extremely; only three said the same thing in public that they had said

Egerton L. Ballachey, *Individual in Society,* New York, McGraw-Hill Book Co., 1962, 511 ff.

[35] R. L. Gorden, Interaction between Attitude and the Definition of the Situation in the Expression of Opinion, *American Sociological Review,* **17**: 50–58 (1952), reprinted in D. Katz et al., *Public Opinion and Propaganda,* New York, Dryden Press, 1954, 425–434.

[36] There was a twelve-item scale on the Soviet Union with five possible responses on each, allowing a range of total scores from 12 to 60, from extreme pro- to extreme anti-Soviet Union opinion. See *ibid.,* Gorden, 53; and Katz et al., 429.

privately. In his appraisal of the two most extreme conformists, Gorden reported that both wanted to become like the other members of the group, which was for them a new and deeply satisfying social experience. Correlatively, one of the two extreme nonconformists continued to associate with high-school chums more than with co-op members, wanted to be different from other members, and at the same time saw the co-op as being a tolerant group. The other of the extreme nonconformists had highly ambivalent feelings toward the co-op members, perversely wishing both to shock and repel them and at the same time to maintain their personal attraction.

In comparing their own opinions with what they guessed was the group judgment, 20 of the 24 individual members saw themselves as being more extreme than the group as a whole. But each such member guessed that the group was closer to his own private opinion than the total actual average of the scores of all members proved to be.[37] This is presented graphically better than verbally, as shown:

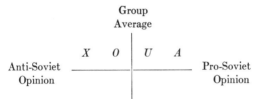

Group
Average

	X	0		U	A	
Anti-Soviet						Pro-Soviet
Opinion						Opinion

X Anti-Soviet individuals' actual score on the scale
     of Soviet items in the questionnaire

0 What X individuals believed the average group
     opinion to be

U What A individuals believed the average group
     opinion to be

A Pro-Soviet individuals' actual score

This half-contrived, half-normal social situation illustrates (more graphically than the line-length experiments) group influence on opinions that per se have no more to do with the group than did the judgments of line lengths. In real-life circumstances group influence is still pervasive, even though mixed with other factors. It most readily appears, or—more exactly—is most easily noticed, when we can momentarily pretend we are observers only and not ourselves group members, and thus can see how group membership influences others only. The

---

[37] *Ibid.*, Gorden, Table 2, p. 53; and Katz, Table 13.2, p. 429.

difficulty is that, since it is easier to see such things in the abstract from a pseudo-objective viewpoint, it is harder for us to realize that these same influences operate on us in exactly the same ways that they do on experimental subjects or on other people in normal life who have been subjected to group influences without knowing it—just as we are, without knowing it.

Over a period of several years in the 1930s, Newcomb gathered data on changes in the political opinions of college students, from the first to the last years that they were in school. The opinions on which he gathered data were not in a contrived experimental procedure. The situation was quite normal; the results are true to life.[38] At this point it should be no surprise that they changed, away from the views which they had acquired in the proximal groups of their childhood and early adolescence toward the views that prevailed in the campus atmosphere. At this particular campus the prevalent views favored the policies of the Roosevelt administration and also favored American aid to the Spanish Loyalist forces then involved in a death struggle with the Falangist rebels under General Francisco Franco. At another campus, a Catholic university, the prevalent view favored success of the Franco rebels and again the students favored the prevalent view.[39]

The psychic situation has become more complicated as we have reached real-life situations. In the Sherif experiments the stimulus was a point of light with no special reference, and the "distorting" came from one or two other group members, each of whom tended to conform to the percept of the other one or two persons. In the Asch experiment the stimulus was a set of lines quite devoid of value content, tradition, or what-not, and other group members were often successful in distorting the percepts of innocent subjects. The nonpersonal symbol-stimulus in both the Gorden and Newcomb research was far more complicated than the point of light or the line in prior experiments. Opinions on political issues are acquired over years, not just minutes or hours as in the case of light and lines, and are therefore probably less susceptible, more resistant, to change as a result of group or any other influence. We can say "have it your way" on how far a point of

[38] See Theodore M. Newcomb, *Personality and Social Change*, New York, Dryden Press, 1943; and Newcomb, Some Patterned Consequences of Membership in a College Community, in T. M. Newcomb and E. L. Hartley, *op. cit.*, 345–357; and the same report in Katz et al., *op. cit.*, 435–446.

[39] Data on changes over the four college years, or differences in the distribution of opinions among the four classes in school at one time, were not reported on the students at the Catholic university.

light moves or how long a line is, without suffering to some degree the loss of face, loss of self-respect (or whatever) that is involved in changing our political views.

Numerous factors are involved in limiting the effect of *present* nonfamily proximal influences on the political opinions of people in the circumstances of those studied by Gorden and Newcomb. Among these numerous factors, the social ones relate back to prior proximal (familial and nonfamilial) groups to which the person has belonged.

The familial influences we have already sketched. We have also noted a hypothetical but not imaginary relationship between young Tom Furumoto's neighborhood playmates' prejudices and his later political conformism. We have also posited a similar relationship between Ken Furumoto's subtler experience with prejudice among his high-school friends and his later political nonconformism. These influences probably occur over and over again, in proximal group context, in any society where there is interstatus or interethnic personal contact.

An adult is the lengthened shadow of a child

All that can be presently stated of general significance is that, starting in early or late adolescence, children are exposed to other influences—personal or impersonal—in addition to their parents. Some of these influences may be "objective" political events of the time, to which young people, with their less firmly established opinions, are more responsive than are old. Others are group influences—friends in their own age group and teachers.[40]

In late adolescence, in relatively immature nonindustrial economies where young people are almost without exception already working, the major proximal group influences are probably quite firmly fixed and unchangeable save by severe political crises. This is another way of saying that peasant-based societies are apt to experience great stability

[40] See the data reported by Herbert H. Hyman, in his *Political Socialization*, Glencoe, Ill., The Free Press, 1959, 99, 101, derived from H. H. Remmers and N. Weltman, Attitude Inter-Relationships of Youth, Their Parents, and Their Teachers, *Journal of Social Psychology*, **26**: 61–68 (1947) and from an unpublished study conducted at Rutgers University. The Remmers-Weltman study reports a correlation of .86 between parents and children on various social issues and of .65 between teachers and pupils on these same issues. See Remmers, Table 3, p. 65. The correlation reported between parents and children on party preference was almost as high as on issue orientation.

of political habits, ideologies, and loyalty,[41] and therefore to change more slowly or not at all—until shaken by strong forces intervening from outside the culture. Even these external influences are proximally mediated through the agency of some personal engagement, as with an agriculture expert, a missionary teacher, a party agitator, or the kaleidoscope of personal influences that operate when the peasant visits the big city. In a mature, industrialized economy, where the young need not go into productive labor as soon as their physical strength, endurance, and neural coordination are up to it, proximal influences remain more diverse for a longer period.

The proximal group influences we have considered thus far have done their influencing of people before they reach full maturity. These prematurity influences are ordinarily the strongest and the most enduring. No one ever quite abandons or forgets his childhood. The experiences, whether pleasant or unpleasant, gratifying or frustrating, remain ever-present in later life, which to a great degree may be described as the process of continuing to work out the tensions (frustrations, anxieties, fears, compulsions) and the gratifications that one experienced deeply in childhood.

It is a common tendency for people to forget this, to assume that as adults they are operating quite freely and rationally in response to the demands of the present, constantly changing situation. So let us just re-emphasize the continuing importance of these childhood influences which have produced such pungent expressions as "the child is father to the man"—and which in their largely unconscious forms are the ones psychotherapists are forever in search of.

Freud, the first person to systematically probe the unconscious, was keenly aware of such influences even in himself, and his own love for his mother and rather intense rivalry with his father are perhaps to a degree the reasons that the Oedipus complex has had such a prominent place in psychoanalytic theory.[42] Two instances—both actual—must here suffice to emphasize how enduring parent-child influences are.

A seventy-five-year-old lady recalled an experience that had occurred when she was ten or twelve. Because of her mother's illness and absence from the home, this girl had to prepare, at her father's request,

---

[41] Hyman, *op. cit.*, 128–129.

[42] Note also the impact of paternal criticism on Freud, who was so long and deeply disturbed by his father's casual remark, when Freud was seven or eight years old, that "that boy will never amount to anything." See Ernest Jones, *The Life and Work of Sigmund Freud*, New York, Basic Books, 1953, vol. 1, 16.

the budget and manage expenses for feeding a household of seven people. At the end of the month she had come within a dollar or so of spending exactly what she had budgeted. She went proudly into her father's study to report to him and to get encouragement for so managing an adult's responsibilities. At the age of seventy-five, she was still chagrined at the reply he had given her some sixty-five years earlier: "Well, you had one less mouth to feed."

The other instance concerns an eighty-two year old Idaho Democrat who turned up in the University of Michigan Survey Research Center random sample for the 1952 election study. When asked from the interview schedule the question as to what he would do if he didn't like his party's nominee, he said he probably wouldn't vote rather than change party allegiance, adding in substance, "If I'd turn Republican, my father, who has been dead for twenty years, would raise out of his grave and say 'Son, what ever made you do such a thing?' " [43]

The contemporary penumbra of adults

Adults do thus continue to live under the long shadow of their childhood, but they are also subject to new influences that develop not during but after what are called the formative years. The most significant of these new influences is generically much like the parental influence, namely the influence of one's spouse, which now supplements but does not displace childhood familial influence. And it is wives rather than husbands, at least in mid-twentieth century America, who are most matrimonially influenced—or most willing to admit it. In the 1952 University of Michigan election study, 27% of the women mentioned being influenced by their husbands in deciding how to vote, in contrast to 6% of the men.[44] Furthermore when there is disagreement between one's spouse and one's parents, there is a greater chance that the contemporary influence will win out over the historical one, rather than vice versa.[45]

[43] On paternal political influence, see R. E. Lane, Fathers and Sons: Foundations of Political Belief, *American Sociological Review,* **24**: 502–511 (1959) or Lane, *Political Ideology,* New York, The Free Press of Glencoe, 1962, ch. 17. Inter alia, Lane suggests that the permissiveness of fathers in the United States and "the low salience of politics" in most American families combine to diminish the amount of rebellion and channel it nonpolitically when it does occur.

[44] A. Campbell, G. Gurin, and W. E. Miller, *The Voter Decides,* Evanston, Ill., Row, Peterson & Co., 1954, Table C.3, p. 205.

[45] H. McClosky and H. E. Dahlgren, *op. cit.,* 769–770. See also Angus Campbell,

For most people most of the time these contemporary and historical influences of spouse, parents, and other close relatives are probably not just the main but *almost* the exclusive proximal group influence on political opinion and action. In an analysis derived from a careful area-probability sample of metropolitan Detroit, the University of Michigan Detroit Area Study found that about three-fourths of those interviewed reported getting together with relatives no less often than once a month, half of the total sample seeing relatives at least once a week. The descending order of proximal-group contacts consists of seeing nonfamily friends, then neighbors, and then fellow workers.[46] Among the working class particularly, extrafamilial sources of influence appear to be rather minimal.[47] In a working-class sample in New Haven, Dotson found that about two-fifths of those interviewed did not even have close friends outside the extended family.[48] With data from nationwide samples, Wright and Hyman came to similar conclusions. Almost two-thirds of all the adults sampled belonged to no voluntary association, whether trade union, fraternal organization, professional group or whatever. And again, those of lower socio-economic status less often belonged.[49]

These latter findings do not of course demonstrate just what the channels of influence are: reasonable as it is to suppose that one is most influenced by those one sees most frequently, we require further data to test such inferred relationships. A close and direct study by Katz and Lazarsfeld of the channels of communication has detailed the patterns of proximal-group influence.[50] Starting with a cross-sectional city sample of 700 women, the investigators asked them whose opinion on public affairs they trusted. Over 350 different people were

et al., *The American Voter, op. cit.,* Table 4.3, p. 77 which by inference agrees with the prior McClosky-Dahlgren finding.

[46] Detroit Area Study, *A Social Profile of Detroit,* Ann Arbor, Michigan, University of Michigan, 1952.

[47] See M. Axelrod, Urban Structures and Social Participation, *American Sociological Review,* **21:** 13–18 (1956), at 17.

[48] F. Dotson, Patterns of Voluntary Association among Urban Working-class Families, *American Sociological Review,* **16:** 687–693 (1951).

[49] C. R. Wright and H. H. Hyman, Voluntary Association Memberships of American Adults: Evidence from National Sample Surveys, *American Sociological Review,* **23:** 284–294 (1958). See also Wendell Bell and M. T. Force, Social Structure and Participation in Different Types of Formal Associations, *Social Forces,* **34:** 345–350 (1956).

[50] Elihu Katz and Paul F. Lazarsfeld, *Personal Influence,* Glencoe, Ill., The Free Press, 1955.

mentioned by the 700. These influencers were in turn asked the same question, producing over 200 second-level influencers, who in turn reported that they were influenced by over 160 others, a third-level of influencers.

Over half the influencers were members of the respondent's extended family, the others being neighbors, friends, and work associates.[51] Thus the most significant single reason for being influential was familial proximity to the person influenced, and the next most significant was nonfamilial proximity. But influential people have other characteristics than proximity. The most common characteristic of influential people was gregariousness, the force that breathes life into proximity. Those people who were members of various organizations and who had most friends with whom they talked from time to time were the most influential regardless of education, social status, or level of information, even though all of these factors intercorrelated in the Katz-Lazarsfeld study. The influential people tended to be better educated, of higher social status, and better informed, but above all they were more sociable.[52]

People nonetheless tended to be more often influenced by persons of their own social status than by those of different status. The interclass influence that existed was generally sought by those of the working class from the white-collar, business, and professional classes and by the white-collar from the business and professional classes. But there was a tendency for the white-collar class to be bypassed by working-class people, who sought influence directly from business and professional people. Correlatively, there was a tendency for business and professional people to seek opinions from working-class people. The cumulative consequence of the pattern of influence (in which those of working-class status looked to white-collar and to business and professional, and white-collar classes looked to business and professional) was, of course, to enhance the relative influence of white-collar and of business and professional, most particularly the latter. Indeed, each of the three successive tiers of influencers contained a larger proportion of higher-status and a smaller proportion of lower-status individuals than the preceding one.[53]

A correlative finding for age status is comparable to that for social status: outside the family, the young people looked mostly to other

[51] *Ibid.*, 140–141.
[52] *Ibid.*, 287–289.
[53] *Ibid.*, Table 41, p. 285 and Table 40, p. 284.

young people for their opinion, but when they did look outside their age group for leadership, it was more often the next older category and less often the oldest category.[54]

There is thus a consistent pattern of proximal-group influence in which equal status makes for greater influence than unequal status: spouse influences spouse more often than father influences adult off-spring; a person of working-class status influences one of the same status more than does a person of white-collar or business and professional status; and a young person influences another young person more than does an old person.

The common factor in each case is an abstract kind of proximity, the proximity of equal familial, social, or age status. In each case there is a closer sense of identity with one's peers: the equal is the most comfortable and, in the broader sense, the most familiar. Proximity is multidimensional: one is associated with his fellow-men in a variety of ways. The family is universal and therefore the most common, but by no means the only one. Two individuals meeting on a South Pacific isle—one a young Polynesian, and the other a middle-aged, middle-class Frenchman who likes to paint—can form a group based on little more than identity on the basic level of being human.

Togetherness forever

Probably the major effect of proximal groups is to homogenize opinions and behavior. The effect is so pervasive and profound as to make it seem like the second law of thermodynamics: if people get together they will in consequence of their proximity achieve the same temperature; more exactly they will tend to feel, think, and act alike—whether the joint activity be judging the length of lines or the stature of political candidates.[55]

An opposite function can occur in groups, a function in which proximity is both a cause and a kind of catalyst. In a study of Ger-

---

[54] *Ibid.*, 292. Old people correlatively were most influenced by their own age category, less by those in the next closest age category, and least by those farthest from them in age. The middle age category looked more often to those older than to those younger for influence.

[55] Homans, following Pareto, uses the concept of equilibrium to describe phenomena comparable to those I analogize to the second law of thermodynamics. See G. C. Homans, *The Human Group*, New York, Harcourt, Brace & Co., 1950, 301–308. As analogies, both terms are equally serviceable.

man prisoners captured during the Second World War,[56] Shils and Janowitz found that a major force—in their opinion, *the* major force—inhibiting disintegration in the German Wehrmacht was the face-to-face solidarity of small military units. It was not appeals to patriotism, to defense of one's family, etc., that kept the army together; it was the solidarity of the members of the military unit. The evidence is not conclusive but persuasive: individuals isolated in foxholes were very likely to surrender; units that had been together for a long time, so that individuals knew each other well, were less likely to give up.

But the investigators also mentioned that when it was possible for units to surrender as units, there was a better prospect of destroying their fighting effectiveness by treating them as units than if an attempt was made to shatter the group. The relevant point here is that proximity did more than prevent surrender: it also facilitated surrender. The variable that intervened consisted of such forces as physical exhaustion, despair, and the individual but common desire to survive. The variable was facilitated in its operation by the fact that men as a group were facing exhaustion and fear of death. They could face it together; they also could turn away from it together.

In another military situation, group solidarity led to Gandhi-like civil disobedience. During the Presidency of Theodore Roosevelt some Negro soldiers stationed in Texas rioted in reaction to discrimination against them by the local townspeople. It became impossible to discover which soldiers in the army companies were the rioters. Roosevelt, the first President in over twenty years to appoint Negroes to nonroutine administrative positions, in 1906 ordered the dishonorable discharge of all troops in the companies containing the rioters—unless the rioters were discovered. When they were not, 160 troops were discharged, including six who had been awarded the Congressional Medal of Honor, the highest combat decoration in America.[57]

Underlying this point is the intervention of forces which operated

[56] E. A. Shils and M. Janowitz, Cohesion and Disintegration in the Wehrmacht in World War II, *Public Opinion Quarterly,* **12**: 280–315 (1948). Reprinted in D. Katz et al., *Public Opinion and Propaganda,* New York, The Dryden Press, 1954, 553–582. Another study found the major reason for soldiers deserting in combat to be lack of integration in their combat outfit. [A. M. Rose, The Social Psychology of Desertion from Combat, *American Sociological Review,* **16**: 614–629 (1951).]

[57] See Richard Lowitt, Theodore Roosevelt, in Morton Borden, ed., *America's Ten Greatest Presidents,* Chicago, Rand McNally and Co., 1961, 199–200.

independently of the group and which first operated on each group member as an individual and then led the group to act together, but contrary to the way it had acted before. The forces had to be powerful to cause this reversal. They were related to the profound desire to survive. In a sense we could say that the group momentarily broke up on the basis of a more profound individual urge to survive, but promptly reasserted its power by making the act of survival a group action. And it merits emphasis that 58% of the changes in opinion [58] (not changers) that occurred between the first and second interview in the Katz-Lazarsfeld study took place without the changers remembering any personal contact. This suggests that more than half of the changes in opinion were either a consequence of nongroup influences or of rather vague impersonal distal group influences. It is to distal group influences that we now turn our joint attention.

[58] Katz and Lazarsfeld, *op. cit.*, 142.

CHAPTER 6

Distal groups in politics

What proximal groups mediate

Now we can move from proximal groups, the ones that serve both as immediate personal parts of the outside world and as mediate relayers of the rest of the outside world. That is, we move now to the distal groups which form that personal part of the outside world with which we are not in direct touch. That distal personal world momentarily includes the neighbor two doors away, about whom we just heard a shocking item of gossip from the neighbor one door away. The distal personal world also includes the astronaut who has returned from outer space and tells his experiences—in a pseudo-proximal contact via television or in a real-proximal contact of a fleeting sort as we personally hear him give a talk or see him wave as we personally watch his parade go down the street.

Understanding the dynamics of distal groups involves an integration of most of the mental processes discussed up to this point. The social ties as such that are involved in distal groups are only the indirect and therefore more remote object of a need for getting together, which ultimately traces back to the organism itself. The tensions that we have and seek to relieve in and through the help of distal groups may range from physical deprivation (food, clothing, shelter, health, and physical safety) to the need for self-actualization—in the form of a sportsmen's club or membership in an international association of antibomb citizens, who can thus express themselves because they, as university students and faculty members, are free of normal concern for food and for social acceptance.

The more or less durable percepts that people develop from day to day also interact with groups both proximal and distal. The hunger for perceiving and making sense of the total environment attracts them to groups ranging from the mother to whom a child fearfully says, "What makes the thunder?"; to the physicist whom a student asks in class, "How do you measure the mass of electrons?"; all the way to the philosopher to whom one indirectly says, "What is justice?" as he reads Plato's *Republic*. The inherent attraction to groups makes people cling to percepts which they get from both the proximal and the distal social groups that they cling to—as we saw in the perception experiments of Sherif, Asch, Crutchfield, and Hovland.

In virtually all situations, therefore, proximal groups—people with whom one is in immediate contact—act as mediators between the individual and the world beyond. When a little Austrian girl learns to fear the Swedish Oxenstierne almost three hundred years after his invasion of Central Europe, she is instructed in this intimate fear—with its temporally and spatially remote object—by a nursemaid or a mother. When a child learns to fear or despise real persons or things, as though they were ghosts, witches, gods, devils, he is taught to do so by real people—whether he knows them well or not, trusts or mistrusts them, or loves or hates them in various degrees. As a growing child casually and gradually learns to feel friendly or hostile toward different categories of people—the rich; the poor; people with white, yellow, brown, or black skins; capitalists; communists; Jews; Christians; Parsees; Catholics; Socialists; Trotskyites; Republicans; Stalinists; Conservatives; Democrats; workingmen; bosses; untouchables; landowners; peasants—it is individual personal contacts that instruct him. The contact may be the child's parents, an uncle, schoolteacher, friend, or other amicable proximal influence. The contact may be a member of an alien, outside group itself, with whom the individual has had only fleeting but deeply impressive proximal interaction.

The first kind of contact, where the mediator is a long-time intimate —whether friend or relative—we have discussed in the preceding chapter. We have scarcely touched on the second kind, which is so very crucial to the development of the patterns of distal group loyalties and hostilities. But we have noted that proximal contacts mediate between outsiders and individuals, who often get their ideas about outsiders via members of their own proximal groups and are therefore predisposed to respond in a particular way when they do come in contact with outsiders. A little Austrian girl who actually met her first Swede in real life might be somewhat apprehensive about the cannibalistic tendencies of this descendant of Oxenstierne. When her mild fear is disappointed, she might come to the opposite conclusion that all Swedes are wonderful people. A child raised to respect ministers or priests as men of great and godly virtue might, upon meeting a corrupt minister or priest, come to the opposite conclusion that all those who are called men of God are minions of the devil. In psychological terms this latter kind of experience is traumatic. There is no distinct name for the former, in which a hostile predisposition is radically contradicted by therapeutic experience.

We may generalize by saying that the more intense the proximal contact a person has with a representative of what is ordinarily a distal group, the more enduring will be the ensuing predisposition toward that distal group. And this predisposition may fall into any one of four categories: a favorable predisposition that is reinforced by personal contact; a favorable predisposition that becomes unfavorable; an unfavorable predisposition that is reinforced; and an unfavorable predisposition that becomes favorable. The presently crucial factor is the sign (plus or minus) that attaches: does the individual like and positively identify with the distal group or does he dislike and negatively identify with the distal group?

We should recall at this point that there must be mental interaction with the distal group—either direct or mediated through a proximal-group member—even though the contact is not face-to-face. If there is no interaction, there is no establishment of positive or negative cathexis. The distal group in such a case simply does not exist in the mind of the individual. Without the occasional direct contact with a usually distal group member—that is, when the predisposition is mediated by a momentarily proximal group member—it is highly labile. Once it is reinforced or radically challenged by direct contact, the predisposition becomes much less subject to change. And we also need to recall that, however univalent is the ultimate positiveness or negativeness of the interaction, its causes or manifestations are highly complicated and subtle—and that in actuality most interactions are both positive and negative.

Adolf, Paul, Abraham, and Vladimir

As an example of occasional or casual proximal contact with distal group members, Hitler in his relationships with Jews is as good as any in modern political life. In his autobiography he recalls that he had had personal contact with very few Jews in his high school days in the

Austrian border town of Linz and considered them to be Germans whose persecution on mere religious grounds was abhorrent.[1] Even when he arrived in Vienna in 1909 at the age of twenty, he recalled that he was repelled by the anti-Jewish press in such a cultivated city.

And then one day he took one of his solitary walks and had an experience as portentous as the Apostle Paul's conversion to Christianity on the road to Damascus. He saw "a being clad in a long caftan, with black curls." The appearance was unlike the Jews he had seen in Linz. "Is this also a Jew?" Hitler thought. "Secretly and cautiously" he "scrutinized one feature after the other" and then asked himself: "Is this also a German?" [2]

This proximal contact with Jews was followed by a distal contact via the anti-Semitic segment of the Viennese press, and then by further, evidently fleeting, personal contacts. The shocking proximal images were reinforced by the distal images, as the two merged inside Hitler's mind. As his despair deepened of ever becoming an artist or an architect or the beloved of a woman, his interaction with Jews became more negative, more intense, and more distal. They became merged with all non-Germans as defilers of German morality, purity, and vitality. In 1913, after four years in Vienna, the forlorn Austrian failure left, not for Linz but for Germany, to await whatever would happen. His proximal and distal contacts with non-Germans had acquired political content; in time produced a party; and finally turned a nation into a war machine.[3]

The contrast with Paul's conversion is striking. Paul ceased to be a Jewish persecutor of a Jewish out-group and came to profess his identification with all mankind, whether proximal or distal, Jewish or non-Jewish. Hitler ceased to be a "weak-kneed cosmopolitan" German and came to identify with Nordics alone and to be a persecutor of Jews. His hatred became intense partly as a result of his casual proximal contact with distal group members in Vienna. The fact that all other Nordics did not become anti-Semites in Vienna reminds us not to credit Hitler with accurate self-insight in suggesting that his contact with Jews was the sole or even primary cause of his conversion

[1] Adolf Hitler, *Mein Kampf*, New York, Reynal & Hitchcock, 1941, 66–67.
[2] *Ibid.*, 73.
[3] From the standpoint of understanding his psychodynamics, it is unfortunate that Hitler did not become a patient of a contemporary Viennese, Sigmund Freud. But it would indeed be magical thinking to assume that psychotherapy might have provided a long enough lever to move the world as it had taken shape in Hitler's head.

to racism. There is nevertheless a close relationship between his proximal contacts and both his intense devotion to the vague distal group, the Nordic race, and his intense hatred of all other distal ethnic groups.

The same relationship exists in two others whom we have previously considered in connection with the problem of intense childhood frustration—Lincoln and Lenin. Famous for freeing slaves, Lincoln as a young man and as a lawyer in central Illinois had little contact with Negroes, who remained a mostly distal group throughout his entire life. Far from identifying with them as equals, he shared the prejudices of his fellow townspeople toward them. But during a trip on a raft down the Mississippi to New Orleans he personally witnessed the sale of slaves and was repelled by the traffic in human beings.[4] Without ever seriously reducing the social distance between himself and Negroes, he developed—in consequence of this and other experiences and forces—a broad sense of humane justice that permanently fixed his attitude toward this distal group. Personal experience, probably more than any reading of Blackstone, Shakespeare, and perhaps even the Bible, shaped his attitude toward slavery.

The same relationship between direct experience and broad ideology was apparent in Lenin. We need not discount or depreciate his reading of Marx to see the deep trauma to him of experiences within his own family. His father's career as a dedicated educational administrator was broken by the recrudescence of reaction following the 1881 assassination of Alexander II, and he died in 1886 at the age of fifty-five. A more serious blow was the execution of his beloved older brother Alexander a year later, for attempting the assassination of Alexander III. Other blows were his expulsion from university as the brother of a would-be assassin and the death in a bad hospital of his gifted sister Olga from typhoid fever.[5] These very proximate tragedies contributed to his becoming a revolutionary. And even his lifelong contempt for liberals developed in part from the way his mother's

---

[4] Lincoln made two trips as a young man to New Orleans, once in 1828 at the age of nineteen and again when he was twenty-two. It was from this second trip that the unverifiable story grew that he had said about slavery: "If I ever get a chance to hit that thing, I'll hit it hard." [Benjamin P. Thomas, *Abraham Lincoln*, New York, Alfred A. Knopf, 1952, 17–18, 24.]

[5] Bertram D. Wolfe, *Three Who Made a Revolution*, 1948, Boston, Beacon Press ed., 1955, 75, 87–88 and Edmund Wilson, *To the Finland Station*, 1940, Garden City, Doubleday Anchor Books ed., n.d., 366–367.

good friends abandoned her after the arrest and execution of her son Alexander.[6]

From private impressions to public cathexes

When Lasswell spoke of the displacement of private aggressions on public objects, he only somewhat overstated and oversimplified a major verity in political behavior. It makes little sense to abstract from personal context the ideology and public actions of either political leaders or ordinary citizens, even though the direct interpersonal, proximal experiences of people are not the sole basis for the formation of political outlook and action. But it is doubtful that ordinary and extraordinary people would ever enter "the stream of history," as it is so loosely called, if they were not pushed into it partly by direct, proximal experience. The founding of a political party, the initiation of a political movement, the inception of a revolution in a turbulent society (indeed its conception in the minds of intellectuals)—all such actions must as a general rule take place in partial consequence of the direct experience which forms people's images of and loyalty or hostility to large and distal groups.

But it also makes little sense to abstract proximal group influences (which are derived from the social, affectional needs) from other influences derived from the physical needs, or from self-esteem or self-actualization. A hungry person is likely to believe some person or group is depriving him of food. A slave who is jailed or lashed, thereby suffering physical deprivation and either shame or disgrace, is jailed or lashed by some one person or by a group. A peasant whipped by a Russian landlord, a Middle-Western American farmer in 1854 who sees his neighbor from the Deep South get rich by the use of slave-labor, a frustrated would-be artist who projects his anger on Jews whom he actually sees in Vienna, or an African who remembers being kicked by a white man—all are abandoning old ties or establishing new ties in politics in consequence of immediate, proximal, personal experience. Ideology may with more or less accuracy rationalize and explain such actions but it has little to do with causing them or the related attitudes. Lenin's eventual conversion to Marxism occurred after his brother's

---

[6] Wolfe, *op. cit.*, 86. Note also that Lenin was moved to prosecute a racketeer river-boat operator, not when he got a vision of Justice but when the racketeer forced Lenin and his sister to hire his steam launch. *Ibid.*, 86–87, and Wilson, *op. cit.*, 367.

death and his own expulsion from university for being his brother's brother.[7] India broke free of its externally exploited past after the Second World War, without its action being sanctified by Marx. China broke free of its internally exploited past about the same time, with an invocation of Marx. The common characteristic is an intense rejection of the past, not the rationale for the rejection.

Political reaction is far more personal, far less abstract and ideological, than either students of citizenry or citizens themselves are wont to recognize. It is easier to study documents written about major public events than it is to study the millions of people (ordinary citizens and leaders) who make these events, often without the benefit of literary effort or even literacy. This is not to say that people are at a loss for words to express reasons for action but that the effect of words is far less than the individual experience—through proximal contacts that mediate distal ones—of assorted and intensely felt deprivations. Revolutions historically have occurred in societies that were overwhelmingly illiterate: the leaders could read and write and speak, but leaders and ordinary citizens shared not so much their verbal as their personal experience. They have been moved far less by ideas than by common grievances that are described verbally but seldom consist of words. And even when the action appears to consist of words, as when a white man swears at a black man, the offense is the contempt—not a construct, an idea, but a feeling which the contemptuous words or tone serve only to communicate.

Routine, everyday proximal group experiences, mainly by way of an individual's family, are the most potent social influences. The limit of these routine influences ordinarily extends no farther than to neighborhoods, work associates, and fellow members of the same church, club, lodge, or local trade union. In a small town the routine proximal influence may be coextensive with the town, but beyond such boundaries such influence probably never exists. Nonroutine, exceptional proximal influence of the sort described as happening to Lincoln in his trips down the Mississippi, Hitler in Vienna, and Lenin

---

[7] See Wolfe, *op. cit.*, 88 and Wilson, *op. cit.*, 369–371, for the vivid impression that a short story by Chekhov, "Ward No. 6," made on Lenin. The picture of hospital squalor in the story is vivid, but it is hard, reading the story in an advanced culture, to appreciate Lenin's horrified reaction. Lenin, however, had recently lost his sister in a wretched hospital. The verbal picture reinforced Lenin's feelings and cannot readily do this to one who has not experienced such tragedy. Not the story but the reality of personal experience appears to have been crucial in Lenin's reaction.

in the loss by death of his father, brother, and sister fill out the picture of proximal influences which—to reiterate—are usually the indispensable mediators between the individual and his distal group identifications.

In group terms an individual becomes a Republican, Democrat, Christian Socialist, or a Laborite either because his family adheres to that particular party or because of some intense personal experiences with individuals outside his normal pattern of associations. The unusual, nonroutine personal experiences are not always like the peasant whipped by his landlord or the African kicked by a white man; the nonroutine experiences are not inevitably ones which alienate an individual from others who are members of the same broad society but of a different social group.

A Catholic suspicious of non-Catholics may have his negative feelings mitigated or changed altogether by a good non-Catholic friend. A business manager with the notion that all trade-union members are lazy may modify his view in consequence of seeing a group of machinists at work. A peasant may hate landlords in general but consider his own landlord a kindhearted person. An African political leader may find the edge of his hostility to white men dulled because of a decent white teacher he had in mission school twenty years before. Such interpersonal contacts across group lines serve to bind a broad society together, along with other forces making for a sense of community.

Small towns mediate the nation

Small towns form a kind of transition community between the proximal family and the clearly distal communities of metropolis, state, region, or nation. Although not necessarily the bridges to distal communities, small towns combine some characteristics of proximal and distal groups. An ordinary citizen in a small town may see the mayor in person less often than he hears or sees the prime minister or the president of his country on radio or television. But when he does see the mayor, it is as a casual acquaintance who is like a neighbor and not like an awesome wielder of great political power. A workingman in the local lumber or cotton mill may act like a worker in a colossal factory in his desire for union organization, higher wages, and job security, but the plant manager or owner whom he sees occasionally cannot easily become a remote or awesome figure like a Wall Street financier or the president of a mammoth steel company.

The social structure of a small town in upper New York State has been subjected to careful analysis. It shows one pattern by which the individual relates to proximal and distal political communities. The village bears the pen name of Springdale and has a population of about 1700, plus about 800 who live on farms or in hamlets socially tied to Springdale.[8]

A proximal community

Despite considerable differences in income, wealth, education, and occupational skill, the citizens of Springdale and environs maintain the social cohesiveness of a proximal group, rather than of a distal group sharing common interests and values without close personal contact. Ordinary citizens sometimes grumble against the established and self-perpetuating coterie of local rulers and even at times listen attentively to opposition leaders. But with at least enough flexibility the local rulers respond to signs of protest and take at least minimal action, co-opt potential opponents in the matter emphasized in a European trade-union context by Roberto Michels, and stay in power.

Cohesiveness is maintained not just by the rulers' adaptiveness and use of co-optation. Cohesiveness is also maintained by sloughing off or discharging into other political arenas those problems on which conflicting positions may be taken by different groups within the community. In the case of public education, citizens as taxpayers inevitably oppose citizens as parents interested in better school buildings and teachers. The result is to rely on financial support from the state government, even though this involves loss of local autonomy on educational standards.

Divisions within Springdale are avoided also by what the authors call "the technic of particularization." Rather than generalize about the well-off being able to buy things that poorer people simply cannot afford, people limit their comments to a specific object acquired by a specific person. And rather than generalize about the effect of state- and nationwide marketing and employment problems, local citizens talk about the price of milk as set by a state agent, the threat to local merchants of chain stores, and (with some abstraction) about seasonal

[8] Arthur J. Vidich and Joseph Bensman, *Small Town in Mass Society*, 1958, Garden City, Doubleday Anchor Books ed., 1960. On the power structure in a comparable community, see Robert E. Agger and Vincent Ostrom, Political Participation in a Small Community, in Heinz Eulau et al., eds., *Political Behavior*, Glencoe, Ill., The Free Press, 1956, 138–148.

changes in jobs in an automobile components factory because of national fluctuations in automobile production. Stark appraisals of sources of dissent and tension are seldom expressed, even though indeed they are made on one level of consciousness and in time of serious crises (career disappointment, job loss, or loss of retail business) are clearly expressed.[9]

Cohesiveness is also maintained by a significant consensus on equalitarian values. On the verbal level these values iterate a belief that the people of the area are "just plain folks" and on the action level show a deference that is more mutual and reciprocal than one-sided. Along with the tendency to establish distinctions, there is a tendency to avoid making them pronounced.

Springdale links itself with the larger society by its voluntary decision to accept state and national aid and regulation rather than raise local taxes. Ideology is defeated by economic rationality: the town gets far more aid from the state than it does from locally assessed taxes, and about 95% of the state tax receipts come from the big cities in the state. It dissipates the hostility which the dependence and loss of indigenous individualism produce by a variety of means, which include a reaffirmation of small-town virtue against big-city vice, small-town Christianity against big-city atheism and other un-Americanisms, a recognition that local rulers have been triumphant in getting aid for road construction, and a denial that this means the state determines where the road goes.[10]

Partly by choice and partly by necessity Springdale is in some specific ways integrated into even the national community: 2500 people identify themselves and their local community with a community that consisted of 150 million people at the time of the study. Thinking

[9] Vidich and Bensman, *op. cit.*, 297–302.

[10] *Ibid.*, 30–34, 40–42, 300. In a somewhat diluted form the same processes seem to operate in "Elmtown," an urban-rural complex with a population of about 10,000. Although the here-relevant data were not so central as in the Springdale analysis, the study of Elmtown shows the same domination by a similarly constituted ruling group, the same pattern of relationships with the state government, at least with regard to the school system, and the same particularization of criticism so that its impact is limited to the specific situation. But social groupings in Elmtown are somewhat larger, more impersonal, more abstract. For example, in student elections of high school officers, there is some evidence that the adolescent portion of the community divides along class lines and coheres across class lines: students in the lower classes help elect students from the upper classes. [A. B. Hollingshead, *Elmtown's Youth*, New York, John Wiley & Sons, 1949, 68–82, 134, 146–147, 201.]

about local public problems is highly specific and usually excludes the broad generalization. Thinking about the public problems of the state and nation tends to be expressed in local tangibles—jobs, prices of goods bought and sold, etc.—or else in rather vague and quite stereotypical terms that reaffirm with a casual certitude the superiority of small towns over big cities, yet vaguely recognize a broad community of interests.

Springdale's ties with larger communities go beyond the state-financial nexus mentioned. Dairy farmers depend on a metropolitan market. New inhabitants in the village are university-trained members of highly skilled occupations, ranging from engineers to state administrators, physicians, ministers, and lawyers, and they did not become such in the village. Both informally and formally, these and industrial workers employed in large factories away from Springdale act as proximal mediators between older inhabitants and distal societies. Having had proximal contact with various aspects of the vague and awesome outside world—in industry, government, and university education—these mediators in their role as local residents soften the contrast between near and far, small and large, pure and impure. On occasion, notably through local politicians of state-party connections, these marginal residents serve directly the interests of the town.

It seems more probable, more like reality, to explain the loose coherence between small towns and the vast national culture of which they are part in such tangible, behavioral terms. To explain the ties in broad terms of unity derived from symbolic, ideological ties facilitates scholarly communication far more than it produces actual intercommunal solidarity. Enormous as is the influence of what are stereotypically called mass media, it does not have either the quality or the intensity of proximal contact in which subsocieties are linked by contacts extending from the back fence to the chat with the local lawyer to the personal lobbying of the lawyer in the state legislature or bureaucracy.

By reversing the telescope but not the objective in sight, we can say that the influence on the general public of a nationwide broadcast or telecast of political candidates is widespread but not very intense. The influence of one's neighbor talking over the back fence is not widespread but much more intense. Everyone can hear a candidate on television and radio, giving the same talk to all. But everyone also has family, friends, neighbors and work associates, who as social influences have far greater impact on the individual than even the most persuasive and sympathetic image or voice coming from television screen or radio speaker. A candidate can by his social and other influences establish a loose sense of community and a vague sense of direction. He can neither generate the community nor the profound forces which put it in nonrandom motion long before he ever steps up to the microphone.

If the discussion of distal group influences up to this point sounds more like a mere continuation of the chapter on proximal influences, the impression is not accidentally conveyed. For virtually everyone, the highly specific pattern of distal identifications is at crucial occasions mediated by proximal contacts. I am saying no more or less than that for almost all people, their social class is the people they associate with. Other social classes are people they occasionally meet or see. Their local community or neighborhood consists of people in those contexts, and their national community and political loyalties are the candidates and programs they have heard about from others whom they personally know and trust (or mistrust). And for most people, prosperity is not a concept but a well-paying job or business, civil rights consist of Negroes and whites together in schools and on busses or trains, and war is the memory of military service or the injury or death of a relative or friend.

Politics is by no means issue-free. Neither does it altogether consist of various patterns of groups holding hands in a vastly extended and cohesive family. But even the broadest issues are discussed characteristically in a social context that is fundamentally and continually proximal. Interactions with others as friends or enemies—positive and negative interpersonal cathexes—are a well-nigh universal ingredient of political thought and action.

After this discussion of the local community we bypass a consideration of class, which is so large a problem as to fit too snugly into anything less than its own chapter. We skip now to the matter of races, of the proximal-distal variety that help form the politics of more than the few people with the intense frustrations of Hitler.

Ethnics and politics

One of the most common and durable sources of friction is race. And race, with which ethnic group is here deemed synonymous, is hard to define. For present purposes our concern is not with the proper racial labels for various people but with what ethnic groups call themselves and others. If a person says he is Cantonese, that may be the most significant self-label in dealing with Manchurians. In

Honolulu, both Cantonese and Manchurians may call themselves Chinese, because in Hawaii non-Chinese do not distinguish between people from the north or south of China. An immigrant from Palermo may at an early stage of living in New York City call himself an Italian—though he had always in Italy considered himself a Sicilian. At a later stage he may call himself an American of Italian birth and at last a New Yorker from the East Side, with his son's Honorable Discharge certificate from the Army of the United States displayed on the wall.

The interaction in which the ethnic becomes prominent necessarily always involves insiders and outsiders. It is another subjective phenomenon; it depends crucially on what an individual *considers* himself and others to be. There were the ancient Greeks and what they called barbarians, that is non-Greeks; Jews who lived not "far" from Greece called themselves God's chosen people and excluded the rest of mankind from selection; Chinese and the similarly inferior balance of mankind; French who say Africa begins just south of the Pyrenees; Spaniards and the barbarous Indians in what Latin Spaniards came to call Latin America; Japanese and hakujin Western devils; Hindus and Moslems; Swedes and Germans; whites and blacks; blacks and blacks— that is, blacks of one tribe who defeated those of another tribe and sold them into slavery. All Nigeria is divided into three parts, in one of which dwell principally the Yoruba, in another the Ibo, and in the third the Hausa. And before the divisions in Nigeria there were the divisions noted by Julius Caesar in Gaul, which the Romans conquered; among the Anglo-Saxons, whom the Gallic Normans conquered; among the Celts, whom the English conquered. And the English in turn were politically won over by three members of ethnic minorities, Benjamin Disraeli, David Lloyd George, and James Ramsay MacDonald.

It may well be, as Madison and Marx have said, that the most common and durable source of political faction is the various and unequal distribution of property. But if this *is* so, it is so by default, because of the common, millennial inability to reduce the largest ethnic problems to political—that is, nonviolent—terms. Nations are the largest political units and are roughly coextensive with broad ethnic groups because it has been usually impossible to contain two or more such groups within one nation when they were of approximately equal power. England subdued the Scotch, Welsh, and Irish people but did not form the federation which would have been a political (non-military) device for exercising constitutional (limited and acknowledged) power. By similar means, Japan subdued the Ainu in ancient times and Koreans and Taiwanese in modern times, but the resultant political unity was like that between Britain and India before 1947, the Netherlands and Indonesia before the same year, France and Indo-China before 1954, and the Soviet Union and its satellites. The Austro-Hungarian empire, composed of Germanic and Slavic groups that shared almost no sense of either ethnic or political community, collapsed almost spontaneously during the First World War. There is little reason to believe East Germany would remain in close economic and political association with the Soviet Union if it had a choice. Tension has in the 1960s often been severe between Russian and Chinese Communists. Neither ethnic group has been able to dominate the other. The ideologies in the two nations are supposedly identical and their histories are economically comparable.

In each of these instances the conflict has not been economic but ethnic. Ethnic differences and conflicts are primarily political and only remotely forcible when they take place within nations where there is a dominant ethnic group and one or more clearly subordinate groups. Otherwise such conflicts appear to be too intense to be manageable by political means. Again, without forgetting economic divisions between rich and poor (which are not the only divisions between rich and poor), one of the largest problems of the twentieth century is to reduce ethnic conflict to political portions between nations. There is too much evidence of ethnic groups as nations making enormous material sacrifices in order to subdue other ethnic groups as nations, or to resist such subjection. We can reduce neither internal nor international conflict to nonethnic categories. Germany under the Nazis sought systematically to destroy Jews and Slavs. The Congo has suffered severe economic dislocation since gaining its independence from Belgium but has shown little inclination to return to economic order if the cost is a re-establishment of the old colonial relationship of racial tutelage and subordination.

Mental processes which cause people to sense ethnic distinction are probably not fundamentally different between and within nations. Psychological economy or Occam's razor or both suggest that there is much in common between the way a self-conscious Irishman feels towards an Englishman in London today and the way an Irish immigrant to the United States felt toward native-born, English-speaking Americans approximately a hundred years ago. The mental processes underlying wars involving "race" must be much like those underlying international conflict. But such analysis as has been done has emerged mainly inside particular nations. We can establish no more than hypothetical relationships between ethnics and politics on the intra- and international levels.

A corps of Soviet citizens on a technical mission in India may include individuals with names that are Ukrainian (Derevyanko), Armenian (Bagramian), or Great-Russian (Suvorov), yet each member of the corps will likely be self-consciously Soviet in the same way that a Prussian or a Swabian is self-consciously German in a foreign land. Middle-class Americans named Polanski, Adams, Conti, Ferrand, Kraus, and Jensen on a guided tour on Southeast Asia would regard themselves as members of a single quasi-ethnic group and would likely be so regarded in the nations they visited. The state of mind is far more crucial than the ancestry, which is important only to the extent the individual and others are conscious of it.[11]

One's self-image depends to a considerable degree on what others think of him, and perhaps this is the basis of ethnic distinction. Suvorov in Moscow is usually unaware of being Russian; Suvorov in Delhi is highly conscious of it. John Polanski in Chicago may think of himself as a Pole, even though he never learned his father's language; in Bangkok with his sport shirt and camera, he becomes aware of being an American. Differences in one or more manifest characteristics can cause others to cause a person to become aware of his "race." It is fairly easily distinguishable signs that produce this self-consciousness: skin color, language, dialect, clothing, and possibly name are among the most prominent. When these differences are classified and lumped together in a particular pattern descriptive of a particular group, ethnicity in the subjective sense has been established.

These distinctive characteristics would have no great political significance if it were not for the common tendency to establish inequality on the basis of racial distinction. A Dane is not just a man who speaks Danish, is easy-going, etc. He is—in his own eyes—not just different but a little better; in the eyes of non-Danes, probably not quite so good. A Jew is not just a person who happens to have been born of Jewish parents but—in his own eyes—is a scion of Zion, of a great race which has never quite been admitted into the society of not-so-great races.

---

[11] Theodore Roosevelt spoke of "the great fighting qualities of our race," by which he meant the American nation, which he no more specifically or objectively defined than to exclude Indians. See Richard Hofstadter, *The American Political Tradition and the Men Who Made It*, New York, Alfred A. Knopf, 1948, Vintage Books ed., 1954, 213.

The distinctions in the eyes of both majority and minority ethnic groups are apt to depreciate the outsider. Welsh consider themselves better than English, Italians in New York better than other New Yorkers. But above all, the majority group—however heterogeneous its ancestry—considers itself better than all minority groups. The rub lies in the numerical inescapability of minority status. Except in consequence of military or other foreseeable conquest, the member of an ethnic minority cannot escape the fact that there are more people who regard him as being inferior than people who—like him—regard his "race" as superior.

Ethnic antagonisms

When these ethnic distinctions become a basis for judging a person as better or worse, which they usually do despite contrary protestations, mutual antagonisms—racial wars—develop. The minority-group member, just as the majority-group member would, resents minimally the denial of recognition. Maximally he resents the overt expression by a majority-group member of revulsion, contempt, fear, or hatred. The antagonism reciprocally reinforces itself and the interaction may become intense enough to produce individual or group acts of violence.

The conflict between minority and majority group members arises from the individual mental conflict between the need to identify with others and the need to stand apart from others. If a person were indifferent to the opinions of outsiders and did not wish to join them, he would not sense separateness and inferiority. If a person did not wish to have his own identity apart from others, he would not likely, as a minority member, become a self-conscious member of the minority, when outside majoritarians regarded him only as an undistinguishable, undifferentiated minoritarian.[12]

This antagonistic mental condition manifests itself in several ways, perhaps the first and last—the beginning and ending—being a defensive self-consciousness as a minority group member. One becomes aware of being attacked or ignored; he reacts by expressing pride at his difference. If he is Italian, that language becomes not just his own language but that of great poets, singers, and philosophers. His ancestors are not just people, but descendants of the Caesars. Besides thinking these reassuring thoughts the minority group member asso-

---

[12] Majoritarian and minoritarian are used here with none of the connotations of Bolshevik and Menshevik.

ciates almost exclusively with others of the same group, living in the same neighborhood,[13] attending the same church, joining the same clubs. These thoughts and actions give him a sense of security which is the saving balm for the wounds of minority status, which contacts with the outside world continually reopen. For Swedes, it may be a particular rural neighborhood in Minnesota; for untouchables in Japan, their quarter of the city; for Jews, the ghetto in Warsaw. Most of the social life for minority group members takes place within such proximate, local, ethnic communities.

But contacts with the outside world are unavoidable, mainly because of economic necessity but also because of contacts by the children in school and at play. The foreman in the labor gang is likely to be of the same ethnic background and to act as a guide and interpreter between the majority society and the newcomer in his economic role. If there is a trade union in the shop, the steward may encourage him to join and thereby enter one group in the larger society.[14] Quite typically a fellow minority-group member who is active in politics will help out in such personal crises as finding a place to live, a job, and, when a fellow member gets in trouble with the law, an easing of the penalty. Historically, big-city political machines in America have acquired a solid core of support for their services to immigrants. The regularizing of such services through the establishment of welfare agencies by city, state, and national governments has contributed to the steady weakening of political machines.[15] These are gradually being replaced by party organizations composed

[13] See Robert E. Lane, *Political Life,* Glencoe, Ill., The Free Press, 1959, 252 on this point and ch. 17 for a sensitive discussion of the politics of ethnicity.

[14] H. Sheppard, The Union as a Political Influence: Ethnic and Generation Factors in Union Members' Behavior, *Journal of Social Issues,* **9** (1): 45–48 (1953). Older Polish members of the CIO were strongly pro-union in their vote for mayor of Detroit, yet ignored the union's stand against anti-Semitism; younger Polish members of the union were not so pro-union in their vote for mayor but were less anti-Semitic. The author's suggested explanation: younger Poles were less tied to traditional Polish anti-Semitism and to the trade union and were more assimilated to the values of American society, which include racial tolerance and diminish the importance of trade unions to the more generally assimilated younger member.

[15] The vote of minority-group members, notably Irish, Italians, Jews, and Negroes is heavily Democratic [see, for example, Bernard R. Berelson et al., *Voting,* Chicago, University of Chicago Press, 1954, 62] and the more intensely felt the minority status, the heavier the Democratic vote [*ibid.,* 72]. But Scandinavians and Germans tend to be Republican. [A. Campbell et al., *The Voter Decides,* Evanston, Row, Peterson & Co., 1954, 77.]

of more strictly amateur political actives. But whether paid or unpaid, it is still party representatives making the personal contact who introduce newcomers to political parties and help establish an enduring sense of political partisan community.

There is a continuous conflict in the minority group member's mind between his acceptance and rejection by the majority and his own acceptance and rejection of the majority. This produces tension manifest not only in tentative efforts to join the larger society but also in deliberate withdrawal. Minority group members apparently vote less at an early state of assimilation than later, but evidently they vote more than others whose ancestry is only remotely foreign.[16] To ascertain this with exactitude would require the canceling out of a variety of factors that relate to frequency of voting, such as income, occupation, education, urban-versus-rural residence, and such "personality" factors as the belief that voting is worthwhile.

The character of ethnic participation indicates that the major concern of minority groups as such is social and political recognition of their group. Members will vote for a candidate because he is of the same national origin, often quite regardless of his stand on any other issues. But it is hard to tell whether a low-income member of a minority is voting for a candidate because he is a member of the same minority or because such a candidate also is an effective spokesman of poor people.

Love those who persecute you

A common tendency of minority group members is to exhibit, along with hostility to the majority, a liking for and identification with the majority. This process of affirmation rather than denial varies greatly in intensity. In extreme form it clearly includes the pattern of what Anna Freud called identification with the aggressor. This has been the case in Nazi concentration camps where some prisoners adopted the style of dress, language, and even the values of the Gestapo guards.[17] In milder form it sometimes produces the anti-Semitic Jew, the Negro who is uncomfortable or ashamed in the presence of lower-status Negroes. This identification with the majority is also characteristic of the superpatriotic conformist who seeks thereby to atone

[16] See *ibid.*, Table 5.4, p. 78. On Negro voting see Angus Campbell et al., *The American Voter*, New York, John Wiley & Sons, 1960, 278–282.

[17] Elie A. Cohen, *Human Behavior in the Concentration Camp*, New York, W. W. Norton & Co., 1953, 177–179, 200–201.

for, forget, or retaliate for his father's Irish (or German) hostility to England and therefore his father's nonconformity to American foreign policy during two World Wars. One of its commonest forms is the tendency of a minority group member to show contempt for other minority groups which have not yet assimilated or which the majority continues to reject.[18] Thus Irish have become politically opposed to Italians in New Haven and to Jews in Boston, causing these latter groups to adhere to the Republican party for a period.[19] And Negroes in the Harlem district of New York, after decades of being on the bottom of the social scale, in the 1950s moved up enough to be able to look down on the newest arrivals, Puerto Ricans.

Such minority group identification with the majority was particularly manifest in the reactions to McCarthyism in America in the early 1950s. There is some evidence that Irish, Italians, and Germans tended to oppose anything that might be deemed even remotely pro-communist or pro-Soviet deviationism.[20] These ethnic groups supported conformism and witch-hunts with an intensity that cannot be attributed altogether to the sustained anxiety of the cold war or the Korean conflict. Like the recruit in the Army who finally learned to march in step, these groups were most vigorous in their denunciation of others whom they regarded as being out of step.

Religion plays a very important role among minority group members. The relationship is so close that Irish, Italians, Hungarians, and Poles have acted as Catholics and Catholics have acted as Irish, etc., so that the ethnic and religious categories are sometimes considered interchangeable.[21] But the independence of religion and ethnicity is emphasized by the clear Democratic majority among Irish Catholics and the Republican majority among Irish Protestants in the

---

[18] See E. S. Bogardus, The Measurement of Social Distance, originally published in 1928 and reprinted in T. Newcomb and E. L. Hartley, eds., *Readings in Social Psychology*, New York, Henry Holt & Co., 1947, 503–507. Excepting their own groups, Negroes and Jews follow the same pattern of maintaining social distance between themselves and other nationalities as do "Americans in general."

[19] Lane, *op. cit.*, 236–237. Samuel Lubell reported that Irish in San Francisco in 1946 opposed a referendum whose effect was to favor civil rights for Negroes. See his *Future of American Politics*, New York, Harper & Bros., 1952, 97–98 and ch. 4, The Frontier Reappears.

[20] See Samuel Lubell, *Revolt of the Moderates*, New York, Harper & Bros., 1956, 64–74 on the ethnic situation in Wisconsin. See also his *Future of American Politics*, ch. 7, The Myth of Isolationism.

[21] As, for example, in Bernard Berelson et al., *op. cit.*, 83, where Catholics are called an ethnic group, along with Negroes and Jews.

1952 election.[22]   Minority group members can get great solace from their religion and from church attendance with congenial members of the same minority.   Along with their consciousness of pride in ancestry, language, etc., goes pride in their religious heritage.   Not until they have become more at home in the larger society does their concern with religion ease somewhat—at least as indicated by a rise in interfaith marriages after the Second World War.[23]

Religion and church-related activities have interacted with ethnicity to play a major role in the political efforts of Negroes in America in the 1950s and 1960s to achieve social and economic equality.   Many of the prominent leaders of the movement are Negro churchmen; churches are the main social centers where joint activity is organized and instigated.   Indeed as I suggest in the following chapter on religion and politics, the vitality of both Protestant and Catholic Christian churches in the twentieth century appears to have been evident almost exclusively in the contest for equal social recognition of ethnic minorities.   Both religious and nonreligious Jews have been prominent in the same effort.

The analysis by Fuchs of the politics of Jews in the United States provides further basis for judging the closeness of ethnicity and religion.   He finds two main reasons for the pattern of liberal and internationalist political tendencies among American Jews.   One relates to their insecurity in a society that has mixed both hostility and admiration in its attitudes towards Jews; the other derives from the values which, in their particular blending, are distinctly Jewish: love of learning, charitable social responsibility (Zedakeh), and "non-ascetism."   The first two are deeply rooted in Judaism as a religious-cultural entity, and Zedakeh has become indistinguishable from the main *social* tenet of the Christianity that emerged from Judaism.[24]

If Jewish values are necessary to explain political behavior of Jews, it cannot be overemphasized how integral to occidental civilization has been the role of Jews precisely because they have been a marginal and chronically condemned body of people.   Without the values they might have died out as a distinct ethnic group.   But without the hostile cooperation of the societies in which they have lived since the Diaspora

---

[22] Angus Campbell et al., *The Voter Decides,* 77 n.   Note that socio-economic status was not controlled and that the number of cases as part of an area-probability sample of the adult population of the United States is inevitably small.
[23] Los Angeles *Times,* 22 February 1958.
[24] Lawrence H. Fuchs, *The Political Behavior of American Jews,* Glencoe, Ill., The Free Press, 1956, 178–184.

in the second century after Christ, it is questionable whether they would have established contact with other people in ways that have enriched and humanized the culture of these other people. Without this contact, Judaism might well have remained distinctly tribal in its influence rather than providing the basis on which Jews individually and collectively have generally written and acted with more humane compassion than their supposedly humane, supposedly Christian hosts.

Ignoring overt difference and covert identity

Just what is the etiology of ethnic conflict within and between nations? We know that minority groups act as groups in politics. And a major line of research traces ethnic hostility back to childhood relationships with parents, implying thereby that it is altogether environmental forces that cause prejudice.[25] Similarly other researchers have blamed one aspect of society or another.[26] But the research is more massive and assertive than it is persuasive.

Socially derived forces do operate. People do despise minority groups because it is part of the ethic of their society to do so: they learn to hate because they are taught to hate. But the process is not, in the sense ordinarily used, by any means altogether social. We can recall the behavior of chickens and dogs to newcomers: individuals do not need cultural osmosis to generate a predisposition to discriminate against those who are different.

It is a bit paradoxical that psychologists who study the ability of

[25] See T. Adorno et al., *The Authoritarian Personality*, New York, Harper & Bros., 1950. Later researchers have found that men who exhibit both ethnic prejudice and "xenophilia" (a preference of foreign things and contempt for one's own society) have a relatively strong "self-dislike." [A. J. Brodbeck and H. B. Perlmutter, Self-dislike as a Determinant of Marked Ingroup-outgroup Preference, *Journal of Psychology*, **38**: 271–280 (1954).] Individuals who were highly xenophobic also were more highly authoritarian than the less xenophobic. [H. B. Perlmutter, Some Characteristics of the Xenophilic Personality, *Journal of Psychology*, **38**: 291–300 (1954).] This American study is corroborated in Australia. See Ronald Taft, Is the Tolerant Personality Type the Opposite of the Intolerants?, *Journal of Social Psychology*, **47**: 397–405 (1958), which found the ethnically intolerant group to be like the tolerant group in ego-defensiveness and "resembles the tolerant group in most respects by contrast with the intermediate group."

[26] E. L. Horowitz argues that "prejudices are derived from social sources rather than through biologically transmitted traits." See Development of Attitude toward Negroes, in T. Newcomb and E. L. Hartley, *Readings in Social Psychology*, New York, Henry Holt & Co., 1947, at page 515.

people to make perceptual discriminations belong to the same profession as do those who see no natural reason why people can and do see distinctions between ethnic groups. People need no more training, for example, to distinguish a white person from a black person than they do to distinguish black words on a white page. Ignoring the natural tendency of people to discriminate limits the possibility of understanding ethnic prejudice. To assume that most human beings who have lived long in one culture will not notice differences in those outside their culture is to assume a measure of mental dullness that in the animal kingdom would make survival difficult for wild zebras who could not distinguish between lions and giraffes. There is a great deal of prudishness and oleaginous sentimentality with regard to prejudice, just as there was with regard to sex fifty years ago.

Probably the major environmental cause for interethnic conflict is the simple fact of manifest difference. To a monkey in a zoo an Englishman and an Italian may look quite alike. To each of these members of the species Homo sapiens the difference may be readily apparent and highly significant. Furthermore, the initial reaction to difference is probably a feeling of threat: if it is different from me I must overpower it before it overpowers me. The reduction of prejudice and its elimination from politics and international power struggles requires not less ability to discriminate but more. It requires ability to discriminate between various levels of difference and similarity between people.

This amounts to a kind of rediscovery of nature, in the sense that it is only by the stripping away of obvious but acquired characteristics like language and dress and other customs that we are able to find similarity and identity with diverse people. Skin color cannot *be* stripped away. What this amounts to is discovering empirically the level on which such moral precepts as "all men are brothers" and "all men are created equal" are valid representations of reality. This in turn includes recognizing the distinction between the objective and the subjective. In Freudian terms this recognition is one way to describe a measure of maturity that probably no one ever reaches. It is hard for people to recognize that subjectively they act and react like other people when it is so easy to point to objective evidence of dissimilar physical features and behavior.

Since cultural and physical differences are here to stay, it is impossible to avoid recognizing them. But by a gradual cultural process people may come to recognize that identity exists on the fundamental, organic level even though it does not exist on the cultural and physical level. The great difficulty of this learning process suggests that the tolerance of ethnic diversity is as slow in coming as is the tolerance of any diversity in others. Interethnic hostility may persist, in a newly independent Nigeria, between Yorubans and Hausans, but various minorities are still faced with discrimination in the United States and the Soviet Union, two cultures which long have prided themselves on a high literacy rate and a dedication to the proposition that all men are created equal and seem sometimes dedicated to the process of making all men alike. Instead of recognizing that this is true only on a very basic organic level, these and other cultures seem occasionally determined to manufacture men who are equal and alike in their thoughts and actions. All of which points out the very limited success of moral exhortation, in contrast to the rather extensive success of direct intergroup association, in the task of reducing ethnic prejudice [27] and recognizing nonethnic individuality.

We cannot do more than conceptualize the environmental and organic aspects of this problem of race. But with some knowledge of how families, local communities, and ethnic and religious groups operate within the individual, we can now more easily consider the complex matter of his identification with political party—which is a special kind of summation of familial and other proximal and distal group identifications.

Party identification

Over half a millennium ago the Guelphs and the Ghibellines formed opposing elitist factions that were the engines of political controversy in thirteenth- and fourteenth-century Florence. In the nineteenth century, political group loyalties began to acquire a broadly popular base, and ordinary citizens developed enduring ties to party. It was thus not until the contest for universal suffrage developed in modern nations that political parties formed their broad popular base.

Probably most people in the world now live in nations that have political parties, but probably live where there is only one party per nation. In most countries there is no chance for an overt opposition group to form (for example, as in the Soviet Union or China). One can exercise his voice in such nations, for the one party, but no more.

[27] On the consequences of integrated versus segregated interracial housing projects, note the research project carried out in New York and Newark: M. Deutsch and M. E. Collins, Interracial Housing, in William Petersen, ed., *American Social Patterns*, Garden City, Doubleday & Co., 1956, 7–61, esp. Table 5, pp. 42–43.

In some nations there is a heavily dominated party with relatively ineffectual opposition (as in India since its independence in 1947, Mexico since Cárdenas, Venezuela of the early 1960s, and the United States during the 1820s, 1830s, and 1860s). In others there has been a multiplicity of parties, none of which could surely command a majority (as in Germany in the 1920s, Sweden, Norway, Switzerland, and Italy and France after the Second World War), and in still others a now normally stable two-party system (as in the United States, England, Canada, Australia, New Zealand, and tentatively Germany of the 1960s).

In nations with a highly developed electoral process, where voters can exercise their choice and not just their voice, party identification is truly widespread. In the United States members of trade unions, farmers' associations or business and professional associations, perhaps even collectively, constitute no more than a minority of the total adult population. In contrast, church and party identifications approach universality, which neither church attendance nor voting does. The proportion of adults in the United States who have no political affiliations is probably about one in eight or nine.[28] The proportion of people who report having no church affiliation probably does not exceed 4% in the United States.[29]

Many of the same forces that make church affiliation so uniform have the same effect on party ties—notably the influence of parents and spouse. But unlike churches, political parties cannot so effectively promise salvation or threaten damnation. Characteristically, non-Communist parties in Western Europe and America do not initiate the apolitical person who wants to join a party in formal ceremonies comparable to religious baptism or confirmation. They never expel an ordinary member, and they very rarely expel a member of the party leadership.

Party ties, though loose and often threadlike, appear to be quite

[28] In national samples taken from October 1952 to October 1958, the University of Michigan Survey Research Center found that the proportion of people who called themselves political independents (with *no* leaning toward Republicans or Democrats) or who were apolitical or "didn't know" varied from 9 to 14%. [A. Campbell et al., *The American Voter*, 124.]

[29] See U. S. Bureau of the Census, *Statistical Abstract of the United States: 1961*, Washington, D. C., 1961, 42, Table 38, Religion Reported by the Civilian Population. . . . : 1957. These data are based on an area sample survey and not on membership reports of churches. The sample includes information on all people fourteen or more years old. The proportion in only the adult population probably does not differ much from the 4% figure.

strong. This apparent strength is not evidenced simply by the intensity of feeling that strong partisans show at election time. It is also not dependent on the fact that if we know a person's party affiliation we can better predict how he will vote than if we know his occupation, religion, income, or education.[30] But the following data indicate that party identification is a distinguishable force.

In America people who call themselves strong (or independent) Democrats or Republicans vote more regularly than self-described weak Democrats or Republicans, and in other ways are more politically active.[31] Strong party identifiers express interest and concern over politics more than others do.[32] They are more likely than not to adopt the recognized stand on issues and to support the party candidacy.[33] They are, if strong Democrats, more likely than not to vote for a candidate of their party even if they dislike him, although strong Republicans are more likely to vote for the candidate of the opposite party.[34] Both strong Democrats and strong Republicans are more likely than not to vote a straight party ticket.[35]

A little reflection on these characteristics of partisanship indicates how reciprocal the relationships may be. A person who votes regularly may in consequence thereof become a strong partisan just as a strong partisan may therefore vote regularly. But the following data suggest that party identification is an independent variable even though it never in actuality functions apart from other variables. This is true of all variables except the ultimate one which is to be found, along with the pot of gold, at the end of the rainbow in Eldorado.

When a national sample was asked in 1958 about possible personal loss from the then current recession, Democrats who said they were hurt mostly disapproved of how the Eisenhower administration was handling the recession. Republicans who reported they were hurt by the recession on the average approved rather than disapproved of how the administration handled it. Those who were hurt were

---

[30] We can even more surely predict how a person will vote by asking him how he will vote, but that does not make the reply the determinant of the vote. It is as yet not possible to say that people vote in particular ways more in consequence of party affiliation than of such other forces as economic or familial interests and loyalties. But there is persuasive evidence that party loyalty is an independent and highly significant phenomenon.

[31] A. Campbell et al., *The Voter Decides*, 101–108.

[32] A. Campbell et al., *The American Voter*, 144.

[33] *Ibid.*, 129–130; and A. Campbell et al., *The Voter Decides*, 145.

[34] *Ibid.*, 95.

[35] *Ibid.*, 95.

stronger in their disapproval or weaker in their approval of the administration than those not hurt. But even when hurt, a person's party identification influenced his opinion of the administration.[36] And there is a higher correlation between subjective, self-labeled class-status and the vote among strong party identifiers than among weak and independent party identifiers. That is, people in 1952 who described themselves both as strong Democrats and as working class were more likely to vote Democratic than those who called themselves weak or independent Democrats and said they belonged to the working class.[37]

The "inheritance" of partisanship

If the phenomenon of party identification does operate independently, how does it achieve this (quasi-) autonomy? The most central group reason—social cause—for this distal identification is probably traceable to exactly the same proximal contact with parents that produces intergenerational stability (i.e., "inheritance") of religion and other aspects of the culture. Roughly three-fourths of all Republicans and Democrats inherit their partisanship from their parents, when both parents belong to the same party,[38] and in the 1948 Elmira Study these overall proportions were roughly the same when measured not by the respondent's party identification but by his vote as compared with his father's usual party preference.[39]

But parental or marital influences are not the only "social" ones, though doubtless the most important. One's friends, work associates, and neighbors all can proximally influence distal affiliation and only parental influence is per se relatively stable over time. If one marries a person of different party affiliation or works, plays, and chats over the back fence with differently inclined individuals, his partisanship may change.

All of these proximal contacts interact with one's socio-economic status, so that he is apt to adopt—particularly if he is upwardly mobile —the politics of a spouse, friends, etc. whose deference he wants to

---

[36] A. Campbell et al., *The American Voter*, 389–390. No apparent attempt was made to distinguish degree of injury from the recession. A man laid off at the factory has been hurt and so has the investor whose stock dividends have declined 10%, but the two men are not likely to be *equally* disturbed by it all.
[37] *Ibid.*, 366–367.
[38] A. Campbell et al., *The Voter Decides*, 99 and *The American Voter*, 146–147.
[39] B. R. Berelson et al., *op. cit.*, 88–89.

receive. He will not only socialize upward but also politicize upward with those he deems above his own family background. When the person is in a presumably stable socio-economic position, any tendencies to wander away from the political fold are apt to be cut short by reminders during the campaign of his status and past partisanship.[40]

Other factors that can influence partisan affiliation (either confirming it or changing it) are age, minority-group status, and economic self-interest. At least judged by studies in the 1950s and 1960s in America, young people have more often than not tended to prefer the Democratic party, and old people have tended to be more Republican than young people. But in either case there is an increase in strength of partisanship as people get older.[41] Minority-group membership tends to produce uniform partisanship, because of internal group pressures,[42] and perhaps also because of an independent but common individual reaction to discrimination.

These largely distal social influences depend heavily on proximal contact in confirming or changing party affiliation. One's family, neighbors, friends, and work associates are to a considerable degree intervening variables, quite literally carriers of more distant influences. The three most significant watersheds of partisanship in the United States have been the 1800 election of Jefferson, the 1860 election of Lincoln, and the 1932 election of Franklin Roosevelt. In the first two instances a party well established in its control over voters' loyalties and over government itself was quite displaced by a brand-new party that promptly established itself in both ways. These elections thus were major shifts in sovereignty, of profound proportions. In the first two cases the election was extremely close, with neither Jefferson nor Lincoln receiving a popular majority.[43] In all three cases the country faced a major crisis, produced a major leader, and established enduring political alignments and for a time almost destroyed partisan opposition. The Federalist party collapsed after the Jeffersonian Democrat-Republicans defeated it. Indeed it did re-emerge as a faction of the Democratic party in the 1820s. The Democratic party

---

[40] *Ibid.*, 254–257.

[41] A. Campbell et al., *The American Voter*, 162.

[42] Lawrence Fuchs argues that Jewish women vote more heavily Democratic than Jewish men because housewives' social contacts are largely limited to Jews, whereas the men at their work come in contact with contradictory political influences. [Fuchs, *op. cit.*, 93–96.]

[43] In Jefferson's case this has to be inferred, because the popular vote was not recorded.

after the Southern secession was out of power for twenty-four years and got back in only by adopting almost the creed and the ritual of the Republican party. One of the factors causing the defeat of Bryan, the Democratic candidate in 1896, was that Democratic President Cleveland had broken the Pullman Strike in 1894 and Republican candidate McKinley appeared to be as concerned as Bryan with working-class interests. And like the pre-Civil War Whigs, the post-FDR Republican party succeeded in winning decisively in 1952 only with a military hero for candidate. This Eisenhowered Republican party won elections in which Democratic voters indulged a temporary amour without contemplating partisan divorcement.

These three watersheds reflected a profound shift in individual partisan loyalties. To oversimplify, in 1800 there was reflected a sense that the new national government was becoming the captive of mercantile, manufacturing, and financial interests. In 1860 was reflected the intransigent hostility between farmers who tilled their own soil and plantationers who had slaves to do it. The free farmers had originally been a major segment of the Democratic party. As Free Soilers, they pulled out to vote for Martin Van Buren in 1848 while the Democratic party came increasingly under slavocratic Southern domination. In 1932 was reflected the growing discontent with business control of government. In each case the victorious party took advantage of widespread, deeply festering popular protest which the established party persisted in ignoring. In this sense the new parties effectively impowered large segments of the population that previously had been unenfranchised or, if franchised, ignored. In intimate terms, this meant to the neglected citizen the establishment of intense devotion to a party which indicated it wanted specifically to help him and proceeded to do so.

This intense devotion at different times, in the case of both Democratic and Republican parties, lost its raison d'être. But it has been handed down from father to son to grandson, as in the case of the little Austrian girl whose nursery rhyme bade her pray because the Swede Oxenstierne was coming (close to three hundred years after his death), and the case of poor farmers who persisted in their Jeffersonian-Jacksonian party loyalties. They did so despite the Democratic party's plantationer domination long before 1854, when the Republican party in the Midwest was created and at last attracted farmers who lacked slaves. Midwestern farmers persisted in their Republican loyalty down to the 1890s when they began to desert first to Populism and then to Bryan. They came back to the fold when economic circumstances improved and the Republican party seemed to be the lengthened shadow of Theodore Roosevelt. If it acts like the Democratic party of the 1850s and 60s and the Republican party of the 1880s, 90s, and 1920s, the post-FDR Democratic party will likely lose its broad and deep popular support and once again promote itself into minority status. If the party loses the basis for its popular support in a mechanical pursuit of tenure, the shades of Ostrogorskii and Michels will nod "we told you so" and those who insist that history need not repeat itself but keeps doing so will assume their wonted air of rectitude.

Having gained power for itself and its adherents among the populace, each new major party proceeds to rectify the injustices done to its righteous adherents. Then each party and its adherents believe justice is now final and complete and proceed vigorously to oppose the interest of other emergent groups. The yeomen farmers of Jefferson's time were satisfied after displacing seaboard men of mercantile and financial prominence. Following the Civil War, free farmers and businessmen became satisfied after displacing the Southern aristocracy from national political power. After the New Deal, labor became generally satisfied and like its predecessors in distributive injustice was now becoming increasingly a conservative force in American politics. In another generation the same may very well happen to Negroes, who in the 1960s are the major indigenous protest group in the entire nation. At least in New York City, Negroes have shown no great enthusiasm for granting equality to Puerto Ricans.

Parties, the churches of politics

Some interesting questions revolve around the reasons for party loyalty. Are parties altogether a matter of socio-economic interest and of cultural "heredity"? Why, in open and closed societies alike—in democracies and dictatorships—have parties been an indispensable or at least ubiquitous political institution? In some nations they have served to protect people individually and even more so collectively from unjust or arbitrary government action. In others they have facilitated control of individuals by the government. But in the twentieth century they are as universal political instruments as broadcasting transmitters and receivers. In a book about individuals, not institutions, this question cannot be properly answered.

But parties clearly have other functions than to control governments or to control citizens. For example, they provide a locus for beliefs and loyalties that are not equivalent to national loyalties or religious ties. Parties therefore may serve as a vehicle of public opinion that is distinct from some hypothetical government-sponsored supraparti-san national interest and may perhaps in time express a supranational partisan interest.

Other institutions have international ties—notably the Catholic church, but also various Protestant churches and increasing numbers of business corporations and trade unions. It is not inconceivable that international ties to political parties may, in decades to come, be established. These can provide a means whereby citizens can have political loyalties that are not considered subversive, in an age when national-ism grows while the world shrinks. A most likely place for this to emerge first is in Europe, by way of the Common Market. Intra-national parties in various member-states are in some instances so much alike as to suggest spontaneously the establishment of inter-national political ties of partisanship. Communist and other con-spiratorial parties work together internationally. There is no inherent reason why Socialist and Christian Democratic parties may not also do so, without subverting anything except antique nationalism or sub-stituting anything but Hammarskjold for Oxenstierne. In their under-standing of how affectionate and hostile ties to percepts can be dur-ably established in childhood, dictatorships show that they sense the relationships between the nursemaid in Austria and the warmaking and peacemaking Swedes. And speaking of war and peace, we can now take up some aspects of religion and churches. We can discuss the origin of those beliefs and institutions in whose name proximal and distal groups kill and embrace one another and with whose help they try to bear the unbearable guilt of having done it to the least of these, their and our brethren.

CHAPTER 7

Religion in politics

Varieties of belief systems

We need not posit religion as a fundamental human need to recognize its virtually universal existence. The basic needs that seem to manifest themselves in religion include the desire to belong, to be *in* society; by belonging to get a sense of recognition, as an object having intrinsic value; and to be able to move from day to day and decade to decade with some sense of purpose—that one's life is not animal-like in its routine producing and consuming but offers some hope that these prior needs, when partially fulfilled, will lead in some direction, to some personal, individual, and unique development. These needs relate to religion but they also relate to other, nonreligious activity.

Other needs are more uniquely relevant to religion and religious institutions (but relate also to other phenomena). These needs are again deep-seated tendencies: the desire to know and the desire to be secure in the satisfaction of a wide range of needs, from the physical to the developmental. The world, as it appears from infancy on, is beset with uncertainties that are related to need satisfaction and to the desire to know. People can ill manage, it seems, to get along without a belief system that presents a complete or at least adequate map of both the microcosm of the individual's life and the macrocosmic universe. Using a small tag to describe this vast problem, we may call it the intolerance of ambiguity. Using a larger tag, we may call it the need for security.

The need for security appears to be a second-order need, derivative from the perpetual failure of the organism to rest in a satisfied condition. In its manifestation as the desire to produce maps coextensive with the cosmos, the deep centrality of this need is far easier to attribute to others than to oneself. Thus a good Christian can describe his belief system as not a belief system but the Truth. A good Marxist can similarly describe his belief system, reaching dogmatic altitudes of unawareness and hyperconformism in the Stalinist era that probably have not been scaled since the Reformation and the Counter-Reformation of the sixteenth century. The tenacity with which such devout believers hold their views indicates how difficult they would find it to live without their Truth. Dostoevski moved in his own mental development from anti-religion to a parochial Russian Christian mysticism, which strangely does not limit the universality of his writing. Koestler, another writer of universal appeal, describes the anguished movement of Rubashov, in *Darkness at Noon,* from denial to acceptance of the Party and Marxist dogma as the Party interprets it—because otherwise Rubashov's life would be without purpose, and now it is too late for him to adapt to or adopt another belief system. Perhaps Stalin's deep need to be sure he was right accounts for much of his intimate savagery toward dissenters.

Even those who have an awareness of this need for a fundamental, holistic cosmic map are not always free from the same need themselves. Thus some scientists have either a conventional belief system (a religion) or are so certain they have no need for a belief system other than Science, which is not a belief but Truth, that they show symptoms of tension (either anxiety or fear) when the question is raised as to the wholeness of their science, at least as a method.

The truth or falseness of any of these belief systems is not here in question. The fact remains that there is so much uncertainty—so little verified fact and tested theory—that all people in one way or another have and continuously employ a belief system, at least methodologically to fill out the vacant parts of the map. And if they are altogether sure (or altogether unsure) that they have a freehold in perpetuity on Truth, they are apt to insist that others agree with them—and either burn dissenters at the stake, shoot deviationists secretly in prison, or impugn the intellectual integrity of colleagues, teachers, or students with whose substantive or procedural beliefs they disagree. This is not an argument for a vacuous uncertainty or an assertion that everyone's dogmas are as good as anyone's. It is an argument for the realization that all people have a belief system and, since all have it, for including in it the possibility that one's belief system may contain at least a few minor defects. That is, it is an argument for a recognition of the reality of uncertainty and of the universal reaction to it. Only for purposes of keeping the discussion within systematic bounds

is the substance of this chapter confined to what are more conventionally known as religions.

We need not reunite church and state, even conceptually, to recognize that churches and their adherents have had enormous influence
on government, and government on churches. In the Western world
these two social groups have been interacting for over two thousand
years. Their interaction would not have political significance if religion were not such a strong force that most people have adhered to
its tangible aspects, churches—sometimes to the point of accepting
death—when governments have tried to control the churches. And
some people, as in Europe in the sixteenth century, have even preferred death to submission when churches have tried to control government or at least assume the functions of government. There have
been martyrs not only in behalf of churches but against churches.
And there have been established churches, like Communism, that became established in the name of anti-clericalism, anti-religion.

Since, in this book, we are primarily concerned with individuals
rather than institutions, it is here appropriate to consider churches
not as institutions, but rather as objects of distal identification of
individuals, whose religious loyalties have had influence on politics.
Unfortunately churches have been studied far more as institutions
than as objects of individual loyalties. This makes it impossible here
to do more than speculate on the relevant group identifications in past
centuries and add what few data are available on the current relation
between the individual, his religious beliefs and religious institutional
loyalties, and government.

Persecution, rule, joint rule, separate rule

From its unpromising beginnings in the first few decades after its
founder was put to death, Christianity developed almost explosively.
From a neo-Judaic sect with some popular support among the poor,
it reached the point where it was tolerated, and then within three
centuries of Christ's death became de facto the established, officially
blessed, and officially encouraged religion of the Roman empire. No
longer despised and rejected of men, the church became so "rich and
mighty," in Burckhardt's phrase, that its history for the next twelve
hundred years was one in which an uneasy balance prevailed between
temporal and spiritual power. Government which had recognized or
been compelled to recognize this extra-legal, at first scarcely respect-
able, incorporation of believers in Christ, found it had permitted the

survival of a healthy body clerical that for over a thousand years sometimes threatened to devour the body politic. If government is that
group which, by its ultimate control over the means of coercion, is the
final maintainer of order, regulator of actions, and adjudicator of
disputes, then during this period the church often became the governor of government and in some areas, government itself.

Neither sacerdotium nor imperium ever quite succeeded in devour-
ing or enslaving the other, but there were some tense periods in which
rulers temporal and spiritual may have regretted ever having established what apparently was a mutual dependence. Around the year
303 government seemed determined to destroy Christianity in a savage pogrom against Christians. In 313 by the Edict of Milan the
Christian church gained official toleration during the reign of Constantine. Ten years later the government began to seek control of the
church. In 324 Constantine put down an anti-Christian revolt led by
his former fellow-ruler Licinius. One year later he called the major
disputants of church dogma to a Council at Nicaea. In doing this
he was not only lending official prestige to the Christian church, he
was also acting as the chief magistrate in the settling of a serious
policy dispute, which had grave consequences for the maintenance
intact of the imperium and of himself as imperator. In twelve years
government had moved from explicit tolerance to implicit control of
the Christian church.[1]

In a doctrinal controversy two hundred years later the Emperor
Justinian had the Pope physically seized. The emperor then (548)
forced him to approve the imperial order establishing Justinian as the
arbiter of a "purely" sacerdotal dispute. Sacerdotium had lost the
battle but not the chronic war. Despite the setbacks, the pressure of
the church to control increased, reaching the point in 1075 where a
vigorous reformist Pope, the son of a peasant, Gregory VII, issued a
forthright dictate that his decisions were absolute, not subject to
criticism by anyone on earth, and that the Pope could take crowns

[1] Compare the intimate, somewhat gossipy and cynical account in Jacob Burck-
hardt, *The Age of Constantine the Great*, Garden City, Doubleday (Anchor Books
Edition), 1956, chs. 8 and 9, 233–324 with the more mature account of Charles
N. Cochrane, *Christianity and Classical Culture*, New York, Oxford University
Press (Galaxy Books Edition), 1957. Burckhardt's work was first published in
1852; Cochrane's in 1940. A history of institutional developments, with regret-
tably little attention to behavior of people, is contained in the *Encyclopedia of the
Social Sciences*, New York, The Macmillan Co., 1934, vol. 13: 246–272, Religious
Institutions, Christian.

from emperors and absolve subjects from allegiance to them. The Pope then proceeded to apply reforms to the clergy in Germany. Some high clerics had been selling divine forgiveness and living with women, in defiance of orders from Rome and without bothering to disavow poverty, chastity, and obedience. King Henry IV of Germany also became the involuntary object of papal reform, to which he responded by calling a council of bishops in 1076. The bishops, some of whom had by now been excommunicated, resolved that Gregory was no longer Pope.

Henry wrote Gregory saying that he was "at present not Pope but false monk" and bade him depart the Papacy with the words "Descend, descend, and be damned through the ages." Gregory replied in the name of Saint Peter, excommunicating both the German archbishop and King Henry and forbidding all Christian subjects to obey Henry. Several potent German princes, fearful that their King would act like a Roman emperor, sided with the Pope. In February 1077, they invited Gregory to come to Germany to decide whether Henry or someone else should rule temporally. But Henry decided that pride indeed might precede a fall and a haughty spirit, destruction. In the dead of winter he traveled over the Alps, and as a humble, ill-clothed penitent he knelt before the Pope and asked absolution from the man he had called "false monk." Gregory could do nothing but grant it and decline the princes' invitation to visit Germany. The dispute continued, with Henry once again deposed and excommunicated by Gregory in 1080—and Gregory deposed and virtually exiled when Henry entered Rome in 1084 and declared his stooge, Guilbert, to be Pope. Whether this conclusion meant that the meek had received or lost inheritance of the earth is hard to determine.

The conflict between these earthly antagonists, each of whom saw himself as the protagonist of God and good government, persisted until the sixteenth century—each trying to control the affairs of the other, each citing the divine origins of his earthly claim to rule. It took the Renaissance and the Protestant Reformation to mark a major turning point in the conflict, after which the power of the church vis-à-vis the state steadily declined. This "turning point" is a short phrase for a long and bitter struggle. But the major contention no longer was between church and state: the dispute was over the question of whether a given country was to have Protestantism or Catholicism as its officially, governmentally sanctioned religion.

Unmodish as it is to consider, in the secular twentieth century, the relation of religion to politics, it is almost impossible to overestimate the role of religion and churches in Western European politics. One consequence of the chronic, often raw struggle between sacerdotium and imperium for a dozen centuries is that there has never been deeply entrenched, in Western conventions about political power, the belief that either the members of the clergy *or* the members of the government have complete hegemony. This is in contrast to relationships between sacerdotium and imperium in that branch of Christianity that remained under Byzantine control in Eastern Europe. The Orthodox clergy never seriously contested the authority—even the spiritual authority—of the long line of Russian rulers. The path for absolutism was never in Imperial Russia blocked by clerical resistance. The church-state conflict in Western Europe produced a tacit concensus of mutual tolerance. Both kings and clerics and later Protestants and Catholics exhausted themselves in savage conflict. Had there been decisive victories, the only victor would have been arbitrary power. In Eastern Europe there was no group that could or at least would oppose governmental omnipotence, and there was thus never a tradition opposing absolutism. Traditions of law and constitutionalism, which began long before Christianity in Babylonian, Judean, Greek, and Roman culture, were reinforced by the church-state struggle in Western Europe. These traditions virtually expired a-borning in Eastern Europe, even before Russia became known by that name.

The appeals of Christianity

Judging from the directly expressed "reasons," these church-state and church-church-state struggles seem futile, because the results denied conclusive victory to each antagonist. Why then did they occur? If Catholics and Protestants and free thinkers can live peaceably in modern states now and if the establishment of government as final but constitutionally restrained arbitrator has not destroyed the autonomy of churches in, for example, England and North America, why such a fuss, from 325 to 1517 (or 1648)? [2]

Why did Christians oppose pagans in a Roman culture that was quite civilized and at last succeeded in gaining the support (and shortly before his death, the conversion to Christianity) of Constantine the Great? Why did Popes oppose emperors and emperors Popes? Why did Protestants oppose Catholics in a series of wars so intense

---

[2] The dates refer to the Council of Nicaea, Luther's posting of his Ninety-Five Theses, and the Treaties of Westphalia.

as to seem to bathe Europe in blood? Were people bored? Quixotic? Were they unleashing from rational control their Freudian death instinct in an orgy of killing and destroying? Were they separately and collectively so pure of heart that all they saw was a fundamental struggle between good and God on their side and evil and the Devil on the other? How did distal groups come into being that allied Constantine with a growing body of Christians; pitted the inhabitants of Rome against Tuscan Gregory VII after the Norman armies sacked the city in 1084 in revenge against the German Henry IV; aligned German noblemen with Luther against Rome and Anabaptists against Luther; and caused Henry IV of France, a Protestant by upbringing and conviction, to become a Catholic in 1593, four years after he gained the throne but not the power of king?

We could say that these events were the consequence of countervailing group identifications or of the need for rulers to recognize that new groups were becoming powerful and that their support was needed in order to acquire or maintain political power. Emperors opposed or supported churchmen because the latter represented substantial bodies of citizens; churches supported rulers because substantial numbers of communicants supported particular rulers. In a sense this is the substance of the kind of social analysis that explains broad phenomena ultimately in terms of conflict between classes. But let us consider—on a necessarily hypothetical level—how these groups that have conventionally been described as religious came into being.

At first it was poor people who paid attention to Christians preaching the universal brotherhood of all men. Poor people did not have to stretch their imagination to the edge of the universe to appreciate teaching that said poor men were as good as rich and that those of low status would truly have an easier time entering heaven than those of high position. They did not really have to believe in the brotherhood of all mankind to feel (consciously or unconsciously) that the new cult gave them identity, dignity, and worth that they had never had before—that they were indeed as good as anyone else. This reaction to Christianity was ultimately an *individual, private* one.[3] The

---

[3] It is most difficult to describe to literate, psychically quite secure, middle-class people who might read this book, what it must have been like for a lower-class person, despised and rejected of men, to get the Christian message; and these people would never read such a cold, abstract book as this one. The sensation must have been somewhat like that of some nineteenth-century intellectuals, alienated from the bourgeois culture in which they lived, reading Marx for the first time and becoming dedicated Marxists—or of a person wanting to be loved

proximal-group identification came later, when people similarly persuaded by the new belief got together to strengthen their dignity with the psychically and physically potent force of association. The distal group identification came when these people developed religious institutions such that, as individuals, they shared loyalty to a common set of beliefs whose instrument the church was and then developed a loyalty to the church as such. A paradox developed. The brotherhood of all mankind came to constitute less than all mankind. In excluding some people, there developed a sense of in-group against out-group—believers against infidels. This paradox has apparently escaped many if not most Christians. The universalist religion became a tribal belief, in even its broadest terms virtually limited to the white race and virtually excluding people of darker skins.

The relation between proximal and distal group identification cannot be overemphasized. The original disciples were personal, closely proximal associates with Christ. The expanding membership grew from personal context, minimally in gatherings at which the disciples or the apostles (notably Paul) established that intimate contact which exists between speaker and listeners. The personal religious contact has continued without intermission ever since. The most important link has been between parents and children, but is bolstered by the periodic reinforcement of contact between a priest or minister and his mentors and between parishioners and their priest or minister. A group identification which may properly be called distal is constantly reinforced by proximal contact.

But the formation of particular religious societies and the political consequences of those distal groups cannot be explained solely in group terms. It is true that something like Gordon Allport's functional autonomy seems to develop: people declare themselves to be Christians or members of some Christian church for the sake of being members of a broad group.[4] But there is no reason per se why Christian churches should develop and endure rather than any other comparable group, unless Christianity has significance additional to that of any other distal groups, in their socializing function as such.

---

and then finding that indeed some beautiful girl (or handsome man) did love him (or her). The girl or the man was beautiful (or handsome) because he loved him (or her). It must have been like the feelings that drew some Russians and Chinese, like Lenin and Mao, rejected by the old society, into the Communist movement before the respective revolutions.

[4] See G. W. Allport, *Personality: A Psychological Interpretation*, New York, Henry Holt & Co., 1937, ch. 7, The Transformation of Motives.

The Christian belief in the equal dignity of each person probably has been the central though not solitary reason for its great growth over nearly two thousand years, and for its great bimillennial political influence. During the reign of Constantine a series of reforms rather considerably ameliorated some of the harsher aspects of Roman law, and these reforms were a consequence of demands of Christians.[5] Women, children, and slaves were the prime beneficiaries of the reforms, which did not eliminate but did reduce their inferior legal position. Divorce at the whim of the husband was prohibited and could be obtained only for specific reasons. Slaves could not be so sold as to separate a man and his wife. Children born out of wedlock became legitimate when their parents subsequently married.[6] Such legal reforms as these by no means established even at law a classless, casteless society. They nevertheless were so significant as to give real meaning to the power of Christianity and the Christian church, and to people who benefited from its political influence. The Roman church maintained its political power and its emotional hold over people during the Middle Ages, for reasons in addition to the inertia of being the established religious institution. It did not depend on the functional autonomy of the drive of church membership but actively promoted humane social relationships.

Rebirth and reform

The tremendous social and political explosions that caused the Renaissance and Reformation are far too complicated to be reduced to monistic psychological explanations. It can surely be said that the Catholic church had become so complacent and corrupt as to have critically lost the equalitarian appeal which so centrally contributed to its popular support for twelve hundred years. In a long step from the simple church organization in the time of Paul the Apostle, the church hierarchy had become intricate and highly stratified. Top-ranking churchmen tended to come from high social status. Forgiveness of sin could be bought for a price—which automatically discriminated against the poor just as did the later ability to buy oneself draft exemption during the American Civil War. In an era when book printing was developing with explosive rapidity, the church continued

---

[5] Cochrane, *op. cit.,* 197–198.

[6] *Ibid.* See 198–201 for a description of the extent and limits of reform under Constantine.

its resistance to printing Holy Scriptures in popular tongues. Literate nonchurchmen were denied direct access to writings they believed to be divinely inspired. Clerics often lived in an ungodly manner that violated at least the vows of poverty and chastity. Strong forces were pent up and finally burst out of the institutional chambers of a church that had wandered far from its original precepts and whose hierarchs from Pope to priest often enough gave vivid proximal reminders of this vagrancy.

During the Reformation there were profound reorientations of distal group loyalties. The long century of violence and persecution by the protagonists of both Protestantism and Catholicism attests the intensity of the reorientation and indicates the limits of analysis in terms of group identifications. If group loyalties for the sake of belonging were the sole operative force, there should not have been any abandonment of the Catholic church, which to a remarkable degree was co-extensive with society and civilization in itself. It was the failure of the church to meet and adapt to old and new expectations of people individually and collectively—rather than a breakdown in church associations as such—which was the major force breaking the monopoly of the church. Church identifications arose that were sometimes radically new in style and were to remain strong and meaningful for at least four hundred years in the Western world.

Industrial revolution and reorientation

The Catholic church failed to maintain its uneasy equal power position vis-à-vis government and its religious monopoly over Christians. But after the Industrial Revolution the church with renewed vitality sought and to a large degree received the loyalty of much of the working classes. It succeeded notably in societies where the Protestant churches had become heavily dominated by and subservient to middle-class values and persons. In America this occurred in part because of the momentum of continued church membership among major segments of the working class. Starting with the Irish immigration in the middle of the nineteenth century and followed by the Central, Southern, and Eastern European immigrations up to the First World War, Catholicism endured among immigrants as one of the few continuing distal social ties with the Old World.

But, more than this momentum, there was a deliberate effort on the part of the Catholic church, starting no later than the 1891 Papal encyclical Rerum Novarum, to revitalize its ancient creed. It was adapted to the class structure of industrialized society. In industrialized societies the church now became the champion of the downtrodden.

The Catholic church has failed to do this in Latin America, indeed to a degree in Latin Europe, from France to Portugal, Spain, and Italy. This failure has been a significant factor contributing to the alienation of poor people in these regions from the church of their ancestors and to their readiness to accept right- or left-wing radicalism, for example, in the form of Peronism or Communism. The inertia, the functional autonomy, of age-old distal loyalties has weakened. New social identifications have emerged, significantly related to the satisfaction of needs other than the social needs as such.

Society in the fourth century was comparatively undifferentiated. During its early centuries, the "universal" church, no longer a subversive but now an official organization, had available limited means of spreading its beliefs, in a society that had a comparatively simple economic structure consisting of quite small, isolated, and self-contained parochial units. In these circumstances the church was the major, perhaps the sole, social instrument for expressing the desire for subjective equality among socially depressed people. The hold of the Catholic church on poor people has probably continued with few interruptions, down to and beyond the Industrial Revolution. Religious reform in Germany in opposition to the Catholic church in the sixteenth century was led by Protestant churchmen, backed by landed noblemen. This reform either ignored or savagely suppressed peasants. The same was true in sixteenth-century France, when political opposition to the monarchy was led by Huguenots, likewise largely recruited from the landed aristocracy and the mercantile bourgeoisie. The massacres of Saint Bartholomew's Day in 1572, at least in Paris, set the faithful canaille against the apostate, Protestant nobles.

The advent of industrialization has produced more pronounced and objective differences in economic function. Modern communication has made it possible for people of like interests to form new associations that no longer depend on churches to gain either sanctity or popularity. The consequence for Christianity in its institutionalized form has been a widespread dispersion of political protest through new social institutions quite outside and even in opposition to churches. The chartists in England in the 1840s, trade unionists and anti-slavery abolitionists in the United States in the 1830s to 1860s, utopian socialists in late nineteenth-century England and France, and trade unionists in France, Germany, and Italy in the early twentieth century—all these are instances in which reform has been undertaken largely outside the framework of church organization. If many individual English Methodists supported Chartism, clergymen of the Church of England opposed it. There was evidently no bold, specific stand by the established English church on the side of the downtrodden. If individual clergymen after the Industrial Revolution did support the less equal, the large church organizations were indifferent or hostile, until almost the end of the nineteenth century.[7]

This raises the question of the continuing influence of religious distal group identifications on politics. Do they retain any vitality, or have they become so weak, so lost in a considerable range of other identifications that individuals no longer think of their church when political issues are raised? Have churches lost the social appeal that made them such a potent political force for "good" and "evil," [8] from the age of Constantine down to the often courageous anti-slavery efforts of some clergymen in the United States before the Civil War?

Opposing the actions of abolitionists were not only the Christian churches in the South of the United States but also dignified church members in the nonslave states. Protagonists and antagonists of slavery found in the same Holy Scriptures a justification for their views. This contest and the Civil War that climaxed it are reminiscent of the wars of the Reformation in Europe. Both sides appealed to a Christianity that traces back, often arrogantly, to the teachings of Christ. But there is no public issue on which Protestant churches in America have taken such a vigorous stand since 1860. There has been a marked demonstration of the theses of Weber and Tawney on the

[7] On the chasm between Christian principles and Christian churches in early nineteenth-century England, see Mark Hovell, *The Chartist Movement* (T. F. Tout, ed.), Manchester, Manchester University Press, 2d ed., 1925, 82–90, 200, 308; and Elie Halévy, *A History of the English People: 1830–1841* (E. I. Watkin transl.), New York, Harcourt, Brace & Co., n. d., vol. 3, 138–158. The Church of England showed even less interest than did Methodists. And Halévy says: "Possibly the majority of the Wesleyans were Tories. Had not their leading representative, the Rev. Jabez Bunting, declared that 'Methodism was as much opposed to democracy as to sin.' And Conference [the Methodist church organization] had expressly forbidden Wesleyans to become members of the trade unions. . . ." *Ibid.,* 156–157.

[8] I have in mind as "good" actions by churches, the Protestant Reformation which not only gave new life to the ancient Christian faith but also revitalized and purged the Catholic church itself; and as "evil" actions the Catholic Inquisition and the Protestant brutality to dissenters in Germany, Geneva, England, and New England, notably in the sixteenth and seventeenth centuries.

connection between capitalism and Protestantism. American Protestant churches in the late nineteenth and early twentieth centuries adopted a middle-class outlook toward social class relationships. This Protestant outlook reflected an uneasy, very mildly critical dependence on the material support of middle-class entrepreneurs, managers, and members of the professions.[9]

The secularization of reform

Protagonists of the downtrodden, of the less equalized people in a society dedicated to equality, were no longer Protestants but often protestants against Protestantism. The vigorous critics now appeared in academic life, including Charles Beard, Thorstein Veblen, Robert S. and Helen M. Lynd, and Adolph A. Berle, Jr., the last himself a son of a minister. Other critics were extracurricular, like Norman Thomas, another minister's son; or trade unionists like Samuel Gompers, Eugene Debs, John L. Lewis, and Walter Reuther; or writers like Sinclair Lewis and John dos Passos; or the vigorous Marxists, Stalinists, Trotskyites as a small minority of the intelligentsia.

The Protestant churches, although not altogether silent, were not the prominent spokesmen of the downtrodden that these other categories were. The Catholic church, even less silent than the Protestants, quietly served the interests of the large working-class segments of its communicants and formed the Association of Catholic Trade Unionists. But again the Catholic church did not serve as a prominent protagonist of poor people, and in Latin Europe and Latin America it showed the same querulous myopia that it did in eighteenth-century France. The main effective social identification *of* poor people has been with trade unions. Their identification with highly oratorical, stream-of-exalted-religious-experience sects and revivalist preachers has served as an escape rather than as a means of solving the problems of inequality.

In two recent crises American Protestant churches have shown a measure of the same vitality that caused so many of them to take a vigorous stand against slavery a century before. One of these had

[9] For a discussion of church activities in the late nineteenth and early twentieth centuries on social issues in America see Carl N. Degler, *Out of Our Past: the Forces that Shaped Modern America,* New York, Harper & Bros., 1959, 338–351. For a classic report on church-connected social reforms in the case of alcoholism, see Peter H Odegard, *Pressure Politics: the Story of the Anti-Saloon League,* New York, Columbia University Press, 1928.

quite limited popular appeal and an elitist orientation that was almost inherently unavoidable. The other had an appeal to more usual equalitarian beliefs and could not appropriately be described as elitist-oriented.

In the angry public pursuit of noncomformists, known as McCarthyism, in the 1946–1954 period, many individual clergymen and some church organizations clearly and emphatically opposed the anti-constitutional techniques used in the pursuit. With few exceptions, established organizations ranging from the United States Senate to trade unions, newspapers, service organizations, and businesses often expressed a cocky confidence which said McCarthy could be managed and was reminiscent of the way comparable German organizations responded to Hitlerism before 1933. Or these American organizations joined and encouraged the popular sickness. The people primarily affected by McCarthyism—intellectuals, scientists, and administrative employees of government—were not the obvious concern of any of these groups. Neither were they the concern of clergymen and churches. But many churchmen refused to assent by silence—as their antecedents had refused, a century before, in the slavery crisis.

In the second crisis, the one of much more general social concern, many American clergymen and churches, including now the Catholic church, reactivated their historic position by showing a new and outspoken concern about the degradation of Negroes. This reactivation of interest in a less-equal group gained force and focus in the 1930s (when Negroes accused of crimes were still getting a frontier type of summary justice) and continued into the 1960s, in the movement to further economic, educational, and social integration of Negroes. Unlike the McCarthyism issue, in which middle-class churches could be said to be advocating the interest of their own kind, in the Negro issue these same churches were showing a concern for relative strangers —for a social, economic, and ethnic group which was still predominantly low in its status. Nevertheless the major impetus for integration has come from individual Protestant churches whose membership is almost exclusively Negro.[10] Whatever the color of the churches involved, their stand probably will strengthen Negro ties of loyalty to both Protestant and Catholic churches, just as their loyalty to the

[10] Martin Luther King, Jr., the vigorous Negro minister who probably more than any other person has led the integration movement, spoke at a rally in Los Angeles in June 1961. The estimate of the proportion of whites who attended was about 10% of the total rally audience. Los Angeles *Times,* 19 June 1961.

Democratic party was established during the time of Franklin Roosevelt.

Among others, religious influences

Do these observations add up to the conclusion that the vital political influence of religion and religious institutions is now moribund or at least dormant in the world? So it would seem in the European and American continents, with the large exception of Negro integration in the United States. In Latin Europe and Latin America, the Catholic church far more often has appeared to be on the side of urban entrepreneurs and rural landowners than on the side of poor peasants and workingmen. To the extent that any association other than government itself has captured the still fluid loyalty of the downtrodden in countries where the gap between rich and poor is very wide, it has apparently been the group that Christians call the anti-Christ, that is, the Communist party. The Christian church, Protestant and Catholic, thus has found itself willy-nilly in the ironic position of defending the rich nations, and in poor nations, defending the rich people against the importunities of the poor. In terms of doctrine, the position is ironic because the founder of Christianity asserted that it would be hard for rich men to enter heaven and that the humble would inherit the earth. These predictions, expressed in the angry sociological dialect of Marx, Engels, Lenin, and Mao Tse-tung, precisely make up the program of what Christians call the anti-Christ.

As vehicles of widespread popular reform, Christian churches in the modern state have lost vitality but are not yet dead. In some of its pronouncements favoring the interests of poor people, notably since the anti-clerical bias of the Castro regime in Cuba became apparent, the Catholic church has indicated an awareness of the threat to its survival in Latin countries if its landowner and entrepreneurial ties are not broadened to include poorer segments of society. But even in the United States, where opinion research techniques are highly developed, it is difficult to determine just how influential churches remain. It is difficult to separate from other forces operating within individuals those that come from affiliation and identification with a particular church. The research attempt at separation has been made, nonetheless, and with considerable success.

Among the influences that have to be separated out before religious influence is revealed are these: objective class position, subjective class identification, ethnic or national class background, length of residence in a particular community (town or city, region, nation), degree of concern with politics, and strength of religious affiliation. Put in different words, this means that if a person is a Catholic in America, being such does make a political difference, but it is hard to tell how much difference—if he is also a workingman and considers himself a workingman, is a union member born of immigrant parents, has lived for a long time in a city, is not much concerned with politics, and regards the Catholic church as one of the most important groups he belongs to. Several studies on American voting behavior are here relevant.[11]

For precautionary purposes I have stated these religious differences in negative form, saying that being influenced by one's religion operates when other forces of group identification are not operating. This precaution is appropriate because these forces usually tend to operate as vectors pushing people's political behavior in the same direction as does their religion. Religion nonetheless is an independent factor in the same sense in which each person pushing a car down the road is an independent vector quite separate from the other-person vectors.

The closest relevant third-correlate between religious identifications and politics appears to be socio-economic status. Catholics are more

---

[11] *On Catholicism vs. socio-economic status*, see P. F. Lazarsfeld, B. R. Berelson, and H. Gaudet, *The People's Choice*, New York, Columbia University Press, 2nd ed., 1948, 21–25, and B. R. Berelson, P. F. Lazarsfeld and W. N. McPhee, *Voting*, Chicago, University of Chicago Press, 1954, Chart 24, p. 65. *On Catholicism vs. class identification*, Berelson et al., *loc. cit. On Catholicism vs. union membership*, A. Campbell, P. E. Converse, W. E. Miller and D. E. Stokes, *The American Voter*, New York, John Wiley & Sons, 1960, Table 12-1, p. 302 (which contrasts Catholics and non-Catholics; union members and non-union members; thereby uneasily allowing a cross-comparison of the two factors in Table 12-2, p. 306). *On Catholicism vs. ethnicity*, A. Campbell, G. Gurin, and W. E. Miller, *The Voter Decides*, Evanston, Ill., Row, Peterson & Co., 1954, 77 n. *On Catholicism vs. length of urban residence*, see B. R. Berelson et al., *op. cit.*, Chart 26, p. 68. The positive correlation between being Catholic, living long in a city and voting Democratic is attributed by the authors to long association with fellow-Catholics within the city. *Ibid.*, 67. The consistent finding that Catholics vote more heavily than Protestants [A. Campbell and H. C. Cooper, *Group Differences in Attitude and Votes*, Ann Arbor, University of Michigan Survey Research Center, 1956, 23] is probably a consequence in part of the concentration of Catholics in the cities. *On Catholicism vs. concern with politics*, indicating that the *more* politically involved one is, the *less* like other Catholics he will be in voting, see B. Berelson et al., *op. cit.*, 69. *On close subjective identification with Catholic church vs. loose identification*, see *ibid.*, 67 and Chart 26, p. 68.

apt to be workingmen than their proportion to the total population. There is strong suggestion that Catholics vote more as working-class individuals than as Catholics because class-status is a better predictor of vote than religious identification. This strong suggestion is fortified by an extensive study indicating that, in their preference for economic security, for greater political influence for working people, and in their 1944 Presidential voting preference, Baptists were far closer to Catholics than they were to Congregationalists.[12] Baptists, in their attitude toward the Papacy, central control of the church organization, and the direct moral responsibility of individuals to their God, are close neighbors of Congregationalists. Baptists have hardly been on speaking terms with Catholics since the days of Thomas Münzer in the sixteenth century—when the Protestant Reformation got into motion and out of the control of Martin Luther and his followers.[13]

Such influences as class-status, ethnic background, etc., probably outweigh church affiliation in mid-twentieth century America (and similarly in other developed industrial societies) as group determinants of political action. But religious influences still operate, sometimes directly and clearly. In an analysis that has the advantages and disadvantages of depending on gross voting data, Fenton has studied the issues of birth control and right-to-work (anti-closed shop) referenda in the United States. He has indicated that Catholics did vote heavily against birth control in Massachusetts, and (less surely) he has indicated that they voted against right-to-work in Ohio. In both cases, the Catholic church explicitly opposed these measures.[14]

Self-evident as these relationships may appear, Fenton's findings about Negroes in Louisiana are indeed newly persuasive of religious influence in politics. In Louisiana parishes that were predominantly

[12] W. and B. Allinsmith, Religious Affiliation and Politico-Economic Attitude, *Public Opinion Quarterly*, **12**: 377–389 (1948); see Table 3, p. 387. The paper is reprinted in D. Katz et al., *Public Opinion and Propaganda*, New York, Dryden Press, 1954, 151–158 and in Peter H Odegard, ed., *Religion and Politics*, New Brunswick, Rutgers—The State University, The Eagleton Institute of Politics, 1960, 139–151.

[13] Modern Baptists are not organizational descendants of the German Anabaptists but share some of the same views (e.g. on baptism) and in large proportion stem from the same depressed social classes.

[14] John H. Fenton, *The Catholic Vote*, New Orleans, The Hauser Press, 1960, Table 2, p. 17, and Tables 4, p. 31; 5, p. 32; and 6, p. 35. The author also considers popular vote for Congressional candidates who are Catholics and how Catholic Congressmen have voted on labor, civil rights, foreign aid, and aid-to-education measures.

French-Catholic, Negroes were registered for voting purposes much more frequently than in non-French-Catholic parishes. The relationship held up in his data even when the degree of urbanization and the balance of Negroes to whites in the total parish population were controlled.[15] He attributes the difference to the official position of the Catholic church in opposition to segregation and to the position in favor of segregation taken by individual Protestant churches and their ministers in non-French-Catholic Louisiana.[16]

Usually an analysis of the relationship of religion to politics in America has emphasized the influence of Catholicism rather than of Protestantism. One reason for this is that the United States is predominantly a Protestant or nonchurch-oriented country: the influence of widespread and diffuse Protestant identifications is harder to single out. With the exception of such instances as birth control and candidates who are Catholic, there are relatively few occasions on which religion is an issue. In such cases the minority by definition is egregious and pops into view as readily, so to speak, as an orange on top of a basket of apples. But it is also probably true that Catholics themselves are, as one kind of minority, more self-conscious than the majority with whom they associate. This self-consciousness is a process that has its roots in the same phenomena that caused our chickens and dogs (see pp. 148–149) to isolate the newcomer and caused the newcomer to feel different. As such the different person who is not utterly lacking in self-esteem is likely to become defensive about his difference and to cling to it sometimes as the surest basis for self-confidence. This is not per se a religious but a social psychological question.

This same consciousness of difference can operate on Protestants, not just when they find themselves in a Catholic church or household, but also when the cues of difference are much less pronounced. In such instances, where there is political relevance, Protestants are apt to react self-consciously in religious terms, but without the measure of intensity that comes from a sense that one is a member of a minority group. Just what goes on in the minds of Protestants in such cases is probably a milder version of what goes on in the minds of Catholics. Both sets of response patterns merit but have not received serious investigation. We can suppose only that it is a response conditioned by opinions expressed in the family by parents and passed down from

15 *Ibid.*, ch. 4, 39–57.
16 *Ibid.*, 43–44.

generation to generation as a virtually immortal echo of the bitter battles of the sixteenth century, reinforced by carefully selected personal experience.

An example (already twice alluded to in this book) of the durability of such attitudes, in this case involving the prejudice against Swedes and Protestants in Austria, is the following rhyme that was recited to children in the late nineteenth century in Austria.

Bet', Kindlein, Bet'	Pray, little child, pray
Morgen kommt der Schwed'	Tomorrow the Swede is coming
Morgen kommt der Oxenstierne	Tomorrow Oxenstierne is coming
Der friszt die kleinen Kinder gerne.	Who likes to devour little children.

Oxenstierne was a scourge of Central Europe in the early seventeenth century, close to 300 years before children in Austria were taught the rhyme.

For better or worse, these opinions become deeply and thoughtlessly held, like a variety of other predispositions one develops in childhood and adolescence. These predispositions are reinforced by the social segregation that has tended to keep Catholics and Protestants apart except in nonintimate contacts at work and in casual association in the market place.

Whatever the dynamics, the self-consciousness shows up when Protestants are confronted with Catholicism as such in politics. It is hard to say whether or not the suspicion has declined since the time when President Andrew Jackson appointed his attorney general Roger B. Taney, who was a Catholic, to the Supreme Court as John Marshall's successor, or when the slogan "Rum, Romanism, and Rebellion" angered Catholics in the 1884 election. At any rate, Al Smith, the Democratic and Catholic ex-governor of New York was defeated in his try for the Presidency in 1928, in an election where many non-Catholic issues were involved. In 1960 a Democrat and a Catholic, who was then Senator from Massachusetts, was elected to the Presidency. It has been estimated that Kennedy's majority was so very slim precisely because he lost about 1.5 million votes on account of his religion.[17]

It remains to be seen what the future relationship of Catholicism and Protestantism to politics will be, in economically and socially

---

[17] See Peter H Odegard, ed., *Religion and Politics*, New Brunswick, Rutgers—The State University, 1960, 115–127; and P. E. Converse et al., Stability and Change in 1960: a Reinstating Election, *American Political Science Review*, **55**: 269–280 (1961).

mature industrial societies. At present they do not seem to be dominant political forces. What the relationship will be between Christian and Moslem churches and politics in economically, socially, and politically underdeveloped nations also remains to be seen, but the present indications are that at least the Christian churches have become identified in the eyes of the majority of the citizens with the established ruling classes. They therefore have lost the strong loyalties that poor people established with Christianity, ties that started almost two millennia ago and continued with renewed vitality from the Renaissance and Reformation down to and beyond the French and Russian revolutions.

Churches (and parties) in the modern world

As they have been considered in this chapter, churches (and parties) are particular instances of institutions. That is, what can be said of the generation, endurance, and decline of institutions in general can be said of churches (and parties). Yet as members of the genus institution, these two fraternal members of the same species are not in all respects like each other or like all other institutions. And in terms of individual human needs they also are like and different from other institutions.

Any explanation for their rise and fall must include a recognition of how well they serve human needs at a particular point in individual development and in the development of a people in a culture. There is a common American joke about sticking pins in shrunken heads that represent one's enemies. This would be no joke if America were in the stage of advancement where people really believe the routine is effective. There was a belief that the Lord would smite down the man who violated the Sabbath by laboring. This belief would persist if there were not so many unsmitten Sunday workers around. There was a belief in America that Negroes always vote the Republican ticket, out of love for the Great Emancipator. Negroes have voted heavily Democratic since the New Deal began.

As beliefs persist and then change, so do institutions change. Neither beliefs nor institutions ordinarily have functional autonomy for a very long time. The pessimism of Ostrogorskii, who saw political parties as perniciously incompatible with the popular will, presupposes that parties can forever, or very long, persist of their own mass and momentum and independently of the needs of their adherents. The deeper pessimism of Michels, who studied European trade unions and then wrote as though he had studied political parties, similarly fails to relate institutions to human needs.[18]

The persistence of religious (and political) institutions over centuries, like the Catholic church, indicates not their monolithic "nature," but their adaptability. If this is so, there are grounds for neither optimism nor pessimism as to institutions, because they will in time die if they do not meet new stages of development, and they will survive if they do adapt. There will doubtless be forever the problem of sloughing off principles that are both no longer the mode and no longer functional. Churches have faced the problem and survived. And so have political parties. Witness the change in the Republican and Democratic parties over their long history and the symptoms of change in the Communist party. In the 1960s China mothers the orthodox, and the Soviet Union (mother country of the revolutionary movement) the heterodox, reformed party.

We need not sanctify institutions to recognize that they do meet deep-seated human needs and that, like human beings, they can and do change. The problem of their adaptability differs from that of human adaptability precisely in that they have no worth, no value, aside from their service to people in their individual and social aspects. It is only when people who, child-like, utterly depend on institutions and raise them to sanctity—to the position where they are to be served without question—that roles are incongruously reversed, and man becomes servant of the servant rather than master of the servant. In that case, the institution had better prepare to fight for its "life," because the fundamental needs of men are not eradicable but institutions are. At least the species still survives and—to take an example—the institution of royalty is dead or dying everywhere. And the Catholic church still lives, because it survived the profound trauma of the Reformation by adapting specifically and by learning how to adapt generally.

[18] See M. Y. Ostrogorskii, *Democracy and the Organization of Political Parties* (F. Clarke, transl.), New York, The Macmillan Co., 1902 and Roberto Michels, *Political Parties* (E. and C. Paul, transl.), New York, Hearst's International Library Co., 1915.

CHAPTER 8

The politics of status

The unequal distribution of deference

The discussion of social influences, whether proximal or distal, has hitherto avoided as much as possible the phenomena of class status. The reason for this is systematic, to avoid trying to discuss too many social influences at once. But it is self-evident that in everyday living the familial, ethnic, political-party, and religious influences already considered interact with status and that one can no more explain political behavior in any society without considering status than he can explain it without considering these other social influences.

Starting with Marx, modern social theorists have so heavily emphasized the influence of class status and politics, that there is now some tendency to deflate an overemphasis on status to the point where it becomes underemphasized. There is indeed some justification for this reversal of the pendulum. Marxian and post-Marxian thought has seen man as nothing other than the product of his socio-economic relationships, a viewpoint emphasized in the statement of Paul Lazarsfeld that "social influences determine political preference." By this he meant more than socio-economic status, but not much—income, occupation, education, and place and type of residence were the major determinants of how one voted, with one's religion (Protestant or Catholic) producing a cross-pressure that weakened the influence of status.[1]

The argument of this book agrees that social characteristics do de-

[1] Paul F. Lazarsfeld et al., *The People's Choice*, New York, Columbia University Press, 1948 ed., ch. 3, Social Differences between Republicans and Democrats, at 27.

termine political preference but denies the holistic implication of the assertion and emphasizes that not all of these social characteristics can be considered under the rubric of status and that not all of the determinants of political action are social. It is true and as partial to say that nonsocial, individual, organic characteristics determine political action as it is to say that social characteristics are determinants. This chapter is only another in which one segment of the total process of causation is considered, and even this segmental consideration cannot properly avoid mention of nonstatus, nonsocial forces. But at least we can keep them well in the back of our minds and let them shout their potence only from a distance and near the chapter's end.

A word of warning about the order in which the various distal social influences have been presented. Implicit or explicit assumptions that ethnic, partisan, religious, or status influences can be given the same rank-order in all times and places are not worth the microcaloric energy necessary to excogitate them, until we have much more precise means of measurement and validation than are now available. In the sixteenth century in Western Europe religion made more political difference than it does in the twentieth century; in the nineteenth century status probably made more difference than it did in the sixteenth century and more difference than religion does in the twentieth century. In the twentieth century in the subcontinent of India, one could not so surely as in the Western world depreciate religion (witness the Hindu-Muslim conflict) nor status as compared with religion (witness the growing demands of the Untouchable caste).

What then is status? By status I mean those social relationships which are a consequence of one's occupation, education, and property in various kinds and amounts of income and wealth.[2] So defining status does not say anything about its origin. In India one may have a particular status for religious reasons and the accident of birth. In ancient Greece one could lose the status of freeman and acquire that of slave by being on the defeated side in war. The same was true in Africa up to the nineteenth century. In the Arab world one could become a slave by individual capture, and in China by sale by one's parents, even in the twentieth century.

---

[2] Income is here regarded as property that is received periodically in contrast to wealth as property whose ownership has become vested.

The social inheritance of social status

And social status well-nigh universally is to a great degree socially, though not genetically, inherited—Aristotle's notion to the contrary notwithstanding. The son of a slave has been a slave; of a serf, has been a serf. Workingmen beget workingmen; and members of the professions produce sons who fall heir to and perpetuate high status. Status per se is a social influence of such great inertial force as to seem to preclude change; yet status, interacting with other forces, has accounted for much of the social and political change of the modern world. Serfs as serfs have with mute power demanded and gained the elimination of that aspect of their status, while retaining status as peasants. Workingmen as such have demanded change which did not alter their working-class status. And the French Revolution is sometimes characterized as one in which the bourgeoisie demanded de jure recognition of their de facto status.

In some societies status is primarily based on the occupation, education, and property of the particular individual rather than that of his kin; in others status is formally and legally inherited. The former may be called a class-status and the latter a caste-status system. Actually in all nations there is probably an admixture of both social systems, regardless of the formal, legal relationships. In India at one time legal relationships between individuals had a caste basis; in Western Europe and the Soviet Union there is hypothetical equality between all individuals. In India there are now laws designed to establish equality between individuals, though the caste system has by no means yet collapsed. In Western Europe and the Soviet Union when one is born the son of a low-status family, he tends to live in that status the rest of his life despite the equalitarian values and legal institutions in these societies. Class status exists even in societies where class distinctions are either extralegal (e.g., the social separation of people of different statuses) or illegal (e.g., where property ownership is not the basis for voting rights). Many societies have adopted equality as a major premise, but neither by fiat nor otherwise has any society been able to abolish the differences in status which classes represent.

In the European Middle Ages individual rights and obligations were tied to one's status, which was caste-like in being largely determined by birth but which could within a lifetime be changed. The serf's obligations to his lord, the vassal's to his overlord, and the reciprocal obligations of the overlord to his vassal, and the lord to his serf were conventionally established and accepted probably as generally as is equalitarianism now in Europe and North America. Each status carried with it certain rights, notably the right to inherit that status. A serf was obligated to perform services mostly related to tilling the soil; he could not be divested of his right to use the soil to which he was attached. A vassal had the obligation to do military services for his overlord and the right to get military protection from him.

Laws against luxurious display in fourteenth-century England revealed both the legal recognition of a caste-class system and the pressures of some people to break through this system—or more exactly to rise within it. Ermine and gold cloth could be worn only by knights and those who owned land over a specified value; successive lower grades of cloth were permitted to those of lower ranks and graded in accordance with social rank or wealth.[3] In seventeenth-century France there were the same laws and the same violations by the upwardly mobile.[4]

These phenomena amounted to a curious reversal of the twentieth-century condition. In the Middle Ages, status was legally recognized and equality between individuals of different status was either illegal or extralegal; in the modern Western world it is status which broadly speaking is illegal or extralegal and equality which is lawful.

Equal justice and class legislation

It would be pleasant for people in the twentieth century who value the equality of man to draw a nice dichotomy between the distributive, Platonic justice of the Middle Ages and the equal, classless justice of the modern world. But despite modern bills of rights, in many ways we still assume that the shoemaker will stick to his last and that only the ephors or guardians will rule. People of all classes, including the shoemaker class, cannot in democracies be said to rule, but in nations where there are two or more political parties, people have a fairly equal opportunity to choose which party and which guardians shall rule. And each person has no more than the one vote every other person is entitled to. Each person in principle is entitled to the equal protection of law regardless of occupation, education, or

[3] See Bernard Barber, *Social Stratification*, New York, Harcourt, Brace & Co., 1957, 161–162.
[4] *Ibid.*, 159–160.

property. This has real significance in major crimes, not in diminishing the great vulnerability of low-status people to criminal liability but in making those of high status equally liable. Poverty still is an extralegal hindrance to securing justice at law, but wealth is no longer a guaranty of legal immunity in criminal actions. Physicians in America of the 1950s and 60s have been tried and convicted for murder despite the fact that in occupation, education, and property they are in the very highest status category.

As a result in part of Puritan morality, but possibly more because of general wealth in the society, there is a tendency for administration of government in the Western world to become free of the graft that has characterized public administration in cultures where it is the custom of a fortunate person with governmental ties to provide for an extended family at public expense. The effect of this norm of administrative integrity has been felt in India, Africa, and parts of China, where English and at one time German colonial officials administered with minimal graft. The new Puritanical regime of communist China has evidently in some administrative areas vastly improved in integrity over its corrupt predecessor.

Wherever the dominant administrative practice has included honesty, the effect has been to diminish (but not extinguish) the differences of status: one need not have a substantial sum of money to employ lawfully available governmental services, ranging from police and fire protection to incorporation procedures and governmental loans. On the other hand the passage of class legislation—laws designed to favor particular groups like peanut farmers, walnut growers, osteopaths, trade unions, or privately owned public utilities—still depends to a great degree on the monetary resources of the group putting pressure on the government through the legislature. The common business practice of giving gifts and entertainment to prospective customers is not quite so common when the customer is government, but there is nonetheless considerable carryover of intrabusiness morality—or amorality—in relations between government and private groups. A private corporation may make a large contribution to a policemen's pension fund drive. A war-weary general may be hired as a nonworking corporation executive when he leaves military service.

Considered individually, class legislation rather obviously favors a particular group at the expense of the rest of the society. A tariff on imported watches helps domestic watch producers at the expense of watch purchasers. An agricultural price-support program helps farmers and is one cause of rising costs to those who eat. Even legislation establishing employer liability for industrial accidents to employees and minimum-wage or maximum-hour labor laws benefits one group at the expense of others. But considered collectively, the process of class legislation may paradoxically diminish economic differences between various small groups and large socio-economic classes. Old-age insurance directly benefits only old people; health insurance only the ill. Gasoline taxes discriminate against people who drive cars and inheritance taxes penalize the man who accumulates wealth so that his progeny will not be as poor as he was. But underlying such class legislation is not so much the notion of distributive as of equal justice. The farmer must get his fair share of the national wealth and may need a government subsidy to get it. The national loss that accompanies unemployment, illness, accident, or old age is something that should be more equally shared by the entire society. Inheritance taxes assume that it is unjust to perpetuate too easily one's high status by bequeathing a very large amount of the property aspect of status to one's children. Financial aid to college students is designed to give equal opportunity to young people equally endowed with mental but unequally endowed with monetary competence.

Class legislation and classless tyranny

In societies that frankly recognize intergroup conflict of interest,[5] there seems often implicit the anti-Rousseauean notion that the general welfare is coextensive with the sum of all individual group welfares—and that what is good for farmers or workers or automobile manufacturers is good for the nation. But this implicit assumption is probably no more harmful than the assumption that what is good for the nation is good for individual groups. At any rate, a selfless preoccupation with the general welfare has been historically associated with dictatorships (even those supported by majorities). These have, from the French Revolution, the 1861 Southern Rebellion in the United States, the Russian Revolution, the Nazi Revolution, down to the Chinese Communist Revolution, embarked on overt or covert aggression (internally or internationally) which has been far more destructive than creative of either individual liberty or national autonomy.

It is doubtless true that the sybarite does not contribute to the general welfare; it seems equally true that his opposite—the lean, hard,

---

[5] This paragraph and the next are not necessary to the continuity of the chapter. They may be skipped as a frank excursion into the cloud-covered region of Values.

dedicated totalitarian—is no more regardful of the general welfare, whether he act in the name of the classless society or of the racially pure folk. The selfish dedication to the pursuit of wealth can corrupt the people as classes, proximal groups, and individuals. The "selfless" pursuit of political power can accomplish the same result and more speedily, whether individually or collectively. It is not clear that it is more materialistic to stamp out individual or class poverty than it is to place a boot on the face of a prostrate enemy, however evil poverty and domestic or foreign enemies may be. Neither is it clear that the segmental and serial processes by which successive social groups have increased the equality of their status in some nations have been less enduring than the sudden verbal creation of the brotherhood of man under the selfless guidance of Big Brother and his selfless, sharp-toothed, canine vanguard of the standardized mass.

Solidarity in proximity and in distance

Status differences establish social distance, or to use a more exact metaphor produce semi-permeable membranes separating groups that are physically rather close. This distance or this membrane both increases and decreases antagonism between social groups and correlatively both decreases and increases intergroup solidarity. Antagonism increases and solidarity decreases partly as a function of proximity. A workingman may hate his immediate boss, the assistant foreman, because he is the proximal contact with the distal factory manager. Peasants or farm laborers may hate the field boss more than they do the farm proprietor who pays them all. But to the contrary, a worker may despise or hate the distant boss and sympathize with his foreman, whom the worker sees as a fellow victim of the same tyranny. A patient who is facing the cost of a major operation may be grateful to the surgeon for saving his life and displace his resentment at the high fees by a hostility that is generalized against the more distant medical profession. Soldiers sent by a psychically distant ruler to quell a local rebellion may side with the rebels when face to face with them, as in crucial moments of the Russian Revolution. And a person who angrily yells "down with the king" may be awed into silence in the presence of His Majesty.

Neither proximity nor distance assures either hostility or friendship across status lines. In Elmtown, working-class people seemed to resent middle-class people more than they resented those in higher classes; middle-class people resented the proximal newly rich leaders more than they did the usually distal old established families. On the other hand, in each interclass relationship, personal contacts (friendly or hostile) were more frequent between individuals in classes that were immediately adjacent.[6]

Common values in differentiated societies

Status differences and interclass antagonism are apt to lead us to neglect the obvious fact that societies more often than not do hold together. They are held together and function as units because of common values and mutual interests. The deepest mutual interests relate to the basic needs, which can be met only in society. The size—the extent—of a society depends to a great degree on the manner in which needs are fulfilled. Broad social ties are not likely to be strong where each nuclear or extended family performs a wide range of functions from the planting of crops, to the literal manufacture of clothing, and to protection against aggression. Where functions become much more highly specialized the society enlarges, as it did, for example, in the gradual process by which nation-states emerged from feudal domains at the beginning of the modern era in Europe. Two major functions that became increasingly specialized were the protection against violence and, later, the production of material necessities.

The superficial paradox is that as people have become more specialized, more unlike in their day-to-day activities, they have in necessary consequence come closer together. Diversity has made for unity. In emphasizing class antagonism, Marx did not adequately consider the obvious fact that there are not only divergent but also compatible interests between classes. Capitalists cannot accumulate wealth without labor; workingmen cannot produce wealth without capital, which becomes increasingly important as the productive process becomes more intricate and involves less direct expenditure of energy by human beings. And few people prefer either the poverty that is the price of undifferentiated economic production or the primitive jungle liberty that attends this poverty.

The collective settlements (kibbutz and kevutsa) in Israel are a case in point. Originally organized on a deliberately classless basis, with minimal differentiation of function, they appeared in the 1960s to be losing this very central characteristic. The kibbutzim were originally

---

[6] August B. Hollingshead, *Elmtown's Youth*, New York, John Wiley & Sons, 1949, 103, 95, 212–217, esp. Table X, p. 212.

intended to produce agricultural commodities and simple manufactured goods. One became a plywood factory; others came to specialize in producing agricultural equipment, household detergents, plastic tableware, or hosiery. Capital is being imported, kibbutz members with special skills are moving to cities, and mothers are taking more exclusive responsibility for rearing their own children. Close to a third of Israel's agricultural production comes from these collectives. But this itself indicates economic specialization: collectives account for less than a twentieth of Israel's population.[7] Once the communal tasks were accomplished that had evoked so much courage and selflessness in defending frontiers and fructifying reluctant land, the collectives in Israel appeared to be going the way of New Lanark, New Harmony, and the phalansteries.

Status recognition and tranquility

Common values—a common commitment to the same goals and the same ways of achieving them—also contribute to the stability of differentiated societies (as well as simple ones). Class antagonism appears to have been more pronounced in the United States in the earlier stages of industrialization when both workingmen and farmers bitterly resented the dominance of the capitalist-entrepreneur class.

It may be more precise to say that these first two socio-economic groups resented the disproportionate share of the national product which the last class kept, rather than to say that farmers and workingmen wanted to seize political power from businessmen. In 1896 labor contributed considerably to the victory of the economically conservative McKinley over the populist Bryan, and once the farmers had become entrenched politically as a pressure group whose economic interests were diligently served by both Republicans and Democrats, they abandoned their efforts to form a distinct political group. This was true not only in the 1890s when the Populists were swallowed by the Democratic party; it had been true in the 1860s when the Republican party on its initially small-farmer base came under the hegemony of the business class.

The extent of agrarian and proletarian protest has been largely limited to economic grievance. Once these have been met, both farmers and workingmen have not only lost the intensity of their political commitment but have indeed become entrenched groups. They are prob-

[7] New York *Times,* 18 June 1961.

ably no less conservative than the business class, which they oppose now in the same way that buyer and seller oppose one another, rather than as antagonists on the field or barricades of battle.

The effect of increasing equality of economic rewards on the conservatism of the working class may be judged in other ways. Labor productivity is probably more than an index of efficiency. It indicates also the degree of mechanization and correlates with rate of pay in real wages, which in turn correlates with the standard of living of working people. A study by the Stanford Research Institute indicates that in 1950 labor productivity in France was 30% of that in the United States and in Italy 20%. In Italy interclass antagonism, as measured by the strength of the communist vote, was probably the strongest of antagonism anywhere in relatively mature industrialized economies.[8] When working people in one socio-economic system see a direct although not necessarily linear relationship between how hard they work and how much they earn, they are apt to be more committed to that system than to one in which more effort produces no great increase in reward. This has at least been part of the explanation for the supposed greater efficiency of free over slave labor. And it is significant that both the Russian and the Chinese revolutions occurred in countries where landlords exploited peasants, in economies that were still overwhelmingly agrarian.

In no industrialized nation has there been an enduring proletarian revolt. This hardly indicates that working people have regularly and continuously received an altogether satisfying share of the industrial product, but it does suggest that working people by and large have accepted—more often and more generally than they have rejected—the system in which their control in practice has been limited to the withholding of their services by strike or the exertion of political pressure through the ballot box. This is another way of saying that interclass antagonism has been more severe in agrarian than in industrial economies, that political hegemony by industrialists (whether under private capitalism, as in Western Europe and North America or under

[8] Stanford Research Institute, *Research for Industry*, **6** (1): 9–11 (November 1953). A caveat is in order as regards Germany, whose 1950 productivity was only 2% higher than that of France, as both were compared with the United States. But the rate of productivity in Germany increased from 15% in 1947 to 32% in 1950 as compared with the 27% of France in 1947 to 30% in 1950. In one case there was rapid increase and in the other, stasis. On the causes of attachment to Communism in (notably) France and Italy, see Hadley Cantril, *The Politics of Despair*, New York, Basic Books, 1958.

state capitalism as in the Soviet Union) is less resented by working-men than political hegemony by semi-feudal landlords has been re-sented by serfs and peasants.[9]

The misjudgment of the intent of labor strikes as being revolution-ary is no easier to avoid than the misjudgment of a servile attitude among peasants or the citizenry of a colonized people, as in Hungary in 1956 or in the Congo in 1960. The manifest verbal phenomena, as the most accessible aspects of reality, are the ones people go by in appraising the portent of social contentment and discontent. If a labor leader says he likes Marx and favors a revolution, he is taken at face value, becomes to a degree persecuted and by his words in-vites the persecution. On the easily neglected level of reality known as action, he and his union—as in the case of Harry Bridges and the ILWU on the West Coast of the United States—may prove quite un-revolutionary.

At least during the Korean War of 1950–1953 there were no signs that Pacific Coast longshoremen were interfering with the transport of supplies from America to Korea in the war against the Communists whom Bridges verbally favored. To the extent that Bridges and the longshoremen were aware of themselves, some may have wished for a communist victory, some may have wished for an American or United Nations or capitalist victory. But by and large, willy-nilly, they all contributed to the American or United Nations or capitalist war effort by loading cargo in West Coast ports. It is hard to imagine anything other than a catastrophic and unequivocal victory for the Communist Korean and Chinese armies without the labor of the West Coast long-shoremen, with Bridges as their head. Neither Bridges nor his verbally patriotic critics could be accused of insincerity in their mutual hostility, but both sides *acted* basically in harmony, even though both for quite contrary reasons were critical of American foreign policy during the late 1940s, which policy they both supported in action more willy than nilly, during the 1950s.

---

[9] The blunt instrument of revolution tends to be neglected as a measure of social discontent in favor of strikes, which are much milder expressions of discontent, but have the advantage of being more readily quantifiable and amenable to statistical validation. What I am here asserting is that revolutions scale higher on interclass antagonism than do industrial strikes and that revolutions usually have occurred in agricultural economies and not in industrial ones.

Status recognition and upset

The opposite may also occur. An industrialist who is deeply committed to the system that made him the powerful figure he is in a private-capitalist nation like the U. S. or state-capitalist nation like the U.S.S.R. is likely inter alia to claim to "know his people." That is, he claims to know how his employees will act and what makes them act. He sees the signs of docility so regularly that he readily assumes "his" workers are indeed his willing instruments and nothing else. It is clear, he believes, that they are interested solely in their pay checks and want no responsibility and that there is nothing more to these people. And then they strike. Since the most readily available explanation of the strike is contained in the words of the strike leaders, he finds it convenient to blame the strike on irresponsible, radical, and foreign agitators who do not understand "the workingman." The labor leader who helps precipitate the strike may not *understand* the working people much better than do industrialists, but in the direction—though not necessarily the intensity—of his outlook and action, he is likely to be more resonant with the expectations that permanently reside inside workingmen than either he or they fully realize.

Similarly a ruling group may assume that it knows "our" people. The Soviet Politburo or Presidium in the 1930s was a vigorous but subservient body reconciled to expressing a chronic enthusiasm for Stalin, the "sun of the proletariat" who benignly shed life-giving rays of light on a dormant nation. A human being who, like Stalin, has become accustomed to regard himself as a rather special person in his role as national leader will doubtless be shocked at verbal and nonverbal phenomena indicating that some citizens in the 1930s regarded him not as the sun but rather as one who had the life-giving brightness and vital power of the primordial void, the darkness upon the face of the deep. Stalin was unable to witness the intense, bitter, savage attack on his magnificence by Khrushchev within three years after his death, but the marathon polemic apparently shocked Khrushchev's audience.[10]

Similarly, it seemed to be something of a shock to the Soviet government to discover, in October of 1956 (the same year in which Khrushchev had denounced omnipotence in his predecessor), that the Hun-

---

[10] It is interesting to speculate as to what the ingredients of such shock might be: how much was shock that Stalin was in fact less than perfect, how much that a devoted servant of his should now be so violently attacking him, and how much that Khrushchev should think he was surprising his audience with real revelations.

garian nation was in revolt against its colonizers.   In Hungary there had been abundant expressions of docile, eager enthusiasm for the new People's Republic.   The new regime was anti-fascist, and no significant category of Hungarians wanted to return to Hitlerism or the neo-feudalism of Horthy.   A land-reform program had taken the latifundia out of the hands of their feudal landlords and placed their ownership in the hands of the (vanguard of the) proletariat.   So the revolt must be solely the consequence of irresponsible, radical, and foreign agitators and their traitorous Hungarian lackeys who did not understand the true aspirations of a downtrodden nation.

And the embittered procession of Belgian colonials who left the Congo in the savage summer of 1960 also seem to have been shocked at the ugly fact of revolt.   Had they not raised the standard of living of these benighted savages?   Had they not brought to them the message of a long-suffering Christ who died for them on the Cross?   Had they not founded a university with the most modern buildings?   Statistically, morally, and culturally the Congolese were blessed by their association with their Belgian benefactors, who, unlike the Russians in Hungary, were voluntarily laying down the burden of dominion. Why this shocking rebellion, not in the midday heat of colonialism but in its gracious sunset?

The particular reasons for particular industrial strikes and particular rebellions are never identical, but one of the common and central reasons for such varied manifestations of tension is the refusal to remain contented with a vast chasm of difference in socio-economic status between the dominators and the dominated.   That is, those of inferior status can no longer tolerate being inferior to the *degree* and in *ways* that those of superior status demanded.

The course of labor relations in the United States since the 1930s suggests that trade unions have sought more (pay, security, etc.) but not the same amount (of pay, security, etc.) as management has in the salaries, retirement programs, etc. of the executives.   The Presidium of the Supreme Soviet and Khrushchev supposedly were willing to admit that Stalin was, like the Prime Minister of the British cabinet, primus inter pares, but Khrushchev at least resented the demi-deification of Joseph Djugashvili.   Hungarians presumably would tolerate many aspects of Soviet influence so long as they had some real part in the making of decisions and the allocation of resources, but they resented the totality of Soviet control.   And Congolese do not seriously propose to revert to an economy, society, and polity based on tribalism.   But in each instance the group with the power refused really to share either power or deference with those beneath them. They insisted on making decisions and on being shown continuous evidence of their own generosity, kindness, intelligence, sensitivity, magnanimity, inventiveness, fortitude, and other characteristics of magnificence. The resentment appears to be not at the quantitative but at the qualitative distinction—that the dominant group is composed, in its own eyes and as reflected in the pool of humanity into which the elite gaze like Narcissus—of a kind of being quite different from others, who are not even except in the formal, insignificant, biological sense members of the same species.

Recognition by elites of the desire on the part of those of lower status to be deemed equal has consolidated in power and prestige those of higher status. Industrialists after the Second World War, in America and in Western Europe, have, for whatever motives, come to acknowledge that their employees, while primarily interested on the job in making money, having security, and working in air-conditioned factories and offices, are also anxious to be regarded as people, not with a desire to be patted on the head but with at least a minimal desire for power and prestige. This acknowledgment has produced a reconciliation of management to trade unions and at least formal solicitude for employees' individual welfare. It is interesting to speculate whether recognition of their influence through unions is more important to employees than the politeness with which they are treated, partly in consequence of having independent power through trade unions and protections of law. An industrialist can be polite to an industrialist of equal rank as another corporation president; two such people can be polite or rude to each other without much offense. A workingman can be deferential or nondeferential to a boss, and vice versa. Does a boss like deference from one of equal status better than from one of lower status? Does a worker like deference from one of higher status better than deference from one of equal status? Scaling on such questions has not yet been developed.[11]

[11] But an abstract, laboratory study is of provocative relevance. In a contrived game, an experimenter established various kinds of hypothetical partners (O) for the experimental subjects (S). The experimenter then varied O's action in ways that he called Conditional Cooperation, Unconditional Cooperation, and Noncooperation. There were three patterns of power relationship between S and O: in one, O had Absolute Power to cause S to lose the game; in another O had Partial Power to cause S to win more or win less; in the third O had Equal Power with S. The experimenter found that "under conditions of Equal Power, S tends to respond to an Unconditionally Cooperative O with exploitive game behavior

But it is clear the industrial conflict has been more violent between industrialists and workers than between industrialists and industrialists. An entrepreneur may seek to ruin his competitor but not to kill or injure him. An industrialist or a government may injure or kill workers in the course of an industrial stoppage (strike or lock out), and workers may do likewise, without either party feeling (or at least expressing) any sense of identity with the other—or else expressing the sympathy of Lewis Carroll's Walrus and Carpenter for the oysters they devoured. Only in wars between criminal gangs in the twentieth century has there been the anarchy and the lack of commonality that exists between equals when they engage in conflict as equals. Industrial conflict has been characteristically between unequals, like that between Nazi Germany on the one hand and Jews and Slavs on the other. This is no argument for making industrial conflict between labor and management a brotherly war between equals but does suggest that violence of conflict is apt to diminish between groups that regard each other as having equal power and meriting equal deference.

It appears not only impossible but also unnecessary to establish equality in all respects between people. But in a society where majorities and minorities rather than socio-economic status constitute the basis for political power, there appears to be less tension than in a society where superior status entails greater political power and where interclass deference is not reciprocal. More briefly, a society in which equal dignity is an acknowledged value appears to be more stable than one in which—regardless of the stated value system—some are considered more equal, more gracious, and closer either to God (as in the case of the Catholic clergy, notably before the Protestant Reformation and many Protestant clerics since), to Marx (as in the case of the vanguard versus the proletariat, Trotskyites versus Stalinists, Russian versus Chinese Communists), or to humanity (as in the case of some French Revolutionists and some twentieth-century intellectuals).

In his already discussed study of people of relatively low occupational, educational, and property status, Lane found that in general

and less liking, whereas he tends to be cooperative and have a greater liking for the Conditionally Cooperative *O.*" [Leonard Solomon, The Influence of Some Types of Power Relationships and Game Strategies upon the Development of Interpersonal Trust, *Journal of Abnormal and Social Psychology,* **61:** 223–230 (1960), at 229.] If these findings are reminiscent of interpersonal relationships of the intimate sort that exist between husband and wife, parents and children, may they not also help explain relationships between lord and peasant, master and servant, employer and employee—as these personal role relationships help determine impersonal status relationships?

these people did not want either the responsibility or the wealth of those of high status and further thought that leaders deserved what they got because they paid such a high price for it in work and worry. The study further indicated that these same people did consider themselves to be as good as those of superior status.[12] This distinction between subjective and objective equality must be made in order to explain the stability of hierarchized societies. If it is hard to understand, one need only reflect on his own reactions to others. Does he object to others' having competence (in material and nonmaterial ways) that he does not have? Does he object to others regarding themselves as "personally" superior, in addition to being superior in some competence ranging from ability to row a boat, dig a hole, speak a language, or drive an automobile? If one resents a segregating, discriminating sense of superiority in other people toward him, how does he so completely distinguish himself from others as to suppose that they do not resent the same behavior in him?

Industrialization and social mobility

Status and therefore hierarchy appear to characterize all societies, whether primitive, pre-industrial, or industrial. Societies differ in the number of status levels and the distance between levels. The social hierarchy may distinguish groups so markedly that even contact with the shadow of an Untouchable may call for ritualistic purification; it may distinguish them so little that chiefs associate routinely with ordinary tribesmen. The hierarchy may involve the intricate differentiation that distinguishes high from low noblemen by birth from those by royal grant of title, high and low middle class, or the paradoxically intricate yet simple status patterns of mature industrial societies.

These distinguishing status characteristics appear to be of far less political portent than the degree of mobility. Societies in which there is relatively little movement from one social status to another may be stable and dormant or highly unstable and alive. Societies in which there is a comparatively large amount of actual status mobility may be stable (like England and America in the mid-twentieth century) or

---

[12] One of his respondents said, on the question of people being equal: "not financially, not in influence but equal to one another as being a person." Another said: "I think I am just as good as anybody else. I don't think there are any of them I would say are better." [R. E. Lane, The Fear of Equality, *American Political Science Review,* **53**: 35–51 (1959), at 41.]

unstable (like France in the eighteenth and nineteenth centuries), but they are not likely to be dormant.

Before industrialization, societies are by and large much more status-immobile than during and after the establishment of the intricate division of labor that industrialization produces. One of the major reasons for this is that in an agrarian and handicraft society there are fewer places to go. It is possible to move across the landscape, from one village or region to another, but the range of occupations necessary to support a simple existence is rather narrow and unspecialized. One can change from being a peasant to being a blacksmith or other wood-, leather-, cloth-, or metal-worker. One can go into trade, in the simple exchange of consumer goods that occurs in societies more advanced at least than the pastoral ones. But towns are apt to be small and serve to improve life in the countryside rather than life in town.

During and after the process of industrialization, occupational differentiation becomes intricate. One can become fully employed in specialized tasks ranging from extractive industries (mining and forestry) to manufacturing of ever-increasing complexity and specialization. Even more significantly one can work in the host of external service industries (performing services directly for the public) from transportation to insurance to entertainment, and even in the ever-growing internal service category within manufacturing and service industries—in the white-collar jobs like purchasing, engineering, tool design, production control, marketing research, and sales which facilitate the job of the factory worker.

Status mobility does not begin with industrialization, but it almost inevitably increases as a society industrializes.[13] The social distance between a medieval peasant and a Pope may be no greater than that between a modern machine tender and a prime minister, but the opportunities to change status are fewer for a peasant than for a mechanic because there are more kinds of jobs in industry than in a society where the overwhelming majority of the people are engaged in raising crops and livestock for food and clothing. In agrarian-based feudal society, a peasant may become a priest or a soldier but he cannot become an engineer, a tool designer, or a timekeeper; and his chances of entering an ancient profession like medicine or scholarship

[13] Seymour Martin Lipset and Reinhard Bendix, *Social Mobility in Industrial Society*, Berkeley and Los Angeles, University of California Press, 1959, 75.

are slim because the society is too close to subsistence to support such occupations for more than a very few.

But occupational and status mobility are not quite the same thing. The son of a farmer who moves to the city and takes a job as an unskilled worker may have suffered a decline in occupational status, may remain static in his educational status, and may have gained only slightly (though to him perceptibly) in income. Yet the excitement, variety, and individual freedom of action may produce such a markedly superior mental outlook on life that the former countryboy sees himself as being far above his former status. In leaving the land and the ways of his ancestors, he may have left behind him the supposed virtues that his parents (and Thomas Jefferson and the Populists) said are derived from country living, but he has the superior sense that comes from a knowledge that he has discovered the mysteries of the big city.

And he has the hope, however well fulfilled it may be, that the future will see a rise in status that never was possible on the farm. If he remains unskilled or semi-skilled, he may nonetheless earn more money than he ever could on the farm and he can later gain a vicarious sense of improved status through the improved education and improved job and income opportunities of his children. If he improves his own skill and job, so much the better.

So long as there is reasonable opportunity for him to advance (directly or vicariously through his children) he is likely to remain supportive rather than critical of the social system that has allowed him to move freely, though at considerable cost in psychic security and just plain hard work, from the routine simplicity of rural life to the variegated complexity of the city. He will not be seriously frustrated if he fails to become a foreman, factory superintendent, or small businessman. The major change from country to city and its immediate opportunities are enough to absorb his energies and he is likely to see his advancement as limited by his own competence and energy rather than by the system.

It is only when the farmer and the former farmers see the industrial system seriously breaking down, as during the depression of the 1930s in Europe and America, that their commitment to the system is weakened. In that circumstance, it is doubtful whether the one-time agrarian is any more critical than the already established second-generation urban workingmen. The newcomer may indeed be less critical because of the intensity of his interest and commitment to the new urban way of life. Like the superpatriotic immigrant, the nouveau riche, or the nonbeliever recently converted to religion, he may be more conformist than his coworkers and neighbors who can be or are more critical of a system they have long since taken for granted.

Mobility after industrialization

The first prolonged period of individual status change comes with the alteration of society from agrarian to industrial. Perhaps in no society is it quite complete yet, so recent is the advent of industrialization. But it is advanced far enough in some societies so that the problem of status that has become fixed arises once more. Thus far, pressures to maintain status-fluidity have succeeded in keeping open the channels of advancement of restless individuals of low status. One of the reasons Nazism was so attractive to many Germans was its successful effort to stir up a society that was still quite status-stagnant after two generations of industrialization. In other societies, like the Soviet Union, Sweden, France, England, and the United States—whether under autocratic or democratic control—opportunities for individual advancement have probably increased in the 1940s and 1950s.

The second period of status change, after industrialization has already been established, involves social groups rather than individuals as such. It involves upgrading the entire occupational and income structure of those of lower status. The working class remains a working class but gains improved wages, shorter hours, and more refined working conditions which amount to a rise more in absolute than in relative status. The worker does not become richer than his fellow workers or neighbors, but he and they become richer than they were and enjoy better health, more leisure, and longer life.

But these changes—of individuals from one status to another and of status groups en masse—tend to ease tension between status groups without eliminating the groups as such. If individuals can move out of a group while the group persists—like drops of water straying from a continuous waterfall—tension is at a comparatively low level even though society has not descended into one vast level sea of people. If entire status groups get more goods, services, etc., even though they do not get as much as those of higher status, one of the main reasons for status-frustrations is removed, and, as Lane has indicated, such people of relatively low status do not necessarily resent the greater rewards of higher-status individuals.[14]

[14] See Lane, *op. cit.*

Tension is further eased by the tremendous growth of indirect labor and service occupations already mentioned. A tool designer may be paid less than a skilled mechanic who makes the die-tool in the shop, but the designer is partly compensated in the prestige associated with a white-collar job. Similarly the host of clerks who keep records and punch the keys of tabulating machines may be paid less than blue-collar shop workers but gain compensation from the prestige of grime-free hands which tell that they are not manual workers. As the industrial society becomes more and more complicated, the portion of people in what Colin Clark calls "tertiary" (nonextractive, nonmanufacturing occupations) grows disproportionately [15] and provides a new area of opportunity once the first urban frontier is filled with the sons of farmers and peasants (and immigrants of rural backgrounds) who learned the skills and routines of mass-production labor.

As the industrial economy, supported by highly efficient agricultural production, spews forth its surplus, more people have time and money to travel, read, consult the doctor, etc., and thus more people can work at these occupations. For most such newcomers to these occupations, the new job usually means a rise in status from that of their parents. Whatever the changes in occupation, they amount to a decline in the proportion of manual jobs and thus indicate upward mobility, by the old criteria of whether or not one works with his hands.[16]

The question of increased upward mobility is fairly easily answered when a society is undergoing industrialization. There is clearly an increase in the opportunity not only for change but also for improvement in status. If a move to the city from the farm may be to a degree only lateral, in at least a generation's time there is an opportunity to move up, as a result largely of more freely available education in public schools. But the question whether mobility persists after industrialization is harder to answer. In the United States, mobility has been high for at least the half-century since about 1910. Indeed it seems to be increasing, both up and down, notably since the Second World War. Downward mobility is significant in indicating whether the status structure of a society is open. If all the sons of professional people remain professionals and the sons of skilled workers fill all the skilled jobs, and neither set of sons drops in status, a theoretical half of the mobility process does not exist. At such a stage, restless low-

---

[15] See Lipset and Bendix, *op. cit.*, 84, which indicates that tertiary jobs in the United States increased from 16.6% of those gainfully employed in 1850 to 47.1% in 1935.

[16] See Lipset and Bendix, *op. cit.*, 88.

status people can rise only by the third process mentioned, the enlarge-
ment of the "tertiary" service occupations.[17]   Far from declining since
the starry-eyed days of Horatio Alger, the proportion of business leaders in 1950 whose fathers were laborers has doubled since 1900.[18]   The
trend in downward mobility is less clear.

In any case the process of movement from one status to another is
a slow one.   It is fairly common for an individual to improve his status
by only one of three or four steps over that of his parents and to
project his disappointment or other status aspirations onto his children.
It is most common—statistically most normal—for a person to maintain
the status of his parents, whether that status was high or low.[19]   And
it is only a small minority that moves from low status and high status.
Despite the increase in the proportion and number of nonmanual jobs
that follows intensified industrialization, between two-thirds and three-
fourths of all employed people interviewed in three separate surveys
from 1945 to 1952 had kept the status of their fathers as manual or nonmanual workers.   But more than half of the remaining third or fourth
of the manual-labor force had moved up into nonmanual jobs from
manual-laboring families.[20]

Most of the ordinary, day-to-day associations between people tend
to continue status, though these associations do not necessarily perpetuate status.   These association patterns are among the most conservative influences in any society.   One is raised in a family of a
particular status and is most comfortable when he associates with
people who are like his family in status.   One lives in a neighborhood
that is usually homogeneous in status—though not necessarily in the
occupation aspect of status.   Manual and nonmanual workers of comparable income can and do live in the same neighborhoods, because
they can equally afford the same quality of housing.   One works beside people who share his occupational and income status.   Because
of neighborhood stratification one's children are apt to associate in
schools that are to a considerable degree status-segregated; and one
plays—in social clubs, sporting associations, etc.—with people whose
status is like his own.

---

[17] This assumes that the occupational status of the extractive jobs in farming,
forestry, fishing, and mining is roughly on a par with manufacturing.
[18] See Barber, *op. cit.*, Table 32, p. 453.
[19] For relation between son's and father's occupation, see Lipset and Bendix,
op. cit., 89.
[20] *Ibid.*, 88.

Social status and individual development

By a variety of criteria it is clear that high status facilitates and low status inhibits the exploitation by an individual of his native talent. A study of 1000 high school graduates in Milwaukee in 1937–1938 who had intelligence quotient scores of 117 and above shows the effect of parental income. When the study was made, one-fourth of the graduates whose parents had incomes below $1500 were in college and three-fourths of those in the same IQ category whose parents earned $3000 or more were in college.[21] In the Elmtown study, there was similar correlation between status and educational achievement, plus intimate evidence of the ways in which family background and school administration encouraged adolescents of high status and discouraged those of low status.[22] It is far easier for a person to retain the status of his parents than to change it either up or down.

The tension of disappointed aspirations may be weaker among most people than the tension of social alienation from one's status equals, and therefore the tension of alienation operates to inhibit aspirations to rise in status. For those with unusually strong desires to improve their status, the process is available—at the cost of a considerable degree of loneliness as one denies his former equals and is denied by those whose equals he wants to be. But those who have high status may be freer of tension after all. At least Buchanan and Cantril have found that in 1948 individuals "with higher socio-economic status feel more secure than the lower groups" in Australia, Britain, France, Germany, Italy, Mexico, Netherlands, Norway, and the United States.[23]

The mythology of the grand social leap from peasant to prime minister persists in the face of overwhelming evidence that these leaps are rare and that when people advance they usually do so by short, slow steps. Most business leaders in America before and after the Industrial Revolution in the mid-nineteenth century have been the sons of

---

[21] See Barber, *op. cit.*, 400–401.

[22] Hollingshead, *op. cit.*, ch. 8.

[23] William Buchanan and Hadley Cantril, *How Nations See Each Other*, Urbana, University of Illinois Press, 1953, 29. To me, part of the explanation for this necessitates use of a need hierarchy, so that those who are well fed and well accepted by their social equals are nonetheless frustrated in their self-esteem and self-actualization but have less total tension because their physical and social needs are met. The finding of Buchanan and Cantril does not state this; although this explanation helps understand observed phenomena, it remains hypothetical.

business leaders.[24]   Henry Ford II is more typical than his grandfather, the original Henry, as an example of status and mobility. Virtually all of the top political "decision-makers" in American national government have been the sons of farmers, businessmen, and professionals. Correlatively, only 4% of all persons who became either President, Vice President, or a member of the President's Cabinet in the period from 1789 to 1934 were the sons of wage earners.[25] Although John Quincy Adams is the only son of a President who ever became President, he is far more typical in his social status than was Abraham Lincoln, who became the prime exemplar and prime object of the virtual mythology of moving from log cabin to White House. Of course the case of neither Henry Ford II nor of J. Q. Adams is typical, for in fact there is no significant pattern of familial inheritance of high office in nations that have shed quite completely the last relics of feudalism like primogeniture and entailed estates. But believers in the mythology are likely to be shocked and puzzled at these aristocratic phenomena and nonetheless to accept as normal reality the equally atypical cases of the first Henry Ford and Abraham Lincoln.

Beliefs as causes of mobility

What causes social mobility? Recent research has elegantly and yet cautiously described it. Its causes are not yet adequately explored. This has not prevented the persistent existence of folklore which, in its most common expression until at least the Great Depression of the 1930s, has said it was all up to the individual whether he advanced or not. Those who showed initiative, perseverance, unshatterable faith, and did not stop work when the whistle blew at quitting time would surely get ahead. The sluggards would fall behind, settle to the bottom of the heap, and become the social pariahs, the constitutionally weak and sinful sloths who are always ready with arms hopelessly extended sideways in resignation to fate or beseechingly extended forward in search of alms.

A contrapuntal theme finds the cause of mobility in society. One gets ahead because society honors and otherwise rewards people who get ahead. Or—to use the social argument to explain the opposite result—the social system makes it impossible for the downtrodden to

---

[24] Lipset and Bendix, *op. cit.*, ch. 4, Social Mobility and the American Business Elite. Note particularly Table 4.4, p. 134 and Barber, *op. cit.*, 443–462.
[25] Donald R. Matthews, *The Social Background of Political Decision-Makers*, Garden City, Doubleday & Co., 1954, 23.

get ahead, by a variety of sinister (or coldly objective) techniques for maintaining the wealth and power of the rich and potent.

On the face of it, neither of these views has anything to do with the reality of causation of status mobility. But in reality both these views are at least peripheral causes of the mobility pattern in a society. If people *believe* they can get ahead solely by their own efforts, they may indeed rise in social status in part because of this belief even though they also get considerable support from "society." If people believe they cannot get ahead because "society" will not let them, they are less likely to do so, all other relevant forces being equal. One can at least logically factor out the relevance of belief, saying it is a post-hoc manifestation of a socially (or organically) derived social itch to excel, but the causal relevance of belief seems reasonable. It need not reflect a true appraisal of causality so long as it impels or impedes the status-striving activity.[26]

But this set of cognitive maps, crediting either the individual or society for mobility or the lack of it, is itself probably in part derivative of a separate factor that is easily confused with these pseudo-scientific maps. The value system in a particular society inevitably includes a belief in the virtue and/or vice (as distinct from a belief in the "scientific" causation) of social mobility. A society based on the old Platonic notion that the shoemaker should stick to his last or which uses the Aristotelian rationale justifying slavery as being appropriate to the nature of slaves will afford fewer opportunities for individual advancement in status than one based on the proposition that all men are created equal. These inequalitarian or equalitarian values have often been expressed as scientific facts (Aristotle so described slaves and slavery, and Jefferson regarded natural equality as a self-evident truth). But more exactly they are the part of a social belief system which has to do with good and bad. Societies say it is good or bad for people of low station to try to move up the line, and they admire or condemn people accordingly. This *valuation* of mobility is of causative significance just as is the closely related *belief* in what causes it; and both are, for present practical analytical purposes, social in origin.

It is easy to suppose that a belief in equality makes for mobility and a belief in inequality inhibits it, but there would probably be far

[26] By this I mean in effect that the error of Columbus' notion of where he was headed did not impede his progress. Indeed some idea of direction and goal were necessary to his arrival at an unintended destination.

less mobility if there were not simultaneously a belief in both. That is, if people do not generally regard some occupations as superior to others in prestige, they will not have the same degree of impetus for status advancement. This is another way of saying that the social value of hierarchy is necessary to mobility just as is the social value of equality. Societies on this dimension differ not in a belief in hierarchy but rather in what should be done about it and how relatively important it is. If they believe in a *socially* determined hierarchy they are more likely to accept a belief in equality and to depreciate status. Jefferson simultaneously believed that all men are created equal and that a *natural* aristocracy should be allowed to emerge, but free of *social* restrictions on movement from one status to another. If societies believe in a *naturally* determined hierarchy, they are more likely to accept and support laws and conventions designed to perpetuate status by *social* restrictions which they believe are merely in accord with the natural and inherited superiority of high-status individuals.

Belief in hierarchy is widespread regardless of the belief in what should be done about it. In a variety of cultures, all to a degree industrialized but not all Western European, a remarkable similarity in the relative status of various occupations has been discovered. In the United States, Soviet Union, Great Britain, New Zealand, Germany, and Japan, public opinion surveys have indicated substantial consensus as to which occupations outrank which other ones, and data from Brazil and the Philippines correlate with the other findings.[27] Each of these societies is not only industrialized to a considerable degree but also committed to equalitarian values. The implication of this is that in a society with a complicated division of labor the two supposedly conflicting values of equality and hierarchy are necessary to each other. In a society that highly values equality, the conflict is resolved or synthesized, regardless of the expressed values, as a belief in the equality of opportunity.

Industrialization as a cause of mobility

But these cognitive maps, explaining the reasons for status differences and the value-systems that uneasily compromise between equality and hierarchy, are not the only important forces producing mobility. A Polish sociologist comparing the socialist and capitalist sys-

---

[27] See A. Inkeles and P. H. Rossi, National Comparisons of Occupational Prestige, *American Journal of Sociology,* **61**: 329–339 (1956).

tems says that mobility is necessary in both, in the former just as much as the latter, because both so highly value the creation of wealth and both need mobility to elicit the special talents required to produce wealth on a large scale. He says "it is the 'social-economic expansion' and not the revolutionary introduction of a socialist order which can be considered a necessary condition of this increase" in social mobility.[28]

The question is not yet answerable with any real quantitative exactitude. But it does seem quite clear that the great movement off the land into the cities—the first real stage in what we abstractly label mobility—has occurred in the process of industrialization and that the differing and similar belief systems of capitalism and socialism have come *after* industrialization began. These belief systems have given some direction to industrialization but probably have not *directly* caused either it or the mobility which is partly the consequence of industrialization. Indirectly, however, the belief in equality has contributed greatly to mobility, not just as I have previously indicated but as a factor contributing to the following causes, which are related to each other and to the belief system.

Intergroup contact as a cause of mobility

Interaction between members in different status groups is necessary—interaction that is not just formal or involves physical proximity but which also establishes psychic ties. These ties must be established so that individuals not only recognize the differences but also sense that the barriers of difference are surmountable. A person of lower status thus senses that he is in significant ways like the person of higher status and can become like him in status.

The importance of psychic intéraction to mobility may be best shown by illustration. Peasants and the sons of peasants may live near noblemen or other kinds of landlords for generations with little more interaction than that between peasants and their oxen. Sympathy and even affection may develop without there ever being a subjective sense of similarity. Such phenomena as the jus primae noctis or the simple seduction of a peasant girl by her father's lord are not ill regarded—by the lord at any rate—because the one is seen as the instrument, not the equal, of the other. They are different creatures.[29]

---

[28] Quoted in Lipset and Bendix, *op. cit.*, 282.

[29] The phenomenon of social distance did not of course die with the birth of industrialization. On one occasion a person reported to a gentle Christian lady

When and for whatever reasons people of lower status come to know those of higher status as fellow creatures, the state of mind that produces status aspirations can then develop. Until he sees that he has at least enough of the intelligence, ambition, aggressiveness, skill, and ability to compete with others who are above him, the person of low status will stay where he is. Until he sees himself as being equal both in the value sense and in his competence, he will not compete. Once he gets this sense of equality, he begins to resent and to fight against social sanctions which discriminate against him without regard to his competence.

Under such circumstances a low-status person characteristically wants to associate with high status. He wants to climb a rung or two on the ladder—on the same ladder that is available to others. He wants to go to the same schools, live in the same neighborhoods, buy the same kind of clothes and other goods, and to have the same single political vote that others have. He wishes, that is, to establish closer social identity with others. This desire, so often ignored by those not in real-life contact with status problems, is intuitively sensed by both white people who bitterly oppose racial integration and colored people who insist upon it. The rhetorical question by the prejudiced white person—"Would you want your daughter to marry one of them?"—is precisely appropriate, however remote in reality the problem of inter-racial marriage may be. It is appropriate because marriage—as distinct from rape or seduction—is one of the most central manifestations of social equality, at least in the modern industrialized world.

It is no accident that a discussion of status in terms of occupation, education, and property should here touch by implication on ethnic minority status. So interrelated are the economic and ethnic kinds of social distinction that minority groups as such have often, though not always, suffered the displeasures of low social status. The successive waves of non-Nordic non-Protestant immigrants to America have typically entered society at the lowest status levels. During periods of railroad construction in the Southern United States in the early nineteenth century, Irish immigrants were employed as road workers because their death from tropical disease was less costly than that of a sturdy Negro slave. Again, Italians pried the usually willing Irish off the social bottom, and so have Puerto Ricans wedged themselves under

on his visit to a copper mining town in Utah. He expressed puzzlement that the miners could live in such cramped and dingy homes, to which the gentle lady replied: "They don't mind. They're Mexicans."

Negroes, Italians, and Irish in New York City. It cannot truly be said that any ethnic minority as such has in America been forced into a caste, but Negroes in the South until the 1940s and 50s were to all intents a caste. An ethnic minority that has newly arrived, thereby combining ethnicity with immigrant status, has repeatedly acquired the lowest social status in America, to rise inevitably with the passage of time. The refusal to accept forever a lowly state has combined with minority status to produce mobility.

Operating jointly with these other factors, family solidarity appears to be a common factor, though perhaps not necessarily antecedent to status mobility. In the lonely process of establishing identification with people who are alien to them yet dominate the culture, immigrants have to have unusually strong family ties to survive the anguished period of rejection. This is typically associated with ethnic solidarity, so that entire ethnic groups, living in the same neighborhoods and in similarly close-knit families, weather the storms of assimilation and status improvement together. And when a woman marries a man of lower status, she is apt to bring up the children so as to gain back her childhood status or to improve it. There is no reason to believe that such mixed-status families are notably happy; a strong mother is often found to be married to an ineffectual husband. But the interstatus and extrafamilial frustrations do appear to be directed toward status improvement.[30]

Organic causes of mobility

Each of the causes of mobility just described is social, though I do not pretend to have mentioned all of the social causes. But the social causes are not all the causes and, like all behavior, the mobility of individuals is a function of the interaction of the organism and the environment. In a chicken-and-egg polemic that has been hidden behind a massive array of convenient data, environmentalists have so emphasized the social influences that they have implicitly become not only primary but almost exclusive. The chicken causes the egg, so pay no attention to the egg as a cause of the chicken. But there is some evidence that organic factors are involved in mobility—again operating in no more solitude than several social factors do but nonetheless operating discretely. The evidence has been little sought, partly because it does not much interest social scientists and partly

[30] Lipset and Bendix, *op. cit.,* 249–250.

because it is a little hard to separate out. And it is slim. But one study has indicated that rural migrants to cities tend to have higher IQs than those who stay on the farm.[31] It is well known that no means has yet been found to purely test one's native intelligence. It is also known that social factors, mainly parental, influence one's intellectual aspiration level, including performance on IQ tests. But it is also well known that one does not altogether acquire his intelligence through training. Innate differences in intelligence and energy level presumably influence mobility, however these forces are directed and shaped by a variety of social influences, but there is little evidence to indicate how much.

For whatever reasons, again not easily described as altogether social, people who seek higher status have superior ability to defer gratifications, notably marriage, in order to train themselves in more exacting skills or to save money for business investment. Since such people are self-selected within broad categories of people who share the same low status but do not move together out of that status, it is reasonable to explore directly the psychic differences between those who do and do not seek a change of status. But until this is done, we can say no more than that it seems highly improbable that all the factors are environmental.

We must at the same time recognize there remains in the most equality-oriented societies—notably the Soviet Union but also Western Europe and America—a large set of formal and informal barriers which render more difficult the task of rising in status when one is of low birth and make easier the retention and improvement of status when one is born in high status. Nevertheless, to paraphrase Oliver Wendell Holmes, it will take more than the Declaration of Independence to persuade me that all men are created equal in their competence. The author of the Declaration did not even believe that himself. To reiterate, he believed that there was a natural aristocracy but that there should not be one imposed by society. And this takes us back to the

[31] C. T. Pihlblad and C. L. Gregory, Selective Aspects of Migration among Missouri High School Graduates, *American Sociological Review*, **19**: 314–324 (1954). The study also found that city residents who had migrated to cities averaged higher intelligence than city residents who had not become such by migration, that the larger the city, the higher the average intelligence, and the farther one migrated the higher the intelligence. The study makes no claim that geniuses are those who left the farm for the remotest big city or that people who have left Missouri, where the study was done, are really more intelligent than those who leave New York or California or Alabama.

distinction between inherent capacity and inherent worth, a distinction which is often ignored in social science, because the high value placed on human beings sometimes makes their students insist that people are in all inherent respects alike.

Marginality

We have just considered some of the causes of mobility. Now we move to marginality, that consequence of mobility which has great political portent. For it is when people are crossing the barbed-wire fences or the railroad tracks or passing in front of the ticket windows which separate the insiders from the outsiders, the better from the good, the saints from the strangers, that they are most anxious. Before one has passed the boundary he is excited but not fearfully worried. After he is on the other side he senses usually that he can get along. But when he is moving across the border he worries about tearing his pants, getting run down, being denied admission, or being damned forever to the status in which he was born.

Marginality can by no stretch of the sociological imagination be limited to the boundaries between socio-economic groups, that is, classes. A tribesman or peasant who has lived in a rural village of his ancestors but now moves to the big city (Nairobi, Calcutta, or Jakarta) suffers severely from the unease of marginality. So does the immigrant; the member of the racial minority who is moving out of caste-like restrictions imposed by the majority;[32] a skilled workingman's son who goes to technical school; and the able, energetic Scotch immigrant's son who graduates from Princeton and marries the dean's daughter. And so in a very special, highly individual way does the renegade from an upper-class background who becomes the radical leader of the working class.

Two observations are appropriate before proceeding further. Most people are not marginal but are stably located within the segment of society into which they were born. One American study indicates that almost half of the interviewed manual workers had worked at nonmanual jobs. And six out of ten nonmanual workers had worked at manual jobs. But the individual manual workers had spent 80% of their careers in manual jobs, and the nonmanual workers had spent 75% of their working years in nonmanual jobs.[33] Most occupational

[32] For a penetrating, speculative, literate consideration of the problem of racial and status marginality, see Philip Mason, *Prospero's Magic: Some Thoughts on Class and Race*, London, Oxford University Press, 1962.
[33] See Lipset and Bendix, *op. cit.*, 165–169.

mobility is confined to a change within the broad categories of manual or nonmanual and does not produce the tension that attends climbing the higher fence between working and middle classes.

The second observation is that mobility can be up or down and can produce similar although not identical anxieties in either case. A study of 130 American veterans of the Second World War showed that those whose postwar jobs were lower in status than their prewar jobs were racially more prejudiced than those whose jobs involved a rise in social status.[34] A more recent study used the raw data of the extensive Berelson-Lazarsfeld-McPhee Elmira Project, and thus had over four times as many cases to analyze as Bettelheim and Janowitz. This study found that both the upwardly and downwardly mobile were more prejudiced than those not in motion from one class to another. Indeed when it came to saying what they would do, as distinct from saying merely what they thought, the upwardly mobile were more often willing to exclude Negroes and Jews from their neighborhood than were the downwardly mobile.[35] In America, members of the middle class whose fathers were in the working class are more likely to abandon the Democratic party and vote for the conservative Republican party than are middle-class people whose fathers were also middle class. The opposite is consistently true in Germany and Scandinavia; middle-class voters of working class background are more likely to remain nonconservative than those whose background is middle class.[36] This may mean that it is easier to become assimilated to the middle class in America than in Europe,[37] but it does not explain why there is a higher frequency of nonconservative voting among those in America who are from middle-class background than among those who have moved into the middle class from a working-class background. Those who cross class lines, at least in America, apparently overreact, overadapt, to their new social status.

[34] Bruno Bettelheim and Morris Janowitz, *The Dynamics of Prejudice,* New York, Harper & Bros., 1950. The total sample of 130 people included 18 downwardly mobile, 68 not mobile, and 44 upwardly mobile. See Table 4 (IV), p. 59.

[35] J. Greenblum and L. I. Pearlin, Vertical Mobility and Prejudice: A Socio-Psychological Analysis, in Reinhard Bendix and Seymour Martin Lipset, *Class, Status, and Power,* Glencoe, Ill., The Free Press, 1953, 480–491.

[36] Lipset and Bendix, *op. cit.,* Table 2.7, p. 67.

[37] In Sweden, middle-class people from working-class backgrounds appeared more conservative if they owned a car than if they lacked this means of physical mobility. See *ibid.,* Table 2.8, p. 68.

Marginality means tension

Marginality as a consequence of mobility means almost tautologically that the marginal are more active than those who are not changing status. They are shedding major aspects of their personality and adopting new ones. They suffer from a variety of feelings: *guilt*, because they are to a degree renouncing the people (especially their parents) in the status group which nurtured them and set many of the rules for their behavior; *solitude*, because they have severed old ties and not yet established new ones; *conformism*, because they feel they must sedulously adopt the customs of the better status group if they are ever to be accepted by it; and a radical *ambivalence* of the self, as they see themselves from time to time failing the past that nurtured them, failing in their efforts to enter a new status, and failing to measure up to a self-image of virtue in either the Greek or the puritanical sense. They feel neither noble nor free of sin.

Marginality, whether attending upward or downward mobility, reflects upward aspirations which invest the marginal person, whether he freely accepts them or not. The upwardly mobile person wants to achieve the status above him. The downwardly mobile fears he will fall from the gracious status he was born into. Even if a person has neither ability nor desire to rise, the predominant social value is upward mobility, not adjustment to one's own abilities and competence. This makes the reality of movement painful for both, perhaps doubly painful to the downward mover because he is degraded if he moves, whereas the upward mover is upgraded.

In politics this fevered, anxious state of mind is apt to produce at once a conformity to the most conventional and obvious values of the higher status group and a kind of jungle lawlessness because the old rules which have been followed no longer lead to success. There is an eagerness to project outward the sense of personal inadequacy and to blame other people or things for one's own sensed faults. The upwardly mobile, with his new possessions in his new neighborhood, will condemn the flashy, pushy people who try to show off their wealth. The downwardly mobile, with his once expensive car, his rundown house in a once elegant neighborhood, will similarly condemn the pushy ones. Those of higher status, who are used to having political influence that accords with their status, may join extremely retrogressive social movements which will return society to the glorious past when the best and most conforming people ruled. With an exposed root system, such people are prone to bury their roots in the first political soil or night soil differing from that of the group which they have rejected or which rejects them. Rootlessness and norm-lessness, which Durkheim combines in the name anomy, can make for political extremism, which combines conventionality with a mob-like rejection of all law, in what Lubell has called the politics of revenge.

But it is equally important to observe that in their extraordinary activity marginal people can become the leaders of the society and the polity, which are advancing toward both the subjective personal equal-ity of equal inherent worth and the objective equality of more equal possession of both goods and opportunities. Not by any means do all marginal people adopt the anti-constitutional policies of left- or right-wing revenge. If Joseph McCarthy was a marginal man, so was Abraham Lincoln. If some German status-anxious shopkeepers and clerks became ardent Nazis, so did some become dedicated anti-Nazis, and marginality was evident in at least some.[38] Marginality does pro-duce hyperactivity and at least nonaverage anxiety, but the channels in which this tense energy moves are as broad as the political spec-trum, quite regardless of the impressive and unimpressive evidence about the marginal origins of Nazism.

Mental differences between classes

Marx said that one's personality is a result of his social relations, particularly his class relations. Neither he nor those who have been conscious of class since his time have contributed much to a knowl-edge of the mental differences between people in various social groups. To avoid speculating wildly, I will not go much beyond extant data in this still little-explored area and—violating common custom—will start at the bottom, which is the least understood by both the readers and writers of books.

[38] Of the 21 cases of anti-Nazis that David M. Levy studied, only 1 could surely be called upper-middle class (an historian); at least 8 were lower-middle class (for example clerk, druggist, tailor, or farm manager); and 13 were products of the crossing of religious or nationality lines in the marriages of their parents. See his Anti-Nazis: Criteria of Differentiation, in Alfred H. Stanton and Stewart E. Perry, *Personality and Political Crisis*, Glencoe, Ill., The Free Press, 1951, 151–227.

The bottom stratum

By the bottom I mean not the working class but the semi-employed class who give the working class something to look down on as shiftless, improvident breeders of the shiftless and improvident. There is no need to picture this group in detail—as it has been with considerable success by Hollingshead [39]—because politically its members are almost completely inactive and, unlike members of other groups, are marginal to society itself. They engage in minimal contacts of an economic and social sort on the job, at school, and (with abnormally high frequency) with the police. Otherwise—notably as regards politics—they are almost altogether out of society. The extent to which they compose mobs in times of social unrest is quite unknown. They may not even take this part in politics. These are the poor whose annals are short and simple and whose lives, miserable or not, are stunted. Our contact with them has probably not much changed over the sesquicentennium since the following was written:

> Poor people are often censured for want of frugality and economy in the management of their earnings. In particular, they are accused of extravagance in eating wheaten bread; of being over-nice in neglecting as they do the use of potatoes; and of a luxurious excess in drinking tea.
> Wheaten bread may be eaten alone with pleasure; but potatoes require either meat or milk to make them go down. . . . Poor people indeed give them to their children in greasy water, in which they have boiled their greens and their morsel of bacon.
> Still you exclaim, *Tea is a luxury.* If you mean fine hyson tea, sweetened with refined sugar, and softened with cream, I readily admit it to be so. But *this* is not the tea of the poor. Spring water, just coloured with a few leaves of the lowest-priced tea, and sweetened with the brownest sugar, is the luxury for which you reproach them. To this they have recourse from mere necessity: and were they now to be deprived of this they would immediately be reduced to bread and water. . . .[40]

It should not be forgotten that this lowest status group, like the others, is composed of ever-changing individuals. There may be a residuum of people descended from fourteen generations of the bottom, but historically there has been a continuous flow in and out, as can be observed most clearly in America. Irish in the early nine-

---

[39] See Hollingshead, *op. cit.*, 110–120 and passim, on what he calls Class V.
[40] Rector David Davies, *The Case of Labourers in Husbandry*, 1796. Quoted by permission of the Twentieth Century Fund, from W. S. Woytinsky and E. S. Woytinsky, *World Population and Production: Trends and Outlook*, New York, Twentieth Century Fund, 1953, 282–283.

teenth century almost without exception were in the lowest status group and are now spread throughout all statuses. The same has been true of other immigrant groups, including Chinese and Japanese on the West Coast. The same is occurring in that group which an American sectional mythology has quite persistently assigned the bottom-most role by their natural-born characteristics: Negroes at last are gradually merging into all social strata.

The working class and the middle class

The working class—people who work with their hands in jobs requiring more or less skill but also the continuous labor which the bottom-most class does not typically produce—is somewhat better known and can be compared with the middle class. They are more inclined than middle-class people to follow impulses and less inclined to defer gratifications; there is a greater difference between their aspirations and their acts than among the middle class. Their aspirations are nonetheless relatively modest, centering around hopes of going into some small business for themselves or getting more skilled, more interesting, or otherwise pleasant work.[41]

In their social views, no clear-cut pattern of race prejudice appears unequivocally,[42] though there is some slight evidence that working people may be more ethnocentric than the middle class.[43] But there is fairly convincing evidence that the working class is more conformist to the demands for the repression of civil liberties than is the middle class. Large samples in the Stouffer study and in American Institute of Public Opinion surveys have shown that working-class people and the correlative status category of low educational achievement are consistently less tolerant of free speech in America than are middle-class people and those with more education.[44] Such findings may shock people who idealize the working class as being unusually hu-

---

[41] See Barber, *op. cit.*, 307–315.

[42] See R. Centers, Attitude and Belief in Relation to Occupational Stratification, *Journal of Social Psychology*, **27**: 159–185 (1948). Reprinted in Daniel Katz et al., *Public Opinion and Propaganda*, New York, The Dryden Press, 1954, 132–151.

[43] T. Adorno et al., *The Authoritarian Personality*, New York, Harper & Bros., 1950, 265–269.

[44] Samuel A. Stouffer, *Communism, Conformity, and Civil Liberties*, Garden City, Doubleday and Co., 1955, 138, 90. And note an independent finding of comparable class differences in V. O. Key, Jr., *Public Opinion and American Democracy*, New York, Alfred A. Knopf, 1961, Table 6.8, p. 136.

mane and liberal. Humane liberals assume that because they to a degree identify with the working class, the working class also identifies with them.

A major implication of such findings is that the working class is not per se any less conservative than any other class. Indeed it may be more conservative because it is more directly dependent on the uninterrupted operation of an industrial system that furnishes jobs. The working class in a successfully private-capitalist country like the United States is probably less inclined to advocate political change than the working class in a state-capitalist country like the Soviet Union. And since workingmen in both countries are steadily better off than they ever were before and better off than their forefathers, neither is likely to be interested in revolution, whereas the peasant population in a country only beginning to industrialize may very enthusiastically support revolution. This may lead some to the notion that the bright hope of the future is no longer the workingman but the deprived peasant or tribesman of Africa or Asia. If they should also prove to be fallibly human, perhaps a new ethnic group from outer space will come to the rescue of a beloved imagery.

In the case of neither the American nor Russian workingman nor the African or Asian peasant[45] is there profound liberalism or conservatism. In all such cases there is much more persuasive evidence of self-interest, which may be served on occasion by change and on occasion by stasis. It is puzzling why the downtrodden should be expected to show a large measure of humanitarian concern—of liberalism—where working-class interests are not evident. It would indeed be an odd state of affairs if those who get less in a society would be seriously concerned with the welfare of those who get more. Humanitarianism is sometimes a necessity for those who have more; it remains a luxury for those who have less. It is not the people per se, but the condition of their stomachs and pocketbooks that controls. There is no evidence that, within the community that is real for them, workingmen are any less generous than any others in their real communities. But workers live in a less extended community, one that is large in the number of its people but small in the breadth of its interests. If these observations sound too much like an excuse for work-

---

[45] For the hair-breadth escape of some young populists from their intended beneficiaries in a peasant village in prerevolutionary Russia, see W. S. Woytinsky, *Stormy Passage,* New York, The Vanguard Press, 1961, 69–85.

ing-class people, bear in mind that until there is complete equality of opportunity and far more equal income, lower-status people will continue to have situational reasons for lacking the greater breadth of outlook of those in higher-status groups.

The top stratum

The upper class often appears to be nothing more than a tired or aged middle class. It is not the same as the French prerevolutionary bourgeoisie who, in a happy symbiosis with the royal court, exchanged money for royally confirmed feudal, that is, upper-class titles. Such middle-class members are marginal to the upper class but not yet in it —though their children through schooling in the proper institutions and marriage into the proper families may achieve it.

The upper class might be presumed by the public or by itself to be the ruling class, but its power is more apparent than real. It is vigorous members of the upper-middle class, often contemptuous of the upper class yet envious of it, who are bent on becoming rulers and have the energy and acumen to do so.

Occasional upper-class individuals like Thomas Jefferson, James Madison, Woodrow Wilson, Franklin Roosevelt, Winston Churchill, and Jawaharlal Nehru may become rulers, indeed great rulers. Proportional to its size, the upper class doubtless oversupplies rulers to the total society. But it seems far more common to observe individuals like George Washington, Alexander Hamilton, Andrew Jackson, Abraham Lincoln, Herbert Hoover, and Dwight Eisenhower emerging from the lower- or upper-middle class to positions of political leadership in modern society.

Aside from producing rulers, like Jefferson, who as individuals renounce their political loyalties to their own kind, the upper class in politics seems to be a conservative influence that lacks the real power of the bourgeoisie and of the working class. The upper class, however, may—as in Nazi Germany—form a power coalition, so that for a few moments at least the upper class may dream happy daydreams of wielding all power. Their ancestors did wield it with vigor but the upper class must now share it with members of the bourgeoisie and proletariat.

The status of status politics

These considerations of status relationships between classes and political leaders are reserved for consideration in the next chapter. We can meanwhile close but not seal a discussion of status with a brief recapitulation.

It may have been usually true that, as Madison and Marx have said, inequality of property is the most enduring cause of political conflict. But it may be better to broaden the concept to status and say that differences in status, when these become rigid and socially enforced, have been and remain an enduring cause of conflict. By so broadening the concept we can include conflicts like the Protestant Reformation and the process of decolonization in which wars or revolutions have been pursued for other than merely (or even primarily) economic considerations. Economic status is not equal to socio-economic status, which in turn is not coextensive with status. The color of a man's skin, the colors of his national flag, the hue of his religion —all these can establish politically portentous status distinctions.

Social science, interested in human aggregates, has perhaps tended to overemphasize the need for a sense of common interest to emerge before a status category can become a self-conscious class. To some degree class consciousness is necessary for common action, but to say so leaves indistinct, in concept and in research, the difference between a million men who think alike and a million men who share the same thoughts. There is certainly no lingual community consciousness in the fact that all Englishmen speak English. There is not necessarily class consciousness if each unemployed person votes for the same candidate because that candidate appeals to the self- (not class-) interest of each unemployed person.

In his study of social class identification, Centers emphasizes the Marxian concept that class consciousness is necessary to turn a stratum into a class. The puzzling thing is that he finds (but does not discuss) a higher correlation between objective economic status and vote than between subjective class identification and vote—a finding that does not destroy the consciousness theory but weakens it.[46] The same

---

[46] Richard Centers, *The Psychology of Social Classes: a Study of Class Consciousness*, Princeton, Princeton University Press, 1949. In Table 34, p. 114, there is a correlation of .36 between class affiliation and vote, .45 between economic status and vote, and .57 between conservatism-radicalism and vote.

finding appears in a study of the 1951 British election, the investigators finding a "slightly stronger" correlation between objective class status and vote than between class identification and vote.[47]   If these findings, which are little or not at all discussed by their finders, are confirmed, there will indeed be confirmation that an individual need not be conscious of his social position to be politically affected by it, and that indeed having a class consciousness is less portentous than having a class unconsciousness, in the Freudian sense.   Both criteria (objective and subjective) are good predictors of how one will vote, and subjective identification refines the objective category.   When objective status and subjective identification combine in the same individual, both the effect of one's socio-economic self-interest and the effect of one's awareness of the group nature of his self-interest operate as vectors moving the individual in the same direction.

Aside from the difficult problem of objective and subjective class-status, a major remaining difficulty lies in understanding internal, mental conflict between self-interest and various group identifications. In the British election of 1951, the most important issue for all those interviewed was preservation of peace (and yet class status and identification still operated as significant forces).[48]   In deciding whether to vote Conservative or Labour, was a person doing so as a workingman or as a war veteran?   In their study of the 1952 American election, Campbell and associates reported that the portion of trade-union members who voted Democratic dropped from 55 to 43% of skilled and from 52 to 39% of semi-skilled workingmen.[49]   Did these reductions in Democratic support among workingmen reflect a sense that the Republican party had suddenly become the workingman's friend, or that Eisenhower could bring peace out of the nagging Korean conflict? [50]

Socio-economic status continues to operate in politics but not with the monolithic force that Marx attributed to it and by no means with sole reference to economic status.   From time to time noneconomic

[47] R. S. Milne and H. C. Mackenzie, *Straight Fight: a Study of Voting Behaviour in the Constituency of Bristol North-East at the General Election of 1951*, London, The Hansard Society, 1954, 43.

[48] See *ibid.*, 102.

[49] Angus Campbell et al., *The Voter Decides*, Evanston, Ill., Row, Peterson & Co., 1954, Table 5.1 at pp. 72–73.

[50] For discussions of social classes in political transition in the industrially mature American society, see Angus Campbell et al., *The American Voter*, New York, John Wiley & Sons, 1960, ch. 13, The Role of Social Class; V. O. Key, Jr., *op. cit.*, ch. 6, Occupation and Class; and Samuel Lubell, *The Future of American Politics*, New York, Harper & Bros., 1952, ch. 4, The Frontier Reappears.

issues emerge which can quite overwhelm the importance of economic issues. People neither live nor vote by bread alone. There is scarcely anything spiritual about the issue of survival, which cuts across class lines in the democracy of total war. As the production and distribution of material goods in advanced economies becomes stabilized and equalized, and if the issue of survival is resolved affirmatively, it may well be that the basis of politics will shift to noneconomic, nonsurvival issues. There is an abundance of such issues to interest and divide people politically for several generations to come, in even the most prosperous societies. And for the still semi-feudal, semi-agrarian, and impoverished part of the world the various and unequal distribution of status—economic and otherwise—is still of explosive portent.

The balance of this book will consider some of the problems of political leadership and of under- and overdeveloped societies, in the tense and fast-moving contemporary world. We can regret that our notions of the future have proportionally developed no faster than they did when men fought and politicked without the benefit of literacy. But at least we are not at the point where, like Plato and Aristotle, we can only sigh for a better and freer Golden Age of the past. For neither workingmen nor corporation presidents nor the heads of Soviet industrial trusts nor social science students and researchers are worse off than they were in bygone days. And we have not yet destroyed ourselves. The difficulty is that politics is fraught with explosive force when people rise above the subsistence level, want more goods and more liberty, and fear they may lose either or both. And people now are in that frame of mind all over the world. If there are any road signs pointing to a return to the big sleep of the Middle Ages, they are being blown over by the tornadoes of change. The awake are more alert and fearful; the long-somnolent people of low personal, class, and national status are now awake and hopeful. A trying time for the psyches of men.

CHAPTER 9

Political leaders
and followers

Democracy in Iowa

Several social psychologists once did an experimental study of politically different kinds of leadership. The experimental subjects were twenty boys about eleven years old. They were divided into four groups of five each. The boys in each group were matched with those in the others, so that each group was about the same as the others in such factors as intelligence, obedience, socio-economic status, amount of social participation, leadership tendencies, and quarrelsomeness. Their activities in the experimental clubs consisted of handicraft and games and during four months continued for successive six-week periods, with a change in leaders at the end of each period.[1]

The phenomenon that was systematically varied in the experiment was the style of leadership. The experimental leaders were psychologically trained adults (including the experimenters) who acted in distinctly different ways in successive runs of the experiment. One of the styles was called autocratic. In it the leader assumed the highest degree of direct command and responsibility for deciding what the group would do, how they would do it, which group members deserved

[1] This study is reported in several places. See K. Lewin, R. Lippitt, and R. K. White, Patterns of Aggressive Behavior in Experimentally Created Social Climates, *Journal of Social Psychology,* **10**: 271–299 (1939); and R. Lippitt and R. K. White, An Experimental Study of Leadership and Group Life, in T. M. Newcomb and E. L. Hartley, eds., *Readings in Social Psychology,* New York, Henry Holt & Co., 1947, 315–330. The fullest report is in Ralph K. White and Ronald Lippitt, *Autocracy and Democracy,* New York, Harper & Bros., 1960.

praise, who should work with whom, etc. The second style was called democratic, with the leader serving more as a guide for group discussion of what the group should do and for the activity that followed. Decisions were largely group decisions; the leader presented alternatives where appropriate; and responsibility and the allocation of tasks were established by the group. The third style was labeled laissez-faire, with the leader acting as a technical source of information and advice but avoiding both participation and the making of decisions with or for the group. Two of the four groups experienced all three kinds of leadership; two experienced only autocratic and democratic leadership.

In the autocratic situation, the leader praised and criticized individuals personally, arbitrarily (without giving reasons), and often capriciously. In the democratic situation the leader gave reasons for praise or blame; in the laissez-faire he avoided evaluation as much as possible. The autocratic leader stayed aloof from the group, the democratic became personally involved in camaraderie, and the laissez-faire kept apart, as a preoccupied rather than as an aloof person. In each group the leader took occasion to leave the boys alone. While he was gone a strange adult, a psychologist disguised as a janitor or electrician, interrupted the group in its activity and rudely criticized individuals and the group as a whole.

The results of the extensive experiments demonstrated persuasively that the kind of leadership made a difference in the pattern of behavior of the boys in the group, because when the style was changed from autocratic to democratic, democratic to autocratic, laissez-faire to autocratic, etc., the boys acted differently. When released from the autocratic leader to the laissez-faire situation, the boys changed from activity that involved little horseplay to a continued outburst of purposeless fooling around. When the autocratic leader was absent for awhile the boys would slack off on their work, which they took up again with great vigor when he returned. When the democratic leader left the room, work went on at almost the same rate. When the laissez-faire leader was gone, the amount of work stayed the same or increased, in a couple of instances because a boy in the group exerted leadership when the normal leader stepped out. The response to the rude stranger with his insults again varied. Both autocratic and democratic groups expressed some hostility to the interloper. The autocratically led boys displaced their aggressions against this frustrating interloper by mild fighting with boys in the club next door, and the democratic group took out its aggressions against inanimate objects in their own club room.

In the autocratic situation the boys were more dependent on their leader for simply paying attention to them and for taking the initiative in doing things. They showed more signs of rebellious discontent but were less inclined to make suggestions as to what the group should do. In the democratic context the boys established more ties to each other, working together as a group, rather than as isolates each separately tied to the leader. They more often looked for approval to the group than to the leader. In the autocratic group, the granting of status and social approval was more the prerogative of the leader; in the democratic group it was more the prerogative of the group. The autocratically led boys nonetheless had a kind of basic solidarity that was in some circumstances more pronounced than in the democratic groups. When the boys were interviewed at the end of the experiment, all but one who directly compared "their autocratic and democratic leaders" said they preferred the democratic leader. The one boy who preferred the autocrat was the son of an army National Guard officer.[2]

These are not all the findings of a highly suggestive experiment into which were built a set of quasi-political ideas and which produced almost a microcosm of the political world. There was dependence on the autocratic leader, displaced aggression against outsiders, the misery of autocratic society that knits itself together in opposition to the ruler. And most preferred a democratic leader. From this we can safely conclude that young American boys, at least in Iowa where the experiment was carried out, prefer democratically run clubs, but we cannot conclude that all Americans do or that one would get the same result with boys raised in Germany, the Soviet Union, China, India, or Nigeria.[3]

But we can, I think, safely conclude that the very special relationship between leaders and the members of the society which they lead

[2] A collateral attack on the obvious implication appears in a finding that air force flight training cadets were less authoritarian and less stereotyped in their orientation toward superiors after a year of training than after just a week of military life. The air force cadets were more authoritarian and "superior-oriented" than a comparable sample of college students. The authors attribute this to recruitment rather than military training. D. T. Campbell and T. H. McCormack, Military Experience and Attitudes toward Authority, *American Journal of Sociology,* **62:** 482–490 (1957).

[3] But note directly comparable experiments in Japan, reported in Ralph K. White and Ronald Lippitt, *Autocracy and Democracy,* 267–268.

s a highly dynamic, very sensitive one. Thousands of books have been written about hundreds of prominent political leaders—some five thousand, it has been estimated, on Abraham Lincoln alone. This writing would not be done were it not for the enduring fascination of great men, for not only writers but also readers. Perhaps no other single subject save sex has so preoccupied the human race, whether of high or low station, subtle or naive, illiterate or educated. And the most prominent single category of great or at least prominent men is to be found in politics—as statesmen, agitators, theorists, polemicists, philosophers—or all of these wrapped in one man's life, as in the case of Thomas Jefferson, Lenin, Wilson, or Nehru.

Carlyle, Tolstoi, and Mann

The difficulty, as I have hinted, lies in the typical ignoring of the basic fact of leadership, namely, that it involves universally a relationship between leaders and followers. Without this relationship there might be a society, but there surely would be no leaders and probably no politics either. A man who thinks he is Napoleon is ordinarily classed among the insane these days and confined to an institution, just as Napoleon was confined to Elba and then St. Helena. The reason for confining the real Napoleon was that, without his adoring public, he could not so irrepressibly wage war and conquer nations. In short, by removing him from France and his adoring public, he was made into somebody other than Napoleon.

Failure to appreciate the necessary relationship has led to an impossible dilemma, one of whose horns was polished by Thomas Carlyle and the other by Leo Tolstoi. Carlyle tended to see history with heavy emphasis on the role of the great man or the great devil—Cromwell and Frederick the Great being examples of the former and the "thin, acrid, incorruptible, seagreen" Robespierre of the latter. Tolstoi, in writing on the invasion of Russia by France, protests so much that Napoleon's role was insignificant that he raises him to prominence, almost without external confirmation, by repeatedly emphasizing Napoleon's triviality.[4] Carlyle appeared to regard mankind

---

[4] But his view of leaders was nonetheless consistent. In *War and Peace*, Tolstoi drops a very central character, Marshal Kutuzov, the successful defender of Russia who opposed continuing the harassing attack on French forces when they retreated beyond the Russian frontier, just as soon as Russian policy called for moving into Europe. See *War and Peace*, Book 15, ch. 4.

as sheep and leaders as shepherds; Tolstoi would have called leaders wolves, as Jefferson indeed did.

The dilemma is a false one. Some leaders are shepherds, some are wolves, and some fit neither metaphor. But a man would not be a leader without a public which adheres to him and which looks to him for expression, guidance, and the making of most decisions in public affairs. Each is as necessary to the other (but not by analogy) as husband is to wife, and each is as necessary to the subject of leadership as husband and wife are to marriage. And yet virtually all discussions of leadership leave out the public half of the equation. If behavior is a function of the organism and the environment, so also (but not by analogy) is leadership a function of the leader and the public that follows him.

At least two reasons help explain the literary unpopularity of the popular half of the leadership concept. Leaders themselves, as men of nonaverage ability, find it easy to exaggerate their freedom of action and therefore their power. It is easier for them, in their self-image, to see themselves as governing rather than being governed, to see the broad extent rather than the broad limits of their power. Being chief of state over a large area of land is apt to make a leader feel he actually controls it and its people, whereas in reality even the most remarkable, gifted, and humane leaders are able to do little more than accelerate or hold steady or decelerate the rate of social movement through history. The track and the switches along the line are pretty much beyond the control of the locomotive engineer. The role of the engineer is greater than that of even his most travel-conscious passengers, but he is ahead of no one if the travelers get off and climb on another train.

The inevitable, understandable, even incorruptible narcissism of leaders is less excusably furthered by their biographers, most of whom seem to have only the vaguest theoretical awareness that leaders have any connection with anyone below the rank of Congressman, Member of Parliament, General of the Army, or the leading intellectuals of their age. The very central relationship of the leader to his broad popular following gets less mention than do the great man's childhood acquaintances and his close friends and enemies in public life. One does not have to agree altogether with Tolstoi to recognize that without their popular following leaders could not rule over more than a small segment of their nations. How many people did Czar Nicholas II rule over, particularly after his troops fired on the demonstrators in the crisis that touched off the 1905 revolution? How many people did

Chiang Kai-shek ever rule, among close to a half-billion Chinese? These rulers and the ancient Pharaohs may have on occasion successfully used force against individuals, but they lacked a really popular base for their power. They could by coercion produce only a fraction of the united support in action that has been elicited since the Russian and Chinese revolutions, by Russian and Chinese leaders, from their broad publics.

Nevertheless, both Lenin and Mao Tse-tung have also been far more creatures than creators of revolution, and they continued to depend on at least the tacit assent of the populace. It is indeed a paradox that the ruler is most powerful who represents the broadest range of followers among the people and that the one who governs without it thereby is not necessarily impotent but weaker. This relationship is an intricate and specific one, not readily transferable from one time to another, from one place to another, or from one leader to another. The delusions of grandeur that beset powerful men who regard themselves as omnipotent are discussed below in a consideration of charisma. Suffice it to say here that it is hard to conceive of Hitler ruling Saudi Arabia in 1933, of Ibn Saud ruling the Soviet Union or even his neighboring Egypt in 1940, and—more's the pity—of Lincoln ruling Russia in 1861.

The most intellectually successful effort to conceptualize the leader-follower relationship is the work of a novelist. In his classic political allegory, *Mario and the Magician*, Thomas Mann gives to both leader and followers equal prominence. The followers do not become an impersonal mass, which a public never is but which social theorists are apt to convert any aggregation of more than fifty people into. The leader is not simply the embodiment of vast social forces. Both, as individuals, are in very intense interaction, the very aspect of leader-follower relationships which writers are most prone to ignore. If the discussion that follows falls short of Mann's brilliant symmetry and exquisite psychological insight, it is for lack of adequate facts about this powerful and subtle relationship—and a desire to abide by the ground rules of nonfiction.

Intimacy and remoteness

What are the special characteristics of the relationship? It is like that between friends, work associates, brothers, husband and wife, and parents and children in its intimacy. Followers are incessantly curious about the personal life and welfare of their leader. They want to know what he eats, how long he sleeps, what he does for recreation, and what his wife is like. When he is ill they worry. When he is troubled they are troubled. When he triumphs, the victory is also personally their own. Again like these other relationships, the one between the leader and his followers is mutual and reciprocal. Followers depend on their leader and he on them, not just for direct support in their common political program but more personally.

To gain new strength for their unending task of governing, leaders periodically venture out into the sea of citizens, to be refreshed by the salty breezes that seldom penetrate a ruler's mansion or palace. On a popular tour, Wilson was at first shocked and then braced by hearing a voice from the crowd yell, "Atta boy, Woody," an appellation no intimate of his would dream of using. Franklin Roosevelt was similarly buoyed up at a discouraging time during the depths of the depression. Jarred, jolted, often squeezed and twisted by wellwishers who want merely to touch him, a leader nonetheless needs this popular contact in the same sense that brother needs contact with brother, husband with wife, parents with children. As such the relationship is one instance of the basic social need.

The leader differs from his followers most markedly in his role: by and large he is the active and followers are the passive participants in the exercise of political power. That is, he proposes and the public ultimately disposes. The leader decides what to do and how to do it. The public decides whether he shall be permitted to do it. The latitude allowed the leader may be broad or narrow, but his power to effect anything enduring is constantly limited by the public's power to grant or withdraw support. This mutual interdependence of the roles of proposer and disposer obviously applies in societies where the process of popular responsibility is institutionalized by periodic elections. It applies, perhaps equally, in dictatorships, because a leader is in no more political interaction with those who are indifferent to him than he is with the mountains, the forests, and the rivers. By sheer coercion he may be able to elicit labor from many people but this process is no more political than the relationship between a man and a mule or between a prison-warden and a prisoner. The power that is exercised is not political. This of course is not to say that there is no politics in a dictatorship but that dictatorships, to the extent that they rely on political means, are dependent on popular assent and support.

But an almost unique characteristic is the great distance separating leader and follower. If indeed it is intimate, it is for virtually all followers remote. Only a small fraction can ever establish even the thin strand of contact that is involved in attending a parade or other public meeting at which the leader appears. For others, the contact is indirect, mediated through the electronic equipment of radio and television and through the printed page. It is this great distance that apparently causes students to neglect the relation between a leader and his broad popular following, and to neglect the relation between leaders and their students and biographers. But thin though these strands are, their cumulative strength both ways is so great as to bind leaders and followers closely and strongly one to the other in their joint endeavors.

The relation between leader and followers is thus at once intimate and remote, with the unbelievably complex role of the leader as policy formulator, initiator, and executor being exercised within popular limits. What then resolves this paradox of a relation that in most other parts of society could not exist? Why do women sometimes swoon when they see their political leader gaze in their direction? Why have dictators like Peron occasionally received marital and often more casual sexual proposals from ardent female adherents? And why do some men and women cry when their beloved leader dies?

Close identification with leaders

A standard explanation is that such people—which includes, in more or less intense form, all people in any modern nation at one time— are responding to a father or big-brother image and are emotionally tied to a surrogate father or brother. But the pattern of interactions, which is so varied from one nation to the next, does not quite fit this explanation. It makes a species into a genus. More appropriately the relation can be described as identification. To the extent that they interact with their leader, followers are putting themselves in his place. In their own minds they are becoming him. The style in which they do so may in some national circumstances resemble the relation between children and their parents, brothers, friends, or be-lievers and their god. But the genotype for the various phenotypes is identification.

The special character of identification has to do with the remoteness of the intimacy. The followers identify not with their equal but with one whom they look up to as a man of superior virtue (energy, skill, intelligence, wisdom, compassion, patriotism, and other virtues). They identify with a possibly imperfect ideal who represents all that they

are and all that they believe in politically. The leader is not what his
followers are but what they would like to be. If they have particular
enemies and friends in society, they expect their leader to share them,
defeating the former and bringing victory to the latter. If they have
particular aspirations for their country, the leader embodies these aspirations.

An implication of this is that the more completely a citizen has fulfilled his needs and hopes, and the freer therefore he is of frustrations
and anxieties, the less likely he is to need to identify passively with a
political leader. The weaker and more frustrated a citizen is, the
more likely he will want to identify passively with a very strong, very
wise, and virtuous political leader. Indeed a virile leader may politically arouse a following that has been hitherto impotent and with-
drawn from the polity. If a citizen is frustrated and anxious enough,
he will suffer from the same perceptual distortions of leaders that
beset other facets of his outlook on life and will more likely make a
god of his leader and devils of his and the leader's opponents. But
no man in politics, whether citizen or politician, is altogether free of
admiration for superiors. If successful citizens take a more realistic
view of leaders because their need to identify is less, they will nevertheless identify in some degree. Even Hitler in a way identified with
Hindenburg and Bismarck, Stalin with Lenin. And both Nehru and
Emperor Hirohito of Japan have had intense admiration for Lincoln.
The measure of identification is in a sense a measure of the gap between the real and the ideal, a gap that apparently exists in the lives
of all men in all ages. In the intensely religious sixteenth century, the
public's ideal individuals included Luther and Calvin. In the intensely
political twentieth century the major public ideals are politicians, some
of whom have either killed God, shoved Him aside, or clearly implied
that His Major Prophet was now themselves, as chief of state.

The distance between a leader and his followers is ordinarily great
and safe enough to protect those followers who want to believe in
their leader's magnificence and who identify with him even more
strongly because of the distance. The fascination of remote intimacy
is so great that most people seem to marvel at what by identification
should have been obvious—that these leaders are real people after all,
that they smile, laugh, get up, shake hands, sit down just like anyone
else and are actually human. The visitor to the office of a chief of
state may tremble in anticipation and then be disarmed by the utterly
unassuming simplicity of such a complicated, extraordinary person.
They think it a miracle that a leader could be so like themselves, even

though they have for a long time identified with him. The reason for this paradox is hard to find, but its existence is apparent. The awesome commonness of Abraham Lincoln not only set him aside from the pretentiousness of others but also was cause and consequence of his reciprocal identification with common people. Citizens choose and attach themselves to someone they would like to resemble and then are surprised to find out how well they have chosen.

It is sometimes asserted that it is the distance itself which lends enchantment, that no man can be great in the eyes of his intimates. This belief is the basis for the deliberate maintenance of mental distance between officers and enlisted men, employer and employees, teachers and students, and others in a superior-subordinate relationship. In some circumstances it may be true, but perhaps less so among the most enduring leaders. Lincoln's now immortal succession of adherents is not disenchanted but rather enchanted by his simplicity and commonness. Lincoln's partner in law practice, William Herndon, regarded him as perhaps the greatest man since Christ, whose disciples and constant companions did not regard Him with contempt any more than did the disciples of Gandhi so regard their beloved leader. And Harry Hopkins was devoted to Franklin Roosevelt.

Correlatively, a leader, never quite sure of himself, needs other assurance than he can get just from the general public. He surrounds himself with close associates who are more or less critical of the leader's policies but usually quite uncritical of him. They are a staff to lean on and a mirror to hide his personal blemishes and asymmetries. And sometimes a leader gets the help of a spouse, like Mary Lincoln or Eleanor Roosevelt, who reminds him that he is nearer to humanity than to divinity. In any case a leader, however gregarious with crowds and with intimates, at times is in remote solitude.

Convenient, even necessary as it may be for a leader to keep people away so that he can perform his tasks, there is no other reason to believe that familiarity leads to depreciation except among those who wish to be either superior or subordinate in the subjective sense, and do not wish to be of equal dignity with those whose political role and social status differ from their own. It must be remembered that in the process of identification, there is an element of equality: people are the leader and he is they. In an age of popularly responsive government, the course of political development is toward equalitarian values and democratization, though not necessarily constitutionality. In such a time, the prospect of enduring popular admiration would appear greater for leaders who act like Andrew Jackson, Abraham Lincoln, Habib Bourguiba, and Jawaharlal Nehru in their public contacts than with those who stand aloof on a self-made pedestal above the masses. The greater the leader's sense of equality, the greater the identification.

Although not central to the present study of leaders and followers, the role of staff members vis-à-vis their chief and the general public may help distinguish the roles of leaders and followers in various situations. If popular leaders wish not only to be distinct from but also to resemble their following, staff members appear to prefer distinction to commonness. They want to be like the boss and unlike his followers. The kind of role I have in mind is that adopted during the first part of his public career by Alexander Hamilton, who served on George Washington's military staff during war and as a kind of head chamberlain in Washington's cabinet; Martin Van Buren, who was Jackson's Secretary of State, Minister to England, and Vice President; Henry Wallace, who held various posts in Roosevelt's government; and Anthony Eden, Churchill's right-hand man in the conduct of foreign affairs. Among intellectuals who for a time adopted the role are Plato, advisor to the tyrant of Syracuse; Aristotle, the tutor of Alexander the Great; and Trotsky, the brilliant aide of Lenin.

If all such staff members have something in common, it appears to be the desire to share power without undertaking the arduous and dangerous task of acquiring it on their own. They become vicarious wielders of power but are carried to the heights on the back of the boss. In turn they wield little or no *political* power over him, in contrast to those who do act, as legislators or agitators, on their own. Staff members rarely have an influential public following. They therefore are limited to using reason, cunning, and other verbal powers in influencing the boss and almost inevitably give way when the power of the public or influential segments of it is felt.

There can be no more persuasive argument for the true impotence of staff members than their usual inability to succeed politically on their own. Either their judgment fails them—as in the cases of Roosevelt's Henry Wallace and Churchill's Anthony Eden—or they lack the ability to establish rapport with the public, or both. In any event, for public weal or not, their political relationship is quite purely instrumental, not of the popular but of the leader's will. In this sense they have no autonomous part in the political process. They have traded their birthright for the revocable license to play-act in the role of ruler. They get a closer glimpse at power than the general public without ever truly exercising it in the way that at times the public even in an autocracy wields power, as in the case of emancipation of serfs in Russia in 1861. Like scholars who analyze and criticize the work of great philosophers and scientists, they can only pretend to eminence. Administrators effectuate established policy, law, and custom and therefore have the instrumental authority inherent in that role and often the quasi-political affection of the corps they administer. But staff members have only the instrumental power derived from the will of the leader. It is nonetheless fortunate that such a category of people exists, for—despite pretensions he may have of being able to do everything—no leader could perform the complex tasks of government without a staff that is intelligent, energetic, and devoted to the boss.[5]

Special characteristics of leaders

Thus far we have emphasized what binds leaders and followers together. Before taking up in more detail this relationship, which remains the central question in this chapter, we may appropriately here consider what it is that sets leaders apart from followers—what causes them to become the living paradox of identifiers who are markedly distinct from the followers with whom they reciprocally identify.

In Chapter 2, I posited the notion that in terms of basic needs, political leaders are distinct from other prominent people, not in their desire for power but in their sheer enjoyment of the political process. They engage in politics because it is the way they can fulfill themselves most completely, a process related to their skills and capacities. To enjoy political life, one must have the abilities it demands, just as a sportsman needs good physical coordination, strength, endurance, etc. At this point we can emphasize the more common characteristics which distinguish the very heterogeneous category of political activists—the elite from which chiefs of state emerge.

Probably most of the characteristics distinguishing any elite group also distinguish the political elite. Not only business leaders, intellectual leaders, and professional leaders but also political leaders tend to come from middle-class rather than working-class backgrounds.[6]

[5] And great intellectuals, however lucid their writings, also require exegesis. Plato succeeded better as portrayer of the teachings of his master Socrates than as advisor to a tyrant.

[6] Donald R. Matthews, *The Social Background of Political Decision-Makers*, Garden City, Doubleday & Co., 1954, Table 1, p. 23. Note that the "proprietor

A clear majority of the Presidents, Vice Presidents, and cabinet members of the United States from 1789–1934 were the sons of professionals, proprietors, and officials. The rest were the sons of farmers or workingmen, but only 4% were of wage-earning class origin, compared with some 36% of the labor force in the wage-earning class as a proportion of the total population. Some 95% of these same high public officers before they entered politics had trained for careers as professionals, proprietors, and officials.[7] The overwhelming majority of the members of the German cabinets of 1890–1945 came from either the aristocracy or the middle class, though only during the Weimar Republic were cabinet members manifestly political officers.[8]

A study of the mostly political elite in Nigeria indicates the same tendency for the ruling class to come from a status group well above the bottom. A third of the topmost 156 elitists came from old elite families, most of these elitists being the sons of tribal chiefs. The others were of "ordinary stock." All but two members of the group had finished grade school and 45% possessed university degrees. Even in a period of rapid transition, which so upsets established status patterns, high-status backgrounds and education during childhood count heavily in Nigeria.[9] Upward social mobility almost by definition characterizes leaders in the modern political era. And in a political age, unless their fathers were in politics, they are moving up. A slim shred of evidence suggests that before entering politics, leaders had improved over the status of their fathers.[10] But in his study of United States Senators, out of the 180 who served in the 10 years from 1947–1957, Matthews found that 15% "were sons of politicians" and "another 15% had one or more members of their families active in politics during their formative years." [11]

and official" category in the table includes merchants, business executives, publishers, and bankers.

[7] *Ibid.*, Table 7, p. 30.

[8] *Ibid.*, Table 13, p. 49.

[9] See Hugh H. and Mabel M. Smythe, *The New Nigerian Elite*, Stanford, Stanford University Press, 1960, 74–92, especially 78–83 and 87. Of the 156 interviewed, 113 were government officials (including 96 legislators) but only 28 listed government and politics as their major occupation.

[10] R. M. Rosenzweig, The Politician and the Career in Politics, *Midwest Journal of Political Science*, 1: 163–172 (1957). The study was based on interviews of sixteen candidates for public office (mostly the state legislature) in Massachusetts. "Thirteen of the 16 had higher status jobs than did their fathers. . . . This group of politicians was characterized by strong upward mobility" (p. 167).

[11] Donald R. Matthews, *U. S. Senators and Their World*, Chapel Hill, University of North Carolina Press, 1960, 49.

The major relevant point is that if they are more than usually upwardly mobile—which the data suggest but fail to demonstrate—political leaders are therefore apt to be marginal people, loosening old social and moral ties and tightening new ones, either in their movement from one major status group to another or within a major status category. And as marginal people, they are likely to suffer and enjoy the mental consequences of never quite being sure where they belong and what they value. Partly for this reason, they have an unusual desire for public acceptance.

It is reasonable to suppose also that leaders are extraordinary in their energy level. They are better able to work long hours, weekends, holidays, and when they should be asleep and others are. Some of this energy is employed in rising socially, part of it is employed in the simple enjoyment of politics, but part of it is also employed in gaining widespread popular acceptance. If a leader has no desire for this, perhaps he would never go into politics at all.

Alexander Hamilton is an instance of the man of low status, marginality, and high energy who leaped over numerous social barriers to high position, not just as a staff man for Washington but as a backstage politician in his own right. Born out in the periphery of British colonial society on a tiny island in the West Indies, he could not even claim legitimate birth. Moving in late adolescence to New York, a major center of British America, he jumped from King's College (now Columbia University) to Washington's wartime staff, to a brilliant marriage into one of New York's most distinguished families, and then into post-Revolutionary New York state and national politics. His energy was extraordinary, his mind sharp and cutting. He loved power and—it is reasonable to suppose—his hypersensitive reaction to lowborn status combined with these other factors to boost him up and keep him forever seeking new heights. The reason he gave for not declining the challenge of Aaron Burr to a duel was that such apparent cowardice would ruin him politically in New York.

Theodore Roosevelt had many of the same personality characteristics that animated Hamilton, with the sole and gross exception of low status. Born into one of the best families in New York, he needed to seek no formal social status. Indeed his family were so sure of their own social supremacy that they considered it a degradation for Teddy to enter politics. Was he then, with his comfortable status, marginal or not? In his particular instance we cannot at one level find much evidence of genuine social easiness. With his poor physique and weak eyes, however, he experienced a kind of marginality: he always felt that he was on the edge of the world of the big and the strong. He spent his life trying to get into the middle and on top of this world. Even his bravery had a compulsive quality about it, as though he were really not even trying to prove himself to others but—in an extreme kind of marginality—to himself.

Evidence can be found of marginality in the lives of many renowned political leaders—in Andrew Jackson, Lincoln, Hoover, and Eisenhower among American Presidents and Disraeli, Mussolini, Hitler, Stalin, and Willy Brandt among European politicians. On the other hand, Thomas Jefferson, Woodrow Wilson, and Franklin Roosevelt do not appear to have been socially marginal at all, and it would be hard to make out a marginal case for Neville Chamberlain, Churchill, or two successive governors of New York State, Averell Harriman and Nelson Rockefeller—or for the Brahmin Nehru.

It may be that marginality is, as in the case of the father image posited above as one species of the genus identification, only one kind of force which, interacting with a high energy level and other personal characteristics, produces the leader (when the time and place are appropriate). That is, the function which marginality apparently had in impelling Hamilton, Jackson, and Lincoln upward—and in a special way also Theodore Roosevelt—may in other politicians be performed by some other inducer of tension: conflict with father (as in Wilson's case),[12] conflict with mother and with shattering illness (Franklin Roosevelt), or desire to emulate (the two young La Follettes, Robert and Philip, sons of their massively successful father, Robert M. La Follette, Sr.). At any rate, some kind of tension-producing trauma, either in childhood or later life, appears to be a common characteristic among prominent political leaders. It cannot yet be said that it is universal, though it may be. But it may also then turn out to be common to all extraordinary individuals.

All this leaves us, or at least me, back where we were when considering self-actualization as a political driving force. The range of personality types among political leaders is so vast and varied that it does not, at this stage of our very limited *general* knowledge of political leadership, seem to merit any other conclusion than that extraordinary leaders become political because they love it, as a sculptor loves to carve, a painter to paint, and a composer to write music. It is far easier to venture valid judgments about the political involve-

[12] See Alexander L. and Juliette L. George, *Woodrow Wilson and Colonel House,* New York, The John Day Co., 1956, especially 116–117.

ment of general publics, whose interest is (fortunately) not central to their being and therefore falls more readily into such patterns as class status and parental influence, than it is to generalize about the highly individual characteristics of elites, particularly chiefs of state.

Leadership relates to substantive needs

People identify with their leaders, but where the available market of leaders provides some formal or informal kind of choice (i.e., by election or other means), people select the person with whom they identify. They are not identifying solely for the sake of identification but also to satisfy other basic needs and to satisfy them in a particular way.

A common explanation for leader-follower identification is that leaders represent both the chance for relieving insecurity, and success at relieving it. This explanation is consistent with the basic position of this book, but it must be emphasized that insecurity is never a discrete, dissociated phenomenon. People are tense and often seek political relief for their tension, but they are always tense *about* something, about deprivation of particular basic need satisfactions. Hungry people, to the limited extent they can divert their attention from the pursuit of food, seek a leader who offers food. People who fear depredation from enemies foreign or domestic will attach themselves to a leader who either expresses that fear or proposes to do something about it. People who have been angered and humiliated by foreign or domestic exploiters will similarly identify with the leader who best fits the need for relief from these particular tensions. They will therefore not seek a leader who will relieve tension that they do not at the time experience; they will seek a leader who provides a rather specific remedy for specific political ailments.

Regardless of the apparent breadth of his program, followers may decisively reject a leader to whom under differ circumstances they have been devoted. Winston Churchill is a case in point. As the farsighted antagonist in the 1930s of appeasing the Nazis, he promptly became Britain's leader when the appeasement policy was at last popularly repudiated. At war's end—even before the end—when Britons already were turning away in exhaustion with war and anticipation of domestic and economic reconstruction, they rejected the party of Churchill in favor of a party and a leader, Attlee, who was less colorful, less articulate, and in no sense a wartime leader, but who clearly had his heart in domestic reform.

Franklin Roosevelt, who proposed vigorous action to meet the Great Depression of 1929, similarly displaced a President who had been elected to preside over a condition of noncrisis, of turning away from positive governmental action. Roosevelt's later retention of the Presidency when war threatened to involve the United States in 1940 was partly due to his being there. But it was also partly a consequence of his remarkable adaptability to the change in crisis from domestic to international, from economic to military.

William Jennings Bryan, the spokesman of the economic plight of farmers, was unable to elicit support from workingmen in 1896, and with the gradual though halting return of prosperity to the farmers, was unable to keep their support sufficiently to approach victory in 1900, even as closely as he had four years before. Thomas Dorr, leader of the little rebellion in Rhode Island in 1842, lost his broad popular following when the established state government conceded the demands for suffrage that had first attached the unenfranchised to Dorr.

To discuss fully the relationship between the particular pattern of needs whose satisfaction is frustrated and the kind of leadership that results would involve a repetition of the earlier discussion of needs. Suffice it to say here that among the basic reasons for the leader's selection is the perception by the public that a particular leader is appropriate to their salient frustrations.

Leadership relates to procedural preferences

But the sensed appropriateness to solving particular substantive problems is not the only basic criterion by which the public selects leaders. The style, the manner of solving problems, though perhaps of secondary importance to the public, may nevertheless be the more critical factor of the two. That is, if two prospective leaders propose to solve a set of current substantive problems, the difference between them may rest more in the manner in which each proposes to solve them. What leaders propose to do in such cases may be less important than how they will do it. An extreme example may serve to illustrate. Russia at the end of the seventeenth century was both dormant and backward in contrast to Western Europe, whose bursting, exciting developments had started at least a century before, during the Reformation. In Russia a modernizer was needed to draw together the thin strands of new life. He emerged in the vigorous, crude, highly intelligent person of Peter the Great. His style of rule often involved extreme cruelty, harsh and arbitrary judgment, even on occasion the murder by Peter of individuals by striking them with his bare fist. But he took effective steps to modernize, to start industrializing Russia.

With a quite different background, the objective state of the American economy a century later was like Russia's, also backward as compared with Europe. No one leader emerged as the process of modernization and industrialization of an agrarian, subsistence society took place. Alexander Hamilton proposed and fostered the development of manufacture and modern finance, with the vigorous support of an already numerous bourgeoisie and its Federalist party. Jefferson, the protagonist of the yeoman farmer who wanted to retain the agrarian basis of society and to keep the workshops and distaffs safely on the other side of the Atlantic, willy-nilly fostered the growth of manufacture, in the process of avoiding military commitments in the European wars. Neither of these men operated in a style that is in any except the remotest way comparable to Peter the Great. They both used rhetoric and guile in pursuit of this goal of industrialization.[13] Neither used brutal or basically unconstitutional means. It is hard to imagine Jefferson striking anyone in anger, let alone killing anyone.

Analyzing the process by which particular leaders emerge and gain popular support involves far more than considering what it is that appeals to people in the politician of their choice. If they like his integrity, intelligence, his past career, his ability to lead, etc., they select these characteristics within a broader framework which determines both the limits of leadership characteristics and of the awareness of the fact that certain characteristics are appreciated or depreciated. Bizarre as it would have been for a voter in America in 1800 to say he preferred Jefferson because he did not kill people, in a constitutional society the high value placed on nonviolence effectively eliminates the political condottiere who could dominate an Italian city during the Renaissance or a half-savage, half-civilized Peter the Great in Russia. America has its semi-civilized condottieri, but they are seldom considered appropriate candidates for elective office and even less often are they elected.[14] Correlatively one would find it hard to imagine

---

[13] Jefferson's *actions* are more relevant here than the sentimental attachment he retained for a kind of society which his policies—especially in the Embargo Act of 1807 but also in his prior refusal to dismantle the domestic program of the Federalists—were inexorably making more difficult to retain.

[14] A possibly contradictory case is Huey Long, but he did not engage in the use of violent force for political purposes until after he had gained office by popular majority in a free election. Thereafter the freedom of choice was limited by a variety of factors, including the Long-dominated state police.

Jefferson winning support among either the ruling class or the general public in seventeenth-century Russia.

Among the broadly limiting factors that restrict choice are the long-range socio-cultural patterns of behavior and values in a particular society. Are the established modes of social interaction equalitarian or hierarchized, respectful or disrespectful of constituted authority, cooperative or competitive? Is the traditional political unit the local community which is popularly invested with most decision-making, or does the public look to a distant source for the authoritative exercise of power? Is there a church or dominant religious belief which serves as the basic source of moral authority and which judges political leaders, or is the society predominantly secular in its moral foundations? Or does it lack a real moral consensus, as in the case of the world community? Is there a communal sense of joint popular responsibility or does the public tend to consider the process of government a specialized competence beyond popular control?

Leadership relates to circumstances and mood

These and other aspects of the behavior and values prevalent in a particular society limit the range of choice of leaders. So also do the particular circumstances prevalent at a particular time in a particular culture. Relatively short-range circumstances include depression and war, which can install and remove not only presidents and prime ministers but also dictators. Longer-range circumstances include the stage of advancement of a culture. Are its people close to the subsistence level? Do they live in an economy that is approaching what Rostow calls the precondition for take-off into industrialization and highly organized exchange of goods and services? Or has the culture advanced to abundance in a mature industrialized economy? Has the society reached an old age in which the widespread popular reaction to change is negation and rejection?

Closely related to such secular stages of cultural circumstance is the public mood, which is partly a function of—partly, that is, a reaction to—the exigencies of the time. When faced with a war crisis, does the public react to aggression catatonically, in a state of futile resignation, or does it achieve a mental posture of readiness to confront it? When faced with novel problems, does the public react with new vigor or with a mechanical, rote preference for solutions to prior problems? Does the public adopt a righteous or cynical, a messianic and universalist, or a resigned pessimism in outlook toward politics and politicians? Is the public individually self-centered or do people worry about the welfare of others? Publics—that is, nations or Volk or narodi in the generic sense—may show some rather enduring mood characteristics and choose leaders accordingly. (The Kaisers, Hindenburg, Hitler, and Adenauer were radically different kinds of rulers, but each was a strong authority figure.) On the other hand, nations may suffer or enjoy a change in mood, overwhelmingly electing and re-electing an activist innovator, like Franklin Roosevelt, and then almost as overwhelmingly choosing a relatively inactive perpetuator of established policies, like Eisenhower. Two decades of unusual tension were followed in 1952 in America by a mood of determined relaxation, of turning away from a sense of participation in and responsibility for solving problems of depression and war.

To lead, succeed; to succeed, do

Our attention has been focused on the general public in its predilection for particular leaders under particular circumstances. The same phenomena may be more fully appraised by looking directly at the leaders whom the public chooses or endorses or at least tolerates, as long as we never forget that leaders are forever dependent on popular support in any society where politics exists. This of course excludes a consideration of leaders who are free to act as they choose because they have depoliticized a society by violence or fraud or because the society is too poor to exhibit anything but apathy in politics. A Spanish intellectual said in 1961 that current economic, social, and religious affairs are never discussed in his country and that "politics doesn't exist." This is an example of the first kind of depoliticization, although it did not quite fit the Spain of 1961. The other kind exists in primitive societies preoccupied with food, health, the weather, and the anxiety of survival itself. Of course it is an exaggeration to say there is no politics under either condition, because terror can nowhere be completely effective for a long time and because the number of people constantly preoccupied with physical survival is steadily diminishing in the world.

The basic criterion for at least a continued tolerance of leaders is whether or not they succeed. Lord Charnwood pointed this out in comparing Lincoln and General George McClellan, the Democratic candidate for President in 1864. Charnwood invoked Dante and said that men were not first judged "according as they were of irreproachable or reproachable character; they were divided into those who did and those who did not." [15]

We must at least concede to the spirit of Plato's Thrasymachus and of Hegel that power must indeed be exercised, and effectively, in order for people to accept a leader. If there is any one necessary condition for judgment, it is this one, and for better and worse it is in many cases apparently deemed a sufficient criterion for judgment—among general publics and elites alike. If Hitler had at last succeeded in Germany in 1945—if Germany had been the victor in the Second World War—it is doubtful that his posthumous following would have been the relatively small one that it became. The same can be said of Mussolini, Chiang Kai-shek, Farouk, Chamberlain; and, to take some earlier leaders or would-be leaders, Louis XV and Boulanger in France; Van Buren, Stephen A. Douglas, Bryan, and Harding in the United States; and Kerensky in Russia.

But the criterion of success is hard to apply and calls for continued reappraisal, by publics and elites, both during and after a leader's tenure of office. The standard plea for dictators, whether they built Autobahns or made the trains run on time or built bridges in Louisiana, is that they did something. Yet by 1944 in Germany a resolute group within the pre-Nazi elite was convinced not only that Hitler was doing wrong but that he was also a failure because he was destroying culture and civilization both inside and outside Germany. Even assuming Hitler's military success—which would of course involve changing his decision to fight a two-front war and doubtless many other decisions—would his acclaim have endured in the long run, that is, in the eyes of posterity even among his countrymen?

Correlatively, Wilson's failure in his international program after the First World War, a failure emphatically so judged in the 1918 Congressional and 1920 Presidential elections, has seemed less and less a failure with the passage of time. His program, essentially calling for American peacetime commitment to participation in world affairs, animated Franklin Roosevelt and became the enduring program of the American public at the end of the Second World War.

These two leaders are examples of opposite types. Each had success in the early years of holding office, yet Hitler's reputation in the long run will probably, though not surely, continue to diminish and

[15] Lord Charnwood (Godfrey Rathbone Benson), *Abraham Lincoln*, New York, Pocketbooks, Inc., 1952, 312. This most penetrating biography was first published in 1916.

Wilson's probably, though not surely, increase. It is not quite true to say that it makes little difference because in the long run we will all be dead. A civilization is a continuing process, and people as long as they are human beings will be the end product of their physical, organic growth and the gradual growth of their civilization. They judge leaders of the past and present by many standards. If they judge a ruthless Peter the Great successful within his era, they may not judge a ruthless Hitler successful in his, and not simply because his military judgment was wrong. And they may judge Wilson a success because his plans bore ultimate fruit.

The criterion of success can be more fully considered by comparing political with moral leaders, recognizing that Woodrow Wilson is on the borderline between the two categories. Socrates, Christ, and Gandhi were moral leaders whose marginal involvement in public policy in various ways resulted in their violent deaths as martyrs to principle. At least in their lifetimes the first two were hardly accountable as successful. They merely taught; they did nothing else; they stubbornly accomplished only their own death. Yet few people in the Western world would regard the lives and teachings of these three individuals, from the long-run standpoint, as anything less than triumphant achievements of civilization, a continuing process with which politics is inescapably concerned and for which the lives of these three are inescapable criteria.

Politicians are not judged by exactly the same set of standards as moral leaders, but moral considerations inevitably are involved, raising and lowering the reputations of individuals who may or may not have built roads and bridges, established social security programs, or won wars. We cannot surely say that Sun Yat-sen was a failure, even though in some of the skills of statecraft he was deficient. We cannot say so despite the fact that his brother-in-law Chiang Kai-shek fatally and he thought necessarily compromised with a feudality incongruously entrenched in the twentieth century. We cannot judge the gentle Sun a failure despite the fact that the post-Chiang dictatorship, which also honors the name Sun, used a blood bath to cleanse China of feudalism. The wars of the Protestant Reformation, which so tragically devastated Europe, were fought by antagonists who uniformly invoked the name of the Prince of Peace.

But aside from moral aspects, the criteria for political success as such remain crude. In order to do something, leaders must have at least some awareness of the problems of their time. They probably must have more than the expressive awareness that William Jennings

Bryan did of the farmers' problems, as only the mouthpiece for only one of several groups of discontented people of his time. Clear failures, the sort that are sometimes consciously blocked out of the memories of both their contemporaries and later generations, include men who were very dimly aware of these problems, like Louis XV, Nicholas II, and Buchanan and Harding. They also include those who, if aware, made no more than feeble efforts to solve problems, like Farouk of Egypt, Bao-dai of Indochina, and Chiang Kai-shek. They further include those who, if aware, made colossal blunders, like Aaron Burr (notably opportunism) and Huey Long (notably destruction of his opposition), or Adolph Hitler (whose errors ranged from genocide to undertaking and mismanaging war). All leaders who fail do so for more than one reason. There is never the Shakespearean tragic simplicity which can lay blame to rest in one grave of vaulting ambition or indecision or whatnot. And none of these leaders, a product of his time almost as much as his fellow countrymen, is altogether accountable for his failures, even though he had some freedom of action.

Our task in these pages is not finally to bury Caesars or to praise them but rather to understand them and judge them tentatively. We cannot do this exactly, the way Dante assigned various individuals to precise infernal residences. But we can avoid the historical objectivity that Pilate used to deceive himself by asking what truth was and allowing Jesus to be judged by His peers. We can avoid trying scientifically to avoid the problem. We can be sure of neither what political success is, nor that success or failure is even in the long run a sufficient criterion. But we may perhaps agree that among the men just cited, the policy failures outweighed the successes. Probably none of these men was a complete failure. It was Harding who freed Debs after Wilson hounded him into prison. Emperor Franz Josef did try to establish a kind of federalism in the Danube basin and did allow the exciting ferment that was Vienna, a metropolis that for a time mothered not only Hitler but also Masaryk and Freud.

We have already mentioned some very broad limits within which leaders must function in solving their nations' problems, indicating how incongruous it would be for a Peter to act in early nineteenth-century America the way he did in eighteenth-century Russia and for Jefferson to act like Jefferson, in Russia a hundred years earlier. Now let us categorize styles of rule more precisely, so that we more exactly know some of the bases for selection, retention, and adulation or condemnation of leaders by their publics. We must remember that some type of success is always presupposed: we remember but we do not honor Neville Chamberlain and James Buchanan—as failures rather than real leaders.

Autocrats and heterocrats

The basic stylistic distinction is between autocrats and what Friedrich and Brzezinski call heterocrats,[16] between rulers who rule themselves, are ultimate law unto themselves; and rulers who are responsible to some other persons or some other thing. The some other persons may include an entire populace as in a democracy, or a small group of men as in an oligarchy. The some other thing may be a concept like the law of nature or of nature's God or the nation's traditions or its written constitution. The basic distinction is between responsible and irresponsible rule, which is roughly equivalent to constitutional versus unconstitutional rule.

In theory, a broad general public may become so anxiety ridden or otherwise emotionally and collectively disturbed as to be itself quite irresponsible. Since the actual governing process necessarily involves only a small group of men (the governors), I am on empirical grounds excluding the theoretical possibility that an entire populace or a substantial majority of it can become irresponsible and autocratic. This is not to say that a populace may not at least passively support an autocrat, like a majority of Germans during the Hitler era or a majority of Soviet citizens during at least the first forty years of the Russian Revolution, or for a short time and in a limited sense, at least a plurality of Americans, during the McCarthy era of the early 1950s. But these broad publics at no time had a very free chance to accept or reject these dictatorships or demagogues. The most that any large body of people can do is assent to or dissent from the proposals of the actual leader. A mob can dump tea in the harbor of Boston or watch with zest the lynching of rulers on the guillotine, but a large body of people cannot rule. This does not free them from their ultimate responsibility to themselves and their posterity but means merely that they are not rulers, not leaders, and in history usually have not had much chance to choose between alternative leaders.

It is appropriate at this point, before listing various kinds of rulers, to indicate that no ruler or ruling group exactly fits any typology,

[16] See Carl J. Friedrich and Zbigniew K. Brzezinski, *Totalitarian Dictatorship and Autocracy*, Cambridge, Harvard University Press, 1956, 3–4. I may be deviating somewhat from at least their vocabulary in my use of the term.

but each exemplifies to some degree different styles of rule. The statement applies even to the basic distinction between autocratic and heterocratic rule. No ruler acts altogether responsibly or irresponsibly. Even the totalitarian ruler has some limits to his power, established by the simple ability of people to refuse support, to take refuge in apathy. And even constitutional, responsible rulers do acts that are unprecedented. The American Constitutional Convention of 1787 was called to consider a revision of the Articles of Confederation; the Convention promptly proceeded to violate its instructions and to make a new, altogether unprecedented, unauthorized organic law.

Traditional, charismatic, and rational autocrats

Following a typology established by Max Weber, but not following it very strictly, I suggest that there are three major types of irresponsible rule and the same three types of responsible rule: the traditional, the charismatic, and the rational. Perhaps the archetypes of the traditional irresponsible ruler were the Russian tsars, who presumed to be exercising power according to long-established custom but for practical purposes recognized no superior earthly authority. Peter the Great adopted the role of the Russian God's earthly emissary as the effective head of the church. When a delegation of churchmen came to ask that he appoint a head of the state church, Peter pointed to himself and said "here is your patriarch." [17] Besides the tsars, other cases in which a kind of traditional irresponsibility has been prominent include the medieval popes in their capacity as earthly rulers over actual land-territory, the Japanese emperors before the Second World War, and possibly the South African white oligarchy in the 1950s.

A major characteristic of this type of rule is that it is government by grace, a kind of paradoxical omnipotence derived from God, a magical interpretation of the nation's past which derives authority in a misty, romantic history. This style of rule ignores the origins of authority (sanctioned power) in a prior, often savage, and never misty test of strength and cunning, violence and fraud. It elicits apathy in part at least because the manifestations of rule are so often brutal and perhaps because the people fear they are themselves truly

---

[17] Thomas G. Masaryk, *The Spirit of Russia,* London, George Allen and Unwin, Ltd., 1919, vol. 1, 62. Peter nevertheless was restrained by comparison with the early Soviet rulers. He favored religious freedom, saying that "the human conscience is subject to God alone." *Ibid.*, 63.

powerless and that God is indeed on the ruler's side. This apathy, rooted in the sheer struggle for survival, is mistaken for assent. When the apathy changes to antipathy in a revolution, such rulers are apparently often incredulous. The deep popular reluctance, indeed fear, of breaking with the past lends by default a precarious stability to such regimes.

The term charisma—miraculously given power—was transferred by Max Weber from its original religious meaning to politics. He described it as the "absolutely personal devotion and personal confidence in revelation, heroism, or other qualities of individual leadership."[18] The charismatic leader is thus one whose claim to rule is neither as a perpetuator of traditional values nor as one who resolves conflicting interests by reasonable and just means but as one endowed with superhuman powers to solve political problems. In the abstract, pure case he is seen by his followers as being *all*-powerful, *all*-wise, and morally *perfect*. Perhaps Mahomet and Brigham Young, who were simultaneously prophets and political leaders, come close to the pure case.

One of the outstanding characteristics of charismatic rule is its mass base. Unlike the tsar or the palace revolutionary, the charismatic ruler is not content with gaining and maintaining control merely over the machinery of government—the police, administrative offices, legislature, and courts. He consciously seeks to gain control over the individual citizen—not just by the threat of force but perhaps more significantly by appealing for affirmative and enthusiastic devotion. The leader seeks not passive acceptance of his rule but an active identification of the citizens' needs and expectations with his own and those of the nation. The political demands of individuals become uniform, at least on the manifest level, and are absorbed in and merged with the economic, social, and ethnic demands of the nation as these are expressed by the leader. A greater portion of the individual's life finds its expression in politics. The charismatic follower becomes an undifferentiated, cancerous cell on the body politic.

Like other styles of leadership, charisma is not a characteristic of leaders as such but a relationship between leader and followers. It depends both on the construction by a leader and his associates of an image of him as infallible, omniscient, and incorruptible and on a positive, active response to this kind of image-building by those who are

[18] H. H. Gerth and C. W. Mills, eds., *From Max Weber: Essays in Sociology,* London, Routledge and Kegan Paul Ltd., 1948, 79.

predisposed toward such leadership. The "compleat" charismatic follower is oriented in politics toward candidates, and in a particular way, rather than towards parties or issues. He tends to divide political figures on the basis of strength or weakness, omnicompetence or utter incompetence, righteousness or iniquity. He is unable to see any but good qualities in the leader he accepts or to see any good qualities in the one he rejects. Although strong liking for a candidate is not in itself evidential, for charismatics the emotional attraction of a candidate is predominant and is coupled with the feeling that the leader is the incarnation of all virtues.

Pure charismatic followers, like pure charismatic leaders, are ideal types unlikely to be found in actual situations. There are doubtless some charismatic tendencies in all candidates for popularly elected office above the level of sanitation supervisor. The well-known panegyrics of those who introduce candidates at a public gathering as often as not are full of hackneyed phrases suggesting the power of their men to move mountains, stop the tides, and gain or regain Utopia within two weeks of taking office. There are doubtless some tendencies in all citizens to believe that the candidate of their choice is superhuman and that his opponent is infrahuman. For, campaign hyperbole aside, the phenomenon of strong leadership is perhaps only rarely divorced completely from the will to be or to follow a leader who will make no mistakes and suffer no defeats at the hands of malignant, real enemies and hostile, shadowy forces. In politics, neither St. George nor the dragon is ever quite dead.[19]

Charismatic irresponsible rule differs from traditional irresponsible rule in being highly individual and personal. If a Russian tsar could claim some kind of mystical historic justification for his irresponsible rule, the charismatic derives power and gains authority by his own unique attributes. Government is an act of sovereign grace, but the ultimate sovereign is not God or the spirit of the revolution or whatnot. It is the person of the ruler. In an era of predominantly charismatic rule in a nation, the people do not want to cling to the past. Having made the free jump into the future, they reject the past and what it stands for, focusing all their political loyalties on the person of the ruler, to whom they cling all the more intensely for having rejected

[19] For an analysis of charismatic tendencies among voters in the 1952 Presidential campaign, when a military hero was elected, in the United States, see J. C. Davies, Charisma in the 1952 Campaign, *American Political Science Review*, **48**: 1083–1102 (1954), where some of the above ideas were previously expressed.

the past. People who do attach themselves to such an irresponsible ruler of course have not thrown off the major part of their past.

When there has been a popular shift from passive acceptance of traditional irresponsible to charismatic irresponsible rule, a tentative step has been taken from apathy to some kind of passive political involvement. The public has at last and at least come to watch the political circus. With the passage of time this very likely means that the public will become critical judges of the performers. They could never have done this if they had stayed away from the show. There is additional hope of political maturation because, in contrast to the traditional irresponsibility of tsars, charismatic rulers are unable to transfer their own personal popularity to a designated successor, because their authority is derived from personal popular acceptance rather than from some mystic, supernatural, metahistorical force.

Julius Caesar was one of the archetypes of the charismatic, irresponsible ruler. His eager cadre, with little hindrance from their chief, had statues erected to him—even temples built to honor him alone— and various festive days were established in his honor. For whatever reasons, he refused to accept the crown of kingship, which would have lent the aura of tradition to his rule—and possibly have diminished his personal authority. But he did permit himself to receive the reverence bestowed on gods, including chariots to carry his images.

Caesar's successors made a routine out of this personal investment with gracious authority and adopted as the verbal symbol of their power the name Caesar, which thus began its lineal descent down to the last tsar and last kaiser at the end of the First World War. When the later Caesars did this they were to a substantial degree losing the personal basis of their rule and becoming traditional rulers. They were to a considerable degree irresponsible but, despite the symbols, no longer such unique and individual power figures. They wore the investments of Caesarly power like a garment that had been tailored for someone else.

The irresponsible charismatic with his antique prototype has had a renaissance in the twentieth century in the style of rule of Hitler and Stalin, whose cult of personality was a central theme of the "secret" speech which Khrushchev made to the Twentieth Party Congress in February 1956. Not only was Stalin in his lifetime apparently regarded by his followers and seemingly by himself as a supremely competent ruler, he was supreme in other realms as well. A poem appeared in *Pravda* in 1936 that in part goes as follows:

Stalin

O, thou great leader of the peoples,
Thou who gavest man his life,
Thou who fructified the lands,
Thou who rejuvenated centuries,
Made chords sing and blossoms spring,
Our hearts love, our factories work;
In life around us is the strength,
O, father, of thy mighty hands.

Thou art the sun—my youth in bloom,
In hearts of millions reflected;
Thou hast from age-old gloom
My sleeping country resurrected.

And the disease has traveled to the Orient, to rationalist, Confucian, worldly China, which has no use for the spiritual, the supernatural. A poem appeared in *Women of China,* a magazine published in Peking, in 1961, entitled

In Praise of Mao Tse-tung

Mao Tse-tung,
Mao Tse-tung,
You are rain for the planting season,
Breeze for the hottest noon,
You are the red sun that never sets,
Wind for boats that need a sail.
If one never wants poverty to suffer,
He has to follow Mao Tse-tung forever.[20]

Another Chinese magazine reported that a man who suffered for thirteen years from a gastro-intestinal disorder was cured by obeying the prescription of a scroll which Mao gave him, the scroll admonishing "let your body give rise to a power of resistance which will struggle against and finally defeat . . . a chronic disease." The man recovered, finally being healthy enough to shout "it is the party and Chairman Mao that have given me a new life." [21]

Kwame Nkrumah, the Prime Minister of Ghana, like the ancient Caesars, is honored by statues and street-names in his homeland. He has even outdone the Caesars, thanks to a technical advance after two

---

[20] Both the Stalin and the Mao Tse-tung poems are quoted from *Atlas: the Magazine of the World Press,* vol. 1, no. 4, 60 (June 1961), by permission of the Publisher-Editor.

[21] Quoted in the Los Angeles *Times,* 16 May 1961.

thousand years, by appearing on postage stamps. An article in the Ghana press describes him thus:

Kwame Nkrumah has revealed himself like a Moses—yea, a greater Moses . . . with the support of all African leaders he will help to lead his people across the Red Sea of imperialist massacre and suffering.

A newspaper cartoon in Accra in March 1960 showed a man labeled "Africa" tied to a post, with "Christian settler" shooting at him. He cries "Kwame! Kwame!" and out of the sky, clad in a white robe, comes Nkrumah to the rescue, saying "Africa, oh Motherland." It is not quite clear whether Africa is Christ and Nkrumah is God but the pictured scene scarcely implies that Osagyefo (the "great leader") is human.[22]

A third category of irresponsible rule is the rational or pararational. If the traditional, irresponsible ruler founds his authority in the mystic and misty past or in divine sanction, the rational ruler who is irresponsible bases his in reason, more exactly in Reason, which in some manner has been revealed to him exclusively and in the name of which the irresponsible, rationalist ruler is sole interpreter—in a real sense, the embodiment of Reason himself. Notable instances have been the leaders of the French Revolution and the early part of the Russian Revolution. Such rule and also traditional, irresponsible rule differ from charismatic rule because the source of authority lies somewhere outside the ruler himself. In fact, however, the authority of the rationalist, irresponsible ruler is also personal, like that of the traditional and charismatic rulers, because ultimately there is no restraint on any of these rulers other than that which is self-imposed or which is the consequence of the public's ability to withhold support by being apathetic. The latter restraint to the irresponsible, rationalist ruler is an obstacle like climate, topography, and natural resources—a natural phenomenon that has to be contended with and even turned to the ruler's advantage but not an object of solicitude save as the means of achieving the ruler's purposes.

No single label fits any single ruler

There is in actuality no pure instance of any of these three categories of irresponsible rule—quite apart from the very broad limitations imposed by the public's ability to withhold support. The pure case would be a ruler who was altogether free of any inner restraint,

[22] The quotations and the cartoon appeared in the B. B. C. *Listener,* 66 (No. 1685), 46 (13 July 1961).

any inhibition of conscience, and whose knowledge of how to elicit popular support was so complete that he could make an entire populace into his willing instrument. But it may be that the irresponsible ruler who invokes traditional or rational sanction feels less restraint than the purely personal ruler. If one believes that whatever he does is effected with the blessing of a nation's past, its gods, God, or Reason, he may be better able to free himself from feelings of remorse, guilt, or of even the possibility of being in error than the charismatic ruler is.

The traditional ruler who believes it is the national destiny to subdue other races may feel quite virtuous at the enslavement of inferior peoples. The traditional ruler who believes that God commands him to torture and kill the enemy within the nation, who are minions of the Devil, may be altogether righteous in his bestiality. The rational ruler who deems it necessary to induce a cooperative spirit by letting hundreds of thousands or millions of dissident peasants starve may feel equally self-justified because dialectical materialism or history or posterity will inevitably prove his actions to have been correct. The rationalist differs from the traditionalist mainly in his gods. Having dethroned God, he is not thereby free of the need to rationalize irresponsibility by invoking external authority. He replaces God with Reason and rules with no more inhibition than the traditionalist. The rationalist ruler is no more willing to examine the major premises from which he deduces the form and substance of his governing actions than is the traditionalist.

But it is doubtful that there has been or could be an incidence of rule that was altogether free of nonpopular restraints. And it is certain that there cannot be any rule quite free of popular restraint, because rule inevitably involves an interaction between rulers and ruled, and if the ruled refuse to interact, if the ruled respond to the demands of rulers with indifference, there can be no rule. Nonpopular restraints are instances in which the ruler actually is limited in what he does because he does not believe tradition or God will allow it or because Reason forbids. In Freudian terms, the ruler is limited by his Superego or his Ego-ideal. His conscience tells him it will be wrong to kill an opponent or his self-image becomes ugly or imperfect as he looks into the mirror and sees evidence of an irrational enjoyment in the suffering of his enemies.

Abstractly speaking, the charismatic, personal ruler who acknowledges no law outside himself should be quite free of the theoretical and often the actual inhibitions of tradition, reason, and compassion.

But concretely the charismatic may be somewhat limited by nonpopular restraints. This seems so because the altogether arbitrary personal ruler might find it difficult to attract a following unless there is some coincidence of self-interest, such that each member of the cadre finds the leader to be serving some of his major interests. Without this reciprocal interest, there would inevitably arise occasions on which a divergence of self-interest would compel the leader to adjust to the interests of others. The lack of identical congruence of self-interest would compel compromise. If Hitler had insisted that his cadre abstain from eating meat, drinking alcohol, or associating with women to the puritanical degree he did, it is doubtful that he would ever have had a following. He found it appropriate to kill Ernst Roehm and some other socialist members of the Nazi party in 1934, but if he had truly established a fixed hierarchy into which there was no access for the gifted outsider and no recognition of equalitarianism, National Socialism might well have burned itself out before consuming Germany and Europe.

Actual autocratic rulers thus never fall neatly into one category or another. Each will in greater or less degree manifest some traditionalism, some charisma, some rationalism. If the tsars were traditionalists they also in some instances (for example, Alexander I who in a sense was Russia's response to the Napoleonic image) manifest some charismatic tendencies and (again like Alexander) some rationalism along with the mysticism. If Hitler's rule was highly personal, it also appealed to the mystical folk spirit of the ancient Germanic race. And it had a strong appeal for those who thought there should be a more rational relationship between talent, performance, and reward than the rigidly class-based German society had hitherto allowed. The rationalist style of Lenin's rule, despite the early revolutionists' effort to deny the past and magic, could not avoid the popular imputation to Lenin of an historic role as a Russian and the possession of superhuman powers. Typologies such as the present one are useful if they help indicate relative emphasis. If they suggest a simple-minded purity of style they do a disservice, because styles of rule are far harder to isolate in actuality than are even such complicated stuffs as organic compounds in the chemical laboratory. The chemically pure charismatic has never existed.

After this discussion of various combinations of autocratic, irresponsible rule, we can now consider the heterocratic, responsible counterparts.

Traditional heterocrats

Traditional responsible rulers are mainly responsible to the past, to a maintenance of both uniformity and continuity of present with past action. They are highly reluctant to do what has not been done or what the founding fathers, the great monarchs, or the great prime ministers of the past might disapprove of. Like Churchill, they do not feel that they have taken office in order to preside over the liquidation of anything great and glorious or indeed to change anything that has worked fairly well. Some examples include Charles II and George III of England, Franz Josef of the Austro-Hungarian empire, possibly Wilhelm II, and surely Konrad Adenauer of Germany, the Ashanti chiefs of Ghana, such American Presidents as the two Adamses, Mc-Kinley, Taft, and Eisenhower. Like any other rulers, these traditional, responsible rulers may be vigorous and active, such as George III or Churchill or Wilhelm or Adenauer, but they are notably inactive when it comes to real innovation. They wish to restore the power of the king or of the empire or of their beloved fatherland, and they wish only such adaptation to changed circumstances as is absolutely essential in order for the monarchy or the empire or the nation to survive.

Charismatic heterocrats

It is logically inconsistent to include charismatic rule in the responsible heterocratic category. Yet in actuality there are several rulers whose appeal has had an inevitably magic quality about it, with many followers believing the leader to be omnipotent, omniscient, and morally perfect, but with the leader himself being rather strictly self-limited in his actions. Some such rulers who have had considerable charismatic appeal include Andrew Jackson and Franklin Roosevelt in the United States, de Gaulle in France, and probably Bourguiba in Tunisia. Jackson was enormously popular but also had a clear sense that he could not do everything he wanted to. He was limited by the expectations of the middle class, the working class, and the western farmers who supported him so ardently and to whom he was so sensitive. He was also limited by a kind of gentlemanly code of his own that kept him from doing things in defiance of the Constitution or even of due legal process. In his fight with the Supreme Court, the veritable symbol of tradition in the United States, Franklin Roosevelt was only attempting to do what Lincoln and other Presidents had done—alter its composition by enlarging its membership. When he lost, he did not by guile, demagogy, or other autocratic process seek to reverse the emphatic rejection of his plan by Congress. He abode by the decision.

The deep suspicion of his most extreme opponents, who, like some of his ardent supporters, imagined him capable of anything, was a source of puzzled anger on Roosevelt's part because he was severely limited by a set of deeply inculcated values acquired at home, in preparatory school, and in college. These more effectively controlled him than did his extreme opponents. In the very critical, frightened months of 1933 when he first became President, he was probably more restrained from becoming a dictator by these values than by any interference on the part of Congress or any major segment of the public. Yet he retained a magical quality that not only contributed to his victories at election time but to a belief among some that he could do no wrong and could not fail in any of his enterprises, domestic or foreign.

Rational heterocrats

Rational, responsible rulers, the most desirable and perhaps least to be feared category, are inhibited by a "reasonable" outlook. It includes a healthy, reasoned respect for the value and inevitability of tradition or habit but is more immediately responsive to the unprecedented, perhaps nonrecurrent, exigencies of the political dilemma of the era. The appeal is to thought more than to either habit or emotion or personal loyalties and the leader presupposes an ability of people to respond to such an appeal. Among American Presidents, Jefferson is doubtless the most clear-cut instance, with Wilson and Lincoln exhibiting a style that was predominantly rational but less purely so than Jefferson's. Thomas Masaryk, the founder of Czechoslovakia, and Nehru, the father of modern India, are other instances.

The predominance of a rational style does not of course preclude less than rational actions. In a sense Jefferson's Declaration of Independence was a restrained piece of demagogy in its focusing of hostility on the British King rather than Parliament. And Jefferson was capable of decisively defeating a political enemy by every honorable political device he could employ, as in his attack on Aaron Burr in 1807. But probably no American President has depended so heavily on quiet discourse and persuasive appeal to reason in dealing with both Congress and the public. More responsible to what he thought reasonable and proper than responsive to the popular passion, he could be reluctant as a strict constructionist of the Constitution to purchase Louisiana, despite the manifest and widespread popularity of such a move—and later ignore widespread unpopularity in pursuing his policy of embargo and nonintercourse with Europe during the Napoleonic wars.

It seems evident not only that irresponsible autocratic rulers can exhibit in varying degrees all three styles of rule—traditional, charismatic, and rational—but that responsible heterocrats can show the same styles. It is also evident that no actual ruler who succeeds— that is, who does—can be altogether responsible or irresponsible. Even as the charismatic autocrat will limit the arbitrariness of his rule in the interest of staying in power, so even the traditionalist heterocrat will bend tradition slightly and the rationalist heterocrat on occasion act rather arbitrarily on his own authority, unauthorized by tradition, constitution, reason, or popular mandate.

The case of Lincoln

A most remarkable instance of the fluid combination of tradition and rationality, in both autocratic and heterocratic forms, is Abraham Lincoln. His case is so special as to make it contentious to fit him into any category—except that one can easily argue against the notion that he himself made many efforts to encourage a charismatic image. A legend almost as soon as he died, he rather sedulously avoided in his lifetime generating the notion that he was all-powerful, all-knowing, and free of blemish in political morals. His opponents in the Democratic and Republican parties and in the wartime cabinet were even more sedulous to see that the image of him remained mortal. As a reminder that no particular leader's style nicely fits any one of the fixed categories, let us consider briefly the man whose style presents evidence of all six.

We should first, however, establish that Lincoln, in contrast to others in his time, *did*, in Dante's sense, as people must in order to merit our further consideration. Among the major political problems, or more exactly the profound public questions, that called for resolution was the possibility of maintaining a large political unit—large in area and in population—as a unit, in the face of conflicting value systems that were geographically separated. In more concrete terms, could a nation be maintained in which there were such sharp differences on the most desirable economic base for the good society (industrialization versus the production of basic raw materials by agriculture) and the appropriate social base (self-exploiting versus slave-exploiting agriculture).

Another of the major problems was the broad one of whether indeed all people were equal and if so, in what sense. Derivative of this problem was the one of self-rule. If people were equal, then they were competent to share equally in the exercise of basic political power—basic policy making. If people were not, then some system of socio-economic-political exploitation was appropriate. Lincoln expressed all of these basic problems in the Gettysburg Address, which in a sense he had spent his adult life in formulating: ". . . our forefathers brought forth on this continent a new nation, conceived in liberty and dedicated to the proposition that all men are created equal. Now we are engaged in a great civil war, testing whether that nation, or any nation so conceived and so dedicated, can long endure."

Although neither Lincoln nor anyone else could be sure in November 1863, when he delivered the speech, that the great social experiment had succeeded, the scientific testing of the proposition had, by the high-water mark of the Civil War, been carried out to a rough, crude, but decisive conclusion. The Union was maintained; the belief that all men are created equal, denied with increasing candor by Southern leaders, remained the accepted belief in the American society; it did not die on the battlefield. And government of the people, by the people, for the people did not perish from the earth. It could in any event have remained a living idea. The Civil War caused it to remain a continuing practice, however imperfect, in America. The cost was enormous in life, liberty, property, and happiness but that testing of the proposition was successful and affirmative.

The plans and actions of all other prominent politicians of the pre-Civil War era failed in either or both of two ways—in preserving the Union or in maintaining a practice of a belief in human equality. Senator Stephen A. Douglas, who probably came closest to recognizing the total series of grave issues, failed in the emphasis he placed on equality. His resolution of the problem was in a rather mechanical reliance on the techniques of popular democracy and majority rule. He did not much consider the basic presupposition of democracy, that all people are—as ends, not means—of equal worth, that subjectively they are equal. His belief in mechanically achieved popular sovereignty was embodied in the 1854 Kansas-Nebraska act. When his reliance proved ill-founded—a consequence that bathed Kansas in blood, John Brown, and brutality—he had no further proposal but more of the same. The 1860 election, which precipitated the secession from the Union of the Southern states, proved how inadequate was his reliance on majoritarianism on a nationwide scale. There was no majority agreement on any candidate in 1860.

Senator John C. Calhoun, whose death in 1850 portended by fifteen years the death of the system he advocated, proposed as the moral foundation for his social system the frank exploitation of some people by others. In this system, some people were valued exclusively for their instrumentality, their usefulness to others. In an anticipation of later analyses of the exploited society this "Marx of the master class," as Hofstadter called Calhoun,[23] proposed the furtherance of what he called civilization (by which he meant possibly a serene plantation life with Shakespeare read on the veranda as strains of Mozart softly floated from the music room where the children practiced quartets) by the physical exploitation and control of black people.

Looking at society from the interests of a class, Calhoun, like Marx, proposed a moral resolution that was universalistic only to the extent that it was a theory for exploitation everywhere by a particular class. This was the end and the justification for politics. The means for achieving it in Calhoun's system involved some logical and semantic legerdemain whereby a concurrent majority would decide basic issues that divided society deeply. By a concurrent majority he meant that if a minority opposed the majority, the minority could veto, that is, forbid, action by the majority. The minority, which he had in mind but which became an abstract principle as he wrote, was the South, specifically the small slave-holding minority in the South, plus the bamboozled Southern majority which dreamily imagined that slave-owners' exploitation was only of slaves. The specific issue he had in mind was, at bottom, whether indeed all men were created equal, an issue he politically proposed not to face but to ignore, by the instrument of veto. The issue was not one on which people could agree to disagree without acknowledging that equality between blacks and whites was as trivial as whether Alabama corn pone was as good as Wisconsin corn bread.

The abolitionists, whether of the speaking kind like William Lloyd Garrison and Wendell Phillips or the acting kind like John Brown, cannot be charged with suffering from the moral cataracts that impaired Calhoun's vision. But sensitive as they were to the intrinsic

[23] See the analysis of Calhoun in Richard Hofstadter, *The American Political Tradition and the Men Who Made It*, New York, Alfred A. Knopf, 1948, ch. 4.

worth of human beings, they had no understanding of gross political processes—politics by the techniques necessary in a large, diverse society. As means, Garrison chose emotional arguments, Phillips a highly moral rationality, and Brown an atavistic violence. The viability of these methods in a large society is limited and, with the exception of Phillips' inherently moderate style, they are alien to the political process of accommodation.

Unable to adjust to less than total victory, abolitionists had much in common stylistically with their Southern antagonists and with the twentieth-century totalitarians, both of these groups seeking a one-to-one correlation between ideology and polity. The role of such groups as Garrison and Phillips was related to politics but was only proto-political—no more political than the land on which a structure is built is a house. Garrison and Phillips were willing to see the Union destroyed rather than permit the continuation of slavery. Like Calhoun, they would destroy the Union rather than abandon their belief. It is not that their morality was equally as good as Calhoun's, because theirs was humane and civilized, which Calhoun's was not. But slaveowners and abolitionists all equally were incapable of maintaining both their values and their recognition of Union as related to these values.[24]

James Buchanan, the man who presided over the final collapse of the federal Union before Lincoln faced the task of putting it back together again, is so loud a silence, so eloquent a failure, as to make one feel cruel even to resurrect his name. He truly seemed overwhelmed by the savage fury of the growing political storm, so overwhelmed that like the man in battle who is furious at a button that pops off his combat fatigues, Buchanan faced the storm by ignoring it. The Dred Scott decision, like the Kansas-Nebraska act which led to the found-

---

[24] If the symmetry of argument appears overdrawn, bear in mind that slavery probably survived for a briefer period in consequence of secession than it would have otherwise. Lincoln in the Emancipation Proclamation of 1 January 1863 did not free slaves in the states that had not rebelled. And the Southern gentry, as a former slavocracy, would not have fared so ill politically if they had not rebelled. As it was, they were faced with the degrading phenomenon of a succession of demagogues from Tilman to Bilbo to Long. There was never such a threat to the English landed gentry, which pliantly adapted to industrialization and the entrance into politics of unpropertied people and even intellectuals. The Southern gentry as a ruling class has never quite recovered from the Civil War and has therefore become only a romantic would-be ruling class, in practice quite completely displaced by energetic bourgeoisie who only as an afterthought cast themselves clumsily in the role of gentry.

ing of the Republican party on its free-farmer base, did not seem something for the public to get alarmed about. Douglas's insistence on a fair administration of the Kansas plebiscite struck Buchanan as an arrogant kind of intraparty contumacy. He could not decide what to do about beleaguered and besieged Federal garrisons in the South, and when his Secretary of War ordered troops sent by ship to one of them, he countermanded the order—after the ship had sailed. He could not even guide a Republican Congress whose recusancy is reminiscent of the intrasigence, sanctimony, and irresponsibility of twentieth-century Nazis, Fascists, and Communists whenever they have appeared incongruously in the legislatures of constitutional democracies.

Buchanan is the epitome of the failure to do. His tragedy was partly personal because his freedom of action had not been altogether destroyed by the boiling up of rebellion and by the bipolarization of loyalties that two generations before had well-nigh spoken with a single voice that all men are endowed by their Creator with the inalienable rights of life, liberty, and the pursuit of happiness. Unable to think, save in the mechanical terms of party government, Buchanan was unable to recognize a social force as an aspect of reality or to believe that anyone could hold anything more dear than the Democratic party and the Union. He was an American Neville Chamberlain, without even the latter's compassion.

Lincoln indeed benefits partly by contrast with his contemporaries, but notably by contrast with Buchanan. If Buchanan, for reasons of the times and personal obtuseness and his party bureaucratism, could not succeed, Lincoln at least had the opportunity to do so. The obstacles overcome by him and the Northerners were so enormous that the very fact of succeeding in doing so stands out: we overlook how the task was done. In a sense Lincoln represents on a magnificent level a rationale which has so testily been advanced by defenders of modern dictators: "After all, he built the Autobahn, didn't he?" One can say of Lincoln, "After all, he preserved the Union and freed the slaves"—which quite neglects how he did these things. It was so great a task as to lead some to beatify his every act and to refuse to consider his style of rule as anything less than divine.

The flavor of tradition-guided autocracy is not strong in Lincoln, but he did feel, increasingly as his Presidency, the Civil War, and his life approached their simultaneous end, that he and the nation were bound by a kind of fate that was predetermined by God. He seemed at times almost to invite death. When he left Springfield to assume the Presidency in Washington City, he bade his friends farewell, "not knowing when or whether ever I may return." He toured a battlefield near Washington, exposing his six-foot, four-inch frame, plus tall stovepipe hat, heedlessly within the range of enemy fire. Within hours after the Confederate army had left Richmond, he walked the streets of that rebel stronghold with no real means of preventing the reach of a sniper's bullet. On the way back to Washington, where he arrived on the 9th of April, the day of Lee's surrender to Grant, Lincoln read from his favorite among Shakespeare's plays, the report that "Duncan is in his grave; after life's fitful fever he sleeps well . . . , nor steels nor poisons, . . . nothing can touch him further." So spoke Lincoln the words of the regicide Macbeth on Duncan, the killed king, the Sunday before Friday the 14th of April, when a young actor shot Lincoln in the head, leaped on to the stage from the President's box and shouted "Sic semper tyrannis," the final scene of the final act of Lincoln's life.

A sense of inevitable victory accompanied the sense of inevitable suffering that made Lincoln so heedless of personal safety, so resigned to whatever must be. The appalling cost of war ground him down as it did his Northern and Southern countrymen. In his Second Inaugural Address in March 1865, he said,

Fondly do we hope—fervently do we pray—that this mighty scourge of war may speedily pass away. Yet, if God wills that it continue, until all the wealth piled by the bond-man's two hundred and fifty years of unrequited toil shall be sunk, and until every drop of blood drawn by the lash, shall be paid by another drawn with the sword, as was said three thousand years ago, so still it must be said "the judgments of the Lord are true and righteous altogether."

He seemed really to feel that human affairs were in great degree beyond human control, puzzling himself with the irony that both sets of combatants were impossibly convinced that God was on their side. He ruminated that "God wills this contest and wills that it shall not end yet," and that God intended "some great good to follow this mighty convulsion which no mortal could make and no mortal could stay." [25] This feeling grew with the spread of suffering as the war progressed.

This resignation to divine will, it may be argued, is kin to the gov-

[25] Lincoln in his own nonpublic writing spelled the pronoun referring to God with a small "h." See for example Roy P. Basler, ed., *Abraham Lincoln: His Speeches and Writings*, Cleveland and New York, The World Publishing Co., 1946, 655.

ernment by divine grace of the tsars. It is directly descended in Lincoln's mind from a kind of fatalism of a more rational sort in which not God but mind figured as the ultimate controlling force, a Doctrine of Necessity conceived in the eighteenth-century rationalism of Jefferson and dedicated to the proposition that liberty must inevitably spread throughout the world. The day of final liberation of all mankind would come when with "all appetites controlled, all passions subdued, all matters subjected, *mind,* all conquering *mind,* shall live and move the monarch of the world." This speech, delivered almost a quarter of a century before the Second Inaugural, reflected less a substantive belief that later changed, than an earlier way of putting it. If mind ruled in 1842 and God in 1865, it apparently meant to Lincoln that there was a body of natural law discovered by mind that described the workings of human nature, which was God's decree.[26] The change in emphasis seemed to be the consequence of a humbling sense that mind could discover only a small fraction of natural law rather than the consequence of any basic change in outlook.

The image is not of a capricious, gracious God, but of an impersonal force that operated in predictable ways if men (including Lincoln) could only discover what these laws were. To this extent Lincoln cannot be said to have evidenced traditionalism of the autocratic sort. Strong as was his basic self-confidence as a ruler, he does not seem to have thought that he himself had a private wire to the divine residence or a total grasp of the laws of nature. The autocratic, anomic aspect of tradition, of the future as it unfolds out of the past, for Lincoln lay wholly in the ignorance of its regularity, not in a belief that development failed to be in accordance with law. Lincoln's view may put him in the same broad category with Freud, who postulated a kind of dualism: reason (Logos) on the one hand and reality or empirical and logical necessity, natural law (Anangke) on the other, with the former the means of discovering but not controlling the latter.

The problem for Lincoln was the practical one of so guiding public affairs that a bit of reason could discover how to help fulfill the inevitable with a bit less suffering. The difference from traditional autocracy thus lies in a faith that God is not capricious but just. The kinship with autocracy is that Lincoln did not suppose any other person to have as good a notion as he of how the future would emerge

[26] See the discussion by Edmund Wilson, The Union as Religious Mysticism, in his *Eight Essays,* Garden City, New York, Doubleday Anchor Books, 1954, 181–202, especially 192–196.

out of the past. The difference in its practical consequences may have been nothing more than a paradoxical humility which led Lincoln to believe that if others were ignorant, he was also—and his ignorance was only a whit less awesome. He must therefore act cautiously, unlike the self-flattered ruler who feels so close to God that he sometimes forgets the distinction in his own mind.

The breakdown of the mental distinction establishes kinship in outlook between the traditional autocrat who believes in God and the rational autocrat who kills Him. Both in practice make themselves the ultimate source of power. This identification of self with ultimate sources of power is a perceptual, ideational error which Lincoln never fell into. Yet Lincoln made and unmade generals. He interfered on all levels with the routine functioning of the administrative departments. To a general fighting in the field his action must have seemed like bare power quite bereft of predictability in its exercise. To deserted soldiers appealing for a commutation of a sentence of death, Lincoln's frequent beneficence must have seemed like infinite mercy rather than judgments which are true and righteous altogether.

The notion that Lincoln was omnipotent, omniscient, and morally perfect, that he was a truly charismatic person, would logically follow in Lincoln's mind had he himself sought to foster the image. There is no good evidence that he did and much good evidence that the image nevertheless began to emerge in his lifetime, and after a century still persists. How then did the image grow and why did he not foster it? Fundamentally it appears to have been one result of Lincoln's unpromising background. The very commonness of it and the very extraordinary success of his role produced a paradoxical but inescapable juxtaposition that seemed miraculous and therefore in Weberian terms charismatic. His excursion from log-cabin nativity to his sanctification as emancipator has so defied reasoned explanation as to facilitate the notion that he was omnicompetent and morally perfect. His paternal ancestors indeed were farmers; his mother, so at least he believed, was illegitimate; he did have altogether no more than a year's formal schooling; and success, in his loves and his married life and in his career, came only haltingly and after successive failures in both roles. Yet he did become a supremely successful President.

In June 1860, Lincoln prepared a short campaign autobiography, written in the third person, some two weeks after his nomination as Presidential candidate at the Chicago convention of the Republican party. He mentioned all the things in the preceding paragraph except his romantic unsuccess with women, but he made little of these ordinary occurrences, in an account that scarcely reads like the miraculous life of a saint.[27] The myth that surrounds Lincoln, that indeed surrounded him even as he made his way to the White House is thus, as Hofstadter suggests, either self-made or made by Lincoln.[28] Spontaneous generation occurs no more in politics than in the etiology of disease. The myth arose not of itself but of the passionate desire of people to establish continuity between their own ordinary lives and beliefs and values and those of their leader. Lincoln unarguably had a common background and a successful presidency. So people saw themselves in him and in their identification made the impossible for them come true in him.

There could be no easier task for Lincoln and his adherents than to encourage a charismatic image. Some of his adherents tried to do this, with considerable success. In this, Lincoln remained either neutral or discouraged the creation of a miraculous image of himself. He said during the war that he was living proof that anyone could become President, a radical contradiction of the notion that his "Pilgrim's Progress" was a miracle. The miracle, if there were to be one, would be his (Lincoln's) self-restraint in view of his tremendous political ambition. Yet the self-restraint existed and the charismatic label does not fit Lincoln the way it fits Hitler, Stalin, and Nkrumah. The miraculous image of charisma is always spurious and always in some degree the product of the ruler himself. Caesar had the power to keep his bust out of temples. Hitler need not have permitted the swearing of loyalty to him personally. Stalin need not have tolerated the notion that he was the sun that gave life to Russia. Nkrumah could have kept his picture off postage stamps. These demagogues let themselves be styled demigods. Lincoln did not.

The sense, if not the knowledge, of this fact, by people living in Lincoln's time and since, has itself lent a miraculous quality to his life and rule. In this sense, Lincoln succeeded as a charismatic ruler where these self-styled members of the genre only tried too hard to succeed. When devotees of Lincoln among the general and scholarly publics give up the search for an explanation of Lincoln's humanity, his non-divinity, then indeed Lincoln will have become charismatic despite his own efforts and those of students of his life who feel discontented at miraculous explanations.

In a careful speech that he made in 1838, when he was almost thirty

---

[27] See Basler, *op. cit.*, 547–555.
[28] See Hofstadter, *op. cit.*, ch. 5, Abraham Lincoln and the Self-Made Myth.

years old and four years after he was first elected to public office, Lincoln outlined his beliefs as to how "we, the American people" can perpetuate our free political institutions. In language a bit flowery by comparison with his austere Presidential prose, he emphasized the dangers of both mobocracy and tyranny. He attacked, that is, the tyrant in the minds of the public and the tyrant in the minds of their rulers. More specifically he was warning of the dangers inherent in the recent lynching in St. Louis, Missouri, of a free Negro who had apparently just killed someone; implicitly he seemed to be warning of the killing three months before by a mob in Alton, Illinois, of an abolitionist editor named Elijah Lovejoy. At the same time he was warning of the danger of "an Alexander, a Caesar, or a Napoleon, of the man of limitless political aspiration who wanted to rule without legal restraint." He was in this probably talking more to himself than his audience and probably warning others to watch out for people with the ambitions of Abraham Lincoln.[29]

It was this sharp, penetrating look into others, into the general public, that prevented the flattery of the public which characterizes the demagogue. It was the equally sharp and deep look into himself that *helped* prevent his becoming the conscious charismatic—and it should be understood that I do not believe that there can be an unconscious charismatic. When an idolizing crowd came to serenade him at the White House, the day after the Southern surrender at Appomattox, Lincoln bade them return the next night. When they did, Lincoln, having already delayed their natural excitement at victory in so agonized a struggle, did not fall into the mood of celebration but with an intensity reminiscent of his speeches before the war spoke of the task of reconstruction that lay ahead.

Other rulers have fallen into demagogy and charisma in knowledge of what they were doing. Caesar allowed his own idolization, shrewdly drawing back from the proffer of monarchy. It is easier to impute to him an understanding of his public image than a stupid misunderstanding of it. Napoleon and Hitler similarly fostered their own charisma.

How then can one argue, as I am, that Lincoln did not foster this? He was a conscious craftsman in the art of political persuasion. He

---

[29] For the maturation of Lincoln's ideology, see Harry V. Jaffa, *Crisis of the House Divided,* Garden City, New York, Doubleday and Co., 1959, ch. 9, The Teaching Concerning Political Salvation. The author emphasizes Lincoln's fear of both amoral leaders and amoral citizens.

moved people deeply in both speaking and writing. There was something almost disingenuous in the ingenuous statement in the Gettysburg Address of November 1863 when Lincoln said that "the world will little note nor long remember what we say here," less than a year after he said, in December 1862, in his annual message to Congress: "Fellow citizens, we cannot escape history. We of this Congress and this administration will be remembered in spite of ourselves. No personal significance, or insignificance, can spare one or the other of us. The fiery trial through which we pass will light us down in honor or dishonor, to the latest generation." [30]

In his highly conscious effort to build for posterity an image of himself, he wanted it to be a particular kind of image, which if narcissistic was narcissism of the sort that animated Christ and not the revivalist preachers of the twentieth century, of the sort that seemed to animate Adenauer and not to have bestirred Hitler, whose actions did not—in the way he had in mind—have much to do with shaping German history for the next thousand years. And indeed Lincoln's was the kind of self-image that appears to be sought after by Nehru among his own people, an image compounded of devotion, aloofness, warmth and coldness, admiration for and scolding of the citizenry, and a desire to gain immortality but a willingness to wait till after his death to achieve it.

With a dispassionate interest that is supposed also to characterize scientists, Lincoln was the rationalist ruler, calmly observing the world inside and outside his own head. His rationality was again of both the autocratic and heterocratic sort. In the most fundamental sense, in his noting of a relationship between natural law, the Declaration of Independence and its equalitarian postulate, and the United States Constitution as the instrument, Lincoln was bound by a very general kind of law. But this left him free to perform a series of acts which could not in any rigorous sense be constitutionally justified. He started to raise an army when Congress was not even in session, and he did not call Congress into special session until three months after Fort Sumter had been fired on. He withdrew funds from the Treasury without appropriation. He issued an Emancipation Proclamation, which deprived southern slave-holders of chattels worth well over a billion dollars, without due process of law. He suspended the writ of habeas corpus, first in areas quite removed from the military scenes

[30] Basler, *op. cit.*, 688.

of battle and then throughout the nation. At least 13,000 people were detained as political prisoners.[31]

His rationale was that the end—the saving of the Constitution in order to save the Declaration of Independence—justified the means:

My oath to preserve the Constitution imposed on me the duty of preserving by every indispensable means that government, that nation, of which the Constitution was the organic law. . . . I felt that measures, otherwise unconstitutional, might become lawful by becoming indispensable to the preservation of the Constitution through the preservation of the nation. . . . I could not feel that, to the best of my ability, I had ever tried to preserve the Constitution, if to save slavery or any minor matter, I should permit the wreck of the government, country and Constitution altogether.[32]

No American President has governed outside the Constitution quite so much as did Lincoln. And yet no President has exhibited more self-restraint in the face of opportunity to act without restraint, unless it be Franklin Roosevelt in 1933 when the nation was in a mood compounded of sullen anger, frustration, and panic. FDR could have governed by decree, imprisoned his extreme right-wing opposition, and withheld the pay of recalcitrant judges. But laws were passed, the bitter opposition continued beyond his death, and judges got their pay regularly. Lincoln did restrain himself, perhaps, because in the 1838 speech he put himself and the public on notice of the dangers of tyranny and because he had the vision, the patience, and the supreme self-confidence to rest his case with posterity rather than with his contemporaries. He despaired from time to time during the war, notably before the 1864 election in which his opponent was the frustrated General McClellan. But he never got so desperate that he basically altered his policy from one of self-restraint to self-indulgence in power. The statement which Khrushchev in his February 1956 speech attributed to Stalin, that he would crush Tito, the recalcitrant Yugoslav Communist, is inconceivable of Lincoln, whose response to obstacles was political or administrative maneuver rather than force and violence.

Lincoln indeed did exhibit traditionalism, charisma and rationality in his rule. He was by habit the first and the last of these—a Whig in the largely Democratic, Jackson-oriented State of Illinois and a prac-

---

[31] See Benjamin P. Thomas, *Abraham Lincoln*, New York, Alfred A. Knopf, 1952, 376–381.

[32] Quoted in Wilfred E. Binkley, *President and Congress*, 3rd ed., New York, Vintage Books, 1962, 154–155. For Lincoln's quasi-legislative actions, see *ibid.*, ch. 6, esp. 152–154.

ticing attorney capable of an incredible measure of sustained thought. And if he did not always discourage the mantle of competence that was thrust upon him, he nevertheless severely limited his contribution to the image. He seemed to be almost exclusively concerned with the judgment of posterity, a judgment that must rest on the remarkable self-restraint shown in circumstances when he could have extended the blood bath from the battlefield to the political hustings, winning his political victories by force rather than persuasion.

America has world fame for a variety of material accomplishments, but deserves probably the highest acclaim for two major nonmaterial contributions: the principle of federalism whereby the paradox of unity and diversity has been sustained, and the rulership of Lincoln. It is doubtful that there has been in the modern world a more brilliantly successful leader, a man both sustained by and profoundly supportive of the free institutions which until the nineteenth century were never even considered possible on a broad scale. In an era that can best be characterized not as economic or religious, but in the last analysis political, the contribution of Lincoln is no mean one for any nation to make.

It is hard to guess how much America was politically a product of Lincoln at the end of the Civil War and how much Lincoln was a product of America. For it is hard, indeed impossible, to determine how much the environment produces the leader and how much the leader the environment. In Germany, after the First World War, some kind of charismatic leader would doubtless have emerged to meet the crises of defeat, inflation, and depression. But it does not seem inevitable that he be the spoiled child with a gun that Hitler was. America similarly seemed predisposed for a strong leader in its depression crisis of the 1930s, but it got a leader into whom decades of parental, academic, and political civilizing had made effectively impossible the unconstitutional absolutism of Hitler.

The occasional catastrophe of assassination removes towering figures like Lincoln and Gandhi. The catastrophe of accidental death took Ramon Magsaysay from his great role in the new Philippines. The lives of these men made a difference among their people. But their deaths do not seem to have profoundly altered the course of history of the peoples. The crucifixion of Christ did not kill Christianity. The assassination of Julius Caesar did not kill Caesarism. The murder of Gandhi did not precipitate a blood bath to avenge the death of that gentle man. Magsaysay's death did not end the slow process of political maturation in the Philippines any more than that one man in his lifetime ended the still endemic disease of corruption. There may sometime be units of analysis that will make it possible to assess the relative impact of the great man and of the society in producing a particular form of government, a particular degree of political maturation, but such analytical instruments are not yet available.

I have left out of the discussion such considerations as conservatism, progressivism, liberalism, partisanship, and any kind of elaborated ideology. This has been done not in a belief that these considerations are meaningless but that they are less meaningful than the criteria advanced for appraising both the substance and the style of rule. The reason for this may be illustrated by Lincoln, though it applies quite generally. Lincoln was a middle-class Whig, an upwardly mobile farmer's son who entered the prestigeful profession of law and politics. He was a success in the former no less than the latter. As is often the case with lawyers, who are a property-oriented lot because they deal mainly with property rights, Lincoln was a conservative. And, with his one year of schooling, he sent his son off to Harvard.

But his conservatism on class status, property, and other social, perhaps ideological, grounds did not interfere with his successful confrontation of novel problems. "As our case is new, so we must think anew and act anew," he said in 1862. Was his government any less, any more, progressive or conservative or liberal for his middle-class Whig background? If adaptability to changed circumstances is an aspect of progressivism, was Lincoln less progressive than William Jennings Bryan, the evangelistic leader of progressives in the 1890s? Was Stalin, in the supposed interests of speedily achieving a socialist Utopia, thereby progressive when he used the atavistic techniques of secret police, torture, and political murder to fulfill a monstrous five-year plan to produce behavioral homogeneity among the Soviet elite? Are one-time Wilsonian progressives truly such when they oppose the New Deal, or New Dealers progressive when they continue in the 1960s to act politically as though they were still in the 1930s?

The ability to meet new cases in appropriate terms appears to be a basic characteristic of people like Lincoln, Wilson, Roosevelt, Churchill, Adenauer, or Nehru quite regardless of their prior ideology. This ability has to do with the ability to do, in the Dantean sense. Progressives can be more rigid than conservatives; for example, as Stalin became increasingly rigid the longer he stayed in power. And those who do can make their mark as autocrats or heterocrats, again without regard to ideology. The likenesses of Nazi rule under Hitler and Communist rule under Stalin are as striking as the differences, if not more so. Yet the former ideology is reactionary in its racist goals and the latter is in some of its goals progressive. Both movements, as they have used political means of achieving the goals, are in the twentieth-century context reactionary.

Leaders and political maturity

In this discussion we have for a time neglected the central figures in this book, who are not leaders but ordinary citizens, who to a great degree are the cause for the emergence of a particular ruler with a particular style of rule. When a general public is tradition-minded, it will pick a traditional ruler if one is around, or at least considerably circumscribe the freedom of action of a nontraditional ruler who emerges. If a public is looking for a charismatic ruler they will select him out of the alternative candidates—if the public has some choice as a voting electorate or as a spectator electorate. Let us now look at the circumstances which will influence a public to pick a particular leader.

In order to do this we can get some conceptual help from a rather mercurial concept in psychology—a concept which nevertheless, in whatever verbal guise, appears to be almost indispensable. The concept—maturity—again is borrowed by psychology from physiology or biology. Botanists, for example, may speak of a "young" tree, a "young" redwood. Such a tree has a rather shiny long-scaled bark. It changes radically as the redwood lives through time, until it achieves the quite unshiny, deeply striated (and incidentally fire-resistant) bark of the "mature" tree. To the nonbiological category of botanic neophytes like myself, there is only a coincidental similarity between the shiny-barked young redwood, whose time since seedling may be five or ten years, and the shaggy, mature tree, whose age may vary from a hundred to a couple of thousand years. Similarly physiologists may speak of a "young" hamster, a "young" chimpanzee, or a "young" human being. In exact physiological designation, the age in weeks, months, or years is specified, to avoid the indefiniteness inherent in such terms as "young" and "mature." But there is ordinarily no physiological doubt as to the morphological differences at different ages unless the biologist has predicted a difference in form or structure from one age to another and then found none.

The problem, so real, yet easy in the case of redwoods and to a lesser degree laboratory animals, becomes quite difficult when one considers the behavior, rather than the form or structure, of these more complicated organisms. In the broad and indefinite category of living things, which are called animals because such organisms are capable of "self-motion," "voluntary motion," when does the creature become mature? When it can find its own food and shelter? When it is physically capable of reproduction? When it is emotionally ready for parenthood? If a dog has puppies when it is very "young," and develops emotional tensions because it was so quickly thrust into motherhood, how do the behavioral consequences of "early" pregnancy for the bitch and for her perpetually hungry whelps compare with the behavioral consequences to parent and offspring when the routine first pregnancy comes at a later stage of development?

The problem is even more difficult when applied to human beings. When does a human being complete its infancy, so that the subsequent behavior that is like that which is "normal" to infancy becomes "infantile"? When does a human being become "mature"? When he or she marries, earns his or her own living, becomes a parent, a grandparent, or what? What is mature behavior? What is mature political behavior?

We may—like sophists but unlike Socrates, Pilate but not Christ, Berkeley or Hume but not Freud—deflect our minds with a safe philosophical query into the fundamental nature of truth or reality and thereby avoid the very real problem. We can, on the other hand, with less than innocence, struggle with it, knowing that we cannot altogether succeed, yet not surely fail either.

"Society," "law," and "governments" make arbitrary decisions as to what constitutes maturity. There are Boy Scout troops, Hitler Jugend, Comsomols, Young Republican clubs, Junior Chambers of Commerce, Young Democratic organizations, and so on. The issue rarely arises, but usually people who call themselves young men graciously drop out of the Boy Scouts, Hitler Youth, Young Communists, Young Republicans, or Junior Chambers of Commerce at an appropriate time. There is the occasional twenty-four-year-old Boy Scout who will not quit till he makes it to Eagle; a Rudolph Hess who makes a brave, solitary, innocent journey to Anglo-land to bring peace within the Nordic tribe; a Georgian who stays with the young Communists in Tbilisi rather than live dangerously with the Moscow metropolites; or a forty-one-year-old business man and Junior Chamber of Commerce leader in Brooklyn who was an executive prodigy fourteen years ago in the toy train business. But, by and large, such gross distortions of the normal calculus of age are infrequent.

At law, young men are responsible for their own debts, can make contracts binding upon themselves without the consent of their parents, at various ages—usually twenty-one in most jurisdictions. Women can act similarly usually at the age of eighteen, though in ordinary practice legal contracts with women under twenty-one, except marriage, have been avoided.[33] With little systematic knowledge other than accumulated experience, "society" makes these rather artificial classifications so real in their consequences. They work better, probably, than would no classification at all.

At law, citizens are considered no longer junior, and not yet senior, when they can vote, usually no younger than at the age of twenty-one, but increasingly at the age of eighteen, because, inter alia, this is the age at which legislatures say they are old enough to serve in the armed forces in defense of their country.[34] This means that people who have achieved majority by legal definition are declared qualified to choose their leaders, in whatever mixture of tradition, charisma, and reason they may appeal for popular support.

The legal judgments of maturity in private law (contracts, etc.) and in public law (crimes, military service, etc.) work reasonably well. Do these judgments work well in politics? The discussion in this chapter has argued that traditional and rational responsible rulers are generally better, more functional, more stable, better able to solve public problems than are charismatic rulers (and that responsible rulers are better than irresponsible and that successful rulers--whether or not responsible—are better than unsuccessful). For example, I have implied that such primarily traditional rulers as Churchill and Adenauer or such primarily rational rulers as Jefferson, Masaryk, or Nehru have been better than even responsible charismatic rulers like Jackson, Franklin Roosevelt, or de Gaulle. One general reason for this judgment is that rulers who are regarded as incapable of wrong or of error tend to get people out of the habit of political maturity, which I will now pro tempore [35] define as the ability to make responsible choice, both as to public policy and public policy makers. I use the term "responsible" in the same sense that is applicable in private law,

---

[33] This marital exception to general contractual prudence has a nontraditional, irrational, libidinal basis, usually in both contracting parties.

[34] In America, in its Civil War, military service was also common before the age of twenty-one, yet males under that age could not then vote. In America and England, suffrage had been restricted not solely on age but on ownership of various kinds of real and personal property.

[35] I do not claim that this pro tempore definition is made sub specie aeternitatis and will bear no responsibility for its being judged as if it were so intended.

meaning capable and willing to recognize and accept the consequence of one's own choices and the choices of others as they affect oneself and the polity at large.

The case of Germany

Political maturity, though a necessary concept in a theoretical scheme that presupposes nonrandom, evolutionary change, is even harder to observe than to define. There is too much evidence that both general publics and the elite are less than completely competent to exercise responsible political choice. Ordinary citizens—in their images of political bosses, Congressmen, the Cliveden Set, millionaires, New Dealers, landed aristocrats, padroni, the white man, the boss, intelligentsia, imperialist and capitalist warmongers, and other segments or aspects of the ruling class—are apt to miscalculate the avarice or stupidity or cruelty of the elite. Members of the elite, including not only the formal political elite but also intellectuals, are apt similarly to reify their abstract concepts of ordinary people (that is, the masses, stupid country boys, muzhiks, kaffirs, et al.). In the process, both categories —ordinary and extraordinary people—show a noteworthy competence for making extraordinary blunders in the selection of leaders. Each category, unable to understand itself as individuals or collectivities, finds it easier to impugn the others rather than see its own miscalculations.

What I have in mind may be better shown by example. Nazism is blamed by many on the German people,[36] to the neglect of German leaders. Implicitly consistent with this is the notion that it was the German elite which made the first step toward removing Hitler in the abortive plot of 1944.[37] The signs of Hitler's enormous popularity between 1933 and at least 1941 are explicit and very persuasive. He probably could have won even free elections easily after once becoming established as Reichsführer. But such an interpretation, though true, is partial. Hitler did not ever win a majority of the German general public to his side in a free election in which the public had an alternative. In the Reichstag election of July 1, 1932, the Nazi Party candidates garnered 37% of the popular vote. In the November 1932

[36] The kind of analysis I have in mind is Erich Fromm's *Escape from Freedom*, which explains Nazism as the political consequence of the inability of modern man to accept the moral responsibility implicit in the Protestant Reformation.
[37] This of course is not necessarily inconsistent with the notion that there was popular support for the attempt to kill Hitler.

election the Nazis lost some 2 million votes and 34 Reichstag seats. In March 1933, in the last popular election before the end of the second Reich, the Nazi party's vote increased by 5 million votes to only 44% of the total, despite a savage campaign in which violence, in the form of governmentally tolerated Nazi storm troopers, played its intimidating role.[38] It was Hitler's cautious conservatism which made him deem it imprudent to risk the future of Germany—which he identified with the Party's and his own welfare—by campaigning in a free election. He was too conservative to trust that he could win a majority.

How then did this come about? Was it the populace that gave rise to Hitler? In a very real sense, yes. But at each stage of the growth of the Nazi party and Nazi movement, Hitler was able to get either the vacillating or eager support or tolerance of members of the ruling class. Judges lightly sentenced Hitler to five years' imprisonment for trying to take over the government of Bavaria in the 1923 Munich Putsch; he was released after serving only nine months. Industrial and army supporters then kept him politically alive. Hindenburg, whose colossal fortitude was fully matched by his political innocence, allowed Hitler to become Chancellor. All these members of the ruling class must share responsibility with the populace for producing the Third Reich. These elitists seemed to think either that Hitler would be good for Germany or that his minor shortcomings could be corrected or controlled by solid, responsible, leading citizens like themselves. Yet one can truly say of them all that they really did not know what they were doing, or at least were almost as ignorant as the public; that is, the stupid person that every German householder (elitist or ordinary citizen) seemed to think lived next door or at least in the next block or the next town or province, in a regression from infinite wisdom to infinite stupidity, a curve that fell sharply immediately beyond the individual's own self.

Which were more immature—the German general public or the army and industrial leaders who knew Hitler but thought he could be controlled? One can say that the political behavior of all of them was childlike. They tended to divide the perceptual world into clear friends and clear enemies. They were predisposed not to trust their neighbor's judgment as compared with their own, or the strange German's judgment in comparison with their neighbor's, who now became,

[38] William L. Shirer, *The Rise and Fall of the Third Reich*, New York, Simon and Schuster, 1960, 166, 194–196.

by comparison, clear friends—and so on to Hitler, who in comparison with Englishmen, Frenchmen, Russians, Jews, capitalists and Communists, became clearly German and clearly good. Both ordinary and extraordinary citizens of Germany acted without the realistic appraisal of reality that is one characteristic of maturity.

Like children, they felt impotent in the face of vast forces, economic and social and military, that threatened or seemed to threaten them individually and collectively. They wanted a quick and easy solution, like the child who cries for food, affection, and recognition and then stops crying when a placebo is provided. They got jobs. They adored Hitler or thought the man next door did. And as they goose-stepped, they got the recognition and anonymity that are produced by sensing they were one of the millions, a necessary one, that made up a Germany in motion. Those who so acted in Germany during the Third Reich, a group that at times clearly constituted a majority, seemed really not to want to make public policy. They seemed to want to be used as instruments of policies which could not be questioned and which were made by a man or men who had a competence for rule that must not be questioned. They chose or tolerated a charismatic ruler, an omnipotent, omnicompetent, morally perfect man. That no such man ever existed did not matter.

What then made for this immaturity? In general one can say that it was the consequence of the activation of needs which must be met before people can bear the responsibility of decision making in politics. This varied with different groups in Germany. Some actually were hungry, but it is doubtful that these showed much political activity. Almost all suffered from some serious frustration or anxiety—some unbearable tension that for enough people could be relieved by a retrogression to the political condition when the Kaisers and Bismarck took care of things.

For the middle class of small entrepreneurs, who could be made and broken by a volatile postwar economy, the economic crisis produced the tension. For the ex-soldier, who recalled the glory and security of military life, the drab insecurity of dull civility built up tension.[39] For landed aristocrats, the middle-classification of a proud Nordic nation of fighters caused tension. For military officers, immediate descendants of landowners, the same middle-classification plus the threat of Communization were cause enough. And for all, to some

---

[39] It was this syndrome that Hitler experienced. It was among veterans that his earliest appeals were successful in changing a category into a group.

degree, the personal impact of first inflation and then depression—of futile job-holding, futile saving and then the threat of losing jobs and savings—was a cause of tension. Just as an adult, sick abed with an illness, reverts to childhood and demands the care of mother surrogates in the form of wife or nurses, so a sick people regressed to a time when they need bear no ultimate responsibility for making decisions, in the good old days of political infancy, before they articulated their voices (Stimmen) and started making choices (Wahlen) in the second, republican Reich.

The phenomenon of political immaturity is too widespread in particular cultures to lend itself to any easy explanation, even though in a particular culture one part of the total explanation may predominate in a particular case. In Germany, economic factors were important, but so also were such noneconomic factors as the frustrations of déclassés. In Germany, status was of greater significance than it has ever been in America, which never had a landed aristocracy so entrenched for centuries as the German Junkers were entrenched, or a military status group that had suffered the degradation of indecisive defeat. Perhaps also the lack of what Bendix has called "cumulative political experience" [40] was a factor.

Other times, other cases

With a lack of appreciation for the centuries-slow learning process in a particular culture, Americans and Englishmen are likely to forget that political murder of the opposition was practiced by Henry VIII in the sixteenth century, that a century later a jingoistic, brutal, and frustrated parochialism characterized English politics during the Puritan Reformation, the Restoration, and the Glorious Revolution. Nations are not born with a sense of political responsibility; they must learn it just as the individual, born an infant, must learn to speak and later accept responsibility before he can become an adult.

Charisma, inherently a symptom of irresponsibility, of political immaturity, may thus appear under a variety of circumstances in a variety of cultures. The regression in some degree to a state of political infancy [41]—in the root sense of infancy, that is inability to speak—may

---

[40] Reinhard Bendix, Social Stratification and Political Power, *American Political Science Review*, **46**: 357–375 (1952). This essay penetrates into the etiology of Nazism far more deeply than the title indicates.

[41] See the summary of Some Studies of Authoritarianism at the end of this chapter, page 330, for some inconclusive but suggestive findings.

thus follow the first attempts to articulate politically. But charisma may not be regression; it may *constitute* the first attempts. Charisma may thus appear in a highly literate society with centuries of scholarly civilization, as in Germany, the Soviet Union, and the People's Republic of China. It has appeared in Ghana where an agglomeration of people of different tribes are in the process of being united in a new nation, a new nontribal people.[42] It appeared in the United States, during a fifteen-year period of crisis, when Franklin Roosevelt, a responsible charismatic ruler, emerged and became a wartime leader in opposition to Hitler, an irresponsible charismatic leader who similarly emerged and endured in Germany.

The symptoms of this political fever in a populace appear to be pretty much the same, even though the causes may differ. The disease may be diminished by the action of a charismatic ruler who really wishes to make the patient well—that is, to teach the patient to bear political responsibility—and who limits himself to a reluctant, conscience-ridden adoption of the parental-surrogate role. The disease may be aggravated by the deliberate, conscience-free exploitation of popular fears, frustrations, and anxieties of both the elite and the general public. But it cannot be argued that charisma is a healthy enduring condition, any more than it can be argued that it is healthy for a person to stay in bed and be ministered to by physicians, nurses, or wives or to continue a dependency on priest, minister, or analyst beyond the confessional or the analysis.

This may give some basis for judging the greatness of leaders. Do they contribute to political maturation or do they encourage enduring dependency? On this question Lincoln, in my opinion, has achieved the zenith in the modern world and Hitler probably ranks at the nadir, with such rulers as Stalin, Mao, Nkrumah, and Lenin somewhere in between.

We may throw further light on the question of political leaders and maturity by considering in some detail the emerging patterns of political behavior in politically undeveloped nations. In a sense the question of political maturity is a central one of this book. The degree of maturity of a people is indicated rather well by the pattern of relations between leaders and followers, and there is such a wide variety of such relations in politically immature nations as to make them a good testing ground for the central ideas of this book, which have been

---

[42] Note the discussion of charisma in David E. Apter, *The Gold Coast in Transition*, Princeton, Princeton University Press, 1955, 304–307.

mainly derived from analyses and developments in nations that are now pleased to regard themselves mature.

APPENDIX

Some Studies of Authoritarianism

Low status and little education correlate with authoritarianism, which is a kind of political irresponsibility, in its emphasis on the need for strong leaders. One hundred and two students who were administered the F-scale in a Southern Negro university, proved to be more authoritarian than 94 white students at the state university. The mean score of the Negroes was 4.68, of the whites 3.86, compared with the criterion-group score of 4.73 among San Quentin prison inmates. [C. U. Smith and J. W. Prothro, Ethnic Differences in Authoritarian Personality, *Social Forces*, **35**: 334–338 (1957).] Employees in a German cosmetics factory were given the F-scale interview in 1952, with a total N of 140. The mean F-score was 5.26, with those who had gone to Volksschule averaging 5.40 and those who had gone on to Hochschule averaging 4.57. Again these compare with the San Quentin prison average of 4.73. [T. S. Cohn and H. Carsch, Administration of the F-Scale to a Sample of Germans, *Journal of Abnormal and Social Psychology*, **49**: 471 (1954).] Another study found the greatest correlation between experimental subjects' opinions and leaders' when the subjects had the least education and were politically the most apathetic. [F. E. Lowe and T. C. McCormick, A Study of the Influence of Formal and Informal Leaders in an Election Campaign, *Public Opinion Quarterly*, **20**: 651–662 (Winter 1956–1957).] The rule of Munoz Marin in Puerto Rico has been styled personalismo or charisma. [See the careful historical analysis of H. Wells, Ideology and Leadership in Puerto Rican Politics, *American Political Science Review*, **49**: 22–39 (1955).] In a 1956 sample of 602 Puerto Rican university students, another analysis found less preference for Munoz' Popular Democratic party among university students (47.5%) than among the electorate (62.5%) or among the fathers of university students (57.3%). [P. Bachrach, Attitude toward Authority and Party Preference in Puerto Rico, *Public Opinion Quarterly*, **22**: 68–73 (1958).] Note also that one of the supposed correlates of authoritarianism, the absence of roots, does not find validation, at least in one study. Those who on the average had lived longest in their area had the highest authoritarianism score (4.5, compared with the lowest of 3.4, which was for the group living the briefest time in their area) and that this long-residence, high authoritarian category also was lowest in economic status and in percentage of people finishing high school. [I. de A. Reid and E. I. Ehle, Leadership Selection in Urban Locality Areas, *Public Opinion Quarterly*, **14**: 262–284, Table 1, p. 266 (1950), reprinted in D. Katz et al., *Public Opinion and Propaganda*, New York, The Dryden Press, 1954, 446–459.]

CHAPTER 10

The politics
of instability

Varieties of political generation

High tension and deep malaise pervade a mature society about to give birth to a new one. Anguished participants in the portended parturition need be neither sympathetic nor hostile to what will emerge. The new will inevitably come. It may be borne in bitterness by a society so querulously enamored of its serene self as to be incapable of sympathy for anything new and different. Or the new may be stillborn, too small and too premature to survive outside the old—or too large and too late to navigate the narrow birth canal. Or the new may indeed be born alive and healthy and beloved, growing in its time to maturity and to confident procreation itself. In any event, the process of nascence, maturity, renascence, and senility goes on as continually in civilizations as it does in the family.

Politics in a society of the third sort, where the offspring is acknowledged and beloved, is the politics of constitutional processes. The new emerges from the old with such comparative ease that parent and child often seem unaware that any crisis has come and gone. This is the politics, since the industrial revolution and perhaps before, of England, Scandinavia, and North America. Long before the industrial revolution, it was the politics of the Roman empire and the Greek city states, until these civilizations became old in a process which neither Gibbon nor anyone else has yet satisfactorily explained, in ten, hundred, or a thousand pages. More continuously than other civilizations, Judaism as a half-cultural, half-ethnic civilization has survived for over six thousand years and Roman Catholicism as a half-cultural, half-religious social institution for close to two thousand.

In none of these civilizations has the process of rebirth been easy or painless. The Chartist movement in England, the popular demands for reform in Denmark from 1830 until the new constitution was promulgated in 1849, the successful demand for constitutionalism by Norway after Denmark gave it to Sweden in 1815, the suffrage extension in the United States in the early nineteenth century—all these developments were anguished. But few were accompanied by a high degree of intergenerational, primordial fear, hatred, and pain. The most notable exceptions among the civilizations of England and North America have been the Puritan Revolution in the seventeenth century and the American Civil War in the nineteenth. But the pre-existing constitutional structure survived these savage contests. This continuity partially distinguishes these struggles from the French Revolution, the Russian Revolution, and the German Nazi revolution.

Our present concern is not with political processes within a "normal" constitutional society but with the first two kinds of politics. Our focus is primarily on political gestation and birth accompanied by much violence, much hatred, and where the parents deny their own offspring and (if it survives) the offspring denies the parents. Or, where the offspring, with the savagery of retaliation sanctified by the lex talionis, tries to kill the old. The old is a long time a-dying and, in the behavior patterns of the offspring, lives on beyond its time.

Differences between constitutional and nonconstitutional change are nevertheless ones of degree. Qualitatively, the Russian nobleman who has lost his manor and "his" serfs and becomes an embittered monarchist is not, in this loss and reaction, different from the manufacturer who formerly did not but now angrily does pay an "excess" profits tax and reconciles himself to the law which protects "his" workers in their wish to bargain with him collectively and as equals. Although the distinctions are quantitative and arbitrary, we can in looking at nonconstitutional processes include such events as the French Revolution and exclude occurrences like the election of Jefferson, the ministry of Gladstone, the Rooseveltian New Deal, and the remarkably but not completely nonviolent power change from Stalin to Khrushchev.

Leisler's rebellion

We can start with a brief chronology of a little revolution—a rebellion—that was stillborn. This little seventeenth-century rebellion is a microcosm of forces that include the Protestant-Catholic conflict in the Reformation; the rise of mercantile capitalism and local entrepreneurs; and the paternalism which, as a feudal vestige, politically lingered in the control of outlanders by haughty metropolitans. Each of these forces, under the same or novel labels, has lingered on into the twentieth century, and is still helping produce political instability.

In 1609 an English explorer-entrepreneur established a relationship with the Dutch government. Probing the western shore of the North Atlantic, he found a deep river and sailed up it. In the name of the Dutch he laid claim to the territory adjacent to the river, which came to bear his name. A settlement started about a year later, called New Netherland, at the mouth of this Hudson river. Two generations later, in 1664, the British captured the colony—after the end of the Puritan Revolution and during the reign of Charles II, a church-going Protestant sybarite of a king, who just two years before had married Catherine of Braganza, the daughter of the restored Catholic king of Portugal.[1] This captured Dutch territory was placed so exclusively under the rule of the king's brother, James, the Catholic Duke of York, that his new colonial feudality acquired the name of his old one. The Congo similarly was to become the virtual private domain of King Leopold of Belgium more than two hundred years later, in 1885.

In 1673 there was a little revolt of the Dutch settlers, supported by some warships from the Netherlands. For several months British sovereignty was displaced in New York City but then re-established. During the next decade English settlers began to demand a popularly (but not too popularly) elected assembly. Impudence toward the Crown increased to the point in 1681 where a New York merchant secured the indictment of the Collector of Customs, charging him with treason, with having "advisedly plotted and contrived Innovacons in Governm't and the subversion and change of the known Ancient and

---

[1] In contrast to the English Restoration of 1660, the Portuguese of 1640 meant not the defeat of Puritanism but the displacement of Spanish with English suzerainty. The defeated force was not domestic but foreign. By the treaty of 1661, Portugal gave England the city-colonies of Tangier and Bombay, plus Catherine as consort. England promised to protect Portugal (against Spain). Religion was not seriously an issue. [J. B. Trend, *Portugal*, London, Ernest Benn Ltd., 1957, 153–164.]

Fundamental Lawes of the Realme of England." More specifically, the records indicate, the Collector had demanded cash payment of import duties on goods, which henceforth were to be assessed at actual rather than nominal value.[2] He had been acting on orders from his superior, the deputy of the Duke's governor Andros, who had failed to make clear just what should be done about the duties. The Collector and his trial were removed to England. When the complaining witness, the New York merchant, did not show up to accuse the Collector, the case was dismissed.

Such irritations as these between the bumptious bourgeoisie of New York and the semi-feudal English rulers increased. Responding flexibly to the importunacies of the contumacious, the Duke of York in 1683 granted a kind of charter to New York. The charter called for an assembly which was to meet at least once every three years, its members to be elected by landowners and to decide on their own qualifications for office. The charter stated a list of basic rights, including due process of law, jury trials, taxation only by the assembly, and religious toleration of Christians of all denominations.

During this crucial period the governor of New York, in effect the vice-duke and by extension the viceroy, was an Irishman and a Catholic named Dongan. He was appointed in 1683, five years after Titus Oates had discovered the "Popish plot." Among other facets, said Oates, it included a plan of Portuguese Catherine to poison her husband, Charles II. What with his loose life, she might have wished to, but she appears to have been guilty of no more murderous or religious subversion than helping reconcile her errant husband to the Catholic church, just before he died in 1685—seven years after Oates' remarkable disclosures and two years after the New York natives got so restless under their Catholic vice-duke.

This is how things looked to the residents of New York. Charles, the symbol of venery and a death-bed Catholic, was succeeded by his devout Catholic brother James, an incontrovertible symbol of Popery. New York was absorbed into the Dominion of New England, whose new governor, Andros, was not a Catholic but an Anglican. Thus he was no Congregationalist and reputedly was even sympathetic to the church of the new king. And he lived way off in Boston. The lieutenant-governor for the province of New York, "a pretended Protestant," reportedly had gone to mass with the King before leaving Eng-

[2] J. R. Reich, *Leisler's Rebellion: a Study of Democracy in New York, 1664–1720,* Chicago, University of Chicago Press, 1953, 41.

land for service in the North American colony. At any rate, it was a known fact that a Catholic was both on the governor's council and at the same time was in charge of the strategic military post in Albany, near to the savage Indians and to Canada; that the New York customs collector was a Catholic; and that prominent citizens of New York, anticipating the wave of the future, were sending their children to a Catholic school. And the 1598 Edict of Nantes, which in France was supposed to have marked the end of the bloody wars of the Reformation, was revoked after nearly a century, in 1685, causing a flow of refugees from France, some of whom came to England and the North American colonies. These French Protestants were forbidden to migrate to Canada, which was then under French control. The atmosphere was tense both in England and in its Dominion of New England.

For a generation after the defeat of Cromwell and Puritanism, the government in England had drifted from the slack, insouciant indulgence of one Stuart king to the more taught, dedicated Romanism of another. On 28 January 1689 Parliament resolved to end this, declaring that James II had violated "the original contract between king and people" while under the influence of "Jesuits and other wicked persons" and was therefore no longer king. Two weeks later, on the 13th of February, Parliament installed on the throne a Dutch Huguenot king, who had neither religious nor political views of the sort that would be uncomfortable to a Protestant kingdom with a burgeoning bourgeoisie and a vigorous parliament.[3]

Within a matter of weeks after the accession of William and Mary, the anti-Puritan Governor, Andros, was arrested and imprisoned in Boston by colonials. The atmosphere in New York became highly charged. It was rumored that there were Catholics on Staten Island who planned to lay waste New York and kill all inhabitants; that all the English soldiers in the city's fort were Catholic; and that the French commanding officer in Quebec would move down the water-level route from Montreal via the shores of Lake Champlain to take and hold Albany (a mere 200 miles from Montreal) and maybe take New York for the deposed James II.

---

[3] William had the further qualifications of being on his mother's side the grandson of Charles I of England, of having already twelve years been married to the daughter of the just-dethroned James II, and of having served with great skill as Dutch monarch during a period of serious domestic and international crisis in the Netherlands.

On 31 May 1689, the fort in New York was captured by a citizen militia, and the city and province entered a condition of rebellion. A leading merchant, a reliable Protestant who had just recently refused to pay to the Catholic customs collector the duty on a cargo of wine, then became the leader of the new rebel government, by relatively popular demand.

This rebel leader, Jacob Leisler, in a life of close to fifty years, had come a long way. He was born in Frankfurt am Main in 1640, the son of a Protestant minister, at a time when the wars of the Reformation were still continuing after a hundred years and when to be a Protestant meant taking sides willy-nilly in a deathly struggle. Twenty years later, in search of his fortune, he arrived in New Amsterdam, soon married the widow of a wealthy merchant, sued her relatives over his wife's inheritance, became a wealthy merchant himself, and never quite gained a commensurate social status.

This failure in high society may have been a consequence of un-gentlemanly quarreling over wealth acquired by marriage. It may have been the result of hard, sharp business on the part of a poor, unknown preacher's kid who was from a proper professional back-ground but was not from a distinguished Dutch, or English Restora-tion, or from a virtuous New England Puritan family. Leisler may have taken solace by reading of the virtuous man who was with them but not of them, and he was doubtless comforted by his popular esteem. But he could not become a scion of even a latter-day first family of seventeenth-century New York, any more than could Alex-ander Hamilton, another outlander, a century later. In any case his emergence as leader conforms nicely to the pattern of marginal man, whom we have already exemplified, in Chapter 3, in the cases of Lincoln, McCarthy, Masaryk, Hitler, and Lenin.

Leisler's rebels set up a government, promptly and optimistically swearing loyalty to William and Mary. They then proceeded to make their first mistake, which was to rule. That is, Leisler and the govern-ing group, the "Committee of Safety," started to collect customs, which had constituted one of the proximate causes of the rebellion in the first place. Nine months after the rebellion began, a legislature con-vened. This was another mistake, because it included representatives of not only merchants but also the previously quite voiceless farmers. Understandably the merchants, some of whom had complained a decade before of the subversion of ancient and fundamental laws of England when the customs collector began seriously to collect full duties on imports, became indignant and disaffected. In January 1690 some French and Indians massacred about sixty people and burned down the settlement at Schenectady. In the spring Leisler organized an expedition, with the half-hearted support of other colonies, to attack French Canada by land and by sea. It failed in midsummer. This was a third mistake, if for no other reason, because it failed.

The legislature in September 1690 enacted a novel tax on real and personal property and ineffectually established a fine of £75 against anyone refusing to serve in the government or armed forces. Two more blunders.

In October there was a revolt against Leisler's rebel government. Some 300 Leisler troops put down about half that number who were planning to march down to New York. In March of 1691 a new governor, the official representative of the Protestant rulers of Protestant England, arrived, and on 17 March 1691 the fort was surrendered to the British troops that had landed some weeks before the new governor. The rebellion was ended less than twenty-two months after it started—or almost a full two years after it started, if one considers two years a long time as civil disturbances go.[4]

Regeneration begins in Europe

I have considered Leisler's rebellion because it is a manifestation of the long, profound transition from the medieval to the modern world, a cultural transition as slow and deep as the geologically described process by which mountains erupt and erode on the earth's surface. This statement is not profound, but the forces were and are. We can possibly move a step or two from the banal statement to the bathysmal, by indicating the historical perspective in which political instability has occurred in the Western world and then proceeding with a systematic comparative analysis.

After the big sleep of the Middle Ages, after centuries on end of intellectual life and inquiry that did not die but did not develop, quite suddenly in the fourteenth, fifteenth, and sixteenth centuries there was an explosive growth. This explosive growth, in technically altered forms, has continued down to at least the mid-twentieth century in

---

[4] The Spanish Civil War lasted from 1936 to 1939, the American Civil War from 1861 to 1865, and the Wars of the Reformation for over a hundred years (considering that they began in 1522 with the Knights' War in the Holy Roman Empire, the Peasants' War of 1524–1525, and that they ended with the Treaties of Westphalia in 1648.

the Western world and is now, in forms only somewhat unique, spreading throughout the world.

The explosive growth began with discoveries and rediscoveries. There was a rediscovery of the vital ancient world. Erasmus (1466–1536), the illegitimate child who never knew his father (who is believed to have been a priest) and whose mother died when he probably was in his late teens,[5] was a bright young man determined to succeed, in the world of letters. When he started collecting the pungent sayings of the "classic"—that is, mainly Roman—authors and began publishing them at the age of thirty-four, he made an instant hit. When he wrote the allegorical satire, *In Praise of Folly*, he praised in effect the naturalness of man, the desirability of abandoning the precious, hypersophisticated intellection of the Middle Ages for the spontaneity of life refreshed at its passionate and compassionate roots. He made a hit again, and he fell only a little short of saying what Freud said, four centuries later—that civilization is a product of sublimated libido.

In addition to a rediscovery of its cultural parenthood, the Western world in its renascence set about discovering the surface of the earth and the people living in it—people ranging from neighbors on the next manor to those in the next shire or county, the adjoining region, and the farthest continent. Even some of these discoveries, like the Canary Islands in 1341, were rediscoveries of lands known to the ancients.

And so also did discovery of the natural world burst forth in this rebirth. Even here the crust of the dark ages had covered over knowledge that had to be rediscovered, like the notion that the earth moved. First vaguely asserted by Philolaus, a pupil of Pythagoras in the fifth century before Christ, it was reasserted by Copernicus in the sixteenth century after Christ (a lapse of over two thousand years) and in the seventeenth was part of the reason Galileo was found guilty of heresy against the Christian church.

These awakenings inevitably threatened the established power structure of medieval society, because of the relationship between knowledge and power. If a holistic doctrine explaining man and the universe had been long established and accepted, the very questioning of it threatened the custodians of knowledge, mainly the Roman church itself. But curiously it was not the gentle Erasmus, whose neoclassi-

[5] See J. Huizinga, *Erasmus of Rotterdam*, London, Phaidon Press Ltd., 1952, 5. This biography was first published in 1924.

cism and humanism struck at the very roots of church dogma, but Luther, the theological reactionary, who became the political radical rejecting overtly the authority of the church. When the Renaissance and the Reformation joined to form a common stream, the days of stasis and the long nights of sleep were ended.

In addition to new discoveries or rediscoveries of the physical and social environment, new techniques also accompanied cultural renascence. Many techniques are commonly mentioned: new or expanded means of transportation and communication; the accumulation of fluid wealth—which of course presupposes the social acceptance of written symbols of wealth (bills of credit, etc.), that is, a medium of exchange which is itself inherently worthless; and the establishment of the limited liability corporation.[6]

There is further a shift in the value system, with the (re-)discovery of the individual as an entity of inherent, noninstrumental, noncollective, nonsocial worth. Stated in the ancient world by the Grecian Aristotle, the Roman Stoics, and the Judaic Christ, the dignity of the individual as a widely accepted object of value had been overlaid with suffocating dogma and the rottening consequences of fixity in all aspects of the medieval world. It took the humanism of people like Erasmus; the intense, literal orthodoxy of Luther and Calvin disturbed by the vagrancy of the Catholic church; the stubbornness of dissenters among dissenters (Anabaptists among German Lutherans, Puritans and Quakers in Episcopal England, and people like Roger Williams in Puritan New England) to carry on the process "begun" two millennia before.

There was further the establishment of a strong central authority over a broad area that inclosed and then engulfed the particularism of the manor, the county, the region. "Begun" in the Renaissance, it continued down into the twentieth century, with Nazism "completing" the process of national unification in Germany and the Nazi attack against the Soviet Union "completing" the process among the widely diverse peoples in the Union of Soviet Socialist Republics.

---

[6] There is an analogous collectivization of capital resources which pools both money and responsibility for economic enterprise in the Soviet industrial "trust." But a limitation of this technique is that the heads and cadres of the trust may be liquidated for failure to succeed. In this sense the Soviet trust is, or was, an unlimited liability corporation.

Irresistible body meets immobile society

If we could do more than just describe the forces of awakening in the fourteenth to sixteenth centuries in Europe, we could understand with some facility the dynamics of cultural (including political) change in that part of the twentieth-century world that has hitherto been outside Western civilization. But if all these forces are involved—intellectual awakening, the elaboration of new techniques, the emergence of the individual and of the great modern nation—they still do not account for the politics of instability in which cultural evolution takes place in the context of a sharp, violent break in the continuity of sovereign political power (a double tautology).

In most of the world most of the time, continuity of cultural development has been broken in savage, heartbreaking, murderous violence that not only changed sovereignty but invariably produced a large measure of at least transitory retrogression to the jungle. Crimes are committed in the name of the past and in the name of the future. For example, Nazism did much to destroy a rather rigid class system in Germany; it also for a decade and a half destroyed dissent and tens of millions of individuals (Jewish, German, Slavic, French, English, and American). The Bolshevik revolution in Russia similarly destroyed much of the class system in imperial Russia; it also destroyed and degraded its millions—in the Ukraine and in the purge of the late 1930s. The bloody parturition of sixteenth- and seventeenth-century Western Europe has been repeated in the twentieth century in Central and Eastern Europe, Asia, and to a degree Africa.

A basic thesis of this chapter, derived from what I have said in earlier chapters, is that violent civil disturbances result from the confrontation of profound forces in opposition to each other. A basic thesis of this chapter, also derived from what I have said in earlier chapters, is that these profound forces are rooted in the human organism, environmentally catalyzed by discovery or rediscovery of all kinds of knowledge, values, techniques, etc. These *catalyzed* internal forces produce violence when they are frustrated by external forces.

The nonconstitutional political process of revolution is in other words the consequence of frustrating the organic development of the individual. Once there has been a positive organic response in the old society and culture to the seminal ideas and practices of new development, a fatefully new society and culture are irrevocably gestating. We have noted certain historic developments: a rebellion in

New York in 1689, the Renaissance, and then the Reformation. Now we will attempt to sketch in nonchronological comparative analysis how this violent process comes about, and hopefully will give some clues as to why. We will try to explain, so to speak, why Erasmus' *Praise of Folly* struck a responsive chord, why Leislers occasionally rebel, and why—without much help from the Bolsheviks—Russian society exploded in 1905 and 1917. We cannot quite succeed, but we will surely fail if, unlike Columbus, we stay in the comfort of familiar mental surroundings and present guided tours of the restored ruins of earlier thought. In the sections of this chapter we shall successively consider the old elite, the established ruling "class"; the new elite, which wants to disestablish the old; the nonelite general public; and what happens as parturition approaches.

The status of the old elite

Members of the old ruling group are those who serve as the custodians of traditional functions of government and religion. They make the basic policy decisions in the society or—more properly, since they dislike the change which policy decisions imply—they strive to administer the basic policies which were established long, long ago and therefore are to them sacred. They deny, in other words, that there is any basic issue that calls for choosing between alternatives. The elite subgroup that runs the government shares power, more or less, with its sustaining coordinate subgroup, the churchmen in the official church. The churchmen support the governing elite by lending to it the sanctity of divine approval and by forever admonishing the general public to the duty of obedience to God's agent, the governing class. The churchmen may be officials of a Roman Catholic, Greek Orthodox, Protestant Episcopal, or Congregational church, or of the propaganda agencies in a Communist society, or they may be tribal medicine men. But in any event, in a conservative, tradition-bound society they serve the function of encouraging, even enforcing by means short of violence, conformity to the demands of the old elite.

The chasm between elite and general public is old (geologically old, it seems), wide, and traversable only with great difficulty in a conservative society. The elite thus protects itself against incursions and subversions from its broad popular base. Distance lends awe; and to the ordinary citizen, the distance between parishioner and priest is psychically greater than that between priest and God, between tribesman and medicine man greater than between medicine man and the spirits of good and evil. It is greater between the citizen and a minor governmental functionary in a bureaucratized society than between the bureaucrat and the chief of state. And the distance between peasant and magistrate is psychically greater than that between magistrate and Justice.

Various devices are used to maintain these distances. The most universal one, probably, is illiteracy. Knowledge of how to read and write is kept from the general public. This in turn weakens the memory of the public because it cannot effectively store up memories of the past (except tribal legends) and cannot (or is not allowed to) trust its memory of godly and ungodly, just and unjust actions by the ruling class. Rather characteristically, attempts to translate the Bible into popular speech were among the first steps toward modernity and were bitterly contested in England (Wycliffe, in the fourteenth century) and in the Holy Roman Empire (Luther, in the sixteenth century). The ruling elite did not want the public to have direct access to Holy Writ, which would endanger the church's vested role as mediator between man and God.

The lag in public education in the South before the American Civil War was similarly a consequence of the desire to maintain an ignorant general public, and so to a great degree has this been the case in Latin America, Asia, and Africa. Other devices include the ownership or control of land and the attachment of people to it by serfdom; the maintenance of a peasant class on a subsistence level which makes movement economically very difficult; and a discouragement of the economic diversification which will open opportunities in cities for the rural populace. Still other devices are the maintenance of a caste system which fixes social relations by the accident of birth, enforced deference and respect to those of high status, and class distinctions as to dress, sometimes legally enforced.

As long as the system is not subjected to external influences, it remains fairly stable. The nobility, the clergy, and the bureaucracy, residing on an uneducated, calloused general public, perform functions very important in any society. They keep order, protecting lives and property. In addition they protect the ignorant by magic from the natural vicissitudes attributed to evil spirits or to the devil, and at least maintain some hope of delivery from the wretchedness of earthly existence, to those who labor and do not question the sanctified power structure.

But as soon as outside influences enter, the position of the old top orders becomes unsettled. A ground tremor opens fissures in the solidary power structure and threatens to shake it down closer to the popular level. The cracks occur before the house itself gets cast down. That is, within the elite, conflict arises among different subgroups. In a portentous mistake, the old elite admits newcomers to its ranks, who are apt to infect susceptible members of the old elite with novel notions of justice, reality, and religion. Whether it be the natural child of a priest re-examining the classics, the son of a miner who enters holy orders and becomes shocked at clerical corruption, or the son of a Protestant minister seeking his fortune in New Amsterdam, these new members of the established elite change it by their own vigorous action and by their influence on those born to high status.

New tasks call for new leadership, which, involving labor, is deemed degrading by the old elite. In a society sloughing off feudality and the village or the manorial economic system, people turn to the man who lacks family distinction but has money to lend. In a society eager for education, people turn not to nobles but to educators, as they did to Ilya Ulyanov, Lenin's father. In a society demanding health, doctors become prominent. Such new men of influence gradually gain admission into the old elite. They become nobles of the robe and often marry into families of the involuted nobles of the sword, whose posture now is en garde—a ritual posture of defensive readiness no longer backed by adequate force or adequate will. New entrants to the old elite become such by public service, by purchase, or by personal distinction attributable to something other than parental status and ancestral grandeur.

This in itself makes for further fracture of a solidary ruling class. Seeing their distinctive prestige, influence, authority, and power taken over by these manufactured nobles, the old elite becomes contemptuous and hostile. In their hostility, occasional members of the old elite become radical critics of the old, no longer exclusive, regime itself.[7] They send their children to the finest schools, at home or abroad, to get the pure and classic education free of modern commercialism. These children come home, sometimes to turn on their parents.

Fearing a fatal separation from their inherited perquisites, the old elite begins to reassert long-forgotten prerogatives, to counterattack against the new assertion of ancient popular liberties. To the extent

[7] The Progressive movement in America that culminated in the Presidencies of Theodore Roosevelt, Woodrow Wilson, and Franklin Roosevelt is an attenuated example. The old families in America produced members who fought vigorously against the crude scramble for power on the part of the arriviste category of businessmen.

this is no longer really possible, they escape into a fanciful world where it is possible. The old elite come to live romantically, in an exquisite contemplation of a glorious past that never really existed. They exact compulsory labor as the price peasants must pay for being descended from serfs or unassimilated natives. They tax commerce, that novel device which is so pernicious and so profitable. They tax land transfers. And they no longer, as power becomes centralized, continue to protect peasants from violence or injustice. Their reason for being becomes a reason for having been.

Bored by the dull manorial life, they move to the ever-exciting big cities and leave even the administration of their prerogatives to hired agents. No longer content to live with the primitive techniques of their past, their feudal futility becomes mechanized. They exchange the sword for the rifle and pistol, the carriage or the stallion for the motor car, and the lamp for electricity. But they frantically demand the continuance of the prerogatives of a nobility that no longer has anything serious to do. In the Arab world these incongruous noblemen drive Cadillacs over fine handwoven rugs. The money for Cadillacs comes from a modern demand they did not create, from oil they did not create and did not even extract from the ground. And the exquisite, handwoven driveways come from the toil of hands more skilled than their own. In other lands they may even deceive themselves into believing they have modernized, by installing time clocks and a system of punch cards to handle the payroll in the textile mill on their estate. And they have labor agitators jailed.

The old nobility, including those who have just entered it, are apt to crowd closely around the situs of political power. The king or the president is thus insulated from the populace. The old nobles swear over and over their loyalty, which no longer matters because, even if he does not know it, the king is no longer endangered by their long-dead feudal power. The new nobles perhaps press even harder about the king, because they have a better idea of what they must insulate him from. And the clergy assures the court that God (or Marx or Lenin or whatever His name) altogether approves them, their sophistication, their gentility, their valor, their gracious kindness, and their position on top of a well-ordered, well-hierarchized society.

Unable altogether to insulate themselves from the dynamic new world whose watches, automobiles, and radios they readily absorb, the old elite begin to doubt themselves. They accept, even propagate, mordant criticism of their thin and rusted armor. They believe in justice within their class and think the kindness they sometimes show to those beneath them is also justice. They equate custom and law and justice and grace—and themselves with the custody of these virtues. And they ride over the peasant's growing crops or over the weaver's rugs in a frantic escape from reality. With occasional clear vision, they see themselves as they are, as the last king of Egypt said of himself before the 1952 revolution: Farouk fou fou—Farouk is finished.

Their loss of function is accompanied by, precedes, or causes a loss in the sense of belonging. They no longer are an integral part of the newly forming society beneath them. They lose a sense of real dignity and replace it, in the second childhood of a senile group, with the rituals and symbols of ancestral merit. They identify with the past and with good people in other lands who are more like them than their own countrymen. They broaden their sense of time and space in their ever-wider separation from the proximate. As they universalize, they paradoxically identify not with the species but with a moribund cultural efflorescence which, dehydrated, crumbles to dust.

In the words of Cash, writing about the planter class in the South before the Civil War, there was "a kindly courtesy, a level-eyed pride, an easy quietness, a barely perceptible flourish of bearing which, for all its obvious angularity and fundamental plainness, was one of the finest things the Old South produced." [8] The angularity is more broadly social: it is a bearing toward individuals, a bearing that is almost 180 degrees off course.

The old elite is headed backwards, for reasons that may become more apparent as we have a closer look at the new elite and at the general populace. These two groups, with different but compatible interests, are headed in the same general direction that the old elite itself moved, until it acquired the notion that its rights to enter heaven were exclusive and prescriptive as against all those of no family and no inherited property.

The position of the new elite

The vigorous, intelligent, ambitious people who strive for influence in a society in transition are a marginal group. They try to enter

[8] W. J. Cash, *The Mind of the South*, New York, Vintage Books, 1960, 72. In three chapters, this book, first published in 1941, describes almost a prototype of the old elite in an unstable society, which America was in critical degree, from at least 1830 until the internecine War between the States.

the old elite and they sometimes succeed,[9] but it is only their children or grandchildren who can achieve the secure sense of belonging. Sometimes a kind of double marginality operates. In Malaya, the indigenous population has been suffused by an energetic entrepreneural class of Chinese. A Chinese wanting to rise socially in this country thus has both economic and ethnic barriers. Some of these Chinese status-seekers joined the Malayan Communist party precisely because in it they saw chances for advancement in power and prestige. They tended to depreciate and reject their parents in favor of the new and sophisticated values of modernization. In their case, middling social background plus their own ambition pushed them altogether out of the old society into a movement planning revolution.[10]

A basic characteristic, almost a definition, of the new elite is status discrepancy—a lack of consistency between property, occupation, education on the one hand and prestige on the other. In even the stable American society, as one study indicated, relatively high status discrepancy produced a greater willingness to want a change in the relative power position of the major power units (big business, small business, labor unions, state and national governments).[11] In Iran, another study found, revolutionaries tended to come from those groups in which there were marked discrepancies between economic and political power.[12] And the same occurred even in the very microcosmic and seemingly homogeneous society that the American wartime relocation centers for Japanese amounted to. The people who were active enough to attend a series of major riots in at least one of the camps were in a variety of ways more marginal than those who did not join in the angry demonstrations against the camp authorities.[13]

---

[9] The top political group in China before its Communist revolution was the Kuomintang. Of its central committee members whose family background could be ascertained, roughly half were of upper-class and half of middle-class background. [See R. C. North et al., *Kuomintang and Chinese Communist Elites*, Hoover Institute Studies, Series B: Elite Studies No. 8, Stanford, Stanford University Press, 1952, 47.]

[10] See Lucian W. Pye, *Guerrilla Communism in Malaya: Its Social and Political Meaning*, Princeton, Princeton University Press, 1956, ch. 5, esp. 128–135.

[11] I. W. Goffman, Status Consistency and Preference for Change in Power Distribution, *American Sociological Review*, **22**: 275–281 (1957).

[12] B. B. Ringer and D. L. Sills, Political Extremists in Iran, *Public Opinion Quarterly*, **16**: 689–701 (1952–1953). And see Lyford P. Edwards, *The Natural History of Revolutions*, Chicago, University of Chicago Press, 1927, 34–35, 55, 79–81.

[13] G. Wada and J. C. Davies, Riots and Rioters, *Western Political Quarterly*, **10**: 864–874 (1957).

In general, leaders are probably more marginal in one way or another than the populace. A new elite is probably very much like the old elite, and in a few ways quite different. But we do not yet have data to compare revolutionary leaders with nonrevolutionary leaders—or either category with the populace. We can thus note that Patrick Henry was the protagonist of the piedmont planters against the established tidewater planters in Virginia, that Napoleon was a Corsican, Stalin a Georgian, and Hitler a petit-bourgeois Austrian. All these men were leaders of unstable societies, but Lincoln and Masaryk were also marginal yet not arbitrary or anti-constitutional personal rulers.[14]

If there is a distinction between leaders in stable and unstable societies, it seems more likely to be the personal experience of some specific event that had a deeply traumatic influence on individuals in unstable societies, throwing them into active opposition to the established society. It is one thing to be upwardly mobile, ambitious, and status conscious. It is another thing to have access denied to channels of advancement in the existing society. Here we can with some confidence mention the effect of arbitrary administration of import duties on such men as Jacob Leisler or John Hancock; and the tragedy for Lenin when his beloved brother, his father, and his sister died in rapid succession for reasons he could attribute to the old regime. If prior traumata did not permanently alienate dissenters in Imperial Russia, at least the school which Siberian exile amounted to produced graduates of distinction.

It is the consequence of these injuries that directs the person away from old loyalties. He begins to see the society in light of his personal experience. He sees the old regime doing to others what it has done to him.[15] In this experiencing of a *specific* trauma, leaders come, as Lasswell might put it, to displace their private aggressions on public objects. More exactly, the traumatized revolutionary identifies his

---

[14] Charles V, the anti-Reformation emperor, was also in a sense marginal. With a Spanish mother, he was raised a Fleming—somewhat like being an Irishman in England. He cannot be called a revolutionary, though he was a crisis ruler.

[15] The picture of misery that Chekhov's story of "Ward No. 6" created in Lenin's head, in light of his sister's death in a hospital, has already been mentioned. (See Chapter 6, footnote 7.) With Russia's modern and competently run hospitals, would this story strike a Russian in 1960 the way it struck Lenin before the revolution? Would the stories of ancient Chinese outlaws, who destroyed those who exploited the poor and the innocent, have the same effect on non-Chinese residents of a stable society that those stories had on the Communist party leaders during the prepower years?

specific aggressions against the established society with those of the general public. The two—leader and followers—then proceed to displace the old elite.

One of the major immediate consequences of these traumata is the establishment of a new set of beliefs. It should be noted that I am asserting a cause-and-effect relationship, respectively, between the traumata and the new beliefs. Leaders and followers do not revolt so much because of their beliefs as because of their injuries. The new beliefs are used to justify the impending revolt. One of the major tasks of the new elite is to elaborate before the revolt this new belief system, whether the elaborators be Locke, Jefferson, Marx, Hitler, or Gandhi. The established authorities are often good enough to free such people of all organizational responsibilities so that they can think and write undisturbed, in prison.

And a curious conservatism sometimes becomes evident in the new dogma. Christ said he came not to destroy the prophets but to fulfill them. Locke said that removal of a government by a people was not rebellion but an exercise of sovereign power against the errant custodians of sovereignty. In New York in the 1680s there was a similar call for a *return* to legitimate rule by the true monarch, on the eve of Leisler's rebellion. The American Declaration of Independence spoke of deprivations of rights that had previously been exercised. Rousseau advocated a return to principles derived from natural law governing natural man in primitive society.

But the appeal is not simply, like that of Erasmus, for a return to the simple glory of the classic and noble past. It is also an appeal outward to universal principles usable by any men anywhere under comparable circumstances of deprivation by the old regime. The justification is not for Englishmen, Americans, or Frenchmen but for all mankind. And this in a sense takes us back to the beginning of this book, to the relationship between basic needs and the reasons for government. The ultimate justifications of life, liberty, property, and pursuit of happiness, or of liberty, equality, and fraternity derive from characteristics of the human psyche. It is for this reason that these various justifications have a similar orientation and a similarly widespread appeal. The style of expression changes from century to century, but the basic appeal to human nature changes no more than do the common organic characteristics of the untutored, uncultivated species.

Along with this task of elaborating the justification for revolt, in which the new elite reaches both backward and outward, there comes a new outlook. There is an unshakable and chiliastic faith that the return to a glorious past (the beginning of man: the state of nature) and arrival at a glorious future (the end of man: utopia, with no laws, no external restraints) will be achieved. By this new mental attitude (a dimension separate from the *content* of the faith), the new elite come to believe they are instruments—however conscious— of God, of Reason, of Dialectical Materialism, or of the Volksgeist. And now they can righteously divide the world into those who are with them and those who are against.

A kind of universal Platonic realism afflicts revolutionary leaders. In the interests of the real world not yet realized, they can use themselves and others with no fear of repeating the errors of those who are against them, simply because those on their own side are incapable of repeating the mistakes of others. The goal becomes all-important and—if only the true leaders stay in power and elicit or command immediate popular obedience to the Divine, Rational, or Historical Will which the leaders embody—can be promptly realized. This new and narrow faith assumes the ability to achieve, in a year or so, the goals for which mankind has striven since the beginning of striving. And so the new elite becomes opportunistic as to means, and to any outside observer becomes amoral. Sometimes they even appear so to insiders.

In the years before the Russian revolution, the Bolshevik Social Democrats resorted to fantastic methods of raising funds for party work. What were called expropriations were nothing but frank robbery. On at least one occasion, marriage was used to procure the fortune of a wealthy woman. Assassination was common, practiced by both government agents and revolutionaries. When Lenin was called to task for the assassinations, in a party congress in 1906, he bypassed the vote against such violence and under the guise of defensive action continued to carry out the same actions somewhat more discreetly.

If these practices seem shocking, we need only recall the techniques used by European royalty to buy and sell territory with marriageable princes and princesses, the English King Henry VIII's murder of some of his opponents, the expropriation by governments of property of citizens (e.g., of the Loyalists during the American Revolution), and the savagery of the Secret Army Organization in Algeria in 1962—a savagery that was the poisonous fruit of French army brutality in Algeria during the eight preceding years. These actions are comprehensible.

What is hard to comprehend is the apparent absence of guilt as governments and rebels alike savagely kill humans, in the name of some humane principle. There seems to be as little remorse about such actions in the twentieth century as there was when Spain savagely conquered Mexico in the early sixteenth century. A notable exception is the apparent revulsion expressed by Khrushchev in 1956 at the brutality of the Stalin era—a revulsion which appeared genuine, in spite of and perhaps because of Khrushchev's participation in the purges, and which has not yet been followed by a return to the earlier savagery. And perhaps, as I suggested in the preceding chapter, Stalin himself felt a kind of guilt.

As the time for parturition approaches, the old and the new elite draw farther and farther apart. To oppose the vibrant new faith and dedication and confidence of the new men, the old have only a scurfy, inturned, ingrown self-concern, together with an almost complete diffidence. To face the new savagery of the revolutionaries who attack in the name of universals, the old elite can only turn to the savagery of despair, of cornered old beasts fighting merely to survive. And so the fight becomes an elemental one, a kind of perverse jungle battle in which for the duration of the violence, the main issue is survival. In this the vital new elite, with its new gods and young men, is apt to show itself superior to the old elite whose gods are either dead or stolen away by the new. More or less without the benefit of paternal acknowledgment or attention, the revolution is born. The old elite rejects it, denying parenthood. The new elite takes it up and makes the child its own. Now we can turn to the general public, the body politic which truly bears the revolution, to see what has brought its child to full or aborted term.

The circumstances of the general public

The background for political instability is economic and social progress. A populace in a static socio-economic condition is very unlikely to listen to the trumpet or siren call to rebellion. A populace whose progress is not impeded by forces attributable to the ruling class is also very unlikely to rebel. Progress in other words is most of the time a necessary but insufficient cause for violent political change.

A very crude index of progress is the rate of population increase. Its basic validity as an index of growth is that it bears some relationship to both the ability and the willingness to support more people. In the extreme cases, starvation limits the ability, and enthusiasm for large families extends the willingness. France's population in the sixteenth and seventeenth centuries was fairly stable, averaging a growth rate of no more than about a third of a million per decade. This rate then tripled in the first half of the eighteenth century to about a million per decade, dropping off to about two-thirds of a million in the second half of the century. European Russia's population growth similarly took a spurt in the hundred years ending in 1880, rising from a rate of about 1.4 million per decade in the century ending 1780 to about 5.7 million per decade in the next 100 years.[16] Again, as in the case of France, the rate of increase slowed as the revolution approached.

These periods of rapid growth of course took place in economies that were overwhelmingly rural, with—by modern standards—only the beginnings of industrialization. Among the major economic innovations in the prerevolutionary periods was a gradual change in the pattern of land ownership, from one in which the peasant rented from a landlord to one in which those who worked the land had a legally protected interest in it. Land came increasingly to be an object of purchase. In both France and Russia, land values steadily rose in the century before the revolution—the major increase in Russia taking place after the 1861 emancipation of serfs.

A second major economic development in France and Russia was the growth of the factory system and industrial production, which nurtured and was nurtured by the rapid growth of cities. The population of Paris more than doubled in the eighteenth century, but it doubled again in the first half of the nineteenth century. St. Petersburg doubled its population in the eighteenth century, but from 1800–1900 its population quintupled. Moscow in the nineteenth century merely quadrupled its population. In Russia's case there are data on the growth of factories and number of workmen—a crucial figure because many factories were set up on country estates to use the immediately available labor of peasant families—and incidentally to insulate the rural worker from subversive city influences. In the first half of the nineteenth century both factories and workmen quadrupled in number. In the latter half, factories and workmen roughly quadrupled again.[17] This steady progress, both rural and urban, lacks the drama

[16] See J. C. Davies, Toward a Theory of Revolution, *American Sociological Review*, **27**: 5–19 (1962), at 11.
[17] See Thomas G. Masaryk, *The Spirit of Russia*, London, Allen & Unwin Ltd., 1919, vol. 1, 120 n.

of sudden events like the emancipation of serfs but has great long-range consequences.

Along with economic progress goes a series of social and legal reforms, again probably both result and cause of further socio-economic progress. The evidence as to France is less complete than as to Russia. Tocqueville mentions that the peasant suffered less oppression as the old regime approached its end than when law had been administered by feudal lords and that gradually he was acquiring that precious possession, land, and that "he enjoyed civil liberty." But such advancement was not accompanied by freedom from feudal dues. In some areas they were demanded with increased importunacy by a frantic nobility, even in the last three or four decades before 1789.

In Russia, a series of social reforms followed the 1861 emancipation, rather startling because they came so late, but nonetheless joyfully received. The administration of justice was removed from landowners to state officials. Running the gantlet (a virtual death sentence), lashing, and branding were abolished shortly after emancipation, and caning a year before the 1905 revolution. Trials became public, the jury system was introduced, and judges got tenure. Compulsory military service, which before emancipation was haphazardly administered, had called for 25 years in the army. Shortly after emancipation, the term was reduced to 16 years (and it was more consistently administered). In 1874 it was reduced to 6 years for those with less than a primary education, and was graduated down to 6 months for those with university education.

Africa in the twentieth century presents a new case of old phenomena. Highly significant reforms were introduced into African society by the aggressive colonizing powers. We have already noted the abolition of human sacrifice by the Spaniards when they conquered Mexico in the sixteenth century. Comparable reforms were undertaken in Africa by colonial governments. But they took place much later and in the context of technically more advanced European culture. The triumvirate of traders, armies, and missionaries combined to accelerate the rate of development in Africa. Colonial elites did not deal with such comparatively advanced cultures as did the French elite in France and the Russian elite in Russia before their revolutions. Colonists dealt with African cultures that were not only on the economic subsistence level but were also in smaller communal units. There was no written language, only animist religion and scant awareness of any world beyond the local community except a world inhabited by threatening creatures and magical forces.

In Africa the starting point was farther back, and progress was rapid. Truly primitive cultures were with shocking suddenness exposed to the product of six thousand years of literate culture. Africans saw not only machine-made products like watches, rifles, sewing machines, and automobiles; they also saw powerful armies and the administrative techniques of modern centralized governments and trading corporations. Even more significantly from the political standpoint, they saw a culture in which the individual is more nearly the supreme object of value and in which—so said the missionaries—all men are of equal worth. They observed that the white governments administered some kind of justice with nonmagical methods of establishing guilt or innocence. And they saw that modern medicine was more potent than magic potions or incantations. In a bewildering way they had the opportunity to leap through millennia of European cultural developments. Prerevolutionary progress in Africa requires the establishment of new scales to measure the high velocity of change.[18]

If the background for political instability is progress, the profound unease of marginality is in the foreground. When an entire people starts enjoying developments at a more or less accelerated pace, an entire people shows classic symptoms of marginality, like our hypothetical Furumoto family in Hawaii. A people is gradually loosening age-old ties to the past and establishing new ones to the future. Everything from the parent-child relationship to the relationship to tribal gods is so changed as to make endemic the rootlessness and normlessness which Durkheim called anomy.

Old patterns of social relationships have come unfixed. Loyalty and obedience hitherto have been granted to noblemen and chiefs, clerics and medicine men, kings and paramount chiefs. When one's former peers now become a new elite, whom does he now obey? Does the former peasant who now has purchased a noble title get the same deference as the nobleman of ancient title? Is the peasant's son who now talks of rising against the landlord worthy of support? Does one listen to the priest who says we are all children of God, or to the agitator who says all men are brothers? Does one obey the medicine man, who successfully puts a curse on one's enemy, or the missionary who says do unto others as you would have them do unto you? Does one do others as some white traders have done blacks, or does he re-

---

[18] For an analysis of these processes as they have occurred in one part of Africa, see James S. Coleman, *Nigeria: Background to Nationalism,* Berkeley and Los Angeles, University of California Press, 1958.

gard white traders as a rather normal mixture of egoism and altruism?
Does one forswear loyalty to the king in favor of republicanism? Does
one deny the paramount and constitutional chief of the tribe and establish a new, personal loyalty to a man whose followers say he will
save not all Ashanti or Baluba tribesmen but all Ghanaians or Congolese?

The crisis begins

In considering a society headed toward revolution, it is hard to overemphasize the intensity and universality of individual mental conflict.
It can be epitomized in the domestic conflict between father and son
or husband and wife, but this is only one of several major areas of
change and thus of mental conflict.   As we have seen, the official introduction of a new religious ritual in Russia was met with a super-
orthodox revival of old ritualism among ordinary people.   We also
know that peasants in late nineteenth-century Russia often turned over
to the tsarist police populists who came from the cities to preach socialism.   In Africa not only did an occasional missionary end up in the
stew; in Kenya the Mau-Mau movement of the 1950s had strong over-
and undertones of atavistic, tribe-based reaction that often altogether
drowned the voice of progressive development.   Blacks were killing
blacks, but every black killed by a Mau-Mau has been said to represent, in effigy, a white man.

At least two new political loyalties begin to emerge, to help fill the
void as the old becomes senile—loyalty to nation and to a new leader.
These new loyalties, it should be noted, are relatively specific, relatively free of a reasoned kind of ideology.[19]   Both cut across established patterns of loyalty and tend to flatten the pyramid of social
hierarchy and deference.   Luther put man in direct and equal contact with God, making salvation possible through an individual, personal act of faith.   In psychically similar ways, nationalism makes all
men within a particular area subjectively equal as fellow citizens of
a common nation[20] and as brotherly admirers of a common leader

[19] Since it is the intellectual who writes about revolutions, he is likely to impute
his own sophisticated abstraction to the general public, which does not think so
much of ideologies and utopias as about overthrowing the established government
and getting a beloved new leader.

[20] In 1906 in Eastern Siberia, a people called Yakuts and numbering some 250,000
demanded various nationalist reforms for Yakuts against the Russian imperial government.   See Hugh Seton-Watson, *The Decline of Imperial Russia: 1855–1914,*
New York, Frederick A. Praeger, 1952, 241.

with whom each citizen has the same direct, close, personal contact. On some occasions the new leader does not emerge till after the revolution has begun (Lenin in Russia, Napoleon in France, Nasser in Egypt); in others he is already a popular symbol beforehand (Nkrumah in Ghana, Banda in Nyasaland, Castro in Cuba).

As developments accelerate—as land passes from landlords to peasants, factories and payrolls rise, and a more equalitarian outlook becomes popular—the proportionate share of the ordinary citizen diminishes. He may get more than he had, but as factory hand or clerk he gets only such minimum wage as is necessary to keep up the flow of people from the countryside to the city. And—so at least it seems— only such equal justice is meted out as is necessary to keep the populace from an excess of restlessness.

In France during the half-century before the revolution, according to one estimate, prices rose three times as fast as wages.[21] As a feudal carryover, peasants had to perform compulsory labor on major highways, to the neglect of local roads of more importance to peasants. Taxes, notably the taille but also the vingtième and capitation, discriminated against the poor, mainly because the rich and noble bought exemption or otherwise evaded payment. Customs duties and excise taxes on some consumer goods had a similarly retrogressive effect.

In Russia, wages rose after emancipation but not so fast as food prices. There was some increase in real wages after 1883, and urban population almost doubled, 1878–1897. But emancipation of serfs placed such a heavy financial burden on them that for a time their actual landholdings diminished. The redemption prices at which peasants could buy land were set well above the market value, in a blatant favoring of landlords. The Peasants' Land Bank, set up in 1883 to lend money for land purchases, was followed in 1885 by the Nobles' Land Bank, which promptly offered more favorable terms for land mortgages than the Peasants' Bank did to its clientele. And it was mainly the wealthier peasants who were able to buy. As in the earlier case of France, taxes fell most heavily on peasants and workers. Land taxes of nobles, almost incredibly, were based on the landowner's own assessment of his own property; one estimate is that land taxes on peasant holdings were double what they were on noble estates.[22] In

---

[21] Georges Lefebvre, *The Coming of the French Revolution*, New York, Vintage Books, 1957, 93. This book was first published in French, in 1939; it was first translated into English by R. R. Palmer and published by the Princeton University Press in 1947.

[22] H. Seton-Watson, *op. cit.*, 120.

1886–1887 taxes on business enterprises brought in about an eighth of what entered the government treasury from the alcohol tax. In 1878 the sugar tax, also falling on the consumer, produced one-third as much revenue as business taxes; by 1895 the sugar tax produced about 10% more than the business tax and by 1897 some 20% more.[23] Tariffs on tea and cotton also hit the poor hardest.

Laws of general application—a rather redundant qualification—ostensibly do not discriminate. An import duty on tea or cotton presumably affects buyers of tea or clothing regardless of race, religion, color, or status. A law against murder does not say it is more murderous for a poor man to kill than for a rich man. A set of laws, that is, which on its face does not discriminate is therefore presumably related to another redundancy, equal justice.

Perhaps as much as anything else, the general public becomes restless and discontented at the growing divergence between laws and the way they are administered on the one hand and the underlying principle of equality on the other. Where this is the case, peasants get restless not so much because they are poor as because such legal devices as the Nobles' Bank in Russia artificially enforce discrimination in a society whose principles are presumably just and charitable and whose laws or decrees do not discriminate. Import duties in New York in the 1680s are one thing. The arbitrary favoring of certain friends of the governor is another. Being compelled to serve one's country in the armed forces is one thing; being able to buy one's way out of the draft is another—and so is getting virtual exemption because one was able to afford a university education. It is fine to hear a missionary preach the good news, the very good news, that the humblest and darkest-skinned of God's children are as good as the most exalted and lightest-skinned. It is not good news to see the missionary, when the issue arises in action, taking sides with the colonial government or entering the club reserved for Europeans only.

If the old elite, the established ruling class, has ever made an historic mistake, it is in admitting to any kind of general humane principles to justify the established government. If the old elite ever makes a contemporary mistake in a society headed for revolution, it is to act in radical contradiction to these principles, so that kindness degenerates into politeness and courtliness, justice is applied only to the masses and mercy to the classes, equality does not discriminate between rich and poor when one is caught stealing bread, and in prac-

[23] *Ibid.*, 121.

tice the virtue of graciousness degenerates into a grand acceptance of the obsequiousness of those beneath oneself. The narcissism of inequality makes the old elite see themselves as morally beautiful when in fact the animal egotism they attribute to the unwashed, untutored "mass" lies just underneath their own grand manner, as it lies just under the obsequiousness of the nonelite.

The only way an old elite could really succeed is to think and act like Orwell's O'Brien in *1984*, to admit honestly to themselves that virtue is a boot stamping in a human face forever. The old elite is unable to live so consistently in either thought or action, to announce even to themselves principles that accord with their often brutish actions. So the old elite stubbornly digs its own mass grave, while the new elite and the general public look on with a puzzled awe that mitigates their savage anger.

As the old elite continues to preach Christian or Marxist or Islamic virtue and to practice hyper-Nietzschean egotism, both horizontal and vertical ties break down, and egotism becomes endemic throughout the society. Tired of serving a lord whose function of protection against predators or invaders has now been taken over by police and armies, the peasant emulates the lord and pursues his own interest. Tired of working too long hours for too little money, the urban worker loses his gratitude for an employer now growing fabulously wealthy because of the voracious demand for factory-made goods and the almost inexhaustible supply of labor coming from an impoverished countryside. Tired of a decadent old aristocracy whose great action is now only ancestral, the new bourgeois and intellectual elite develops an angry contempt and by cunning and wealth acquires or seeks the trappings of ancient distinction. Each class becomes encapsulated. Within each class, each individual becomes encapsulated. There is a host of barriers within barriers, in which the common interest, the social sense, even the desire to love and be loved gets smothered and seems to die. If society could kill the social sense, in an old society it would surely have died of corruption, cynicism, and the frantic fatalism of a finished Farouk indulging deathbed desires. It gives the appearance of supporting the Freudian theory of the death instinct, of an actual desire to die, not just a resignation to death.

The crisis deepens

As parturition approaches, these long-range developments begin to converge in time. The ideas planted even centuries before and nurtured in the old society meet the smothering, confining resistance of a body politic that no longer nurtures the old ideas because they no longer nurture the body politic. It is at this point in the genesis of revolutions that we have more knowledge of what happens, just as in medicine the knowledge of childbirth is more complete than the understanding of genetics. So it is well to remember that the phenomena now to be considered are more exactly epiphenomena, the consequences of forces rooted in the human organism and nurtured over centuries of slow cultural development.

As the revolution approaches, the first group to emerge as active protestants is mainly from the old and the new elite. That is, the agitators and future ruling class are in large part noblemen, arriviste bourgeois, or the sons of either class. Much more rarely are they the offspring of poor people with no claim to distinction. Those New Yorkers who started the rebellion against James II's minions were merchants. Jacob Leisler was a clergyman's son, certainly a social superior to coopers, cordwainers, and even to the yeoman farmers who rallied to his support after he accepted power.

Other examples lend support to the bourgeois or upper-class origin of new revolutionists. Lenin was the son of a schoolmaster who had been made a nobleman for his distinguished work. Trotsky was the son of a wealthy peasant. Marx was the son of a successful lawyer and married the beautiful daughter of one of the leading local aristocrats. The party functionaries in the Malayan Communist party tended to come from comparatively prosperous backgrounds and to be better educated than not only the rank-and-file party members but (of course) also the ordinary peasants and workers in whose name they were rebelling.[24] A classic case is Henry VIII, who as ecclesiastic-rebel King of England can hardly be said to have lacked social position. Granted the grand title, Defender of the Faith, by a Pope grateful for such a prestigious attack on Lutheran heresy as young Henry produced, the monarch rebelled violently against the Roman church when it stood between him and his Hollywood- or Grecian god-like marital ventures.

There is no particular need to labor this point, except for two considerations. The first is that, folklore to the contrary, it is not the poorest, the most downtrodden people, who initiate civil disorders. On the contrary, it is members of the established middle and upper classes who have the leisure to work at tasks other than survival and

[24] See Pye, *op. cit.*, 129, 149–154.

the accumulation of basic material "necessities" and who for various reasons become disaffected or otherwise alienated from the established classes. The second is that, as a genuine (in contrast to a palace) revolution ripens, it almost by definition does involve the broad citizenry. Events move so fast as revolutions come into being that it is easy to forget or not to notice the sequence in which groups join the revolution.

For example, one can say that a few people, mainly of the intelligentsia, were in revolt when Alexander II of Russia was assassinated. Indeed the turning to the technique of killing government officials was partly a consequence of the failure of these members of the new elite to elicit popular support in their Movement to the People. The 1917 Revolution in Russia began in the cities, themselves a cultural avant-garde in an overwhelmingly rural civilization. The cities themselves had been prepared mentally by a vanguard of disaffected elitists. Only after there had been an effective transfer of the actual governmental machinery out of the hands of the old regime did the peasants join. When they did, they did so with passionate abandon, but not until the cities were securely in control of the revolution.

John Locke in his seventeenth-century justification for rebellion noted the extreme reluctance of the people to rebel. "They are hardly to be prevailed with to amend the acknowledged faults in the frame they have been accustomed to." And they "are more disposed to suffer than right themselves by resistance." [25]   The great gulf between the ordinary citizen and his rulers in a little-developed society is epitomized by a research anecdote. An interviewer in Turkey, as he went through the questionnaire, asked his respondent what he would do to solve Turkey's major problem if he were President. The respondent, a shepherd, replied, "My God! How can you say such a thing? How can I . . . I cannot . . . a poor villager . . . master of the whole world." [26]   Even a generation after great changes began in Turkey under Kemal Atatürk, about half the Turkish population remained in what Lerner calls the Traditional category, and among these Traditionals almost 9 out of 10 did not feel there was anything they could do to help solve Turkey's problems. [27]   These people, poor in goods as

[25] John Locke, *Of Civil Government* (the Second Treatise), London, J. M. Dent & Sons Ltd., Everyman's edition, 1924, page 230, paragraph 223, and page 233, paragraph 230.
[26] Daniel Lerner, *The Passing of Traditional Society*, Glencoe, The Free Press, 1958, 24.
[27] *Ibid.*, ch. 5. This book does a remarkable job of psychologically distinguishing major social segments of societies in transition to the modern world from feudalism.

well as spirit, support but do not make revolutions. They may indeed some day inherit the earth, but they will pay a substantial fee to their counselors at law and in politics—the elite which at the time of revolution is with them but not of them.

What then does finally move a critically large segment of the population into rebellion? The vanguard of revolution, the new elite, are ready, well in advance of the actual outbreak. Indeed some are so far in advance that they are killed by the old elite, often with the tacit or express consent of the populace. My notion is that it is specific grievances, events specifically hurting ordinary citizens, that produce actual popular outbreaks.[28] This is hypothesized not on the grounds that the broad populace is actually thrown back to a desperate condition of living on the edge of survival, but that it fears it will be. Expectations of better material or other circumstances have become habitual and now are met with sharp, ineluctable frustration. People are apt to rebel, not when their rising expectations are satisfied but when they have been satisfied for a prolonged period and are then frustrated by action or inaction blamed on the government.[29]

Parturition

A society that is undergoing change is in a state of considerable (though tolerable) tension in any case. When there occurs some major blockage of the accelerating forward movement, the tension is apt to reach the bursting point. Chronic grievances are aggravated by new, acute ones. The blockage surely varies with time and locale, but one of the commonest is war, which inevitably raises profound anxiety about survival itself. The great Russian revolution in both its phases was precipitated during wars which the populace did not feel had anything to do with them. The war with Japan in popular eyes seemed to be a contest of rival imperialisms, and the war with Germany only nine years later in the same eyes was being fought under the guidance of leaders whose attachment to Germany seemed suspiciously apparent, under the guidance of a Tsar who was under the domination of a Germanborn Tsarina.

[28] For a fuller statement, see J. C. Davies, Toward a Theory of Revolution, *American Sociological Review,* **27**: 5–19 (1962). See also the brief mention of the phenomenon in connection with anomy and suicide in Emile Durkheim, *Suicide,* (1897), Glencoe, Ill., The Free Press, 1951, 252.

[29] On the deprivations immediately preceding the Russian Revolution, see Michael T. Florinsky, *The End of the Russian Empire,* New York, Collier Books, 1961, chs. 6 and 7. This study was first published in 1931.

In America by 1775 a long series of specific irritations and frustrations had occurred. Among them were trade restrictions by acts of Parliament (1733–1767); the closing of the Western frontier by the 1763 Proclamation; the stationing in Boston of British troops, too few to quiet Indians and too numerous to ease fears they had come to quiet Bostonians; and a succession of clashes with these British troops from 1768 till the running battle on the road from Lexington to Concord in 1775. Some frustrations hit merchants, some hit ordinary citizens who had to quarter British soldiers in their own homes, but all were specific and not particularly ideological. Thomas Jefferson and Thomas Paine wrote to justify a turn of events that had already taken place.

A rebellion can be headed off before its actual outbreak, sometimes by concessions (as in Dorr's rebellion in 1842 in Rhode Island),[30] sometimes by superior force (as in the 1956 Hungarian rebellion). If it is not, it moves in a course that seems almost blind and inexorable, with the justification appearing as an almost madly rational aspect of a primeval procedure. Like a husband with an abstract turn of mind telling his wife in childbirth that the forthcoming infant will be a credit to the human race, an ideologue may more or less correctly appraise the purposes of revolution, but all the parturient society can think of at the moment is pain and pressure.

Once there has been a final precipitation of conflict, such as soldiers firing into a crowd or someone in a crowd throwing a rock at patrolling soldiers, the process is in usually irreversible motion. As Le Bon pointed out in his study of crowds, a skillful person can divert a crowd from its momentary purposes.[31] But it is asking too much of any single human being—or any number less than a battalion or division of disciplined, unequivocally loyal troops—that they reverse a process that is so deep in its origins and massive in its accumulated force. Once parturition has begun, no midwife or physician is so insane as to imagine it possible to keep even a premature fetus from being born.

The draft riots in New York in July 1863 ran a course for five days, with the city police quite incapable of maintaining any semblance

---

[30] See Davies, *op. cit.,* 8–10.

[31] Gustave Le Bon, *The Crowd* (1895), New York, The Viking Press, Compass Books ed., 1960. See also W. A. Westley, The Nature and Control of Hostile Crowds, *Canadian Journal of Economics and Political Science,* **23**: 33–41 (1957), which, based on interviews with police officers, corroborates some of Le Bon's findings a half-century later.

of order.[32] The riots in Cairo in January 1952, while briefer, were comparably uncontrollable or uncontrolled. And it is utterly impossible to imagine what any force could have done in Russia in February 1917 to stop that revolution. The troops could not be forced into stopping the crowds. A kind of ultimate incongruity between constitutional and unconstitutional processes is reached when a legislature "deliberates" under the machine guns of a new leader, as did the Congolese parliament in September 1960 when Lumumba asked for complete authority to rule.

The physical violence, so central a characteristic of revolutions, has at least four consequences. It induces a sense of shock so severe that people observe and take part in the events with a kind of mental dissociation, like that with which a soldier in combat faces the reality of death or mutilation, with a dazed yet calm and rational detachment. Like concentration camp internees protected by the shock of an incredible real world, citizens in a revolution can be calm and detached, relatively free of panic.

A second consequence is a kind of apathy, a paradoxical indifference to what happens. The apathy is partly the result of fear that getting involved in anything will endanger life and limb. It is also in part, immediately after or alternating with periods of extreme excitation, a consequence of simple exhaustion. Some of the tension that has built up is released by direct or vicarious participation in popular demonstrations, and people are for a time emotionally unstrung. The experience is somewhat like that which tens of millions of people in Europe, Asia, and America had in 1945 when the war, which had scraped and hammered and plucked their nerves raw for six years, came at last to an end. Such a profound sense of relief, after the resolution of long-enduring tensions, apparently is causally related to a state of apathy that prevails for awhile, after the old elite has abdicated or been destroyed.

A third consequence of the physical violence is a kind of equalization of people in all ranks and conditions. Almost everyone has experienced the ease of association that follows a common disaster, or a happy event like the achievement of peace. People with whom one would not have dared or deigned to speak are now the willing objects of the reciprocal exchange of the sense that is a consensus. But there is a further reason for this equalization than the delight or comfort in sharing joy or sorrow. People are thrown back on basic resources, on

[32] See Irving Werstein, *July 1863*, New York, Julian Messner, 1957.

basic individual human resources, which test and expose them to the core. Courage is observed and admired without regard to status, and so is cowardice. Generosity, fear, selfishness, and quite simply the shedding of blood or life are root experiences which for a time slough off the more subtle effects of enculturation. A semi-permanent consequence is the reminder of what people do have in common and of the inadequacy of long-established criteria (like property, occupation, education, and religion) to test people very deeply.

A fourth consequence, related to the first three, is a heightened sense of national community. For a time, sectional and individual conflicts are pushed into the background by a strong, new, and larger social sense. This new socializing is also partly the result of the excess of egotism in the prerevolutionary period, an overreaction from individualism in the old society to the suppression of the individual in the new national community.

The shock, apathy, equalization, and socializing that follow the period of physical violence provide a metaphase during which there is a lining up of forces that will determine the style of revolution and the sort of leadership to come. Members of the new elite share their rejection of the old regime and their desire to take power, but they do not share a desire to share power. They all want to lead the downtrodden masses straight to Utopia, but each small group of new elitists is altogether convinced of the incompetence of all other groups. As the struggle progresses, the public outside—without a particular awareness of its crucial role in resolving its own transitory chaos and the struggle for power in the palace and the legislature—becomes a major arbiter of the dispute because it is to the public that leadership groups appeal for support.

The elite group most likely to succeed, more often than not, seems to be the one that has the hardest, least conciliatory program—and the hardest men. Any group which proposes to maintain any continuity with the old regime has less chance to succeed than one which at least says it will make a complete break with the past. Almost by definition a populace that has thrown off the old does not want even to be reminded of any connection with it—any more than a teenager on a Saturday night wants to be reminded of the parents he is escaping. Even compromise within the contesting new, would-be ruling groups is apt to be seen by the populace as a sign of wavering, of uncertainty as to the location of the obviously easy and direct path to the good society. And the group that calls for the most sacrifice, of present comfort for future perfection, is apt to win over the one that says people are still individuals and let us proceed slowly into the foggy future. For a populace that wants to escape from a miserable world, talk of a direct path that the leaders say, and may even believe, they clearly see is more welcome than talk of the uncertainty of success and the possibility that the old elite was not altogether malignant.[33]

But the old society, even the old regime, gradually begins to reassert itself from the grave. There is no real return to the previous landed and haut-bourgeois basis for the political power structure. But in a wide variety of ways the old manner reasserts itself.

The attempt by some people after the American revolution to establish a constitutional monarch is only one instance. When Napoleon became emperor, when Nkrumah became prime minister, there was an adoption of some external forms of the old regime. Far more significant than such forms are the more intimate stylistic relationships between the rulers and the public. A populace long accustomed to a monarch who was the symbol of national unity, authority, beneficence, and grace cannot move suddenly to more abstract representations. The new elite must—and readily does—produce a new leader who becomes the living, personal symbol of unity, authority, beneficence, and grace. He may even go a step beyond. If the old monarch was supposed to be perfect but obviously was not, the new leader becomes in the eyes of his followers not the symbol but the reality of perfection, the omniscient, omnipotent, morally perfect, charismatic leader.

The charismatic leader of course is the embodiment of justice and of grace. In this light, Stalin (in his own eyes) and perhaps even the highly rationalist Lenin (in the eyes of some of his followers) appeared as the successors of the supposedly finished line of tsars. The secret police were an intensified carryover from the empire, and so indeed were the collective farms, however spurious was the new measure of local communal self-rule that had begun in the zemstvos and mirs. As Wolfe points out, Stalin was repeating the experiences of his youth when he encouraged informing, which in his seminary days he had so bitterly resented; and when he followed the catechis-

---

[33] Pye attributes an unrealistic appraisal of actual time needed to achieve goals, among Malayan Chinese Communists, to the uncertain time-categories in the Chinese language. [Pye, *op. cit.*, 126.] More reasonable is the explanation that men frustrated by misery want much and want it now. At least there has been the same impatience in Russia, and the Russian language has no such vagueness about time.

tic style in his writings, he was acting like the hated priests.[34] In a speech in Budapest in December 1959, Khrushchev justified his intervention in the Hungarian revolt of 1956 by reminding his Hungarian audience that Tsar Nicholas had helped the Austrian Emperor suppress a Hungarian revolt in 1849.

And perhaps the strength of the appeal of Marxism, with its demand for the destruction of the exploiting class, derives from a simple appreciation of the Marxist anger at exploitation as such, because an exploiting class has caused anger in the society undergoing revolution. Certainly one cannot explain why Marxism has taken strongest root in the least economically developed, most feudal agrarian societies on grounds that Marx called for the overthrow of capitalists. The style may be more important than the content because it provides a rationale for revenge—it rationalizes a mood.

But this has already taken us too far beyond the causes of revolution. Before we start speculating on what happens when a revolution becomes stabilized, we had best stop. In the meantime and without much benefit of academic analysis, organic forces within individual human beings continue to interact with external and internalized cultural forces, to maintain a continuing process of political evolution and revolution. A French bishop, who was a friend of Petrarch, in the fourteenth century wrote of the value of the secure life (vie seüre) in the country as opposed to insecure life at court.[35] Six hundred years later and as long as people maintain their nature—that is, forever—they cannot and will never be able to escape the problem of security and insecurity. The ever-emerging needs of man interact with an environment that ever falls short of fulfilling these needs and so generates the tension that causes civilization to emerge and evolve.

[34] Bertram D. Wolfe, *Three Who Made a Revolution,* Boston, Beacon Press, 1955, 411, 413, 459.
[35] See Johan Huizinga, *The Waning of the Middle Ages,* London, Edward Arnold Ltd., 1924, 117–118.

List of sources

with occasional comments

The writings that follow are ones I have used in developing the notions in this book and presenting the evidence in their support. The writings are varied, indeed variegated. Some are as old as the hills—or at least as old as Greece and Judea. Others are from more recent professional and technical publications. Still others (not included in the following list) are from the daily newspaper. If there is any meritorious conclusion to draw from the wide variety, it is that the often elusive mental phenomena I have tried to make some sense out of are everyday, real, and common ones. They have been continuously probed by philosophers, kings, statesmen, demagogues, citizens, and scientists. The phenomena are, as has been said in a different context, deep enough for an elephant to swim in and for a child to bathe in.

The reader is invited to have a look at any or all the writings. Above all, he is invited to look around him for relevant observations that this book has overlooked. Thomas Hobbes said three hundred years ago: "He that is to govern a whole nation must read in himself, not this or that particular man, but mankind. . . ." This book purports to be a jumping-off place for exploring human behavior in politics and ourselves as part of the governing process. For those who can tolerate ambiguity that is sometimes chilling, the following books and articles may serve not as a stagnant, dark pool to gaze into but as a navigable stream that leads to the oceanic depths of the human mind. And if he will but turn his mind to it, each of us may thus better explore his own political self.

Books

Adorno, T. W., Else Frenkel-Brunswik, Daniel J. Levinson, and R. Nevitt Sanford, *The Authoritarian Personality*, New York, Harper & Bros., 1950.

Allee, W. C., *Animal Aggregations*, Chicago, University of Chicago Press, 1931.

Allee, W. C., *Cooperation among Animals*, New York, Harry Schurman, 1951. A biologist's synthesis of research on the clustering, the grouping, of mainly some lower forms of plant and animal life.

Allport, Gordon W., *Personality: A Psychological Interpretation*, New York, Henry Holt & Co., 1937.

Apter, David E., *The Gold Coast in Transition*, Princeton, Princeton University Press, 1955.

Aristotle, *The Nicomachean Ethics* (H. Rackham, transl.), London, William Heinemann Ltd., rev. ed., 1934.

Aristotle, *Politics* (H. Rackham, transl.), London, William Heinemann Ltd., 1932.

Asch, Solomon E., *Social Psychology*, New York, Prentice-Hall, 1952. Contains a very detailed report of the author's studies of group effects on perception, in addition to a sophisticated general treatment of the subject that titles the book.

Bakke, E. Wight, *Citizens without Work*, New Haven, Yale University Press, 1940.

Barber, Bernard, *Social Stratification*, New York, Harcourt, Brace & Co., 1957.

Basler, Roy P., *Abraham Lincoln: His Speeches and Writings*, Cleveland and New York, The World Publishing Co., 1946. A very useful, calm-eyed, one-volume compilation of Lincoln's main writings—with lucid and germane comments.

Bauer, Raymond A., et al., *How the Soviet System Works*, Cambridge, Harvard University Press, 1956.

Beck, F., and W. Godin, *Russian Purge and the Extraction of Confession*, London, Hurst & Blackett Ltd., 1951.

Benedict, Ruth, *Patterns of Culture* (1934), New York, The New American Library of World Literature (Mentor Books), 1949.

Berelson, Bernard R., Paul F. Lazarsfeld, and William N. McPhee, *Voting*, Chicago, University of Chicago Press, 1954. The so-called Elmira Study. An analysis of mainly social-status correlates of voting in a constitutional democracy in 1948.

Binkley, Wilfred E., *President and Congress*, New York, Vintage Books, 3rd ed., 1962.

Bowlby, John, *Maternal Care and Mental Health*, Geneva, World Health Organization, 1952. A synthesis of research in the catastrophic mental consequences of infantile deprivation of normal maternal care.

Buchanan, William, and Hadley Cantril, *How Nations See Each Other*, Urbana, University of Illinois Press, 1953.

Burckhardt, Jacob, *The Age of Constantine the Great* (1852), Garden City, Doubleday Anchor Books, 1956.

Burger, G. C. E., J. C. Drummond, and H. R. Sandstead, eds., *Malnutrition and Starvation in Western Netherlands, September 1944–July 1945, Part 1*, The Hague, General State Printing Office, 1948.

Campbell, Angus, Gerald Gurin, and Warren E. Miller, *The Voter Decides*, Evanston, Ill., Row, Peterson & Co., 1954.

Campbell, Angus, and Homer C. Cooper, *Group Differences in Attitude and Votes*, Ann Arbor, University of Michigan Survey Research Center, 1956.

Campbell, Angus, Philip E. Converse, Warren E. Miller, and Donald E. Stokes, *The American Voter*, New York, John Wiley & Sons, 1960. A meticulous sociological and psychological analysis of correlates of voting in a constitutional democracy. Based mainly on a large national sample-survey of the 1956 election in the United States.

Cash, W. J., *The Mind of the South* (1941), New York, Vintage Books, 1960. The first three chapters of this book present a deeply probing analysis of the mentality of an ancien régime, in this case the pre-Civil War aristocracy of the American South.

Centers, Richard, *The Psychology of Social Classes: A Study of Class Consciousness*, Princeton, Princeton University Press, 1949.

Chamberlin, Roy B., and Herman Feldman, eds., *The Dartmouth Bible*, Boston, Houghton Mifflin Co., 1950.

Charnwood, Lord (Godfrey Rathbone Benson), *Abraham Lincoln* (1916), New York, Pocketbooks, Inc., 1952. A psychologically very sensitive biography, more penetrating than some more recent studies of Lincoln.

Cochrane, Charles N., *Christianity and Classical Culture* (1940), New York, Oxford University Press (Galaxy Books), 1957.

Cohen, Elie A., *Human Behavior in the Concentration Camp*, New York, W. W. Norton & Co., 1953. A nonsensational analysis of the mental consequences of living constantly almost in extremis, written by an introspective, involuntary participant-observer.

Coleman, James S., *Nigeria: Background to Nationalism*, Berkeley and Los Angeles, University of California Press, 1958.

Crossman, Richard, ed., *The God That Failed*, New York, Bantam Books, 1952.

Degler, Carl N., *Out of Our Past: The Forces That Shaped Modern America*, New York, Harper & Bros., 1959.

Detroit Area Study, *A Social Profile of Detroit*, Ann Arbor, University of Michigan, 1952.

Diaz, Bernal, *The Discovery and Conquest of Mexico: 1517–1521*, G. Garcia, ed. (A. P. Maudslay, transl.), London, George Routledge & Sons Ltd., 1928.

Dollard, John, et al., *Frustration and Aggression*, New Haven, Yale University Press, 1939.

Donnelly, Ignatius, *Caesar's Column* (1890), Chicago, Syndicate Publishing Co., 1906.

Dunn, L. C., and Th. Dobzhansky, *Heredity, Race, and Society*, New York, Penguin Books, 1946.

Durkheim, Emile, *The Division of Labor in Society* (1893), Glencoe, Ill., The Free Press, 1933. To date, perhaps the classic social-psychological analysis of the personal consequences of industrialization.

Durkheim, Emile, *Suicide* (1897), Glencoe, Ill., The Free Press, 1951.

Edwards, Lyford P., *The Natural History of Revolutions*, Chicago, University of Chicago Press, 1927.

Erikson, Erik H., *Young Man Luther*, New York, W. W. Norton & Co., 1958. An exquisite probing of a gigantic marginal and ultra-conservative man who rebelled. Compare with the like biography of Erasmus, an elder acquaintance of Luther, by Johan Huizinga (see below).

Farber, Seymour M., and Roger H. L. Wilson, eds., *Control of the Mind*, New York, McGraw-Hill Book Co., 1961.

Fenton, John H., *The Catholic Vote*, New Orleans, The Hauser Press, 1960.

Florinsky, Michael T., *The End of the Russian Empire* (1931), New York, Collier Books, 1961.

Freud, Anna, *The Ego and the Mechanisms of Defence*, New York, International Universities Press, 1946. A major advance in theory and research over the work of her father, in a very difficult area.

Freud, Sigmund, *Group Psychology and the Analysis of the Ego*, London, The Hogarth Press, 1922. An only moderately successful effort to treat of social psychology. Freud relies rather heavily on Gustave Le Bon instead of first-hand investigation.

Freud, Sigmund, *Civilization and Its Discontents,* London, The Hograth Press, 1930. One place to start in trying to understand Freud's views on and some of the psychodynamics of civilization.

Freud, Sigmund, *New Introductory Lectures in Psycho-Analysis,* London, The Hogarth Press, 1933. A succinct statement of Freud's major contributions.

Freud, Sigmund, *An Autobiographical Study,* London, The Hogarth Press, 1935.

Freud, Sigmund, *Totem and Taboo* (1918), New York, Vintage Books, 1960. Again, as in *Group Psychology,* Freud relies rather heavily on written sources for his synthesis on social primitivism.

Friedrich, Carl J., and Zbigniew K. Brzezinski, *Totalitarian Dictatorship and Autocracy,* Cambridge, Harvard University Press, 1956.

Fromm, Erich, *Escape from Freedom,* New York, Rinehart & Co., 1941. A sweeping thesis about man's inability to bear the responsibility of political maturity. This book fertilized an enormous spawn of research in authoritarianism after the Second World War.

Fuchs, Lawrence H., *The Political Behavior of American Jews,* Glencoe, Ill., The Free Press, 1956.

Gerth, H. H., and C. Wright Mills, eds., *From Max Weber: Essays in Sociology,* London, Routledge & Kegan Paul Ltd., 1948.

George, Alexander L., and Juliette L. George, *Woodrow Wilson and Colonel House,* New York, The John Day Co., 1956. A psychological study of Wilson, notably in his relationships with his father. Fails to consider the possible impact on a hypersensitive child of being raised in the devastation of the American South during and after the Civil War.

Halévy, Elie, *A History of the English People: 1830–1841* (E. I. Watkin, transl.), New York, Harcourt, Brace & Co., n.d.

Hebb, D. O., *The Organization of Behavior: A Neuropsychological Theory,* New York, John Wiley & Sons, 1949.

Hicks, John D., *The Populist Revolt,* Minneapolis, University of Minnesota Press, 1931.

Hitler, Adolf, *Mein Kampf* (1925, 1927), New York, Reynal & Hitchcock, 1941.

Hobbes, Thomas, *Leviathan* (1651), Michael Oakeshott, ed., Oxford, Basil Blackwell, n.d. Perhaps the most brilliant attempt to found a political theory on a systematic theory of human behavior and on a dour view of the human race.

Hofstadter, Richard, *The American Political Tradition and the Men Who Made It* (1948), New York, Vintage Books, 1954. Sometimes with a scalpel, sometimes with a cleaver, the author dissects the minds and careers of history-making political leaders in the United States.

Hofstadter, Richard, *The Age of Reform: From Bryan to F. D. R.,* New York, Alfred A. Knopf, 1955.

Hollingshead, August B., *Elmtown's Youth,* New York, John Wiley & Sons, 1949.

Homans, George C., *The Human Group,* New York, Harcourt, Brace & Co., 1950. A major attempt to construct a basic theory of mostly small, proximal groups.

Hovell, Mark, *The Chartist Movement,* T. F. Tout, ed., Manchester, Manchester University Press, 2d ed., 1925.

Hovland, C. I., I. L. Janis, and H. H. Kelly, *Communication and Persuasion,* New Haven, Yale University Press, 1953. A synthesis of highly significant research in the psychodynamics of social communication.

Huizinga, Johan, *The Waning of the Middle Ages,* London, Edward Arnold Ltd., 1924.

Huizinga, Johan, *Erasmus of Rotterdam* (1924), London, Phaidon Press Ltd., 1952. A dispassionate analysis of a marginal and profoundly radical man who discreetly avoided rebellion. Compare with Erikson's penetration into the marginality of Luther (see above).

Hunter, Edward, *Brainwashing: The Story of the Men Who Defied It,* New York, Farrar, Straus & Cudahy, 1956.

Hyman, Herbert H., *Political Socialization,* Glencoe, Ill., The Free Press, 1959. A synthesis of research in mainly proximal group influences on the formation of opinion. Covers the same general area as Verba's *Small Groups* (see below), though not in the same manner.

Jaffa, Harry V., *Crisis of the House Divided,* Garden City, Doubleday & Co., 1959.

Janis, Irving L., *Psychological Stress,* New York, John Wiley & Sons, 1958.

Jones, Ernest, *The Life and Work of Sigmund Freud,* New York, Basic Books, 1953.

Kardiner, Abram, *The Individual and His Society: The Psychodynamics of Primitive Social Organization,* New York, Columbia University Press, 1939.

Kardiner, Abram, et al., *The Psychological Frontiers of Society,* New York, Columbia University Press, 1945.

Katz, Elihu, and Paul F. Lazarsfeld, *Personal Influence,* Glencoe, Ill., The Free Press, 1955.

Key, V. O., Jr., *Public Opinion and American Democracy,* New York, Alfred A. Knopf, 1961.

Keys, Ancel, J. Brozek, A. Henschel, O. Mickelson, and H. L. Taylor, *The Biology of Human Starvation,* Minneapolis, University of Minnesota Press, 1950. Volume 2 contains the report of experiments in mental consequences of extreme deprivation of food.

Kluckhohn, Clyde, and Henry A. Murray, *Personality in Nature, Society, and Culture,* New York, Alfred A. Knopf, 1948.

Koestler, Arthur, *Darkness at Noon,* New York, The Macmillan Co., 1941. A psychologically penetrating fictional account of man in a totalitarian society, written precociously before many nonfictional corroborations of Koestler's observations.

Koestler, Arthur, *The Invisible Writing* (1954), Boston, The Beacon Press, 1955.

Krech, David, and Richard S. Crutchfield, *Elements of Psychology,* New York, Alfred A. Knopf, 1958.

Krech, David, Richard S. Crutchfield, and Egerton L. Ballachey, *Individual in Society,* New York, McGraw-Hill Book Co., 1962. A major and coherent synthesis of theory and research in social psychology.

Lamy, M., M. Lamotte, and S. Lamotte-Barrillon, *La dénutrition, clinique-biologie-therapeutique,* Paris, G. Doin et Cie., 1948.

Lane, Robert E., *Political Life,* Glencoe, Ill., The Free Press, 1959.

Lane, Robert E., *Political Ideology,* New York, The Free Press of Glencoe, 1962. A deep probing of the origins of the basic political outlook of some lower-middle- and working-class Americans.

Lasswell, Harold D., *Psychopathology and Politics,* Chicago, University of Chicago Press, 1930.

Lasswell, Harold D., and Abraham Kaplan, *Power and Society,* New Haven, Yale

University Press, 1950. Partly in the guise of definitions, a systematic political theory.

Lazarsfeld, Paul F., B. R. Berelson, and H. Gaudet, *The People's Choice*, New York, Columbia University Press, 2d ed., 1948. The pioneering social-psychological study of voting behavior.

Leach, Jack F., *Conscription in the United States: Historical Background*, Rutland, Vermont, and Tokyo, Japan, Charles E. Tuttle Publishing Co., 1952.

Le Bon, Gustave, *The Crowd* (1896), London, Ernest Benn Ltd., 1952 and New York, The Viking Press, 1960.

Lefebvre, Georges, *The Coming of the French Revolution* (1947), New York, Vintage Books, 1957. A systematic discussion of the antecedents of the first major postindustrial revolution.

Leighton, Alexander, *The Governing of Men*, Princeton, Princeton University Press, 1945.

Lerner, Daniel, *The Passing of Traditional Society*, Glencoe, Ill., The Free Press, 1958. A sociopsychological analysis of publics in transition from agrarian to urban society, based on extensive opinion surveys in the Middle East.

Lewin, Kurt, *Principles of Topological Psychology*, New York, McGraw-Hill Book Co., 1936.

Lifton, Robert Jay, *Thought Reform and the Psychology of Totalism: A Study of "Brainwashing" in China*, New York, W. W. Norton & Co., 1961. A deep and deeply disturbing analysis of Chinese communist attempts to restructure the minds of twenty-five captive Westerners.

Lipset, Seymour Martin, *Political Man: The Social Bases of Politics*, Garden City, Doubleday & Co., 1960.

Lipset, Seymour Martin, and Reinhard Bendix, *Social Mobility in Industrial Society*, Berkeley and Los Angeles, University of California Press, 1959. A careful analysis and synthesis of research on a difficult subject.

Locke, John, *Of Civil Government* (the Second Treatise), London, J. M. Dent & Sons (Everyman's Library), 1924.

Lubell, Samuel, *The Future of American Politics*, New York, Harper & Bros., 1952.

Lubell, Samuel, *Revolt of the Moderates*, New York, Harper & Bros., 1956.

McClosky, Herbert, and John E. Turner, *The Soviet Dictatorship*, New York, McGraw-Hill Book Co., 1960.

Maier, Norman R. F., *Frustration: The Study of Behavior without a Goal*, New York, McGraw-Hill Book Co., 1949.

Mann, Thomas, *Buddenbrooks* (1902), New York, The Modern Library, 1924.

Mann, Thomas, *Mario and the Magician* (1929), in Mann, *Death in Venice and Seven Other Stories*, New York, Vintage Books, 1954.

Masaryk, Thomas G., *The Spirit of Russia*, London, George Allen and Unwin Ltd., 1919. A brilliant analysis of the antecedents of the Russian Revolution, written before the revolution by the Czech sociologist who became the founder of a nation.

Mason, Philip, *Prospero's Magic: Some Thoughts on Class and Race*, London, Oxford University Press, 1962. A subtle, speculative, literate consideration of the common problem of racial and status marginality.

Matthews, Donald R., *The Social Background of Political Decision-Makers*, Garden City, Doubleday & Co., 1954.

Matthews, Donald R., *U. S. Senators and Their World,* Chapel Hill, University of North Carolina Press, 1960.

May, Rollo, *The Meaning of Anxiety,* New York, The Ronald Press Co., 1950. A mature, fruitful analysis of a concept and phenomenon that remained stubbornly jejune even in the hands of Freud.

Meerloo, J. A. M., *The Rape of the Mind,* Cleveland and New York, The World Publishing Co., 1956.

Merton, Robert K., *Mass Persuasion: The Social Psychology of a War Bond Drive,* New York, Harper & Bros., 1946.

Michels, Roberto, *Political Parties* (E. and C. Paul, transl.), New York, Hearst's International Library Co., 1915.

Milne, R. S., and H. C. Mackenzie, *Straight Fight: A Study of Voting Behaviour in the Constituency of Bristol North-East at the General Election of 1951,* London, The Hansard Society, 1954.

Morton, H. V., *A Stranger in Spain,* New York, Dodd, Mead & Co., 1955.

Murray, Henry A., *Explorations in Personality,* New York, Oxford University Press, 1938. A durable landmark in the continuing search for motivation theory.

Myers, H. A., *Are Men Equal?,* Ithaca, Cornell University Press, 1955.

Newcomb, Theodore M., *Personality and Social Change,* New York, Dryden Press, 1943.

North, R. C., et al., *Kuomintang and Chinese Communist Elites,* Hoover Institute Studies, Series B: Elite Studies No. 8, Stanford, Stanford University Press, 1952.

Odegard, Peter H, *Pressure Politics: The Story of the Anti-Saloon League,* New York, Columbia University Press, 1928.

Odegard, Peter H, ed., *Religion and Politics,* New Brunswick, Rutgers—The State University, The Eagleton Institute of Politics, 1960.

Ostrogorskii, M. Y., *Democracy and the Organization of Political Parties* (F. Clarke, transl.), New York, The Macmillan Co., 1902.

Parsons, Thomas Richard, *Fundamentals of Biochemistry in Relation to Human Physiology,* Cambridge, W. Heffer & Sons Ltd., 6th ed., 1939.

Pavlov, I. P., *Conditioned Reflexes: An Investigation of the Physiological Activity of the Cerebral Cortex* (G. V. Anrep, transl.), London, Oxford University Press, 1927, and New York, Dover Publications, n.d.

Plato, *Symposium* (W. R. M. Lamb, transl.), London, William Heinemann Ltd., 1925.

Prescott, William H., *History of the Conquest of Mexico* (1843) and *History of the Conquest of Peru* (1847), New York, The Modern Library, n.d.

Prince, Samuel H., *Catastrophe and Social Change,* New York, Columbia University Studies in History, Economics and Public Law, vol. 94, no. 1, 1920.

Pye, Lucian W., *Guerrilla Communism in Malaya: Its Social and Political Meaning,* Princeton, Princeton University Press, 1956.

Reich, Jerome R., *Leisler's Rebellion: A Study of Democracy in New York, 1664–1720,* Chicago, University of Chicago Press, 1953.

Riesman, David, Reuel Denney, and Nathan Glazer, *The Lonely Crowd: A Study of the Changing American Character,* New Haven, Yale University Press, 1950.

Rostow, W. W., *The Stages of Economic Growth,* Cambridge, The University Press, 1960.

Schachter, Stanley, *The Psychology of Affiliation*, Stanford, Stanford University Press, 1959.

Seton-Watson, Hugh, *The Decline of Imperial Russia: 1855–1914*, New York, Frederick A. Praeger, 1952.

Sherif, Muzafer, *The Psychology of Social Norms*, New York, Harper & Bros., 1936.

Shirer, William L., *The Rise and Fall of the Third Reich*, New York, Simon & Schuster, 1960.

Smith, M. Brewster, Jerome S. Bruner, and Robert W. White, *Opinions and Personality*, New York, John Wiley & Sons, 1956.

Smythe, Hugh H., and Mabel M. Smythe, *The New Nigerian Elite*, Stanford, Stanford University Press, 1960.

Sorokin, P. A., *Man and Society in Calamity*, New York, E. P. Dutton & Co., 1942.

Spiro, Melford E., *Kibbutz*, Cambridge, Harvard University Press, 1956.

Stouffer, Samuel A., *Communism, Conformity, and Civil Liberties*, Garden City, Doubleday & Co., 1955.

Thomas, Benjamin P., *Abraham Lincoln*, New York, Alfred A. Knopf, 1952.

Thomas, Dorothy S., and Richard S. Nishimoto, *The Spoilage*, Berkeley and Los Angeles, University of California Press, 1946.

Tischendorf, C., ed., *Novum Testamentum Graece*, Leipzig, J. D. Hinrichs, 1877.

Trend, J. B., *Portugal*, London, Ernest Benn Ltd., 1957.

United Nations, *Report on the World Situation*, New York, United Nations, 1957.

United States Bureau of the Census, *Statistical Abstract of the United States: 1961*, Washington, D. C., 1961.

Verba, Sidney, *Small Groups and Political Behavior*, Princeton, Princeton University Press, 1961.   A synthesis of research in mainly proximal group influences on political behavior.   Covers the same general area as Hyman's *Political Socialization* (see above), though not in the same manner.

Vernadsky, George, *A History of Russia*, New Haven, Yale University Press, 4th ed., 1954.

Vidich, Arthur J., and Joseph Bensman, *Small Town in Mass Society* (1958), Garden City, Doubleday Anchor Books, 1960.

Wallas, Graham, *Human Nature in Politics*, New York, Alfred A. Knopf, 3rd ed., 1921.

Werner, M. R., *Bryan*, New York, Harcourt, Brace & Co., 1929.

Werstein, Irving, *July, 1863*, New York, Julian Messner, 1957.

White, Ralph K., and Ronald Lippitt, *Autocracy and Democracy*, New York, Harper & Bros., 1960.   Doubtless the definitive report of the extensive research of the Iowa group on the internal government of small experimental groups.

Wilson, Edmund, *To the Finland Station* (1940), Garden City, Doubleday Anchor Books, n.d.

Wolfe, Bertram D., *Three Who Made a Revolution* (1948), Boston, Beacon Press, 1955.

Woytinsky, W. S., *Stormy Passage*, New York, The Vanguard Press, 1961.

Woytinsky, W. S., and E. S. Woytinsky, *World Population and Production: Trends and Outlook*, New York, Twentieth Century Fund, 1953.

Articles

Agger, R. E., and V. Ostrom, Political Participation in a Small Community, in Heinz Eulau, Samuel J. Eldersveld, and Morris Janowitz, eds., *Political Behavior: A Reader in Theory and Research*, Glencoe, Ill., The Free Press, 1956, 138–148.

Allinsmith, W. and B., Religious Affiliation and Politico-Economic Attitude, *Public Opinion Quarterly*, **12**: 377–389 (1948).

Allport, G. W., The Composition of Political Attitudes, *American Journal of Sociology*, **35**: 220–238 (1929).

Allport, G. W., and J. M. Faden, The Psychology of Newspapers: Five Tentative Laws, *Public Opinion Quarterly*, **4**: 687–703 (1940).

Asch, S. E., Forming Impressions of Personality, *Journal of Abnormal and Social Psychology*, **41**: 258–290 (1946).

Axelrod, M., Urban Structures and Social Participation, *American Sociological Review*, **21**: 13–18 (1956).

Bachrach, P., Attitude toward Authority and Party Preference in Puerto Rico, *Public Opinion Quarterly*, **22**: 68–73 (1958).

Bauer, R. A., Some Trends in Sources of Alienation from the Soviet System, *Public Opinion Quarterly*, **19**: 279–291 (1955).

Beam, J. C., Serial Learning and Conditioning under Real-Life Stress, *Journal of Abnormal and Social Psychology*, **51**: 543–551 (1955).

Bell, W., and M. T. Force, Social Structure and Participation in Different Types of Formal Associations, *Social Forces*, **34**: 345–350 (1956).

Bendix, R., Social Stratification and Political Power, *American Political Science Review*, **46**: 357–375 (1952).

Bettelheim, B., Joey: A "Mechanical Boy," *Scientific American*, **200** (3): 116–128 (March 1959).

Bogardus, E. S., The Measurement of Social Distance (1928), reprinted in Theodore M. Newcomb and Eugene L. Hartley, eds., *Readings in Social Psychology*, New York, Henry Holt & Co., 1947, 503–507.

Bondy, C., Problems of Internment Camps, *Journal of Abnormal and Social Psychology*, **38**: 453–475 (1943).

Brodbeck, A. J., and H. B. Perlmutter, Self-Dislike as a Determinant of Marked Ingroup-Outgroup Preference, *Journal of Psychology*, **38**: 271–280 (1954).

Brozek, J., Semi-Starvation and Nutritional Rehabilitation: A Qualitative Case Study, with Emphasis on Behavior, *Journal of Clinical Nutrition*, **1**: 107–118 (1953).

Bruner, J. S., and C. C. Goodman, Value and Need as Organizing Factors in Perception, *Journal of Abnormal and Social Psychology*, **42**: 33–44 (1947).

Bruner, J. S., and L. Postman, Symbolic Value as an Organizing Factor in Perception, *Journal of Social Psychology*, **27**: 203–208 (1948).

Bruner, J. S., and L. Postman, On the Perception of Incongruity: A Paradigm, *Journal of Personality*, **18**: 206–223 (1949).

Campbell, D. T., and T. H. McCormack, Military Experience and Attitudes toward Authority, *American Journal of Sociology*, **62**: 482–490 (1957).

Carothers, J. C., A Study of Mental Derangement in Africans, and an Attempt to Explain Its Peculiarities, More Especially in Relation to the African Attitude to Life, *Psychiatry*, **11**: 47–86 (1948).

Centers, R., Attitude and Belief in Relation to Occupational Stratification, *Journal of Social Psychology,* **27**: 159–185 (1948), reprinted in Daniel Katz, Dorwin Cartwright, Samuel Eldersveld, and Alfred McClung Lee, *Public Opinion and Propaganda: A Book of Readings,* New York, The Dryden Press, 1954.

Cervin, V., Experimental Investigation of Behaviour in Social Situations: I. Behaviour under Opposition, *Canadian Journal of Psychology,* **9**: 107–116 (1955).

Cohen, A. R., E. Stotland, and D. M. Wolfe, An Experimental Investigation of Need for Cognition, *Journal of Abnormal and Social Psychology,* **51**: 291–294 (1955).

Cohn, T. S., and H. Carsch, Administration of the F-Scale to a Sample of Germans, *Journal of Abnormal and Social Psychology,* **49**: 471 (1954).

Collins, M. E., Interracial Housing, in William Petersen, ed., *American Social Patterns,* Garden City, Doubleday Anchor Books, 1956, 7–61.

Converse, P. E., et al., Stability and Change in 1960: A Reinstating Election, *American Political Science Review,* **55**: 269–280 (1961).

Cowen, E. L., The Influence of Varying Degrees of Psychological Stress on Problem-Solving Rigidity, *Journal of Abnormal and Social Psychology,* **47**: 512–519 (1952).

Davies, David, *The Case of Labourers in Husbandry* (1796), quoted in W. S. Woytinsky and E. S. Woytinsky, *World Population and Production: Trends and Outlook,* New York, Twentieth Century Fund, 1953, 282–283.

Davies, J. C., Some Relations between Events and Attitudes, *American Political Science Review,* **46**: 777–789 (1952).

Davies, J. C., Charisma in the 1952 Campaign, *American Political Science Review,* **48**: 1083–1102 (1954).

Davies, J. C., A Note on Political Motivation, *Western Political Quarterly,* **12**: 410–416 (1959).

Davies, J. C., Toward a Theory of Revolution, *American Sociological Review,* **27**: 5–19 (1962).

Dotson, F., Patterns of Voluntary Association among Urban Working-Class Families, *American Sociological Review,* **16**: 687–693 (1951).

Dukes, W. F., and W. Bevan, Jr., Size Estimation and Monetary Value: A Correlation, *Journal of Psychology,* **34**: 43–53 (1952).

Duncker, K., The Influence of Past Experience upon Perceptual Properties, *American Journal of Psychology,* **52**: 255–265 (1939).

Edwards, A. L., Political Frames of Reference as a Factor Influencing Recognition, *Journal of Abnormal and Social Psychology,* **36**: 34–50 (1941).

Eisenberg, P., and P. F. Lazarsfeld, The Psychological Effects of Unemployment, *Psychological Bulletin,* **35**: 358–390 (1938).

Engel, L., The Troubled Monkeys of Madison, *New York Times Magazine,* 29 January 1961.

Esfandiary, Fereidoun, Is It the Mysterious—or Neurotic—East?, *New York Times Magazine,* 24 March 1957, 13 ff.

Fischer, J., Government by Concurrent Majority, a 1948 *Harper's Magazine* article, reprinted in H. M. Bishop and S. Hendel, *Basic Issues of American Democracy,* New York, Appleton-Century-Crofts, 4th ed., 1961, 266–278.

Frenkel-Brunswik, Else, Intolerance of Ambiguity as an Emotional and Perceptual Personality Variable, *Journal of Personality,* **18**: 108–143 (1949).

Frenkel-Brunswik, Else, Interaction of Psychological and Sociological Factors in Political Behavior, *American Political Science Review,* **46**: 44–65 (1952).

Fromm, Erich, Die Entwicklung des Christusdogmas, *Imago,* **16**: 305–373 (1930).

Geiger, K., Deprivation and Solidarity in the Soviet Urban Family, *American Sociological Review,* **20**: 57–68 (1955).

Gilchrist, J. C., et al., Values as Determinants of Word-Recognition Thresholds, *Journal of Abnormal and Social Psychology,* **49**: 423–426 (1954).

Goffman, I. W., Status Consistency and Preference for Change in Power Distribution, *American Sociological Review,* **22**: 275–281 (1957).

Goodstein, L. D., Intellectual Rigidity and Social Attitudes, *Journal of Abnormal and Social Psychology,* **48**: 345–353 (1953).

Gorden, R. L., Interaction between Attitude and the Definition of the Situation in the Expression of Opinion, *American Sociological Review,* **17**: 50–58 (1952), reprinted in D. Katz et al., *Public Opinion and Propaganda,* New York, The Dryden Press, 1954, 425–434.

Greenblum, J., and L. I. Pearlin, Vertical Mobility and Prejudice: A Socio-Psychological Analysis, in Reinhard Bendix and Seymour Martin Lipset, *Class, Status, and Power,* Glencoe, Ill., The Free Press, 1953, 480–491.

Grimes, P., India's "Wolf Boy," *New York Times Magazine,* 30 October 1960.

Haire, M., and W. F. Grunes, Perceptual Defenses: Processes Protecting an Organized Perception of Another Personality, *Human Relations,* **3**: 403–412 (1950).

Harlow, H. F., Mice, Monkeys, Men, and Motives, *Psychological Review,* **60**: 23–32 (1953).

Harlow, H. F., The Nature of Love, *The American Psychologist,* **13**: 673–685 (December 1958).

Harlow, H. F., and R. R. Zimmerman, The Development of Affectional Responses in Infant Monkeys, *Proceedings of the American Philosophical Society,* **102**: 501–509 (1958).

Hebb, D. O., Heredity and Environment in Mammalian Behavior, *British Journal of Animal Behavior,* **1**: 43–47 (1953).

Hebb, D. O., E. S. Heath, and E. A. Stuart, Experimental Deafness, *Canadian Journal of Psychology,* **8**: 152–156 (1954).

Heron, Woodburn, The Pathology of Boredom, *Scientific American,* **196** (1): 52–56 (January 1957).

Heron, W., W. H. Bexton, and D. O. Hebb, Cognitive Effects of a Decreased Variation in the Sensory Environment, *American Psychologist,* **8**: 366 (1953).

Heron, W., B. K. Doane, and T. H. Scott, Visual Disturbances after Prolonged Perceptual Isolation, *Canadian Journal of Psychology,* **10**: 13–18 (1956).

Hoffman, M. L., Some Psychodynamic Factors in Compulsive Conformity, *Journal of Abnormal and Social Psychology,* **48**: 383–393 (1953).

Horowitz, E. L., Development of Attitude toward Negroes, reprinted in T. M. Newcomb and E. L. Hartley, eds., *Readings in Social Psychology,* New York, Henry Holt & Co., 1947, 507–517.

Hovland, C. I., and W. Weiss, The Influence of Source Credibility on Communication Effectiveness, *Public Opinion Quarterly,* **15**: 635–650 (1951).

Ichheiser, G., Frustration and Aggression or Frustration and Defense: A Counter-Hypothesis, *Journal of General Psychology,* **43**: 125–129 (1950).

Iisager, H., Factors Influencing the Formation and Change of Political and Religious Attitudes, *Journal of Social Psychology,* **29**: 253–265 (1949).

Inkeles, A., and P. H. Rossi, National Comparisons of Occupational Prestige, *American Journal of Sociology,* **61**: 329–339 (1956).

Janis, I. L., and S. Feshbach, Effects of Fear-Arousing Communications, *Journal of Abnormal and Social Psychology,* **48**: 78–92 (1953).

Katz, D., and H. Cantril, An Analysis of Attitudes toward Fascism and Communism, *Journal of Abnormal and Social Psychology,* **35**: 356–366 (1940).

Kay, H., Toward an Understanding of News-Reading Behavior, *Journalism Quarterly,* **31**: 15–32 (1954).

Khrushchev, N., The Crimes of the Stalin Era (Speech to the Twentieth Party Congress in Moscow), *New Leader* edition, New York, 1956.

Killian, L. M., The Significance of Multiple-Group Membership in Disaster, *American Journal of Sociology,* **57**: 309–314 (1952), reprinted in Dorwin Cartwright and Alvin Zander, *Group Dynamics: Research and Theory,* Evanston, Ill., Row, Peterson & Co., 1953.

King, J. A., Closed Social Groups among Domesticated Dogs, *Proceedings of the American Philosophical Society,* **98**: 327–336 (1954).

Lacy, W., et al., Foreknowledge as a Factor Affecting Perceptual Defense and Alertness, *Journal of Experimental Psychology,* **45**: 169–174 (1953).

Lane, R. E., Fathers and Sons: Foundations of Political Belief, *American Sociological Review,* **24**: 502–511 (1959).

Lane, R. E., The Fear of Equality, *American Political Science Review,* **53**: 35–51 (1959).

Langfeld, H. S., Heredity and Experience, *Année Psychologique,* **50**: 11–25 (1951).

Lazarsfeld, P. F., An Unemployed Village, *Character and Personality,* **1**: 147–151 (1932–1933).

Lazarus, R. S., et al., Hunger and Perception, *Journal of Personality,* **21**: 312–328 (1953).

Levine, J. M., and G. Murphy, The Learning and Forgetting of Controversial Material, *Journal of Abnormal and Social Psychology,* **38**: 507–517 (1943).

Levy, David M., The Strange Hen, *American Journal of Orthopsychiatry,* **20**: 355–362 (1950).

Levy, David M., Anti-Nazis: Criteria of Differentiation, in Alfred H. Stanton and Stewart E. Perry, *Personality and Political Crisis,* Glencoe, Ill., The Free Press, 1951.

Lewin, K., R. Lippitt, and R. K. White, Patterns of Aggressive Behavior in Experimentally Created Social Climates, *Journal of Social Psychology,* **10**: 271–299 (1939).

Lewis, Flora, Clues to the Communist Lingo, *New York Times Magazine,* 1 September 1957, 11.

Lidz, T., et al., The Intrafamilial Environment of the Schizophrenic Patient: IV. Parental Personalities and Family Interaction, *American Journal of Orthopsychiatry,* **28**: 764–776 (1958).

Lilly, John C., Mental Effects of Reduction of Ordinary Levels of Physical Stimuli on Intact, Healthy Persons, *Psychiatric Research Reports,* **5**: 1–28 (June 1956).

Lippitt, R., and R. K. White, An Experimental Study of Leadership and Group Life, in T. M. Newcomb and E. L. Hartley, eds., *Readings in Social Psychology,* New York, Henry Holt & Co., 1947, 315–330.

Lipscomb, F. M., German Concentration Camps: Diseases Encountered at Belsen, in H. L. Tidy and J. M. B. Kutschbach, eds., *Inter-Allied Conferences on War Medicine,* London, Staples Press Ltd., 1947, 462–465.

Lipset, S. M., Some Social Requisites of Democracy: Economic Development and Political Legitimacy, *American Political Science Review*, **53**: 69–105 (1959).

Lowe, F. E., and T. C. McCormick, A Study of the Influence of Formal and Informal Leaders in an Election Campaign, *Public Opinion Quarterly*, **20**: 651–662 (1956–1957).

Lowitt, Richard, essay on Theodore Roosevelt, in Morton Borden, ed., *America's Ten Greatest Presidents*, Chicago, Rand McNally & Co., 1961, 185–206.

McClosky, H., Conservatism and Personality, *American Political Science Review*, **52**: 27–45 (1958).

McClosky, H., and H. E. Dahlgren, Primary Group Influence on Party Loyalty, *American Political Science Review*, **53**: 757–776 (1959).

McGinnies, E., Emotionality and Perceptual Defense, *Psychological Review*, **56**: 244–251 (1949).

McGinnies, E., and H. Sherman, Generalization of Perceptual Defense, *Journal of Abnormal and Social Psychology*, **47**: 81–85 (1952).

Mäder, Hannes, The Tongues of Tyrants, *Atlas*, **4**: 92–99 (August 1962).

Maslow, A. H., The Dynamics of Psychological Security-Insecurity, *Character and Personality*, **10**: 331–344 (1942).

Maslow, A. H., A Theory of Human Motivation, *Psychological Review*, **50**: 370–396 (1943).

Mason, W. A., The Effects of Social Restriction in the Behavior of Rhesus Monkeys: I. Free Social Behavior, *Journal of Comparative and Physiological Psychology*, **53**: 582–589 (1960); II. Tests of Gregariousness, *op. cit.*, **54**: 287–290 (1961).

Masserman, J. H., and C. Pechtel, Conflict-Engendered Neurotic and Psychotic Behavior in Monkeys, *Journal of Nervous and Mental Disease*, **118**: 408–411 (1953).

Montague, M. F. A., The Origin and Nature of Social Life and the Biological Basis of Cooperation, *Journal of Social Psychology*, **29**: 267–283 (1949).

Muensterberger, W., On the Biopsychological Determinants of Social Life, in Werner Muensterberger, ed., *Psychoanalysis and the Social Sciences*, New York, International Universities Press, 1955, vol. 4, 7–25.

Newcomb, T. M., Some Patterned Consequences of Membership in a College Community, in T. M. Newcomb and E. L. Hartley, eds., *Readings in Social Psychology*, New York, Henry Holt & Co., 1947, 345–357.

Nkrumah, K., African Prospect, *Foreign Affairs*, **37**: 45–53 (1958).

Pace, C. R., The Relationship between Liberalism and Knowledge of Current Affairs, *Journal of Social Psychology*, **10**: 247–258 (1939).

Pastore, N., and M. W. Horowitz, The Influence of Attributed Motive on the Acceptance of Statement, *Journal of Abnormal and Social Psychology*, **51**: 331–332 (1955).

Patch, Richard W., Life in a Peruvian Indian Community, *American Universities Field Staff Reports*, West Coast South America Series, vol. 9, no. 1, 1962.

Perlmutter, H. B., Some Characteristics of the Xenophilic Personality, *Journal of Psychology*, **38**: 291–300 (1954).

Pihlblad, C. T., and C. L. Gregory, Selective Aspects of Migration among Missouri High School Graduates, *American Sociological Review*, **19**: 314–324 (1954).

Postman, L., J. S. Bruner, and E. McGinnies, Personal Values as Selective Factors in Perception, *Journal of Abnormal and Social Psychology*, **43**: 142–154 (1948).

Rabin, A. I., Some Psychosexual Differences between Kibbutz and Non-Kibbutz Israeli Boys, *Journal of Projective Techniques*, **22**: 328–332 (1958).

Reid, I. de A., and E. I. Ehle, Leadership Selection in Urban Locality Areas, *Public Opinion Quarterly*, **14**: 262–284 (1950), reprinted in D. Katz et al., *Public Opinion and Propaganda*, New York, The Dryden Press, 1954, 446–459.

Remmers, H. H., and N. Weltman, Attitude Inter-Relationships of Youth, Their Parents, and Their Teachers, *Journal of Social Psychology*, **26**: 61–68 (1947).

Richet, C., Experiences of a Medical Prisoner at Buchenwald, in H. L. Tidy and J. M. B. Kutschbach, eds., *Inter-Allied Conferences on War Medicine*, London, Staples Press Ltd., 1947, 454.

Ringer, B. B., and D. L. Sills, Political Extremists in Iran, *Public Opinion Quarterly*, **16**: 689–701 (1952–1953).

Rokeach, M., Generalized Mental Rigidity as a Factor in Ethnocentrism, *Journal of Abnormal and Social Psychology*, **43**: 259–278 (1948).

Rokeach, M., and B. Fruchter, A Factorial Study of Dogmatism and Related Concepts, *Journal of Abnormal and Social Psychology*, **53**: 356–360 (1956).

Rose, A. M., The Social Psychology of Desertion from Combat, *American Sociological Review*, **16**: 614–629 (1951).

Rose, A. M., Social Psychological Effects of Physical Deprivation, *Journal of Health and Human Behavior*, **1**: 285–289 (1960).

Rubin-Rabson, G., Intelligence and Conservative-Liberal Attitudes, *Journal of Psychology*, **37**: 151–154 (1954).

Sanai, M., The Relation between Social Attitudes and Characteristics of Personality, *Journal of Social Psychology*, **36**: 3–13 (1952).

Sanford, R. N., The Effects of Abstinence from Food upon Imaginal Processes, *Journal of Psychology*, **2**: 129–136 (1936).

Schiller, Paul H., Innate Constituents of Complex Processes, *Psychological Review*, **59**: 177–191 (1952).

Schnierla, T. C., Problems in the Biopsychology of Social Organization, *Journal of Abnormal and Social Psychology*, **41**: 385–402 (1946).

Secord, P. F., et al., The Negro Stereotype and Perceptual Accentuation, *Journal of Abnormal and Social Psychology*, **53**: 78–83 (1956).

Sheppard, H., The Union as a Political Influence: Ethnic and Generation Factors in Union Members' Behavior, *Journal of Social Issues*, **9** (1): 45–48 (1953).

Sherif, M., Group Influences upon the Formation of Norms and Attitudes, in T. M. Newcomb and E. L. Hartley, eds., *Readings in Social Psychology*, New York, Henry Holt & Co., 1947, 77–90.

Shils, E. A., and M. Janowitz, Cohesion and Disintegration in the Wehrmacht in World War II, *Public Opinion Quarterly*, **12**: 280–315 (1948), reprinted in D. Katz et al., eds., *Public Opinion and Progaganda*, New York, The Dryden Press, 1954, 553–582.

Smith, C. U., and J. W. Prothro, Ethnic Differences in Authoritarian Personality, *Social Forces*, **35**: 334–338 (1957).

Smith, M. B., The Personal Setting of Public Opinions: A Study of Attitudes toward Russia, *Public Opinion Quarterly*, **11**: 507–523 (1947), reprinted in D. Katz et al., eds., *Public Opinion and Propaganda*, New York, The Dryden Press, 1954, 295–305.

Smock, C. D., The Influence of Psychological Stress on the Intolerance of Ambiguity, *Journal of Abnormal and Social Psychology*, **50**: 177–182 (1955).

Solomon, Leonard, The Influence of Some Types of Power Relationships and Game Strategies upon the Development of Interpersonal Trust, *Journal of Abnormal and Social Psychology*, **61**: 223–230 (1960).

Spitz, R. A., The Role of Ecological Factors in Emotional Development in Infancy, *Child Development*, **20**: 145–155 (1949).

Stagner, R., Attitude toward Authority: An Exploratory Study, *Journal of Social Psychology*, **40**: 197–210 (1954).

Stanford Research Institute, *Research for Industry*, **6** (1): 9–11 (November 1953).

Taft, Ronald, Is the Tolerant Personality Type the Opposite of the Intolerants?, *Journal of Social Psychology*, **47**: 397–405 (1958).

Taylor, J. A., The Effects of Anxiety Level and Psychological Stress on Verbal Learning, *Journal of Abnormal and Social Psychology*, **57**: 55–60 (1958).

Taylor, J. A., and K. W. Spence, The Relationship of Anxiety Level to Performance in Serial Learning, *Journal of Experimental Psychology*, **44**: 61–64 (1952).

Thompson, L. J., German Concentration Camps: Psychological Aspects of the Camps, in H. L. Tidy and J. M. B. Kutschbach, eds., *Inter-Allied Conferences on War Medicine*, London, Staples Press Ltd., 1947, 466–467.

Vernon, J., and J. Hoffman, Effect of Sensory Deprivation on Learning Rate in Human Beings, *Science*, **123**: 1074–1075 (1956).

Wada, G., and J. C. Davies, Riots and Rioters, *Western Political Quarterly*, **10**: 864–874 (1957).

Wax, R. H., The Destruction of a Democratic Impulse, *Human Organization*, **12** (1): 11–21 (1953).

Weininger, O., Mortality of Albino Rats under Stress as a Function of Early Handling, *Canadian Journal of Psychology*, **7**: 111–114 (1953).

Weiss, W., A "Sleeper" Effect in Opinion Change, *Journal of Abnormal and Social Psychology*, **48**: 173–180 (1953).

Weld, H. P., and M. Roff, A Study in the Formation of Opinion Based upon Legal Evidence, *American Journal of Psychology*, **51**: 609–628 (1938).

Wells, H., Ideology and Leadership in Puerto Rican Politics, *American Political Science Review*, **49**: 22–39 (1955).

Westley, W. A., The Nature and Control of Hostile Crowds, *Canadian Journal of Economics and Political Science*, **23**: 33–41 (1957).

Wilson, Edmund, The Union as Religious Mysticism, reprinted in Edmund Wilson, *Eight Essays*, Garden City, Doubleday Anchor Books, 1954, 181–202.

Wright, C. R., and H. H. Hyman, Voluntary Association Memberships of American Adults: Evidence from National Sample Surveys, *American Sociological Review*, **23**: 284–294 (1958).

Wylie, Philip, Panic, Psychology, and the Bomb, *Bulletin of the Atomic Scientists*, **10**: 37–40 (1954).

Zawadzki, B., and P. Lazarsfeld, The Psychological Consequences of Unemployment, *Journal of Social Psychology*, **6**: 224–251 (1935).

Authors' index

Adorno, T. W.   164n, 203n, 268n
Agger, R. E.   191n
Allee, W. C.   32n
Allinsmith, W. and B.   229n
Allport, G. W.   112, 112n, 118n, 220n
Apter, David E.   329n
Aristotle   35n, 48, 48n, 236, 284
Asch, Solomon E.   113n, 171, 171n
Axelrod, M.   178n

Bachrach, P.   330
Bakke, E. Wight   168n
Ballachey, Egerton L.   63n, 171n
Barber, Bernard   237n, 254n, 268n
Basler, Roy P.   86n, 313n, 316n
Bauer, Raymond A.   19, 20n
Beam, J. C.   119n
Beck, F.   19n
Bell, W.   178n
Bendix, Reinhard   250n, 253n, 254n, 259n, 261n, 264n, 328n
Benedict, Ruth   96n, 97n
Bensman, Joseph   191n, 192n
Berelson, B.   199n, 201n, 208n, 228n, 264
Bettelheim, B.   151n, 264n
Bevan, W., Jr.   137
Bexton, W. H.   106n
Binkley, Wilfred E.   319n
Bogardus, E. S.   201n
Bondy, C.   145n
Bowlby, John   152n

Brodbeck, A. J.   203n
Brozek, J.   12n, 13, 13n, 14, 14n, 15n
Bruner, Jerome S.   114n, 119n, 137
Brzezinski, Zbigniew   297, 297n
Buchanan, William   255, 255n
Burckhardt, Jacob   216n
Burger, G. C. E.   15n

Campbell, Angus   57n, 164n, 166n, 200n, 206n, 207n, 208n, 228n, 272n
Campbell, D. T.   276n
Cantril, Hadley   122n, 243n, 255, 255n
Carothers, J. C.   99n
Carsch, H.   330
Cash, W. J.   345n
Centers, Richard   268n, 271, 271n
Cervin, V.   80n
Chamberlin, Roy B.   49n
Charnwood, Lord   293–294, 294n
Cochrane, Charles N.   216n, 221n
Cohen, A. R.   108n
Cohen, Elie A.   200n
Cohn, T. S.   330
Coleman, James S.   353n
Collins, M. E.   205n
Converse, Philip E.   228n, 231n
Cooper, Homer C.   228n
Cowen, E. L.   79n
Crossman, Richard   82n
Crutchfield, Richard S.   63n, 171n

Dahlgren, H. E.   166–167, 167n
Davies, David   267n

Davies, J. C.   53n, 132n, 169n, 300n, 346n, 351n, 360n, 361n
Degler, Carl N.   225n
Denney, Reuel   46
Detroit Area Study   178n
Diaz, Bernal   43n, 44
Doane, B. K.   106n
Dobzhansky, Th.   3n
Dollard, John   83n
Donnelly, Ignatius   40n, 41–42
Dotson, F.   178n
Drummond, J. C.   15n
Dukes, W. F.   137
Duncker, K.   114n
Dunn, L. C.   3n
Durkheim, Emile   141, 141n, 142, 360n

Edwards, A. L.   122n
Edwards, L. P.   346n
Ehle, E. I.   330
Eisenberg, P.   168n
Engel, L.   149n
Erikson, Erik H.   82n
Esfandiary, Fereidoun   97n

Faden, J. M.   112, 112n
Farber, Seymour M.   21n
Feldman, Herman   49n
Fenton, John H.   229, 229n, 230, 230n
Feshbach, S.   78, 79n
Fischer, John   133n
Florinsky, Michael T.   360n
Force, M. T.   178n
Frenkel-Brunswik, Else   79–80, 80n, 120, 120n, 164n, 203n, 267n
Freud, Anna   39n, 82n
Freud, Sigmund   7, 8, 32, 32n, 37n, 81n, 115n, 116n, 157n
Friedrich, Carl J.   297, 297n
Fromm, Erich   49, 49n, 325n
Fruchter, B.   119n
Fuchs, Lawrence H.   202, 202n, 209n

Geiger, K.   168n
George, Alexander L. and Juliette L.   288n
Gerth, H. H.   299n
Gilchrist, J. C.   137
Glazer, Nathan   46
Godin, W.   19n

Goffman, I. W.   346n
Goodman, C. C.   137
Goodstein, L. D.   120n
Gorden, R. L.   172–174, 172n
Greenblum, J.   264n
Gregory, C. L.   262n
Grimes, P.   151n
Grunes, W. F.   113n
Gurin, Gerald   57n, 166n, 177n

Haire, M.   113n
Halevy, Elie   224n
Harlow, H. F.   108n, 149–150, 149n
Hebb, D. O.   4n, 105–106, 106n
Henschel, A.   12n
Heron, Woodburn   106n
Hicks, John D.   36n, 40n
Hitler, Adolf   186n
Hobbes, Thomas   16, 19n, 34, 52
Hoffman, J.   106n
Hoffman, M. L.   164n
Hofstadter, Richard   42n, 45n, 197n, 310, 310n, 316n
Hollingshead, A. B.   192n, 241n, 267n
Homans, George C.   180n
Horowitz, E. L.   126n, 203n
Hovell, Mark   224n
Hovland, C. I.   125n, 126n, 128n
Huizinga, Johan   338n, 365n
Hunter, Edward   21n
Hyman, Herbert H.   175n, 178n

Ichheiser, G.   83n
Iisager, H.   165n
Inkeles, A.   258n

Jaffa, Harry V.   317n
Janis, I. L.   78, 79n, 81, 81n, 126n
Janowitz, M.   180–181, 181n, 264n
Jones, Ernest   176n

Kaplan, Abraham   2, 2n
Kardiner, Abram   2, 2n, 96n, 97n
Katz, D.   122n
Katz, Elihu   178, 178n, 179n, 180n, 182, 182n
Kay, H.   81n
Kelly, H. H.   126n
Key, V. O., Jr.   268n, 272n
Keys, Ancel   12n, 14n, 15n

Khrushchev, N.   20–21, 21n
Killian, L. M.   168, 168n
King, J. A.   148n
Kluckhohn, Clyde   3n
Koestler, Arthur   19n, 82n, 214
Krech, David   63n, 171n

Lacy, W.   137
Lamotte, M.   15n
Lamotte-Barrillon, S.   15n
Lamy, M.   15n
Lane, Robert E.   46, 46n, 177n, 199n, 201n, 248–249, 249n
Langfeld, Herbert S.   4n
Lasswell, Harold D.   2, 2n, 57, 57n
Lazarsfeld, P. F.   16–17, 17n, 141, 168n, 178, 178n, 182, 182n, 228n, 234, 264
Lazarus, R. S.   108n–109n
Leach, Jack F.   6n
Le Bon, Gustave   127n, 361n
Lefebvre, Georges   355n
Leighton, Alexander   18n
Lerner, Daniel   359n, 360n
Levine, J. M.   122n
Levinson, Daniel J.   164n, 203n, 267n
Levy, David M.   148n, 164n, 266n
Lewin, Kurt   2, 2n, 274n
Lewis, Flora   123n
Lidz, T.   164n
Lifton, Robert Jay   21n, 34n
Lilly, John C.   107, 107n
Lippitt, R.   274n, 276n
Lipscomb, F. M.   14n, 34n
Lipset, Seymour Martin   26, 27n, 250n, 253n, 254n, 259n, 261n, 264n
Locke, John   359, 359n
Lowe, F. E.   330
Lowitt, Richard   181n
Lubell, Samuel   102n, 201n, 272n

McClosky, Herbert   21n, 118, 118n, 166–167, 167n
McCormack, T. H.   276n
McCormick, T. C.   330
McGinnies, E.   137, 140
Mackenzie, H. C.   272n
McPhee, William N.   264
Mäder, Hannes   123n
Maier, Norman R. F.   77–78, 78n

Mann, Thomas   11n, 279
Masaryk, Thomas G.   298n, 351n
Maslow, A. H.   8n, 8–11, 60–62, 65n, 145
Mason, Philip   263n
Mason, W. A.   149n
Masserman, J. H.   78n
Matthews, D. R.   57n, 256n, 285n, 286
May, Rollo   81, 81n, 103n
Meerloo, J. A. M.   21n
Merton, Robert K.   127, 127n
Michels, Roberto   191, 232–233, 233n
Mickelson, O.   12n
Miller, Warren E.   57n, 166n, 177n, 228n
Mills, C. Wright   299n
Milne, R. S.   272n
Morton, H. V.   116n
Montague, M. F. A.   32n
Muensterberger, W.   4n
Murphy, G.   122n
Murray, Henry A.   3n, 7n, 7–9
Myers, H. A.   53n

Newcomb, Theodore M.   174, 174n
Nishimoto, Richard S.   18n
Nkrumah, K.   135, 135n
North, R. C.   346n

Odegard, Peter H   225n, 231n
Orwell   135
Ostrogorskii, M. Y.   232, 233n
Ostrom, Vincent   191n

Pace, C. R.   118n
Parsons, Thomas Richard   14n
Pastore, N.   126n
Patch, Richard W.   44n
Pavlov, I. P.   76–77, 77n, 129n
Pearlin, L. I.   264n
Pechtel, C.   78n
Perlmutter, H. B.   203n
Pihlblad, C. T.   262n
Plato   31n, 284
Postman, L.   114n, 137, 140
Prescott, William H.   45n
Prince, Samuel H.   33n
Prothro, J. W.   330
Pye, Lucian W.   346n, 358n, 364n

Rabin, A. I.   165n
Reich, Jerome R.   334n
Reid, I. de A.   330
Remmers, H. H.   175n
Richet, C.   12n
Riesman, David   46
Ringer, B. B.   346n
Roff, M.   115n
Rokeach, M.   120n
Rose, A. M.   33n, 181n
Rosenzweig, R. M.   286n
Rossi, P. H.   258n
Rostow, W. W.   11n
Rubin-Rabson, G.   119n

Sanai, M.   118n
Sandstead, H. R.   15n
Sanford, R. N.   108n, 164n, 203n, 267n
Schachter, Stanley   33n
Schiller, Paul H.   4n
Schnierla, T. C.   32n
Scott, T. H.   106n
Secord, P. F.   137
Seton-Watson, Hugh   354n, 355n, 356n
Sheppard, H.   199n
Sherif, Muzafer   170, 170n
Sherman, H.   137
Shils, E. A.   180–181, 181n
Shirer, William L.   326n
Sills, D. L.   346n
Smith, C. U.   330
Smith, M. B.   114n, 119n, 123n
Smock, C. D.   79, 79n
Smythe, Hugh H. and Mabel M.   286n
Solomon, Leonard   247n–248n
Sorokin, P. A.   14n, 15n
Spence, K. W.   80n
Spiro, Melford E.   165, 165n
Spitz, R. A.   152n
Stagner, Ross   164n, 168n
Stanford Research Institute   243n
Stokes, Donald E.   228n
Stotland, E.   108n
Stouffer, Samuel A.   111n, 268, 268n

Taft, Ronald   203n
Taylor, H. L.   12n
Taylor, J. A.   80n
Thomas, Benjamin P.   187n, 319n
Thomas, Dorothy S.   18n
Thompson, L. J.   13n
Tischendorf, C.   31n
Trend, J. B.   333n
Turner, John E.   21n

United Nations   27
U.S. Bureau of the Census   206n

Verba, Sidney   153n, 169n
Vernadsky, George   116n
Vernon, J.   106n
Vidich, Arthur J.   191n, 192n

Wada, G.   169n, 346n
Wallas, Graham   7, 7n
Wax, R. H.   18n
Weininger, O.   150n
Weiss, W.   125n, 128n
Weld, H. P.   115n
Wells, H.   329
Weltman, N.   175n
Werner, M. R.   40n
Werstein, Irving   6n, 362n
Westley, W. A.   361n
White, Ralph K.   274n, 276n
White, Robert W.   114n, 119n
Wilson, Edmund   187n, 188n, 189n, 314n
Wilson, Roger H. L.   21n
Wolfe, Bertram D.   187n, 188n, 189n, 365n
Wolfe, D. M.   108n
Woytinsky, E. S.   27
Woytinsky, W. S.   27, 269n
Wright, C. R.   178n
Wylie, Philip   109n

Zawadzki, B.   16–17, 17n
Zimmerman, R. R.   149n

General index

Africa 352–354
  anomy in 353
  Congo 196
  Mau-Mau rebellion 354
  Nigerian elite 286
  origins of instability 352–354
Agrarian politics:
  in early industrial conditions in America 36, 40–42
  in preindustrial conditions 342–345, 351, 355–356
Anomy 101, 266
  in Africa 353
Anti-Nazism:
  and family background 164
  and marginality 266
Anxiety:
  and basic needs 101
  and dependency on leaders 96, 101, 327
  and frustration 66–67
  and identity 81–82
  and McCarthyism 103
  and mental rigidity 119–120
  and newspaper reading habits 80–81
  and Soviet purges 103
  annihilation, perception, and 109–110
  causes 70–74
  diagram illustrating 69
  distinguished from fear 67–69
  during brainwashing 18–19
  experiments on 76–80

Anxiety (cont'd)
  Freud on 66, 71
  in backgrounds of political leaders 85–94
  in industrial society 102–103
  in preliterate society 95–98
  in pre-Nazi Germany 327–328
  in the populace 94–103
  in transitional society 98–102
  irrational responses to 82–83
  of retrogression 100–101, 360
  of social estrangement 97, 101, 266, 353
  of survival 97, 109–110, 360
  of transition 95–96, 98–102
  of unfulfilled expectations 97–98
  optimum 70, 80–81, 84, 103
  rational responses to 83–84
  symptomatic relief of 82-83
  see also Fear, Frustration, Insecurity, Tension
Apathy and apathetics (i.e., apoliticals):
  a definition 25–26
  and assimilation 169
  and autocratic rule 298–299
  and starvation 13, 15, 26–28
  and unemployment 16–17
  proportion of 53–54
  purges and brainwashing 23, 26
  right after revolution 362
Aristotle 22n, 31, 35n, 48, 48n
Assimilation and depoliticization 169

Authoritarianism:
    and education   330
    and lack of roots   330
    Germans   330
    Whites and Negroes   330
"Autokinetic effect"   170

"Basic personality structure" and human
        nature   2
Belief systems:
    and religion   213–214
    and social mobility   256–258
    of "Rubashov"   214
    of Dostoevski   214
    universality of   214
Bourguiba, Habib   284, 306
Brainwashing   18–23
    and need hierarchy   33–34
    de-individualization during   19
    in Chinese People's Republic   21–23
    in Hungarian People's Republic   21–
        22
    in Korean War   26
    insecurity of the victims   18–19
    in Soviet purges of 1930s   18–21
    recovery from   33–34
Bridges, Harry and Korean War   244
Bryan, William Jennings   41n, 290,
        294, 295–296, 320
Buchanan, James   311–312

Caesar, Julius   301
Caesar's Column   41–42
    projection in   41–42
Calhoun, John:
    and Lincoln   132–133, 310–311
Calorie consumption:
    in concentration camps   12n, 14n
    in selected countries, chart on   27
Calvin, John   19, 22n
Carlyle, Thomas   277-278
Caste:
    distinguished from class   236–237
    rights and obligations of   236–237
Catholic church   221–230
    alienation from poor   223, 225, 227
    and Leisler's rebellion   333–336
    and Negroes   226, 229–230
    and Reformation   221–222
    and subjective equality   223

Catholic Church (*cont'd*)
    and voting in U. S.   228-230, 228n,
        229n
    and working class   222–223, 225,
        227, 228, 228n
    in Latin America   223, 227
    in Latin Europe   223, 227
Charisma   299–303
    a definition   299
    Alexander I of Russia   305
    Bourguiba   306
    Caesar, Julius   301
    De Gaulle   306
    Hitler   304–305
    Lenin   305
    Lincoln   308, 315–316
    Mahomet   299
    Napoleon   305
    Nkrumah   302-303
    Roosevelt, Franklin   306
    Stalin   301-302
    tsars and Stalin   364
    Young, Brigham   299
Charles II of England   333-334
Charles V of the Holy Roman Empire
        43, 60, 347n
Chekhov's "Ward No. 6"   189n, 347n
Chiang Kai-shek   278-279, 294, 295,
        296
Christ and Christianity:
    and basic needs   232–233
    and Communism   227
    and criterion of success   295
    and family   220
    and proximal groups   219–220
    and rich vs. poor   219, 227
    and social reform   223–227
    appeals of   218–221
    Byzantine and Roman compared
        218
    Chartism and English churches   223–
        224
    church-state conflict   215-218
    conflict between Henry IV and Greg-
        ory VII   216–217
    Constantine and   216, 218–219, 221
    Council of Nicaea   216
    equality and dignity   48–49, 219–
        221, 219n–220n, 223
    influences in politics   227–232

Christ and Christianity (*cont'd*)
    love   31, 31n
    Reformation and   221–222
    social reforms under Constantine
      221
    universalism and tribalism   220
Churchill, Winston   288, 289
Cicero on equality   48
Civil disobedience and proximal groups
    181
Civil liberties:
    and need hierarchy   111n
    and Protestant churchmen   226
    and tension   103
Civil War (American):
    and draft riots of 1863   5–6
    old elite in South   345, 345n
Class:
    and caste   236–237
    and civil liberties   268–269
    and Nazism and Communism   340
    and personality, Marxist view   234
    and racial prejudice   268
    consciousness and unconsciousness
      271–272
    identification with   271–272
    interclass antagonism and solidarity
      240
    interclass solidarity and division of
      labor   241
    justice, legislation, and   237–240
    liberalism and self-interest   54, 269–
      270
    of political leaders   270, 285–286
    personality differences in classes
      266–270
    workingmen, conservatism of   242–
      244, 268–270
Class legislation   237–240
    and classless tyranny   239–240
    and economic equality   238–239
Classless society and class legislation
    239–240
Columbus and a sense of direction
    257n
Concentration camp internees:
    caloric intake of   12n, 14n
    need hierarchy   14, 33
    recovery of   33, 34n
Concurrent majority   133

Conditioned reflexes   76–77, 129–130
    and rationality   129–136
    extinction of   129–130
    Pavlov's experiments   76–77
Conformity:
    class status and conformity   268–269
    family influence on   163–169
    nonfamily group influence on   170–
      175, 180–181
Conservatism   114–121
    and changed church identification,
      Reformation   222
    and continued church identification,
      twentieth century   230–232
    and party identification   210–211
    and utopianism of revolutionaries
      348–349
    causes of   118–121
    intelligence and   119
    of Lincoln   319–320, 321
    of working class   242–244, 268–270
    personality correlates of   118–119
    related to tension   119–120
    status as conservative force   236
    vs. adaptabilitiy of leaders   321–322
Constantine   216, 218–219, 221
Constitutionalism:
    and background of elite   29
    and economic conditions   26–29
    and popular government   54
    and propaganda limits   135–136
    and self-interest   54
    during revolution   362
Cortes, Hernando   43–44
Council of Nicaea   216
Crisis:
    effect on family   167–169
    proximal groups in   180–181
    see also Ch. 10
Crypto-Platonic realism   51, 52
    and reaction to word "socialism"
      117
    and Soviet "socialist competition"
      117
    in interclass antagonism   244–245
    of revolutionaries   349

Darkness at Noon   19n
    and social need   107n
    and "stimulus-action" hunger   107n

Darkness at Noon (*cont'd*)
  "Rubashov" and religion   214
Death instinct:
  among old elite   357
  in Hitler   90
De-individualization in brainwashing
    19
Depoliticization:
  among French war prisoners   15
  and assimilation   169
  and physical deprivation   15–23
  at detention centers for Japanese
    17–18
  crisis, and the family   168–169
Deprivation, physical:
  after-effects   13, 13n, 14–15
  and alienation of Soviet citizens   19–
    20
  and apathy   13, 15, 26
  and depoliticization   15–23
  and forced political participation
    22–23
  and limits to propaganda   134–136
  at detention camps for Japanese   17–
    18
  fear of bodily harm or death   5–6,
    109–110, 360
  hunger and starvation   5–6, 11–15,
    27–28
  in Chinese People's Republic   21–23
  in Hungarian People's Republic   21–
    22
  in Soviet purges of 1930s   18–21
  recovery from   33–34
Deprivation, sensory:
  Darkness at Noon   107n
  experiments in   105–107
  Hebb's experiments   105–106
  Lilly's experiments   107
  separation from self and   106, 107
Deprivation, social:
  effects of   150–152
  experiments in   149–150
  in brainwashing   22
  in infants   151–152
  in "mechanical" boy   151
  in "wolf" boy   150–151
Desocialization:
  and unemployment   16–17
  of family   168–169

Desocialization (*cont'd*)
  of brainwashing victims   19, 22
Detention centers for Japanese:
  deprivation and depoliticization   17–
    18
  riots at   18, 346
Dictatorship, equality, and suffrage
    51–52
Disaster, effects on community   168
Discrimination and prejudice, racial:
  and class   268
  causes of   203–205
  see also Ethnic groups
Displacement   39, 82
  of aggressions in revolutionary leaders
    347
Dissociation, mental, right after revolu-
    tion   362
Distal groups:
  and Christianity   220, 222
  ethnic groups   198–200
  influence on party identification
    210–211
  in prerevolutionary conditions   341–
    342
  mediated by small town   190–193
  mental interaction of, with individual
    185
  mobility of entire status groups   252
  occasional proximal contact   184–188
  of working class   269
Division of labor:
  and kibbutzim   241–242
  and social mobility   250–254
  Durkheim on   101
  growth of tertiary occupations   253
"Don," starvation experimentee   12–14,
    16, 26, 33
Dorr, Thomas   290
Dostoevski, Fyodor, change in his belief
    system   214
Douglas, Stephen A.   294
  and Lincoln   309–310, 312
Draft riots in New York, 1863   5–6,
    361–362
Durkheim, Emile   101, 141, 142, 266

Economic progress and instability
    350–352
Eden, Anthony   284
Edict of Milan   216

Edict of Nantes 335
Eisenhower, Dwight 293
Elite, political:
    and self-actualization needs 56–60
    Chinese and Indian compared 29
    see also Leaders, political; Old elite;
        and New elite
"Elmtown," interclass antagonism and
    solidarity in 192n, 240–241
Emancipation Proclamation 311n
Environment (i.e., situation) 2–5
    and human nature 2
    and the organism 3–5
Equality (i.e., self-esteem, dignity)
    needs 9, 45–53
    and class legislation 238–239
    and ethnic minority status 197–200
    and hierarchy in groups 144
    and natural law 52–53
    and political stability 47–48, 243–
        244
    and power 247n
    and status 246–249
    and suffrage 51–52
    and utopian socialists 46–47
    Aristotle on 48
    Catholic church and 223
    Christ on 48–49
    Cicero on 48
    in America 50
    in early Christianity 49, 223
    in prerevolutionary conditions 354–
        356
    in Protestant Reformation 49–50,
        339
    in Soviet Union 52
    Jefferson on 48–49
    Judaic expression of 48–49
    Kant on 48–49
    Lincoln on 48–49
    lineage of the idea 48
    manifestations in law 50–51, 356
    Marshall, George C., on 48
    objective and subjective, distinguished
        46–48, 249n
    relation to social needs 45–46
    right after revolution 362–363
    subjective and self-esteem 47–49
    suffrage, dictatorship, and 51–52
Erasmus 338–339, 341, 348
    and Freud 338

Ethnic groups and ethnicity 194–205
    and conflict between Soviet Union
        and China 196
    and Congo independence 196
    and marginality 264
    and mobility 260–261
    and religion 201–203
    and status 260–261
    basis for nonpolitical conflict 195–
        196
    causes of discrimination 203–205
    identification 195, 198
    prejudice and class 268
    social and self-esteem needs 198
    subjective aspect 194–195
Experience, traumatic and therapeutic:
    and party identification 207–208,
        209–210
    and political participation 185–190
    Hitler and Jews 185–187
    Lenin's and his politics 187–189,
        188n, 189n
    Lincoln's and slavery 187
Extremism, political:
    and Hitler's background 88–90
    and McCarthy's background 87
    and marginality 164, 266

"Fairgrieve" family: *see* "Furumoto"
    family
Family:
    and anti-Nazism 164
    and crisis 167–169
    and dictatorship 164, 167–169
    and economic depression 168
    and political participation 35, 163–
        169, 175n, 177
    and religious belief 220
    and social mobility 261
    and social needs 35, 155–156
    parental influence 166–168, 176–
        177, 177n
    spouse influence 177
    the "Furumoto" family 4–5, 153–
        155, 157–163, 165–167, 169
Farmers, American:
    conservatism of 242–244
    identification process 40–41
    projection process 41–42
    socialization of 36

Farmers and peasants in politics:
  conservatism of   242–244
  in early industrial conditions, in
    America   36, 40–42
  in preindustrial conditions   342–345,
    351, 355–356
Fear:
  causes of   71–74
  diagram illustrating   69
  distinguished from anxiety   67–69
  experiments with monkeys   78n
  Freud on   71
  optimum   70
  toothbrush experiment   78–79
Food consumption in selected countries
  27
Freud, Anna:
  and identification with aggressor
    200
  on defense mechanisms   82
Freud, Sigmund   5, 19, 36–37
  and Erasmus   338
  and Lincoln   314
  Oedipus complex   37
  on anxiety   66, 71
  on love   32
  on "oceanic" feeling   81–82
Frustration:
  and anxiety   66–67
  and insecurity   66
  and tension   66
  in Lenin's background   90–92
  Maier's experiments on   77–78
  Pavlov's experiment and   76–77
  unpleasant tension   66
Functional autonomy:
  Allport   220
  and church membership   220, 223
  and institutions   233
  and social needs   152
  Durkheim   141
"Furumoto" family:
  and desocialization   169
  and political involvement   161–163
  Kentaro Kawashima   161–163, 165–
    167
  Thomas Fairgrieve   161–163, 165–
    167
  Tom   4–5
  Tom and Mary   4–5, 153–155, 157–
    161

Gandhi   283, 320
Garrison, William Lloyd   310–311
General public:
  decline in progress   355–356, 360
  economic progress   351–352
  in prerevolutionary conditions   350–
    360
  insecurity and   94–103
  political participation of   23–29, 53–
    56
  rationality, compared with elite
    130–136
  reluctance to rebel   359–360
  social reform and   352
Germany:
  and genocide   196
  and political maturity   325–328
Graft (political corruption) and justice
  238
Gregory VII   216–217, 219
Groups:
  a definition   142–144
  and categories   142–143
  chicken experiment   148
  distal, a definition   145–147, 183
  dog experiment   148
  family influences   163–169, 176–177,
    177n
  influence on conformity   170–175
  in war combat   180–181
  monkey experiments   149–150
  neighbors and friends   178–179
  nonfamilial   175–176, 178–181
  of equals and unequals   144
  origins of   146–153
  proximal, a definition   145–147, 183
  status group influence   179–180
  table of types   147
  teachers' influence   175n
  see also Distal groups; Proximal
    groups
Guilt and innocence:
  among American farmers   40–42
  and ignorance (i.e., innocence)   22,
    22n
  and marginality   265
  and moral relativism   44–45
  Calvin and   19
  Freud and   19

Guilt and innocence (*cont'd*)
  identification and   38–39
  in *Caesar's Column*   41–42
  in purges and brainwashing   19–21
  Khrushchev's, re Stalin's purges   21,
    21n, 350
  of old and new elites in revolution
    350
  projection and   42

Hamilton, Alexander   284
  marginality of   287
Harding, Warren G.   294
  and Eugene Debs   296
Henry IV of France   219
Henry IV of Germany   217, 219
Heredity   1–4
Hierarchy of needs   10–11, 60–63
  among French war prisoners   15
  and constitutional democracy   16,
    26–29
  and social status   255, 255n
  and support for civil liberties   111n
  charts showing   62
  in concentration camps   14, 33
  in Russian 1918-1922 famine   14
  physical vs. social needs   32–34, 33n,
    145n
  Rostow and *Buddenbrooks*   11n
  social vs. "self-assertion"   148n
Hitler, Adolf:
  and death instinct   90
  and Lincoln   318, 320
  and success   294–295, 296
  background of tension   88–90
  charismatic rule   301, 304–305
  contact with Jews   185–186
  in Vienna   89, 186, 296
Hobbes, Thomas   16, 34, 52
"Horatio Alger"   254, 255–256
Human nature   1–6
  and appeal of revolution   348
  and "basic personality structure"   2
  and the environment (situation)   2
  and the person or personality   2–3
  and the situation (environment)   2
  the organism   2
  see also Organism
Hume, David, on cause and effect   129,
    129n

Hungary:
  Soviet misperceptions in 1956   245–
    246
  Khrushchev on Russian intervention,
    1849 and 1956   365
Hunger:
  and constitutionalism   27–28
  and limits of propaganda   135–136
  and perception   108–109
  and political community   27–28
  and political participation   27–28
  food consumption, various countries
    27
  see also Starvation

Identification   36–39
  a definition   37
  among American farmers   40–41
  and projection   39, 45
  church and party compared   206
  ethnic   195, 197
  of ethnic minority, with majority
    200–201
  origins of   36–37, 155–156
  political party   205–208
  racial   195, 197
  with aggressor   83–84, 200
  with Christian church   219–220
  with class   271–272
  with defender   83–84
  with leaders   83–84, 218–283, 289–
    290
Identity:
  and anxiety   81–82
  and appeal of Christianity   219
  and "oceanic" feeling   81–82
  and social needs   156
  ethnic or racial   197, 198–199
  Luther's anxiety about   82n
  origin of, in infancy   155–156
Ideology and personal experience   188–
    190
Imprinting and social needs   150–152
Industrialization:
  and interclass conflict   243–244
  and social mobility   250–254
  in prerevolutionary period   351–352
Innocence (i.e., ignorance) and guilt
    22, 22n
  among American farmers   40–42

Innocence and guilt (*cont'd*)
  and marginality   265
  and moral relativism   44–45
  Calvin and   19
  Freud and   19
  identification and   38–39
  in *Caesar's Column*   41–42
  in purges and brainwashing   19–21
  Khrushchev's, re Stalin's purges   21,
    21n, 350
  of old and new elites in revolution
    350
  projection and   42
Insecurity:
  and anxiety   66
  and frustration   66
  and religion   213–214
  and social status   255
  and tension   66
  during brainwashing   18–19
  in background of political leaders
    85–94
  in the populace   94–103
  in primitive societies in transition
    97–100
Interclass antagonism:
  and common values   242–243
  and increased division of labor   241
  and misperception   244–245
  and solidarity   240
  and subjective equality   247–249
  in agrarian vs. industrial economies
    243–244
  physical proximity, psychic remote-
    ness   259–260
  strikes and revolutions compared
    244n
Intolerance of ambiguity:
  and mental rigidity   119–120
  and religion   213–214
  Frenkel-Brunswik on   79–80, 119–
    120, 120n
  experiments on   79–80
  in appraising political leaders   93–94
Irrational (dysfunctional) action:
  among political leaders   85–94
  and tension   74–76, 82–83

Jackson, Andrew   284
James II of England (Duke of York)
  333–335

Jefferson, Thomas:
  and social mobility   258
  on equality   48–49
  Populists and   40, 41
  style of rule   291–292, 307–308
Jews and Judaism:
  value system   48–49, 202–203
  Zedakeh   202
Jus primae noctis and equality   259
Justice:
  and graft   238
  and poverty   237–238
  distributive, Platonic   237–239
  equal   237–240
  law, and grace   356–357

Kant, Immanuel, on equality   48–49
Katz-Lazarsfeld study   178–180
Khrushchev:
  compares 1956 intervention in Hun-
    gary with tsar's intervention   365
  misperceptions of Hungarian revolt
    245–246
  on Stalin   20–21, 21n, 245, 245n,
    246, 350
Kibbutzim   164–165
  and division of labor   241–242
Koestler, Arthur   19n, 82, 107n, 214
Korean War of 1950–1953
  and brainwashed captives   26
  and Harry Bridges   244

Lasswell, Harold D.   57, 188, 347
Law:
  and equality   356
  justice, and grace   356–357
  prerevolutionary breakdown of   356
  see also Justice
Leaders, political:
  adaptability vs. conservatism and pro-
    gressivism   321–322
  authority figures   293
  autocrats and heterocrats   297–298
  backgrounds of tension   85–94
  characteristics of   56–60, 285–289
  charismatic autocrats   299–303, 327
  charismatic heterocrats   306–307
  class backgrounds of   40n–41n, 256,
    270, 285–286
  creatures of their times   277–279
  criterion of success   293–297

Leaders, political (*cont'd*)
  dependency on 101, 327
  energy level of 289
  father- or big-brother image 281
  genetic makeup of 93
  great man theory of 277–278
  identification with 83–84, 281–283,
    289–290
  Iowa experiments in 274, 277
  marginality of 85–94, 287–288,
    345–348
  misperceptions by 244–247
  narcissism of 247
  needs of the time for 101, 289–290
  personal traumata of 347–348
  public mood and 292–293
  rational autocrats 303
  rational heterocrats 307–308
  relation to followers 277–285
  revolutionary, from old elite 343
  revolutionary, loyalty to 354
  sense of equality in 283–284
  social status of 270, 285–286
  socio-cultural context for 92–93
  staff of 283–285
  style of rule 290–292
  traditional autocrats 298–299
  traditional heterocrats 306
Leisler, Jacob, background of 336, 358
Leisler's rebellion of 1689–1691 333–
  337
  and Catholicism 333–336
Lenin (V. I. Ulyanov):
  and Chekhov's "Ward No. 6" 189n,
    347n
  as creature of revolution 279
  background of tension 90–92
  contact with tsarist government
    187–188
  traumatic adolescence 90–91, 187–
    188
Lincoln, Abraham 25, 308–320
  and abolitionists 310–311
  and Buchanan 311–312
  and Calhoun, compared 132–133,
    310
  and charisma 308, 315–316
  and Douglas 309–310
  and Freud 314
  and inevitability 313–314
  and McClellan 293, 319

Lincoln, Abraham (*cont'd*)
  and Stalin 319
  and success 308–309, 312
  autocratic ruler 314–315, 318–319
  background of tension 85–87
  conservatism of 319–320, 321
  contact with slaves 187
  Herndon on 283
  introspects on ambition 316–317
  on equality 48–49
  rationalist ruler 318
Line-length experiments 171
Locke, John 359
Lodge, Henry Cabot, and Wilson
  133–134
Long, Huey 291n, 296
Love 31
  Aristotle on 48, 48n
  Christ on 31
  Greek words for 31n
  Paul on 31, 31n
  Plato on 31, 31n
Lumumba, Patrice 362
Luther, Martin:
  and Erasmus 338–339
  identification anxiety 82n

McCarthy, Senator Joseph, background
  of tension 87
McCarthyism:
  and Protestant churchmen 226
  and public tension 103
McClellan, George B. 293, 319
Magsaysay, Ramon 320–321
Mahomet 299
Majority rule and social status 248–249
Mao Tse-tung:
  as creature of revolution 279
  charismatic rule 302
  poem eulogizing 302
Marginality 263–266
  ambivalence as to extremism 94
  and anti-Nazis 164, 266
  and political extremism 164, 266
  and racial prejudice 264
  and tension 265–266
  Durkheim on 266
  frequency of 263–264
  in background of political leaders
    85–94, 287–288, 345–348
  in Charles V's background 347n

Marginality (*cont'd*)
  in Hitler's background   88–90
  in Leisler's background   336
  in Lincoln's background   85–87
  in McCarthy's background   87
  in Masaryk's background   87–88
  in revolutionary leaders   345–348
  lack of, in Lenin's background   90–92
  varieties of   263
Mario and the Magician   279
Marshall, George C., on equality   48
Marx, Karl, and Marxists:
  and class basis for personality   234
  and class consciousness   271–272
  and human nature   1
  and morality   45
  interclass antagonism and solidarity   241
  Marx's personal background   358
Masaryk, Thomas:
  background of tension   87–88
  in Vienna   296
Mau-Mau rebellion   354
Mental rigidity:
  and anxiety   119–120
  and "intolerance of ambiguity"   119–120
  in old elites   344-345
  levels and areas of   120–121
Mexico, conquest of   43–44
Minnesota starvation experiments   11–14
  perceptual effects   108
Mobility, social:
  and early industrialization   250–252, 258–259
  and ethnic minorities   260–261
  and family solidarity   261
  and growth of tertiary occupations   253
  and occupational mobility distinguished   251
  and the organism   261–263
  and social stability   249–250
  and specialization   250–251
  and urbanization   251
  belief in hierarchy   257–258
  beliefs and   256–258
  causes of   256–263

Mobility, social (*cont'd*)
  in already industrialized societies   252–254
  intergroup contact and   259–260
  Jefferson on   258
  lack of, in primitive societies   97–98
  of entire status groups   252
  of political leaders   287
  upward and downward   253–254, 264
Monkeys:
  fright experiments   78n
  Harlow's research on social deprivation in   149–150
Morals (i.e., values):
  of revolutionaries and old regimes   349–350
  origins   46, 46n
  relativism and   44–45
Mozarabic ritual in Toledo cathedral   115–116

Napoleon   277
Narcissism:
  of old elites   357
  of political leaders   246–247
Nasser, Gamal: Aswan Dam, Dulles, and hunger   111, 135
Nationalism:
  and religious conversion   123–124
  right after revolution   363
Natural law:
  and equality   52–53
  and the human psyche   52–53
Nazism:
  and class system   340
  background for   327–328
Needs (i.e., drives or wants)   6–11
  and institutional change   232–233
  and limits of propaganda   134–136
  and religion   213
  anxiety about   101–102
  basic   6–11
  distinguished from tension   6, 64–65, 74–75
  Freud's list of   7, 8
  hierarchy of   10–11, 60–63; and *see* Hierarchy of needs
  Maslow's list of   8–11
  Murray's list of   7–9

Needs (*cont'd*)
   physical 9, 11–23
   relation of leader selection to 289–290
   Wallas's list of 7
Negroes:
   and Catholic church 226, 229–230
   and Protestant churches 226–227
   Emancipation Proclamation 311n
   party loyalty of 232
Nehru, Jawaharlal 276, 284
   admiration for Lincoln 282
   compared to Lincoln 318
New elite:
   alienation from old elite 345–348
   follows style of old rulers 364
   hardness of 363–364
   in prerevolutionary conditions 345–350
   lack of sense of guilt 350
   marginality of 345–346
   social background 348
   see also Political leaders
New York draft riots of 1863 5–6, 361–362
Nineteen Eighty-Four 135, 357
Nkrumah, Kwame:
   charismatic rule 302–303, 329
   on political reality 135

Oates, Titus 334
"Oceanic" feeling 81–82
   and identity 81–82
   and sensory deprivation 106, 107
   de-individualization during brain-washing 19
   Koestler's experience of 82
Oedipus complex 36–37
Old elite:
   alienation from society 344–345
   death instinct and 357
   in prerevolutionary conditions 341–345, 355–357
   lack of sense of guilt 350
   mental rigidity in 344–345
   resurgence of its style after revolution 364
   see also Political leaders
Old Ritualists in Russia 116

Organism, the 2
   and environment 2–5, 150–152, 156–157, 234–235
   and human nature 2
   and political behavior 3, 5–6
   and revolution 340–341, 358
   and social change 340–341
   and social mobility 261–263
   growth, and imprinting 150–152
Oxenstierne 184, 210, 231

Parents: political influence of 166–168, 176–177, 177n
Parties, political:
   identification with 205–208
   "inheritance" of identification 208
   international ties 212
   other causes of identification with 208–211
Pavlov, I. P.:
   and extinction of conditioned reflex 129–130
   experiments 76–77
Peasants and farmers in politics:
   in early industrial conditions, in America 36, 40–42
   in preindustrial conditions 342–345, 351, 355–356
Perception:
   and church identification 230–231
   and conservatism 114–121
   and consistency 113
   and ethnic discrimination 204–205
   and expertness of carrier 125
   and identification with carrier 127
   and liking the familiar 114–121
   and mental rigidity 119–121
   and persistence of past percepts 114–121
   and physical needs 108–110
   and race prejudice 204–205
   and reality 128–132
   and religious conversion 124
   and resistance to change 114–121
   and self-actualization needs 111
   and self-esteem, equality needs, 111
   and social needs 110–111
   and trustworthiness of carrier 125–126
   and values 121–124

Perception (*cont'd*)
  carriers of percepts 124–128
  distorted by values 121–124
  line-length experiments 171
  of words and misperception of acts
    244–246
  "sleeper effect" 127–128, 128n
  social effects on 169–175
  symbols and resistance to change
    114–118
  tendency to make percepts complete
    112–113
  tension and persistence in 79–80
Peron, Juan 281
Person, the (i.e., personality) 2
  and human nature 2–3
  Marx's class basis for 234
Peter the Great 290–291, 295, 298,
    298n
Phillips, Wendell 24–25, 310–311
Physical deprivation:
  after-effects 13, 13n, 14–15
  and alienation of Soviet citizens 19–
    20
  and apathy 13, 15, 26
  and depoliticization 15–23
  and forced political participation
    22–23
  and limits to propaganda 134–136
  at detention camps for Japanese
    17–18
  fear of bodily harm or death 5–6,
    109–110, 360
  hunger and starvation 5–6, 11–14,
    27–28
  in Chinese People's Republic 21–23
  in Hungarian People's Republic 21–
    22
  in Soviet purges of 1930s 18–21
  recovery from 33–34
Physical needs 9, 11–23
  and desocialization 17–18, 19, 22
  and perception 108–110
  and politics 15–23
  annihilation and perception 109–110
  vs. social needs 32–34, 33n
Plato 31
  on love 31, 31n
Political change:
  and need for equality 50–53

Political change (*cont'd*)
  and self-righteousness 41–42, 45
  and the organism 340–341
  and war 360
  constitutional and nonconstitutional
    331–332
  group influence on 180–181, 210
Political extremism:
  and Hitler's background 88–90
  and McCarthy's background 87
  and marginality 164, 266
Political leaders:
  adaptability vs. conservatism and pro-
    gressivism 321–322
  authority figures 293
  autocrats and heterocrats 297–298
  backgrounds of tension 85–94
  characteristics of 56–60, 285–289
  charismatic autocrats 299–303, 327
  charismatic heterocrats 306–307
  class backgrounds of 40n–41n, 256,
    270, 285–286
  creatures of their times 277–279
  criterion of success 293–297
  dependency on 101, 327
  energy level of 289
  father- or big-brother image 281
  genetic makeup of 93
  great man theory of 277–278
  identification with 83–84, 281–283,
    289–290
  Iowa experiments in 274–277
  marginality of 85–94, 287–288,
    345–348
  misperceptions by 244–247
  narcissism of 247
  needs of the time for 101, 289–290
  personal traumata of 347–348
  public mood and 292–293
  rational autocrats 303
  rational heterocrats 307–308
  relation to followers 277–285
  revolutionary, from old elite 343
  revolutionary, loyalty to 354
  sense of equality in 283–284
  social status of 270, 285–286
  socio-cultural context for 92–93
  staff of 283–285
  style of rule 290–292
  traditional autocrats 298–299
  traditional heterocrats 306

Political maturity   322–325
   a definition   324–325
   and charisma   328–329
   and leaders   329
   England   328
   Germany   325–328
   leaders and citizens compared   325–327
Political participation   23–29
   active   23–25
   a definition   23–26
   and apathy distinguished   23, 25–26
   and the family   35, 163–169, 175n, 177
   and personal experience   185–190
   and physical deprivation   15–23
   and social needs   34, 36, 40–42
   and teachers   175n
   degree of   24
   in China   29
   in India   28–29
   in Peru   28
   in Soviet Union   28–29
   passive   23–25
Political stability and equality   47–48
Popular government (i.e., democracy) and free government   54
Population growth:
   as index of instability   350–351
   in France before revolution   351
   in Russia before revolution   351
Populists, American   40–41
   identification process   40–41
   leaders of 40n–41n
   prior socialization   36
Portugal   333, 333n, 334
Prejudice and discrimination, racial:
   and class   268
   causes of   203–205
   see also Racial groups
Prerevolutionary conditions:
   breakdown of law   356
   crisis approaches   354-360
   fear of regression   355–356, 360
   general public in   350–360
   industrialization under   350–352
   new elite in   345–350
   new loyalties   354–355
   old elite in   341–345, 355–357
Pressure groups and equal justice   238–239

Priority of needs   10–11, 60–63
   among French war prisoners   15
   and constitutional democracy   16, 26–29
   and social status   255, 255n
   and support for civil liberties   111n
   charts showing   62
   in concentration camps   14, 33
   in Russia's 1918–1922 famine   14
   physical vs. social needs   32–34, 33n, 145n
   Rostow and *Buddenbrooks*   11n
   social vs. "self-assertion"   148n
Projection:
   a definition   39
   among American farmers   41–42
   among Spanish conquistadors   43–44
   Anna Freud on   39n
   by governments   42–43
   in *Caesar's Column*   41–42
   of vice   42, 45
Proletarian revolt and agrarian revolt   242–244
Propaganda, extent and limits of effectiveness   134–136
Protein consumption in various countries   27
Protestant churches:
   and alcoholism   225n
   and English Chartism   223–224, 224n
   and McCarthyism   226
   and Negroes   226–227
   and rich vs. poor   223–224, 227
   and slavery   223, 224
   class orientation of   222–225
Proximal groups:
   a definition   145–147
   and church identification   219–220
   and lack of identification   259
   and party identification   208–209
   chicken experiment   148
   dog experiment   148
   family influences   163–169, 176–177, 177n
   mediator for distal groups   184, 188–200
   monkey experiments   149–150
   nonfamilial   175–176, 178–181
   of equals and unequals   144
   origins of   146–153

Proximal groups (*cont'd*)
   table of types 147
   teachers' influence 175n
Public, general:
   decline in progress 355–356, 360
   economic progress 351–352
   in prerevolutionary conditions 350–360
   insecurity and 94–103
   political participation 23–29, 53–56
   rationality, compared with elite 130–136
   reluctance to rebel 359–360
   social reform and 352
Purges of 1930s, Soviet 18–21
   and tension 103
   compared to McCarthyism 103
   insecurity of purgees 18–19
   Khrushchev's speech on 20–21

Racial groups and racism:
   and conflict between Soviet Union and China 196
   and Congo independence 196
   and marginality 264
   and mobility 260–261
   and religion 201–203
   and status 260–261
   basis for nonpolitical conflict 195–196
   causes of discrimination 203–205
   identification 195, 198
   prejudice and class 268
   social and self-esteem needs 198
   subjective aspect 194–195
Rationalism and reason 22n
Rationality:
   and conditioned reflex 129–130
   and reality 128–132, 136
   and tension 83–84
   of elite and general public 130–136
   of Lincoln and Calhoun 132–133
   of Wilson and Lodge 133–134
Realism, crypto-Platonic 51, 52
   and reaction to word "socialism" 117
   and Soviet "socialist competition" 117
   in interclass antagonism 244–245
   of revolutionaries 349
Reality and perception 128–132

Reality-testing:
   and propaganda limits 134–136
   and rationality 128–132, 136
   of elite compared with general public 130–136
   perceptions of commodity-market slump 131–132
Rebellion:
   conservatism during 348
   Leisler's of 1689–1691 333–337
   Mau-Mau 354
Reformation, Protestant
   and equality 49–50, 339
   and frustration 73–74
   and Jacob Leisler 336
   and Renaissance 337–339
   class orientation of 223
Relativism, moral 44–45
   and Marxists 45
   and Populists 45n
Religion:
   and various needs 213
   churches and functional autonomy 220, 223, 233
   science, and scientism 22n, 214
Renaissance and Reformation 337-339
Retrogression, tension about 5–6, 100–101, 355–356, 360
Revolutions:
   and human nature 348
   and illiteracy 342
   and new elite 345–350
   and old elite 341–345, 364
   atavism in 350
   contrasted with labor strikes 244, 244n
   immediate consequences 362–363
   leaders, from old elite 343
   war as precipitator 360
   see also Prerevolutionary conditions
Riots:
   at detention centers for Japanese 17–18, 346
   Cairo in 1952 362
   marginality of leaders 346
   New York draft 5–6, 361–362
Roosevelt, Franklin D.:
   and Hitler 320, 329
   and the public 280
   conflict with mother 288

Roosevelt, Franklin D. (*cont'd*)
  illness 288
  responsiveness to popular needs 290
Roosevelt, Theodore 181
  on the American race 197n
  marginality of 287–288
Rousseau, J. J. 22n

St. Bartholomew's Day massacre, class
    orientation of 223
St. Simeon Stylites 25
Science and scientism 22n
  and religion 214
Scientific socialism, socialists, and
    morality 45
Security needs 9–10
  and politics 10, 54
  and religion 213
  and social status 255
  distinguished from basic needs 9–10
Self-actualization needs 9, 53–60
  and perception 111
  and social status 255–256
  general public, political participation,
    and 53–56
  of political elites 56–60
  special groups and 54–55
Self-esteem (i.e. dignity, equality)
    needs 9
  and appeal of Christianity 219–221,
    219n–220n
  and ethnic minority status 198
  and perception 111
  distinguished from social needs 45–
    46
Sensory deprivation:
  Darkness at Noon 107n
  experiments in 105–107
  Hebb's experiments 105–106
  Lilly's experiments 107
  separation from self and 106, 107
Separation of self from other:
  child and mother 155–156
  social and self-esteem needs 45–46
Sin and error 22n, 23
Situation, the (i.e., environment) 2
  and human nature 2
  and the organism 3–5
Social deprivation:
  effects of 150–152

Social deprivation (*cont'd*)
  experiments in 149–150
  in brainwashing 22
  in infants 151–152
  in "mechanical" boy 151
  in "wolf" boy 150–151
Social determinism 141–142
  Durkheim 141
  Lazarsfeld 141
Social groups and categories 142–143
Social groups, table of 147
Social mobility 249–263
  and early industrialization 250–252,
    258–259
  and ethnic minorities 260–261
  and family solidarity 261
  and growth of tertiary occupations
    253
  and occupational mobility distin-
    guished 251
  and social stability 249–250
  and specialization 250–251
  and the organism 261–263
  and urbanization 251
  belief in hierarchy 257–258
  beliefs and 256–268
  causes of 256–263
  in already industrialized societies
    252–254
  intergroup contact and 259–260
  Jefferson on 258
  lack of, in primitive societies 97–98
  of entire status groups 252
  of political leaders 287
  upward and downward 253–254,
    264
Social (i.e., love, affection, belonging-
    ness) needs 9
  a definition 31
  among American farmers 36
  and ethnic minority status 198
  and family 35, 155–156
  and identity 38
  and imprinting 150–152
  and perception 110–111
  and sensory deprivation 107n
  and starvation 14–15
  deprivation of 149–152
  during prerevolutionary conditions
    357

Social needs (*cont'd*)
    experiments on   148–150
    in infancy   151–152, 155–156
    origin of   146–153
    right after revolution   362–363
Socrates   285n, 295
Soviet expatriates, study of   19–20
"Springdale"   191–193
Staff members of leader   283–285
Stalin:
    and Lincoln   319
    and style of rule of old regime   364–
        365
    charismatic rule   301–302, 364
    misperceptions of self   245
    poem eulogizing   302
Starvation   11–17
    after-effects   13, 13n, 14–15
    and apathy   13, 15, 26–28
    effect on social ties   14–16
    in Nazi concentration camps   12n
    in the Netherlands, 1944–1945   15n,
        16
    Minnesota experiments   11–14
Status:
    a definition   235
    and ethnic minorities   260–261
    and graft   238
    and individual development   255–
        256
    and insecurity   255
    and justice   237–240
    and majority rule   248
    and need hierarchy   255, 255n
    and politics   271–273
    and self-actualization   255–256
    and subjective equality   246–249
    class and caste   236
    class legislation   238–240
    discrepancy   346
    marginality and race   263–264
    mobility of entire status groups   252
    of political elite ("decision makers")
        40n–41n, 256, 270, 285–286
    social inheritance of   236–237
Stimulation, need for   104–105, 107–
    108
    and need for cognition   104
Strikes, labor, contrasted with revolu-
    tions   244, 244n

Suffrage (i.e., the vote):
    and equality   51
    and Soviet 1936 Constitution   52
    equality and dictatorship and   51–
        52
Survival needs:
    and concentration camps   33–34
    and group influence   181–182
    and need hierarchy   33–34, 33n
    and political apathy   13, 15, 23, 26–
        28, 298–299
    anxiety   97, 109–110, 360
Symptomatic relief of tension   82–83

Tension:
    a definition   65
    and ambiguity   79–80
    and anxiety, frustration, insecurity
        66
    and identity   81–82
    and irrational (dysfunctional) action
        74–76
    and McCarthyism   103
    and marginality   265–266
    and mental rigidity   119
    and need distinguished   6, 64–65,
        74–75
    and newspaper reading habits   80–
        81
    and persistence in perception   79–80
    and Protestant Reformation   73–74
    and Soviet purges   103
    and tendency to make percepts com-
        plete   113
    causes   71–74
    experiments on   76–80
    in backgrounds of political leaders
        85–94
    in industrial society   102–103
    in preliterate society   95–98
    in the populace   94–103
    in transitional society   98–102
    of dependency   96
    of retrogression   100–101
    of transition   95–96, 98–100
    of unfulfilled expectations   97–98
    optimum   70, 80–81, 84, 103
    quantification   80–81
    symptomatic relief of   82–83
Tolstoi, Leo   277–278

Toothbrush experiment   78–79
Transition:
  anomy and   101, 266
  anxiety of   95–96, 98–102
  in Africa   352–354
  in Turkey   359
Trotsky, Leo   284

Unemployment:
  and apathy   16–17
  and desocialization   16–17
Utopian:
  and conservative views of revolution-
    aries   348–349
  communities   46–47, 241–242

Values (i.e., morals):
  and interclass antagonism   242–243,
    247–249
  and interclass solidarity   241, 242–
    244
  and perception   121–124, 137, 140
  and social identification   38
  Christian   48–49
  during Renaissance and Reformation
    339
  Jewish   48–49, 202–203
  nationalism   123–124
  origins   46, 46n

Wallace, Henry   284
Wants (i.e., needs or drives)   6–11
  and institutional change   232–233
  and limits of propaganda   134–136
  and religion   213
  anxiety about   101–102
  basic   6–11
  distinguished from tension   6, 64–
    65, 74–75
  Freud's list of   7, 8
  hierarchy of   10–11, 60–63; and *see*
    Hierarchy of needs
  Maslow's list of   8–11
  Murray's list of   7–9
  physical   9, 11–23
  relation of leader selection to   289–
    290
  Wallas's list of   7
Weber, Max   298, 299, 299n
Wilson, Woodrow
  and Lodge 133–134
  and success   294–295
  and the public   280
  conflict with father   288
  Harding, and Debs   296
Working class: conservatism of   242–
  244, 268–270

Young, Brigham   299